A
COVERT
LIFE

RANDOM HOUSE · NEW YORK

A
COVERT
LIFE

JAY LOVESTONE

COMMUNIST,

ANTI-COMMUNIST,

AND SPYMASTER

TED MORGAN

Copyright © 1999 by Ted Morgan

All rights reserved under International and Pan-American
Copyright Conventions. Published in the United States by Random
House, Inc., New York, and simultaneously in Canada by Random
House of Canada Limited, Toronto.

RANDOM HOUSE and colophon are registered trademarks of Random House, Inc.

Library of Congress Cataloging-in-Publication Data

Morgan, Ted.
    A covert life : Jay Lovestone, communist, anti-communist, and
spymaster / by Ted Morgan.
        p.   cm.
    Includes index.
    ISBN 0-679-44400-9
    1. Lovestone, Jay.   2. Communists—United States—Biography.
3. American Federation of Labor—Officials and employees.   4. United
States.   Central Intelligence Agency—Officials and employees.
I. Title.
HX84.L68M67   1999
335.43′092—dc21
    [B]   98-39514

Random House website address: www.atrandom.com

Printed in the United States of America on acid-free paper

9 8 7 6 5 4 3 2

First Edition

BOOK DESIGN BY MERCEDES EVERETT

This book is dedicated to

Louise Page Morris and Sam H. Schurr,

without whom there would be no book

During the four years that I spent on this book, when friends asked me what I was working on and I replied, "A biography of Jay Lovestone," most of them asked, "Jay who?" Of those few who remembered him, fewer still knew why he was worth remembering: "Boss of the American Communist Party, wasn't he?" "Expelled by Stalin, as I recall." "Started his own party, what were they called, the Lovestoneites?" "Handled foreign affairs for George Meany in the AF of L." "Something to do with the CIA, under the cover of the labor movement." "Some kind of éminence grease, wasn't he?"

Lovestone was all of the above but is largely forgotten in our collective memory. He probably would have wanted it that way, for his method was to work behind the scenes, unheralded. Lovestone was a Zelig-like figure, the one in the photograph you can't quite place, standing behind the president, or shaking hands with a foreign chief of state. The one whispering into the ear of the secretary of state. The one seen scurrying from the national security adviser's office whose name does not show up on the appointment calendar.

Lovestone never ran for office and never held a government post. He had no private wealth and commanded none of the usual levers of power. He did his best to stay out of the papers. But his friend Ernest Cuneo described him in his syndicated column, "The National Whirligig," as "one of the half dozen most powerful men in the hidden power structure of America."

According to Cuneo, "Lovestone was a maker of foreign policy for forty years as organized labor's Secretary of State." He was the quintessential "man behind the man," secretly summoned to the White House to confer with presidents. "With his uncanny ability to sniff the diplomatic winds," wrote Cuneo, "he is the veritable Sherlock Holmes of diplomatic affairs." He was also, added Cuneo, the premier Kremlinologist of the free world, a onetime Communist, the first outsider to take Stalin head-on. He had known Lenin, who had once advised him, "Remember, a good housewife finds use for even a broken shoestring."

In 1982, when he was an old man musing on the past, Lovestone lapsed from his habit of avoiding the press and gave a long interview to a Canadian reporter, Peter Worthington of the *Toronto Sun.* "In some ways he is the most remarkable man in America, if not anywhere," Worthington wrote. "Not only for the history encountered face to face, but for the history he has influenced, shaped and even changed. . . . He more than anyone probably saved the unions in Europe after World War II from going Communist. . . . He was instrumental in saving post-war Europe from Stalin and his successors. . . . No one has fought for freedom and organized labor as relentlessly and effectively as Jay Lovestone. Though his life is intriguing and unique, no biography has been written about him."

But how to write the biography of a man who cultivated anonymity, was obsessed with secrecy, worked through surrogates, unseen and unheard? Most of the time he covered his tracks, but with posterity in mind he squirreled away his papers, which he left to the Hoover Institution and which were opened to researchers in 1995. With his papers and those in other archives, including the Comintern papers in Moscow, and with the recollections of those who knew him and survived him, the outline of his life becomes visible. Yet he remains an often elusive figure, as though seen in the pulses of a strobe light, brightly illuminated for a moment, then retreating into darkness.

CONTENTS

A
COVERT
LIFE

1

THE BLOND BEAST

As it often happened, the father came first with his oldest daughter to take care of the house, leaving the rest of the family behind. In the great hall of Ellis Island, divided by railings, they inched forward in the endless line, where federal inspectors processed as many as five thousand immigrants a day. Would they get through or be sent back? The father, his scraggly beard covering his shirt collar, had brought his prayer shawl and phylacteries. God did not refuse the pious. But was God present in the midst of this bustle, this polyglot confusion?

The doctors were the keepers of the gates, one inspecting their eyes, another asking them to cough. Not carrying trachoma or tuberculosis, they were let through, into another line, finding themselves at last before a uniformed man at a desk. Barnet Liebstein was allowed to keep his name, unlike so many others, such as the man who was told an Americanized name to give the inspector but forgot it and blurted out in Yiddish *Shane vergesse* (I forgot), ending up James Ferguson.

As for his age, or even his daughter Mary's age, he wasn't sure. In the old country Jews were not given birth certificates; they were nonpersons from the day they were born. He figured he was in his forties, while Mary was in her late teens. Once the rest of the family arrived, he would assign birthdays to all of them.

The year was 1906, in the second wave of Jewish migration from the

Russian empire. In tsarist Russia, which included the Baltic states and part of Poland, Jews were assigned to a large boundaried district called a pale. They were not allowed to own land, or attend universities, or travel outside the district without papers. But they were allowed to serve in the tsar's army. Essentially they were a minority under surveillance, the targets of a sly bureaucracy. Depending on the whim of the tsar, the pendulum swung from repression to relative ease.

America beckoned, with its policy of open immigration. In 1882 the United States had 100,000 Jews; by 1920 it had 4 million. The great bulk of them came from the Pale, which they fled for practical reasons: to avoid conscription, to travel without an internal passport, to escape a small life as a herring salesman at town fairs.

One of these immigrants seeking a fresh start was Barnet Liebstein, a pious and orthodox man who took his own food for the crossing because the food on the boat was not kosher, and who did not neglect his prayers amid the stench and blare of steerage. Barnet came from a village too small to figure on most maps: Molchad, in the then Polish (and later Lithuanian) province of Grodno, south of the Lithuanian capital of Vilnius and west of the Belorussian capital of Minsk. Barnet was the rabbi of Molchad, a respected figure to whom people came for more than religious services. They came to him in a marital dispute or over a contested inheritance, rather than go to the civil authority.

But in America he was no longer the head of his community. He was not even the head of a congregation, for there was a glut of rabbis on the Lower East Side, which offered by the time of his arrival in 1906 a ready-made Yiddish-speaking quarter, a reconstituted ghetto, not unlike Minsk. Hester Street, where he found a tenement, smelled of garlic and fish and rang with the calls of pushcart peddlers—"I cash old clothes," and "Fresh pike for the Sabbath." Here everyone was poor, and people haggled over a penny. And here the roofs were flat, with clothes on ropes fluttering in the wind.

Barnet found a place as sexton or *shammes* in one of the storefront synagogues. He was responsible for its care and upkeep, and lit the candles. In his spare hours he taught Hebrew. Detached from worldly things, uneasy in the new world, Barnet found a refuge in scrupulous orthodoxy. He never shaved his beard. He never touched a coin on the Sabbath, or lit a match, or used gas. He wrapped himself in protective Judaism.

But Mary had a good business sense; she managed the finances so that in little more than a year they had saved enough money to bring the rest of the family over: Barnet's wife, Emma, who was about five years older than he was and who wore a wig that covered most of her brow, which she continued to wear in New York; and in descending order of birth, Morris, Sarah, Esther, and Jacob. They boarded the *Zeeland* in Antwerp and arrived in New York on September 15, 1907.

The family was reunited on Hester Street in the small-roomed building where the tenants moved often, when they found something better or couldn't pay the rent. Jacob, born in 1897, was not quite ten. He was assigned December 15 as a birthday but when asked found it more dramatic to say he was born on Christmas Day.

Jacob was strikingly different in appearance from his siblings, who were brown-haired, brown-eyed, and more or less olive-skinned. In a childhood photograph he stands barefoot in a park with Sarah and Esther. The sisters are wearing what look like homemade rather than store-bought dresses, and their long, brown hair flows over their shoulders. Between them stands Jacob, in a T-shirt and short pants, flaxen-haired and blue-eyed, with his arms akimbo and one knee bent on sloping ground, suggesting the body language of the man being photographed after climbing Mount Everest.

With his straight blond hair cut short and his arched eyebrows, the resolute and unsmiling set of his mouth, and the direct stare of his blue eyes, young Jacob looks like a displaced little Aryan, and his expression seems to be saying: "You want to mess with me? You'll get the worst of it." In later years, after being told by Arthur Koestler about a tribe of blond Tatars in Central Asia who adopted the Jewish faith, Jacob claimed he was a throwback to that tribe.

In the year of Jacob's arrival in New York, President Teddy Roosevelt, then in his second term, was going after the "malefactors of great wealth" and trying to make the Republican Party the party of reform. In New York the union movement was gaining momentum, and the International Ladies' Garment Workers' Union led the march. By 1904 there were two hundred thousand Jews in the garment industry. The Socialist Party was on the upsurge, running Eugene Debs for president in the 1900 and 1904 elections. In 1908 Debs came to New York and spoke in Hamilton Fish Park, but Tammany stole the vote with repeaters. By then the Jewish socialists in New York were themselves learning the machinery of electoral politics. Street meetings were a form of free entertainment and a part of neighborhood life. Registering to vote was a ritual of participation. The Jewish socialists grew their own leaders, among them Morris Hillquit, the garment union lawyer who ran for Congress in 1906 and 1908 (losing both times), and Meyer London, a Marxist who was elected to Congress three times, in 1914, 1916, and 1920.

With the Lower East Side overflowing, the Liebsteins moved to the

Bronx, at 2155 Daly Avenue, close to the park and the newly built subway. Barnet and Emma, who by now were called Barney and Minnie, settled in. Barney found a better synagogue, the Ocean Parkway Jewish Center in Brooklyn, where he spent long hours teaching Hebrew. Minnie, as a good Orthodox housewife, cooked and took care of the children and parented by precept: "A Jewish boy doesn't climb trees," and "Why do you play stickball when you could play chess?"

A harsh decision had to be made. The boys, Morris and Jacob, would be educated while the three girls would work in the needle trades. Sarah went into millinery, the other two into dresses. They found work in the sweatshops, and spent ten hours a day bent over their machines, turning their wages over to their parents to help put the boys through school.

Morris took courses at the Cooper Union and then enrolled in the New York College of Eclectic Medicine, which took a holistic approach. He set up a practice on Central Park West and founded the Maimonides Hygienic Association, named after the great Hebrew scholar and physician who practiced in twelfth-century Spain. Morris saw himself as a latter-day Maimonides, "a public servant of ailing humanity," as he said. Although bombastic and self-important, he was in some ways ahead of his time, for he recommended proper diet and herbal medicines, and recognized tobacco as a dangerously toxic substance. He was one of the first doctors in New York with a no-smoking sign in the window of his office.

As for young Jacob, he went to public school until midafternoon and after that to Hebrew school, trading baseball cards as the teacher droned on. His days were followed by long hours of homework in the evening. Of the old country, village life in Molchad, he retained only one or two mental snapshots: his mother baking cookies and selling them at fairs. Mornings, sneaking under the house where the chicken coop was, puncturing eggs with a pin and sucking out the contents.

Now he was a child of the city, playing stickball in the street, saving soap coupons until he could buy his own roller skates (over Minnie's objections), and when he could get his hands on an extra quarter, renting a bicycle for an hour. His *tsidderike* (trembling with fear) mama worried herself sick. If he was five minutes late it was a calamity.

In high school, at Townsend Harris Hall, Jacob's desire for spare change became acute. He needed those pennies and nickels to buy the newspapers and magazines his parents did not read—the *Freiheit,* the *Call, The Masses.* Jacob had developed into a strong, well-built young man. A natural pugnacity and the promise of prize money led him to take up boxing. In those days the tenement roof had many uses. Dances were held up there, to the music of a harmonica. Pigeons were kept in make-shift coops. Boxing rings were improvised with clotheslines tied to chimneys, and bouts were advertised in flyers by fledgling promoters. Jacob was billed as "The Blond Bum" or "The Blond Jew." He didn't have a knockout punch, but he was scrappy and fast on his feet, and the money was good—three dollars when he won, two when he lost.

He was making three more often than two and building up a neighborhood reputation when one sweltering summer evening he took on Dutch Schaefer, a muscle-bound lump of Teutonic granite who outweighed him by twenty pounds and who beat him up so badly that when he got home, swollen-eyed and bleeding, he had to tell his horrified mother that he'd fallen down the stairs. His boxing career came abruptly to a close.

His father, easygoing, lost in his thoughts, did not try to impose his orthodoxy on the children. Barney never learned English, never became a citizen, and never involved himself in the rough dynamics of American democracy. Jacob turned away from his heritage and his religion, forging his American identity. Jacob's views on religion were sardonic. Once on a train he sat next to a rabbi who asked him what he did for a living. "I'm a pig bristle salesman," he said.

Jacob's three sisters married and moved out of the house. Mary ran a drugstore at 761 Gravesend Avenue in Brooklyn with her husband, Paul Gavza. They owned the building the store was in and lived above it. Esther and her husband, Louis Matis (shortened from Manishevitz at Ellis Island) ran a pawnshop in Brooklyn. Their three-story house at 703 Ditmas Avenue became a sort of community center, where the warmhearted and welcoming Esther was always ready to feed an army.

Sarah, the youngest daughter, described as "the most placid of the five kids," married Charles Gray (shortened from Grabow), known as Max. He had plenty of good ideas, but somehow they never panned out. At the time of his marriage to Sarah, he ran Graybow Silk in Paterson, New Jersey. Each year he laid out his capital to buy the silk in Japan. But one year an earthquake wiped out the silkworms and he was ruined.

It was only natural that Socialism should take root among the Jewish immigrants in New York, who by 1910 numbered one million out of a population of four million. Some of these immigrants had been Socialists in Russia, as a way of resisting tsarist injustice. Once in the new world they could laugh at the tsar. On an old Victrola record of Yiddish jokes that Jacob Liebstein remembered, there was one that went "I pray for the tsar—that he should be far, far away."

But though the tsar was far away, the Jewish immigrants brought with them the deep conviction of a persecuted people that personal liberation depends on the liberation of society. Their own situation as an oppressed minority in the old world made them take up Socialism in the new, where instead of tsarist injustice they had to contend with made-in-America oppression in the form of gouging employers and corrupt political bosses.

When the Liebsteins arrived on the Lower East Side in 1907, they found a society in ferment, a downtrodden Jewish proletariat looking to the unions for remedies. And though the mark of the shtetl was still on them, and though they spoke in that mishmash of Russian and German and Hebrew known as Yiddish, they soon began thinking in terms of mass action and political goals, for they knew they were in a country where change was not only possible but prescribed.

When the Liebstein girls went into the needle trades, they were charged for the needles they used and the chairs they sat on. They were fined for being late and had to rent their clothes lockers. If you had three sisters working in the needle trades, as Jacob Liebstein did, conditions in the sweatshops were brought home on a daily basis. Mary, the oldest girl, not only joined the International Ladies' Garment Workers' Union but secretly took her brother to the Jewish Socialist Sunday school, where they sang union songs instead of hymns and the sermon consisted of a discussion on piece-good rates.

Like other Jewish children, Jacob Liebstein learned enough to be bar-mitzvahed, but his true interests were elsewhere. Jacob was drawn to the radical speakers of the day, Big Bill Haywood of the Wobblies, and Emma Goldman the anarchist, who fueled his youthful capacity for indignation. At the north end of Central Park, he was one of the faithful who gathered not only to listen to but also to argue with the soapbox orators. Not to mention the "kitchen table" politicians who held never-ending debates on the issues of the day in one another's homes. It seemed that a good radical was defined by the extent of his stamina for marathon discussion.

Jacob was also a voracious reader, who went through piles of penny radical papers and nickel magazines, such as *Mother Earth,* the *Daily People,* the *Freiheit,* the *Forward,* the *Call,* and *The Masses.* He spent hours in the library, studying the works of the nineteenth-century thinkers who sought an alternative to the cutthroat capitalism of the industrial revolution.

Thus was the teenage Jacob Liebstein radicalized, in somewhat the same way that a goose is force-fed, although in his case it was voluntary. His reading told him that, for the first time in the history of man, there were enough goods so that everyone could have a decent standard of living. There should thus be a social system that would distribute the goods and give everyone a fair share. It all seemed perfectly reasonable. Socialism was based on cooperation rather than competition and would lead to a society with no private ownership, where the lion's share of the wealth was not hoarded by a tiny number. Of the thinkers that Jacob studied, Marx had a great impact, for he posited not a utopian but a scientific socialism, and an inevitable progression from capitalism to socialism and communism. It seemed ordained that just as man had evolved from lower forms of life, he would rise through the class struggle to communism.

But the thinker under whose spell Jacob Liebstein fell was his contemporary Daniel De Leon, then the leading Marxist theoretician in America, who translated Marx and Engels and wrote for the Marxist newspaper *The Daily People.* De Leon was an immigrant from the Dutch island of Curaçao, off the coast of Venezuela, descended from Sephardic Jews. His father was a doctor prosperous enough to send him to school in Germany and Holland. De Leon came to America in 1876 and studied and taught at Columbia Law School. In 1890 he veered to the left, becoming a Marxist and joining the splinter Socialist Labor Party, which he promptly took over.

De Leon's central idea was that one powerful industrial union would eventually take over the government via the ballot box. A government of trade unionists would run America. For Jacob Liebstein, knowing the experiences of his three sisters in the sweatshops, this scenario was mightily appealing. Alone, as he saw firsthand from a life of grinding poverty, the workers were feeble, but united with others of their class they would have tremendous power.

In his plan for an authentic Socialist trade union, the main target of De Leon's attacks was the American Federation of Labor, founded in 1886. He heaped invective on the federation and its leader, Samuel Gompers, whom he called a "labor-fakir." Gompers hit back, saying: "De Leon came of a Venezuelan family of Spanish and Dutch descent with a strain of colored blood. That makes him a first-class son of a bitch." One of De Leon's impulses was to reinvent his past once he became a Marxist. Repudiating his Jewish ancestry, he claimed to belong to an aristocratic Venezuelan family directly descended from Ponce de León.

In 1905 De Leon was one of the founders of the Wobblies (Industrial Workers of the World), the kind of radical industrial union he had dreamed of, but he was such a compulsive factionalist and troublemaker that he was drummed out in 1908. He spent his last years brooding over his expulsion and died in 1914. Even though he had failed to build a mass movement, he was a popular figure in New York leftist circles, and *The New York Times* reported that three thousand people attended his funeral, and that more than fifty thousand lined the streets through which the procession passed. Some were on their knees in prayer. One of those who came to mourn the Marxist intellectual was his disciple Jacob Liebstein.

Daniel De Leon died in May 1914, and that August, Jacob Liebstein saw a newsboy hawking an extra that had a one-word headline: WAR. By then he had been sufficiently radicalized to declare his opposition to what he thought of as an imperialistic struggle between Britain and Germany to dominate world markets. Soon after, at the age of seventeen, he joined the Socialist Party. Then, in the fall of 1915, he entered City College.

In many if not most Jewish families, college was not debatable, even though it meant that the boundaries of intellectual inquiry were removed, and that the process of political radicalization might be furthered. Thus, the mother of Morris Raphael Cohen, the renowned City College philosophy professor, said: "If need be, I'll go out as a washerwoman and scrub floors so that my Morris can have a college education." Even with free tuition college was seen as a luxury—but a necessary one. Of course it was understood that parental sacrifice would be matched by good grades; Jacob's oldest friend, Bert Wolfe, whom he met at City College, was told by his mother: "If you ever flunk a single course, out you go."

When Jacob Liebstein entered City College, the children of Jewish immigrants made up 70 percent of the student body of thirteen hundred. The college, which in 1908 had moved its campus from Lexington and Twenty-third Street to leafy Harlem, at 138th Street and Convent Avenue, where gabled buildings surrounded a grassy plaza, was known as the Harvard of the proletariat. It was in fact—long before open admissions—a meritocracy where only students with good high school grade averages got in.

Thus, Bert Wolfe, who grew up on Berriman Street in East New York saying "boids" for *birds,* won the Ward Medal for proficiency in German language and literature and graduated Phi Beta Kappa. In addition, he was an incurable joiner, who belonged to the Clionia Literary Society, the Deutsche Verein, the Philosophical Society, and the Varsity Debating Team.

Jacob Liebstein also won a prize, as he reported to the alumni secretary in May 1978 after attending the sixtieth reunion of the class of 1918, the best-known member of which was the lyricist E. Y. "Yip" Harburg, who wrote the words to "Brother, Can You Spare a Dime?" and "Over the Rainbow." "I do not usually go to social gatherings because I believe in Girth Control," Jacob wrote. "Yip was in great shape, he has lost none of his fire or talent. . . . We survivors of six of the stormiest decades in human history have no complaint. . . . CCNY deepened my interest in economic, social, and philosophy of law problems. This led me to win the highly coveted philosophy prize awarded by professors Harry Overstreet and Morris Cohen. Of the seventeen in his class, he gave me the prize, a fifty-dollar government bond. I refused to accept it unless the other sixteen students got a passing mark, so that their diplomas would not be held up."

That Jacob Liebstein was able to pressure Morris Raphael Cohen, a notoriously tough teacher, quick with sarcasm and reticent with praise, into passing the entire class sounds like a bit of sixtieth-reunion hyperbole. But the real revelation in Jacob's letter is that he accepted a fifty-dollar war bond at a time when he was militantly antiwar. Jacob, however, admired Morris Cohen, a fellow disciple of Daniel De Leon. Like Jacob, Cohen had made the leap from religious orthodoxy to social reform.

Jacob joined the Intercollegiate Socialist Society, then the most radical student organization on campus, founded in 1905 under the sponsorship of Upton Sinclair, who said that "since the professors would not educate the students, it was up to the students to educate the professors." As secretary and then president of the ISS, Jacob tried to avoid a head-on collision with the school administration, hoping to conform to the ISS motto, "Light, Not Heat." He tried to be effective in small, practical ways, such as obtaining jobs for needy students in the library and the student co-op. In 1916, when the streetcar workers went on strike, he took a detachment of ISS members to picket alongside the strikers and collected food for them.

Then came 1917, a watershed year for the left, the year the United States got into the war. The year the tsar was overthrown in Russia and the Bolsheviks took power and pulled out of the war. For young antiwar militants like Jacob Liebstein and Bert Wolfe, America's entrance and Russia's exit opened a large credit for the Bolsheviks. That April, three days after President Woodrow Wilson asked Congress for a declaration of war, the Socialist Party Congress in St. Louis passed a resolution announcing its "unalterable opposition to the war just proclaimed by the government of the United States."

Jacob Liebstein, as president of the ISS, tried to maintain an antiwar stance without getting into hot water. In a 1917 letter to the Socialist Congressman Meyer London, he expressed disdain for those who "continually yelp their r-r-r-revolutionary position." The ISS was converted into the Social Problems Club, in keeping with the wishes of the board of trustees to "avoid any name that would imply a connection with a political party." The Social Problems Club played the role of loyal opposition, protesting that the school administration had no business pressuring students to buy Victory Bonds but not actually campaigning against the bonds. When the fire-eating prowar evangelist Billy Sunday appeared on campus, the Social Problems Club provided the hecklers.

In June 1918, after only three years, Jacob graduated from City College. He was twenty years old and five feet, ten inches tall, with a narrow face and a beaky nose. Not exactly handsome, but with the kind of looks that convey vitality. In his half-formed personality grappled the forces of idealism and opportunism, and it was not always possible to discern which side prevailed. Jacob felt strongly about social injustice but also had the schemer's tactical cunning. At City College, in the radicalized climate of 1917, he became a political activist, not as a passing phase (like so many of his classmates) but as a lifetime vocation. Brash and self-assured, quick-witted and outgoing, he was an obvious go-getter, but in what direction would he go?

His two best friends were Bertram Wolfe and William Weinstein. The third of four children, Bert did well in his studies while working after school as a candy butcher and newsboy on the Long Island Railroad and as a messenger boy for Western Union.

Bert also liked to play tennis in Prospect Park. One day when Bert was sixteen, his friend Alex Tendler arrived for a game of doubles with a fourteen-year-old girl by the name of Ella Goldberg. She was only about five feet tall, but there was such intelligent curiosity in her brown eyes, and such charm and vivacity in her manner, that Bert was captivated. On the tennis court Ella teamed up with Bert, who said: "Alex tells me you're his girl." "That's a surprise to me," she answered. "If you were my girl," Bert said, "I'd marry you and take you to the Black Forest for our honeymoon."

Ella soon became Bert's girl, and in 1917, when Bert was twenty and Ella was eighteen, they were married. When they went to the municipal building for the ceremony and Bert kissed the bride, the judge said: "Kissed like a pro." Instead of going on a honeymoon in the Black Forest, they moved into a small place in Brooklyn, and their first guest was

Jacob Liebstein. "He had a way with people, an engaging smile, an engaging manner," Ella recalled, "but he always treated me like a man." Ella became his confidante, the one woman he could kid around with, who gave as good as she got, the only one to whom he revealed himself, suspending a natural secretiveness.

With Will Weinstein it was different. Ella had to fight him off because he had a crush on her. He was at City College too, a year behind Jacob and secretary of the ISS when Jacob was president. Will and Bert and Jacob formed a politically conscious triumvirate and seemed to be conducting some sort of gargantuan discussion that was interrupted but never concluded. At that time Jacob and Will were close friends, though Ella sensed in Will, who was a pontificator and a hairsplitter, a latent jealousy of Jacob, who had more energy and a better mind.

Ella and Bert and Jacob enrolled in New York University Law School in 1919. They wanted to be union lawyers helping the workers and were filled with confidence that Bolshevik Russia would solve the problems of the world. Eventually the revolution would spread to the United States. It all seemed so logical, so . . . right. Overwhelmed by events, all three dropped out of law school to become political militants.

Jacob Liebstein went through a sea change. Perhaps inspired by Daniel De Leon and his claimed descent from Ponce de León, Jacob resolved to shed his past and his name. When he was naturalized at Bronx Supreme Court on February 7, 1919, he changed his name to Jay Lovestone. Will Weinstein followed suit, becoming Weinstone.

The change of name demonstrated the change in political direction. Jay had been swept up in the political ferment of the war years, at a time when there were so many soapboxes at Central Park West and 110th Street that it was known as Trotsky Square. The Bolshevik Revolution made a tremendous impression, and now he supported the regime that had overthrown the tsar and brought about the rule of the working class, a regime threatened by a civil war that the allies—France, Britain, and the United States—encouraged. "If it wasn't for the 1917 revolution," he told Ella, "I would have become a lawyer." Instead, he became a career Communist, caught up in the business of the party, wanting to advance within it, maneuvering for position, as one does in any career. The struggle of a young party trying to survive in a hostile climate became his struggle.

In addition, perhaps thinking it would be preferable not to have any identifiable family ties in case he had to do secret work for the party, Jay made up a little biography for himself, which he dispensed in later years the few times he was interviewed: He had been born in the small town of Naponoch in upstate New York, of a Jewish father and an English mother. His father was a baker and a member of the bakers' union.

And so, like the quick-change artist who walks offstage costumed as a Spanish Gypsy and emerges moments later as a New England Pilgrim, Jacob Liebstein walked in one door and Jay Lovestone walked out the other—a new man, twenty-one years old, self-invented, a sort of crafty utopian with an Aladdin-like future before him.

2

PRESENT AT THE CREATION

Before the Russian Revolution, American radicals had no place to go but the Socialist Party, which was making progress in running candidates for state and national office. After 1914 the Socialists became the antiwar party, rallying young pacifists like Bert Wolfe and Jay Lovestone. But as the mood of the country changed toward preparedness, the Socialists were attacked as unpatriotic. The war helped to split the party into a temporizing right wing and an increasingly radical left wing.

The Russian Revolution sent a strong signal that the capitalist world was doomed. If it could happen in this backward land of illiterate peasants, it could happen anywhere—even in America. In May 1917 there were only eleven thousand Bolsheviks in Russia, and five months later they had taken power. Here in the United States people were waiting every four years for the next election, but over there they were voting every day of the week with rifles, and they had shot the Romanov dynasty out of existence.

Out of these events five thousand miles away came the American Communist movement. The Russians inspired it because they were the first to conduct a successful socialist revolution. They had the patent on revolution and could franchise it. As Lovestone told the Dies Committee in 1939: "In the first days of the October Revolution—that is the Bolshevik Revolution—the Russians were the leaders through prestige, through achievement, through the fact that they had conquered one sixth of the world for Socialism. We had an attitude of almost religious veneration for the Russian leaders."

Having dropped out of law school, Lovestone was working for the Jewish Protectory and Aid Society as a "big brother" to juvenile delinquents. As an antiwar Marxist he naturally gravitated toward the left wing of the Socialist Party, which was trying to take over the various city branches. A young Socialist labor organizer named David Dubinsky remembered meeting him in 1918 at the Lower East Side branch, where he was trying to mastermind a secession of the left wing. "He was a young guy fresh out of City College with a very effective debating style, but we licked him," Dubinsky recalled.

Manhattan remained the fortress of Morris Hillquit and the right wing of the party, which was taking prowar positions and had in the spring of 1918 voted in favor of the Fourth Liberty Loan. But the "City College boys"—Lovestone, Weinstone, and Wolfe—were making inroads. Benjamin Gitlow, the head of the Retail Clerks' Union, who in 1917 had been elected assemblyman from the Bronx on the Socialist ticket, recalled that at one meeting "we lost the discussion by one vote due to the tactics of Jay Lovestone, who kept disturbing the meeting to such an extent that a number of members left the hall in disgust." When Lovestone spoke, Gitlow said, "in a sharp sarcastic tone as was his custom, his face would become livid and break into a contemptuous sneer, his words coming at a rapid clip." At another meeting, in the Bronx, Lovestone baited the fabled John Reed, who had actually seen the revolution and written about it, calling him "the so-called proletarian who lives on a sumptuous estate in Westchester." After the meeting was over, Lovestone, according to Gitlow, "rushed up to Reed like a young puppy and offered his hand. Reed told him to go to hell."

In February 1919 the left wing formed a City Committee of Fifteen, which included Reed, Gitlow, Wolfe, and Lovestone, and which saw itself as the heart and soul of the Socialist Party. They issued membership cards, charged dues, and published their own newspaper, *The New York Communist.*

Meanwhile in Moscow, Lenin had convened the first Congress of the Communist International on March 2, 1919, to demonstrate that the Russian Revolution was a world revolution, destined for export. The Communist International, or Comintern, was the agency that would manage all Communist parties outside Russia from 1919 until its dissolution in 1943.

The Comintern was established at a moment when the survival of the regime was in doubt, with the Bolsheviks fighting a civil war on four fronts. Fifty-two men and women met in the Kremlin for five days of anticapitalist harangues. Leon Trotsky, the commissar for war, made a dramatic entrance, fresh from the front, the smell of gunpowder clinging to his uniform, and read the Comintern manifesto, which he had written on the train. The capitalist states were doomed, he intoned. The hour of proletarian dictatorship was about to strike, for the peasant in Bavaria who could not see beyond the spires of his village church, for the small French wine producer driven into bankruptcy by the merchants who adulterated his wine, and for the American farmer fleeced and cheated by bankers and congressmen.

As the delegates sang the Internationale, Trotsky strode out to battle the Whites on the Asian marches. Gregory Zinoviev, Lenin's right hand, was made head of the Comintern and predicted that "in a year the whole of Europe will be Communist." He also called for a "merciless" fight against the right-wing prowar Socialists.

In America the growing strength of the left-wing Socialists led to a split in the party that May. But even within the left wing there was a split between the English-speaking group and the powerful language federations, such as the Russians, Balts, and Finns. The question was: should the left wing form a pure Bolshevik party or try to capture the Socialist Party?

The Russians thought of themselves as the only real Bolsheviks and were in no mood for compromise. They were leaders, not what Lenin called "tailists." They would form a Communist party that was unsullied by right-wing Socialists and called for a convention on September 1 at their Chicago office on Blue Island Avenue.

But in July 1919 part of the English-speaking left wing went over to the Russians, led by the Ohio Socialist Charles E. Ruthenberg, who thought that this was the quickest way to attain a Communist party. Tall and storklike, this son of German Lutherans had run for city, state, and national office eight times between 1910 and 1919, always on the Socialist ticket and always losing. His reputation was enhanced in 1918 when he was indicted for obstructing the draft in his speeches, and he spent most of the year in the Canton, Ohio, jail. It was there that he had the time to read Marx and Lenin, and converted to Communism. But C.E., as he liked to be called, was no hotheaded radical, he was a bridge builder, a compromiser by nature, and he was hoping to avoid the disaster of two competing Communist parties.

For the moment Ruthenberg cast his lot with the Chicago-based Russians. By this time Lovestone had become a Ruthenberg disciple. He convinced Bert Wolfe to go along, even though Wolfe disliked the Russians, who were in his eyes just off the boat and ignorant of American politics. The remainder of the English-speaking left wing, led by Reed and Gitlow, still clung to the hope of taking over the Socialist convention that was also being held in Chicago, on August 30. But when they showed up at Machinists Hall on South Ashland Boulevard with eighty-two delegates, they were thrown out. So they regrouped in the billiard room downstairs and created the Communist Labor Party of America, which proposed "the overthrow of the capitalist rule and the conquest of the political power by the workers."

On September 1 at noon, the second Communist convention opened at 1221 Blue Island Avenue, known as Smolny Hall, after Lenin's Moscow headquarters. The 128 delegates represented the language federations, which claimed more than fifty thousand members, plus the Ruthenberg group. Ruthenberg was elected national secretary, and Lovestone was seated on the Central Executive Committee of Fifteen, while the young Boston radical Louis Fraina was made international secretary.

Although loyal to Ruthenberg, Lovestone had misgivings concerning a party that was overwhelmingly foreign-born and non-English-speaking. How could it recruit outside its ethnic groups and become a mass party? How could its foreign-language newspapers gain a following? Ruthenberg himself later complained that the party did not have "five speakers who could present its case in English and the same was true in regard to writers and editors."

Balding at age thirty-eight, with bright blue eyes, a jutting nose, and a pronounced overbite, Ruthenberg was now the leader of one party, the Communist Party of America, while Gitlow and Reed formed the Communist Labor Party, which claimed to be the real American party. The tragedy of the American Communist movement, puny to begin with, was its separation at birth. The two parties expended their energies in quarrels, and the movement was paralyzed as comrade fought comrade. The history of its first decade can be described as one long faction fight, in which Jay Lovestone was a principal combatant.

In 1919, however, a more immediate crisis menaced the two parties, for hard on the heels of their creation came the Red Scare. No sooner were they born than they had to go underground. The war years had spawned an anarchist movement that escalated from draft resistance to bomb throwing. Bombs started going off all over the place. Thirty-six mail bombs, disguised as parcels from Gimbel's, were sent from the main New York post office in April and May 1919. Sixteen of them were held for insufficient postage and turned over to the bomb squad by an alert clerk. The other twenty went to their destinations, usually injuring the servants and secretaries of the prominent men for whom they were intended. The series of bombings killed thirty-five and injured two hundred. The anarchists were mostly Italian and hated Communists, who had confiscated the estates of the anarchist leader Prince Pyotr Kropotkin, but both groups were lumped together as Reds.

The general dislike of "Reds" was not only a result of the bomb throwing. In 1918 the Bolsheviks had sued for peace, concluding a treaty with Germany. This was seen by the allies as a stab in the back, for now the Germans could redeploy dozens of divisions to the Western Front. Nor was it forgotten that the Germans had facilitated the exiled Lenin's voyage back to Russia.

In Washington, on June 2, 1919, Attorney General A. Mitchell Palmer, a Pennsylvania Quaker and Democratic wheelhorse, was himself the victim of a bomb that did extensive damage to his house on R Street. Shaken by the attempt on his life, Palmer studied an intelligence report which noted that 90 percent of radicals were foreign-born and that a 1918 deportation statute would be the most effective way get rid of the bomb throwers. He asked Congress for five hundred thousand dollars to carry out a number of raids in cities with large numbers of radicals and for a law providing for the automatic deportation of aliens belonging to "Red" organizations.

Meanwhile in New York, State Senator Clayton R. Lusk held hearings on Bolshevik activity, although the Bolsheviks had nothing to do with the mail bombs. On November 8, 1919, the Lusk Committee task force of seven hundred police raided seventy-three radical centers throughout the state and arrested five hundred "Reds," about seventy-five of whom were charged with "criminal anarchy." Among those arrested in the raids, only two months after the formation of the two Communist parties in Chicago, were Ben Gitlow of the CLP, and Charles Ruthenberg, Jay Lovestone, and Harry Winitsky, a CPA organizer in New York City.

Bert Wolfe, who was editing the newspaper *The Communist World*, saw a headline after the Lusk raids that said: SEVENTEEN REDS ARRESTED. He knew every name on the list and realized that he was next. He and Ella moved to San Francisco, where he called himself Arthur Albright and got a job as an accountant for Union Carbide.

On January 2, 1920, Palmer's agents under the command of J. Edgar Hoover struck in thirty-five cities, picking up 2,600 aliens. Anyone who could not supply proof of citizenship was detained or taken to Ellis Island to await deportation. There was a second round on January 3, and on January 5 Palmer announced that he would deport 2,720 "alien Reds" (about 800 were actually deported, most of them after hearings).

Palmer was targeting not Communists but Italian and Russian aliens. However, a lot of Communists got caught in his net. The Palmer and Lusk raids succeeded in driving the Communist parties underground, tying up the leadership in the courts, and badly reducing the membership—from twenty-three thousand in December 1919 to fewer than two thousand dues-paying members in January 1920.

Everywhere comrades were being arrested, for distributing leaflets or simply for being at party headquarters. Party funds were depleted by payments for bail and lawyers. From Warren, Ohio, Ed Smith wrote Ruthenberg on March 3, 1920, that "Agent Roach came into the house where I live last Sunday without a search warrant and ransacked my belongings. He stole my membership card in the Communist Party and also my IWW card. He also stole 50 blank membership cards."

From Nucla, Colorado, W. F. Liebenberg reported on March 23 that "I have tried to get contributions for the Communist cause but it is hard to find men and women here in this bourgeois community that are not afraid of jeopardizing themselves to the American czar. . . . We have failed so far, now that the persecution is on. . . . Since the headquarters was raided we have been without an address. . . . Under our next President there will probably be death penalties added." In fact Warren Harding took office in March 1921 and announced that "too much has been said about Bolshevism in America," though it took time for the hounding to die down.

Back in New York City, Ben Gitlow was the first of the Communist leaders arrested in the Lusk raids to be tried, in January 1920. His lawyer was Clarence Darrow, noted defender of the underdog, who told him: "Oh, I know you are innocent, but they have the country steamed up. Everybody is against the Reds." In Gitlow's case, the jury was out less than an hour. He was sentenced to five to ten and went to the big house up the river—Sing Sing.

Lovestone at first escaped arrest but decided in January 1920 to attend Gitlow's trial, which was a way of turning himself in. He was arrested when he walked into the courthouse and charged with criminal anarchy. He was taken to the Tombs while his friends raised the thousand-dollar bail. But while awaiting his own trial, he was subpoenaed to appear as a witness in the February trial of his friend Harry Winitsky, a huge twenty-two-year-old known as the "baby elephant." District Attorney Alexander

Rorke offered Lovestone immunity if he testified, which meant that the charges against him would be dropped. Ruthenberg told him to go ahead and testify but not to give them anything of value. So in February 1920, Lovestone testified for the state in Winitsky's trial. He said that after the September convention in Chicago, he had come back to New York to turn the Socialist Party branches into Communist Party branches. The new CPA branches were organized along assembly district lines. Lovestone was in charge of the branch for the Fourth Assembly District.

He said he saw Winitsky occasionally at party headquarters, 207 East Tenth Street. They discussed the need to teach English to foreign members. Lovestone told the jury that after the Palmer raids in January, he had lamented to Winitsky: "The whole thing has gone up in smoke—they won't permit us to carry on the work." He could not conduct his classes because "they broke into headquarters, destroyed the furniture, and took away all the materials . . . we had no place to teach."

That was all Lovestone said about Winitsky, and there was nothing in his testimony that could help convict his colleague from the Jewish Protectory. So the D.A. tried to get Lovestone to incriminate himself, asking: "Have you ever said that the use of force and violence for the overthrow of the government was justifiable?"

"I did not put it in that form," Lovestone said. "What I said was that we want the revolution to come without violence and that we cannot answer by yes or no whether it must come by violence because we are not prophets."

The jury found Winitsky guilty of criminal anarchy, and the judge, Bartow S. Weeks, set March 29 for the sentencing. On March 28 a despondent Winitsky wrote Lovestone from Cell 113 in the Tombs: "Now I am in here and can do nothing, my folks are hysterical, and I can't expect anything from them. . . . Get after the defense committee and see that the minutes of my case are printed so that an appeal can be taken immediately."

On March 29, Winitsky's lawyer, William J. Fallon, pleaded with the judge for leniency, saying: "The boy's mother is here, and her heart is broken to think that a boy born in America should hold the views he holds. There is not a criminal strain in his entire being. He has a sense of honor far in advance of that we find in most people."

"After your arrest," Judge Weeks said to Winitsky, "you made a speech in which you stated to your fellow Communists that the public officials in the Tombs searched you for bombs. They asked if you had any bombs in your whiskers. Did that conversation take place?"

"Yes, sir," Winitsky replied. "When I was searched on the third tier, one of the men said, 'It is peculiar, you do not seem to have a beard like the rest of the Bolsheviks.' It was said in jest. . . ."

"I am unable to see, Mr. Winitsky," said Judge Weeks, "any excuse for a young man of reputable parents, afforded every opportunity in this land of freedom, who used his education to obtain a position, who had manifestly a clear mind, entering deliberately on a campaign to destroy the government to which he owes everything in his life except breath. He has brought sorrow to his family who have done so much for him. . . . This offense is a serious one. The line between treason, which is punishable by death, and criminal anarchy is so narrow as to be indistinguishable. The punishment for this crime is imprisonment for ten years. The court must fix a term of one half of that period. It is the sentence of this court that you be imprisoned in state prison at hard labor for a minimum of five years and a maximum of ten."

On March 31, Winitsky wrote Lovestone a second letter to say that

I was glad to hear from you. If I thought that you had not played fair with me, I would not have even written to you. I know the position you was [sic] in and I am not complaining, in fact I am exceedingly glad you are free. I hope you will continue to work in the movement. I have spoken to my parents but it does no good. I can't change their opinions. They will get over it, however. I was on my way to Sing Sing yesterday but I was brot [sic] back again. Fallon got a stay in that Supreme Court. All I ask of you is to do your level best. Having your assurance I am satisfied that you will do whatever is possible. . . . Your friend and comrade, Harry.

Soon Winitsky joined Gitlow in Sing Sing. The guards said, "They'll have to blast the cell block to get him in." In October, Ruthenberg arrived, also sentenced to five to ten. He tried to lift the spirits of his fellow Communists, saying that beauty could be found in the most dismal surroundings. From his cell, for instance, he could see the Hudson River, and the wind whipping up the whitecaps, and the hills enveloped in a blue haze. Ruthenberg was quite a ladies' man, and a comrade in New York who was in love with him, Ray Ragozin, came to see him. According to Gitlow, C.E. wooed her in the visitors' room, but as soon as he got out he ditched her.

The Winitsky case, however, was maliciously exploited over the years in the Communist Party faction fights in order to smear Lovestone. This was because District Attorney Rorke said in court that the indictment against Lovestone was dismissed "on the ground that his testimony in the Harry Winitsky trial was a valuable service to the people."

Right after the trial Lovestone's rivals demanded that he be removed from the executive committee for "the distortion of Communist principles and tactics." An investigation was conducted, and it exonerated him completely. Yet the gossip persisted that he had ratted on Winitsky to save his own skin. Five years after the event, in March 1925, William Z. Foster, then Lovestone's main adversary in the faction fights, brought charges before the Control Commission of the Comintern in Moscow, which ruled on April 11, after reviewing the evidence:

> Comrade Lovestone made some statements in this trial which do not entirely correspond to the dignity of a member of the Communist Party. In view of the fact, however, that the examination of Comrade Lovestone lasted eight hours, and the replies in question constituted a very small part of the testimony, and that Comrade Lovestone himself does not now regard the answers as being entirely beyond reproach, and that such answers are to be explained by the fact that the party was then in the process of formation . . . the International Control Commission declares the case settled finally and for all time.

After the Palmer raids, both American Communist parties were in limbo. Many members had been deported, while a number of leaders were in jail. At the same time Ruthenberg was getting fed up with the domination of the language federations in the Communist Party of America. They had a ghetto mentality with no interest in reaching out to a broader base. Also, they promoted violence, and in February they drafted a leaflet that called upon railroad strikers to launch an armed insurrection. Ruthenberg, who came from the mainstream of the Socialist Party, thought that this sort of incitement would get nowhere.

In April 1920 he split with the federations and formed an alliance with the Gitlow-Reed Communist Labor Party. In effect he did what Gitlow and Reed had done at the Chicago convention in September 1919, that is, break away from the Russian-controlled group to create an American party. Lovestone went with him. In May the two groups held a unity conference—though many could not attend, being in jail—and formed the United Communist Party.

There were still two Communist parties, however, and the question was which one would be recognized by the Comintern at its Second Congress. Each American party sent its emissary. John Reed was the trump card of the newly formed United Communist Party, since he was friends with Lenin and the rest of the Bolshevik leadership. Louis Fraina, after some delays, arrived in June to represent the Communist Party of America, now consisting of the language federations.

The Second Comintern Congress lasted from July 17 to August 7, 1920. Unlike at the improvised and meagerly attended First Congress, 169 delegates from thirty-seven countries showed up. Zinoviev, Lenin's "maid of all work," was in charge. Then at the apex of his power, he was determined to make the infant Comintern into a highly disciplined world party in which each national party was a section. To enforce discipline he introduced the twenty-one points, which were conditions of membership, specifying that all parties were subordinate to the Comintern and could be expelled from it. The national parties themselves had to expel "all unreliable elements" and were ordered to create an illegal organization, which would "do its duty at the time of revolution." Subversives would be sent into the armed forces to carry on illegal work. By joining the Comintern, a national Communist party became the agent of a foreign power, its members committed to the subversion and overthrow of the country they lived in as citizens.

In Europe the growth of Communism was phenomenal, with a party of a hundred thousand in Germany and fifty thousand in Italy. But in America the party was not only tiny but split in two. Zinoviev cracked down on the contentious Americans, telling Reed and Fraina that they must attend the congress as members of a single movement. He gave them a deadline of October 10, 1920, to unite their two parties.

When the congress was over, Reed was invited to accompany Zinoviev and Karl Radek, a prominent member of the Comintern Presidium, on a thirteen-hundred-mile train trip to Baku, a major port on the Caspian, for the Congress of the Peoples of the East. Reed caught typhus in Baku and was brought back to Moscow, where he died in October 1920. He was thirty-three years old, a hero of the revolution who had outlived his usefulness but who was nonetheless buried at the foot of the Kremlin wall.

Zinoviev's deadline for American unity came and went, but the bickering continued. Lovestone reported to Bert Wolfe on January 7, 1921, that merger talks were taking place but getting nowhere: "At a recent meeting I had a stormy ovation, all the emphasis on the ova, and rotten ones at that. Malicious slander, vile bluff, reeking filth and base calumny were sung in my dishonor. . . . The merger is most distant. In spite of our superior finances and sales force we are ready to talk agreement on a basis of equality. A $5,800,000 concern—no watered stock—can't yield much more to a cesspool of nuts." Since the party was illegal and underground, Lovestone and his colleagues used the vocabulary of business correspondence, so that the party became the corporation.

On March 12, 1921, Lovestone wrote Wolfe that "apathy, disgust, and disintegration reign supreme . . . the failure to merge has led to the flame of disruption. It is next to impossible to work up a half-effective interest among the rank and file. . . . I came under fire for my activity against the Board of Directors." Lovestone, who liked puns and displayed a touch of youthful cynicism, also called the rank and file "the rank and vile" or "the rank and filth."

Out of patience, Zinoviev ordered a unity convention, which took place at Woodstock, New York, in May 1921. It was a shotgun wedding with a facade of unity to please the Comintern. The new party was called the Communist Party of America and included twenty-one language federations. Lovestone wrote that June to Wolfe in San Francisco none too happily: "Well, our firms have merged."

In the meantime, in Moscow the Comintern line was now in favor of working with non-Communist unions. This led to the creation in early 1921 of yet another agency, the Red International of Labor Unions, or Profintern, which held its first congress in Moscow in July 1921. William Z. Foster, a radical trade unionist with a record of achievements—not yet a Communist but on the verge—attended. Lovestone, who became his archfoe in the party, called him "zig-zag" for changing his line at the slightest hint from Moscow.

Foster was born in 1881 in dire poverty. His father was a militant Irish nationalist, passing down the insurgent gene to his son. His mother bore twenty-three children, of whom four survived as adults. As a young man Foster was a drifter, moving from job to job—a lumberjack in Florida, a streetcar motorman in New York City, a dockworker in Portland. He moved to Spokane in 1909 and joined the Wobblies and the Socialist Party. Thus was formed in youth a seditious temperament. Tall, thin, and high-domed, with blue eyes that slanted downward and jug ears, Foster had a rather pinched, clerical face.

During World War I, Foster became an organizer for the AFL Brotherhood of Railway Carmen. He adopted some of the positions of the despised Samuel Gompers and carried out campaigns for the sale of Liberty Bonds. As one of his biographers, Max Nomad, put it: "You could no longer tell if he was deceiving his opponents, misleading his friends, or deluding himself." In 1917 he organized the Chicago meatpackers, holding back his radical urges to win an eight-hour day, over-time, and raises.

In 1919 with the halfhearted backing of Gompers, he launched a na-tionwide steel strike. Within a month a quarter of a million steelworkers went on strike in the biggest single walkout the country had ever seen. Foster grabbed the headlines, becoming the best-known labor organizer in America. But in spite of the momentum, the strike was broken with the help of Negro scabs. As Foster put it, the only way black workers could advance was to "stick in with the boss and then when there is a strike to step in and take the jobs that are left."

At the Profintern Congress in Moscow in July 1921, Foster ardently agreed with the new line, having long held that the only way for Com-munists to get anywhere in America was to join the existing unions and burrow from within. He also made friends with the head of the Profintern, Solomon Lozovsky, a short, stocky man with a black beard who had once run a small union of hatmakers in Paris.

When Foster got back to Chicago in September 1921, he joined the Communist Party. His aim was to infiltrate the AFL with radical trade unionists. To this end he created the Trade Union Education League (TUEL). Thanks to Foster, the American Communist Party was now in actual contact with American workers. It was positioned to build a mass base in keeping with the Comintern line: "Burrow from within, win over the workers."

In Moscow, however, the American Communists were still consid-ered a pathetic band of slackers. Lenin himself said so, asking why they had boycotted the 1920 presidential election instead of backing the So-cialist candidate, Eugene Debs. And why did they not connect with the working masses? Lenin's prodding seemed to do some good, for Love-stone wrote Wolfe on July 25, 1921: "The corporation is at present in a state of flux. The stockholders are beginning to see the light. Most of us realize that 'money makes money.' We must get new fields of invest-ment. We must get new stockholders. We must get some air . . . we must win a name for our corporation by actually rendering service to the 'people.' . . . I am feverishly pushing things."

The party was still underground, and Lovestone was pushing for the formation of a legal party, which could recruit new members and adver-tise its activities. On November 14, 1921, a cable arrived from Moscow using the corporate vocabulary: "President Chamber of Commerce [Zi-noviev] sent you letter approving immediate manufacture new goods for open market declaring delay not permissible now." Lovestone saw this as a mandate for the formation of a legal party, without "the Russian federation madmen," as the Kansas City–born, onetime Wobbly James Cannon called them.

With the Comintern's blessing, the long-desired Workers' Party was born at a convention at the Star Casino in New York City from December 23 to 26, 1921. This was the second act in the drama of the party, as it broke out of the language-federation ghetto into the world at large. The membership was down to ten thousand, but some new blood came in when the large Finnish and Jewish federations joined up. The Comintern approved "in the most emphatic manner," for its new line was "the United Front." "An open, legal party, accessible to the wide masses, is an absolute necessity for the purpose of enabling the Communists to reach the masses," said the new Comintern instructions.

The twenty-four-year-old Lovestone was so overworked that he wrote Bert Wolfe on April 18, 1922, that "for the first time in my life I broke down in health. . . . My family [he was living with his sister Esther in Brooklyn] then instituted a rigorous blockade against everything that they suspected had anything to do with the movement. . . . I raised hell and put a stop to the farce of trying to save me from myself. I don't know when I'll break down next, but so what?"

Lovestone, who hadn't joined the party for the money, could not afford his own apartment and lived with the bighearted Esther on Ditmas Avenue. Esther provided him bed and board, hocked his watch, waited up for him at night, and gave him bagels and lox for breakfast—he had to have Nova Scotia. So he was a Communist—so what? In the twenties so was half the neighborhood. Cables from Moscow in the corporate vocabulary arrived at Ditmas Avenue regularly, and on numerous occasions Esther entertained the entire American Communist Party Politburo. She was proud of her kid brother, who had gone beyond the shopkeeper mentality to espouse an unpopular political cause that seemed to be fighting for social justice and the rights of the common folk. Already people regarded Jay as one of the up-and-coming party leaders. He was the real spark plug behind Ruthenberg, it was said. Jay in turn was grateful to Esther for her openhandedness. She was someone he could always turn to. When she died in 1971, Jay, who was not overly sentimental, wrote her daughter Mildred: "I was intensely touched by Esther's death. In the whole family she and I were closest over the years."

Ruthenberg was out of jail and wanted to abolish the illegal party, which led to constant infighting. Lovestone was nominally an editor of *The Worker,* the party newspaper, but in fact he was Ruthenberg's "maid of all work, slaving like hell," he wrote Wolfe. "My confidence in men and things has been rocked to its very bottom. I am a thoro' cynic today. . . . It's 4:50 A.M. and just got in from a session. I am tired and depressed. Gee, its [*sic*] hell. Wish I could shake it and go west. . . . Too tired to sleep. I might as well watch the dawn."

For the young, dynamic Lovestone, the endless diatribes were frustrating. The party ideologues could argue for hours on whether the proper phrase was "mass action" or "action of the masses." Lovestone wanted less talk and more action, but still the faction fight raged. The Workers' Party now operated in the open; it held public meetings and published a newspaper. But a minority, known as Geese, refused to give up the underground party, while those who wanted to abolish the illegal party were called Liquidators.

To bring an end to this dispute, the Comintern sent over three special envoys that July 1922: H. Valetski, whom Gitlow described as the cartoon version of an old Bolshie, with disorderly hair and a scraggly beard; Boris Reinstein, who had once operated a drugstore near Buffalo; and the Hungarian revolutionary Joseph Pogany.

The plan was to hold a convention in an out-of-the-way place and unite the factions. Someone knew a farmer who rented out cottages to groups on Lake Michigan near the village of Bridgman, a whistle-stop about an hour's train ride from Chicago. On August 17 forty-five delegates—including Ruthenberg, Lovestone, Bert Wolfe, and Bill Foster, all under assumed names—arrived at the farm. One of the delegates, Francis Morrow, a small man in his forties who was going gray, worked for the Justice Department as Agent K-97.

It was like summer camp, Wolfe recalled, with walks in the woods along paths that led to the sand dunes and the lake, and roll call three times a day. Bert thought the Comintern man, Valetski, was a little high-handed and spoke up to say that "we don't want to be dictated to by someone outside our ruling body." Pogany leaned toward Valetski and said in a stage whisper, "This man thinks he's the American Lenin." "I have no such thought," Bert said, "but I do know that I am an American, at an American convention of the American Communist Party."

At night, outdoor meetings were held by lantern light. Foster, who was new in the party, told those assembled: "The fate of the Communist Party depends on the control of the masses, through the capture of the trade unions, without which revolution is impossible."

By August 20 four agents, notified by Morrow, had moved in on Bridgman. One of the delegates, who went into the village to buy papers, came back and said, "The whole Chicago bum squad is there." The Communists had only one car, and that night it drove out with the three Comintern reps. Some stayed behind to bury documents, while others walked in the dark to St. Joseph, fifteen miles away, where they could catch a train to Chicago. When the agents moved in at dawn, they arrested seventeen Communists for violation of a Michigan criminal syndicalism statute. Among those locked up in the county jail in St. Joseph were Ruthenberg and Lovestone. Bert Wolfe escaped and fled to Mexico with his wife. Foster was arrested on August 26 in Chicago.

The result of the Bridgman convention was to maintain both underground and open work. The Justice Department raid seemed to make the best case for remaining underground. There matters might have rested, but the Comintern had the last word, for at the Fourth Congress in November 1922 Zinoviev formed an American Commission, which gave its blessing to the full legalization of the Workers' Party.

There was a quick transition to legality on December 24, 1922. The illegal party simply dissolved itself, in keeping with Comintern instructions. The Workers' Party was the only American political party under the control of a foreign government, obeying instructions from Moscow as Holy Writ, though pretty feeble as parties went, with a membership of about twelve thousand. Most of these members were still foreign-born, with the Finnish federation accounting for almost half the total and the English-speaking group for only about 5 percent. But its aspirations were great—the defeat of capitalism and the overthrow of the United States government.

These aspirations, however, were known only to the leadership, for the party decreed that its true aims be hidden from the rank and file. Deceit was a necessity. As one of the party theoreticians, Alexander Bittelman, who spoke and read Russian, and whom Lovestone called the Rabbi for his pontificating manner, put it: "The whole truth does not mean telling the workers, at every turn of the game, that the seizure of power will have to be accomplished by force of arms. . . . Telling the workers the whole truth about a given situation does not mean giving the workers the full Communist program. A Communist program is not a Bible to be brought to the workers always in full, with all its implications. It is a guide to action for the advanced guard of the working class—the Communist Party."

3
LOVESTONE IN LOVE

At the age of twenty-five, Jay Lovestone was the wunderkind of the party, a workhorse who would take on any assignment, as well as a brilliant theoretician who turned out articles and editorials for the *Daily Worker* under half a dozen noms de plume. He lived and breathed for the party, or rather the Ruthenberg wing of the party, with a single-mindedness that some admired and others envied. In November 1922, as a veteran of the faction fights, Lovestone wrote Bert Wolfe, still in his Mexican exile: "Life is indeed strenuously complicated, and very few succeed in beating the orgy of stains. . . . Over the years I have lived the life of a bureaucrat, of a feudal baron having his castle, retinue, and petty little kingdom."

Ruthenberg, released from Sing Sing in 1922 and now the New York–based titular head of the party, used Lovestone as his troubleshooter. In June 1922 Lovestone was sent to Berlin, as an American delegate to a Friends of the Soviet Union conference, to lobby for U.S. recognition of the Bolshevik regime and also to collect some funds for the American party—which Lovestone called "getting some oil for our machinery at home." He wrote Wolfe that "Berlin is a beautiful city. Here one sees how little we Americans know about life and how to live it. . . . We seem to be swiftly pouring hell in and out of ourselves. Not so here. The war has left some ugliness and dejection. But go to the streets and all is throbbing with life."

Lovestone may have been impressed by a country with a large and thriving Communist party, while in his own land the Workers' Party of America, although now legal and aboveboard, had a paltry ten thousand members. He did not realize, however, that by 1922 he was under FBI surveillance. In a June 22 report the bureau noted that his party name was L. C. Wheat and described him as "stockily built . . . said to have worn a small mustache. . . . He is understood to have a thin face and to be a member of the Jewish race, although this would not be noticed in his conversation . . . and is inclined to be stoop-shouldered."

Roger B. Nelson was another pseudonym Lovestone used in the party organ *The Communist*. Adopting the tactic of masking the party's true purpose, he wrote that "we might talk ourselves blue in the face about our holy cause, about the wonders of Communism, about the necessity for shouldering guns against capitalism, and yet not enhance the revolution by an iota. But let us talk to the workers about their long hours, their disemployment, their hardships, and the why and wherefore of these, and they will be ready listeners and doers."

Lovestone was trying to "make the party cut some kind of figure in the life of the country," as he wrote Wolfe, and the way to do that was to latch on to a hospitable mass organization. One likely candidate was the Farmer-Labor Party of Minnesota, a grouping of trade unionists and agrarian radicals that had become a major political force in that state, electing two representatives to the House in 1920 and a U.S. senator in 1922. Ruthenberg sent Lovestone to Minnesota, since the party was trying to inject itself into national politics but was having no success on its own. In 1922 it presented only four state tickets.

Lovestone was burning to attend the Fourth Comintern Congress that November in Moscow, but Ruthenberg told him, "The party cannot spare you at this time." He wrote Wolfe that he felt "like a soldier who has not seen a moment's furlough." He was working on famine relief in Russia with the slogan "Give not only to feed the starving but to save the Russian workers' revolution. Give without imposing reactionary conditions as do Hoover and others." On the anti-imperialist front, he was working toward the independence of the Philippines. He was also running a Lenin study group and fighting off the Chicago-based Foster faction, writing Wolfe that "we are in the midst of fathomless turmoil. . . . Today my uncle is crowned, tomorrow he's beheaded. . . . My 99th assassination is probably being prepared, this time to the tune in *Lohengrin*." Jay even did "Jimmy Higgins" work, such as passing out leaflets. No task was too small.

In addition, he produced a veritable Niagara of articles and pamphlets, among the latter "The Party Organization," "America Prepares for the Next War," "Soviet Foreign Policy and World Revolution," "Blood and Steel" (an exposé of the twelve-hour day in the steel industry), and "Labor Lieutenants of American Imperialism" (an attack on the AFL). His magnum opus was a 368-page book published in 1923, *The Government Strikebreaker,* described in an advertisement in the *Daily Worker* as "an arsenal of incontrovertible facts gathered from authentic sources showing how the government has stood back of the employing class in the miners' strike, the railroad strike, in every big industrial conflict, and against the workers when they demand union recognition, better wages, and humane living conditions." The country was still more than ten years away from collective bargaining, and Lovestone's interest in the rights of workers went back to his admiration for Daniel De Leon.

Behind these tactical prolabor pieties, however, Lovestone remained a true believer in world revolution and a fervent admirer of the Soviet Union (which he had yet to see). He had the sense of being in tune with history and gave full vent to his passion in a 1923 speech in Chicago's Ashland Auditorium to celebrate the American party's fourth anniversary. He began by paying homage to "the unstinted sacrifice, the indomitable spirit of the Russian masses . . . the inestimable progress made by the Communist Party of Russia in rebuilding the war-shattered agricultural economy. . . . The Communist spirit has given tongue to the tongueless millions of yesterday in at least fifty lands. . . . The sun never sets on the lands where Communist hearts beat in unison, inspired by the hope of a better day. . . . The Soviet government stands today as the granite foundation of the Communist system."

Lovestone then went on to explain how the party could succeed in the United States only by building a mass base. "Because we have in the United States the highest developed industries," he said, "the most productive working and farming masses in the world, and such vast natural resources, it is necessary and practical to Sovietize America. . . . We must have a united front under the leadership of the Communists. . . . We must engage in direct political struggle for direct political power. . . . We must build a powerful mass Communist party to unify the working class and lead it to as complete a victory as our brave sister party in Russia. . . . The road to revolution is not as smooth as Michigan Boulevard. . . . Prepare for new and sharper conflicts. Prepare for gigantic open-shop drives. There is no title higher for any worker than that of being a member of the Communist International."

Whether it was his workload or the rarefied air of pure Communism,

Lovestone was beginning to feel trapped in his all-consuming party activities; he wrote Bert and Ella Wolfe on January 8, 1923: "I have the social blues all the time. I get tired of having no friends to whom I could talk and with whom I could agree and disagree over other matters than the party routine. . . . I need to break my chains, get out and see the world, say farewell to my narrow confines."

But right there in the headquarters office, a three-room apartment in New York's Washington Heights, was a bewitching young woman, Clarissa Ware, who ran the Research Department. Always to be seen with a briefcase full of clippings, she had written a pamphlet entitled "The American Foreign-Born Worker," replete with statistics and colored charts, which the party sold for fifteen cents. She was, Ben Gitlow said, "as ambitious as she was pretty," a curly-haired brunette with long lashes, a cat's greenish, large-pupiled eyes, and a flirtatious smile.

As the wife of Harold Ware, Crissie, as she was known, had married into one of Communism's first families. Her mother-in-law, Ella Reeve Ware, was better known as Mother Bloor, a charter member of the Communist Labor Party in 1919. At the age of nineteen, in 1881, Ella had married her first cousin Lucien Ware. His father, Dan Ware, had been an ardent abolitionist during the Civil War, in charge of the Underground Railroad in New Jersey. In some families the streak of social activism was passed down the generations, in this case from abolitionism to Socialism to Communism, as in other families property was handed down. Recent genetic studies in fact suggest that "radicalism is 65 percent heritable."

Harold Ware joined the Communist Party at the same time as his mother. He was unprepossessing, with a plain and open face, and wore rimless pince-nez glasses. When he went hoboing out West, his Wobbly friends ribbed him about his "sissy specs." In 1921, when the famine hit Russia, Hal raised seventy-five thousand dollars with the help of the party and bought twenty-two tractors so that he could teach the Russian peasants mechanized agriculture. In May 1922 he left for Russia with the tractors, nine farmer-instructors, a medical unit, several tons of food, and his wife, Clarissa.

All this cargo went aboard a Baltic-American liner headed for the Latvian port of Liepaja, from which they took the train to Moscow. When they got there they found that the food and tractors were scattered in half a dozen freight yards, which seemed like deliberate sabotage. But because his project had the support of Lenin, Ware was able to appeal to Felix Dzerzhinsky, the ruthless head of the Cheka (security police), who was also commissar for transport. Dzerzhinsky pushed a button on his desk and said: "Call every stationmaster where those cars are scattered and give them three days to have the train assembled at the correct station. Immediate removal and other consequences if the train is not ready."

In less than three days the train was ready, and Ware and his people proceeded to a collective farm in the Kuznetsk Basin, about four hundred miles east of Moscow. There, in spite of the local priest, who called the tractors "devils," Ware and his North Dakota sodbusters taught tractor plowing to the Russians. Soon he had forty-four peasants working the twenty-two tractors on two seven-hour shifts. They plowed and harrowed four thousand acres, sown to rye and harvested. Hal Ware ended up staying in Russia eight years, with trips back to the States to raise funds and buy equipment. He was promoted to even larger farms, one a former tsarist estate in the north Caucasus, between the Black and Caspian Seas, another a fifteen-thousand-acre state farm called Maslo Kut. When he went home in 1930, he was a legend in Russia, the man who had brought the one-horse peasants into the age of mechanized farming.

In the thirties Hal Ware had a second career as a covert Comintern agent whose mission it was to penetrate the old-line U.S. government agencies. The so-called Ware cell has in recent years gained some notoriety, for one of its members was Alger Hiss. But Ware's espionage activities were cut short on the night of August 13, 1935, as he drove on a twisty mountain road in Pennsylvania. He collided with a truck and died the next morning in a hospital in Harrisburg at the age of forty-five.

On Ware's first farm in 1922, Clarissa learned to drive a tractor and helped train the young Russian drivers. But she missed their daughter, Judy, who had been left behind with relatives, and went home after six months. Through her party connections she found work in the headquarters office.

Back on the collective farm in Russia, Hal fell in love with the beautiful, honey-haired Jessica Smith, a Quaker pacifist who was in the Volga region doing famine relief work for the Friends Committee. She stayed on the farm with Hal, who divorced Crissie on one of his trips home and married Jessica in a ceremony performed by the Socialist leader Norman Thomas. After Hal's death Jessica married John Abt, a fellow member of the Ware group and later the lawyer for the Communist Party. For many years Jessica worked at the Soviet embassy in Washington as the editor of the propaganda magazine *Soviet Russia Today*.

At the time Lovestone was bemoaning that his days were all work and no play, there was Crissie Ware at the desk next to his, taking out a pocket mirror and putting on her lipstick, or bantering with him over an editorial he had written, or asking him whether he had a girlfriend. They spent many hours together, and it turned out they were both lonely. Crissie was divorced from Hal, while Jay felt youthful longings that had nothing to do with the party line.

Jay fell in love, for the first time, with the same kind of intensity that he applied to his work. Crissie, who was a few years older and had been through marriage and childbirth, responded playfully, flattered by his ardor but wary of his possessiveness. The affair did not last long. In April 1923 Crissie went to St. Joseph to cover Ruthenberg's trial on the charge from the Bridgman raid. Sentenced to three to ten years, he was released pending appeal. He may have impressed Crissie as a heroic martyr to the cause. According to Ben Gitlow, she zeroed in on Ruthenberg in a deliberate and calculating manner, saying that if a woman wanted to make a career for herself in the party, she must attach herself to one of its leaders.

Soon she was attached to Ruthenberg. Gitlow noticed that the arrangement of the office changed. Before, you had to go through the Research Department to get to Ruthenberg's office. Lovestone had his desk right up against the partition between the two offices. But upon his return from the trial, Ruthenberg moved Lovestone out of the Research Department. When he wanted to be alone with Crissie, he locked the door. "The amorous proclivities of Crissie Ware," wrote Gitlow, "threatened to create a political crisis."

It should be noted that, along with the political line of the Comintern, there was a line on love. In the euphoria of the early years after the overthrow of tsardom in Russia came a loosening of social restraints and a reaction against "bourgeois" standards. This was the period of free love, easy divorce, and legal abortion. Outside Russia the various parties did their best to carry out the line and rid themselves of bourgeois inhibitions. Gitlow wrote that when he got out of Sing Sing, he was propositioned by the wife of a member of the Central Executive Committee, who said: "I will be frank with you, Ben. I like you. I'd like to go to bed with you." "But you are the wife of a good friend of mine," Gitlow said. "You and I are revolutionists," the woman replied. "My husband understands my position perfectly, and has no objection if I occasionally go to bed with another man."

But Lovestone was not so broad-minded. For the one and only time in his life, he was brokenhearted over a woman. His armor of brash self-confidence and witty cynicism was pierced. His mentor had stolen his girl. This romantic disappointment came at a time when things were going unusually well in the party. As he wrote Bert and Ella Wolfe on June 23, 1923: "The party was never as unified as it is today. The Geese and the Liquidators have been liquidated. For the first time in our stupid history there are no groupings along the lines of ancestry or intention or hope."

In the same letter Lovestone could not resist venting his spleen toward Ruthenberg and Crissie Ware:

> Ruthenberg and I are not getting along as well as we used to. . . . He is just gone mad with a rabid form of egomania. . . . Notoriety is his middle name. . . . Then he made another female conquest. This one is a shrewd, husky female afflicted with a college education and totally devoid of any mental integrity. She is a personification of a woman at her worst and typifies the animal that makes all women so repugnant to me. . . . Since she has become Ruthenberg's undermate, she has gone all blooey and nuts. . . . Ruthenberg, because of this Cleopatra no. 231 or so, is making many mistakes in his work . . . here and there, instigated by the foul bird, he goes off the handle and reacts against me and my work. . . . But no one is going to get away with any fake stunts with me.

There was chaos in the office. Jay now held a grudge against his boss, while Crissie had brought out in him a strong misogynist streak. Of course in those days the party itself, with its all-male leadership, was sexist. Women were routinely referred to as undermates rather than comrades. Ella Wolfe, who was immensely fond of Jay while sizing him up dispassionately, replied from Mexico City on June 30: "Why should you lead the attack? Why is it that you always make yourself so much disliked? What is there in you that is always itching for a fight? When oh when will you grow up? . . . C.E.'s love affairs are personal, they don't concern you nor the party, insofar as they do not hinder his work. You who only six months ago thought so much of the man's ability to reason, were willing to follow his policy, and now you have done a complete somersault. I feel again your adolescent tendency towards fragmentation."

Jay was so upset that he unburdened himself to Hal Ware, who was back in the United States on a purchasing mission. From Salina, Kansas, where he was buying tractors, Hal wrote Jay: "All this about Cris and C.E. is one I'm sorry to say panned out and I can't feel happy about it. Cris responds to him and as you say is free, white and 21. . . . You see I pulled out because I felt Cris could be happier with you or someone else. I consciously played a game and built up my shock absorbers to give her a chance. She's taken it head on and I'm not going to holler. . . . Nevertheless I feel spiritually sick. . . . I suppose Cris didn't take the role I figured she would."

Jay, however, was hollering. The man who in the eyes of some of his colleagues in the party was a cold and calculating conniver in this one instance revealed an absolute loss of self-control, releasing his emotions in a lovesick epistle that Crissie found so irritating she sent it back to him with her comments in the margin:

He wrote:

My rapidly fading but evermore charming *Schickselle,* I am going through the worst and most serious crisis of my life. . . . Crissie I have prepared a lifetime to live for you. For a while you believed you also found in me the ideal. [*Not correct,* Crissie commented.]

Today I am crude, I am rough, I am childish, I am mechanical, I am not good enough for you. [*Not correct.*]

You love Ruthenberg, you don't love me. [*How can you say such things?*]

I know your love for Ruthenberg will be only a brief spell. [*You have no right to use that word.*]

But Brownie dear, I know love can't be ordered. [*Damn you how can you use that word?*]

I will find you only when you find yourself. [*As long as you go on this way you can never find me.*]

Jay has loved and loves evermore his Crissie. [*That's a goddam lie.*]

Ruthenberg is now your ideal. [*Another goddam lie but you can be sure you are not.*]

Someone else in my place might find solace in another woman, in sex intercourse. But I can't. [*A damn shame you are so perfect.*]

I am begging you to give me a chance. [*How can I love a weakling—a mad, insane, jealous male thing?*]

Come back, My Crissie. . . . Come back, my *Schickselle.* Come back my Brownie. [*The use of "back" is quite typical.*]

But Crissie did not come back. This spirited, adventurous, tough-minded, lovely young woman died only a few months after Jay's moonstruck letter. Pregnant, probably with Ruthenberg's baby, she had an abortion and died on the operating table. Jay wrote Ella Wolfe on September 22 that "it was a dreadful shock to me." The shock may have come in part from wondering whether it could have been his baby, since Crissie's affairs with Jay and C.E. overlapped.

In any case Lovestone never married and had no children, though he found time for affairs with a succession of women. His misogyny, which was aroused when Crissie dumped him but subsided into a lingering suspicion of female disloyalty, did not prevent him from being attracted to women, and they were attracted to him, drawn to his vitality as if from a residue of the animal competition for the best breeder, the lion with the mightiest roar. In our society today high-energy performers such as athletes and rock musicians are followed by groupies; when Lovestone was in the party, it too had its share of groupies circling the leaders.

It was Jay's bad luck that C.E. was his boss. When Ruthenberg went on trial in April 1923 in St. Joseph, Michigan, on charges of "advocating criminal syndicalism" (the trial that Crissie Ware covered for the *Daily Worker*), Lovestone was called as a defense witness. Under cross-examination he revealed the existence of Communist front groups, primarily Friends of Soviet Russia, which he admitted was under party control and had collected $725,000 in cash and $450,000 in supplies up to July 15, 1922. He also disclosed that the news agency Federated Press was party-controlled and of great service to the party in meeting the attacks of Samuel Gompers and Secretary of Commerce Herbert Hoover. The FBI found Lovestone's testimony so interesting that it ordered a copy of the 135-page transcript from the court reporter.

By September the party headquarters had moved to Chicago, which Lovestone considered "a darned dirty city and a disgrace to America." He was in the dumps, mourning Crissie and missing New York.

In 1923 a very different Workers' Party emerged, freed to some extent from the albatross of the language federations but now under the influence of the inimitable Joseph Pogany, alias John Pepper. His life in the party shows that the Comintern became a depository for all sorts of picturesque rogues, who used Communism as they might have floated a Ponzi scheme, to advance their careers and unleash their personal extravagance. In March 1919, Béla Kun proclaimed a Bolshevik government in Hungary and made Pogany his commissar for war. The first foreign soviet, nicknamed Russia on the Danube, lasted about five months, after which Kun and Pogany fled to Moscow and were given Comintern jobs.

Pogany, or Pepper, was one of the three Comintern representatives who came to the Bridgman convention in August 1922, but he stayed behind when the other two went home and appointed himself commissar of the American party. Short, balding, and bespectacled, strutting about like a plump pigeon, Pepper could barely speak English but thought of himself as an expert on American political trends. When agricultural prices dropped in early 1922, he predicted a farmers' revolt. He also foresaw a black secession in the South, writing that the region's 8 million Negroes were on the verge of a spontaneous uprising. Although in the country illegally under an assumed name, he loved renown and signed his articles in the *Daily Worker.*

Pepper's plan in 1923, in accordance with the Comintern's "united front" line, was to bring the party into mainstream American politics by finding a hospitable ally, which was a little like a virus looking for a welcoming host. Pepper's choice was the Chicago-based Farmer-Labor Party, one of those regional movements then in vogue as a result of the 1920–1922 depression and an emulation of the British Labour Party. When Pepper saw that the party was growing into a national movement of left-wing unionists and agrarian radicals, he decided to bring the Workers' Party under its tent.

John Fitzpatrick, a onetime Irish blacksmith who had launched the Chicago Farmer-Labor Party, called a convention for July 3, 1923, to which the Workers' Party was invited. Pepper saw his chance and masterminded the packing of the convention with Communist delegates. On July 3 somewhere between four hundred and seven hundred delegates (estimates vary wildly) arrived in Chicago's Ashland Auditorium claiming to represent six hundred thousand workers and farmers. Even though the Workers' Party had only ten delegates in its own name, many others came in the names of bogus fraternal societies such as the Lithuanian Workers' Literature Society and the United Workingmen Singers. Thus the Communists had about two hundred hidden delegates and were able to steamroll the convention.

On July 5, Fitzpatrick walked out of his own convention, saying that what the Communists had done was "on the level of a man being invited to your house as a guest and then once in the house seizing you by the throat and kicking you out the door." Ruthenberg called for the formation of a new party, the Federated Farmer-Labor Party, which a majority of delegates endorsed.

Pepper was exultant. He thought the Communists were now in control of a mass party. Bill Foster said it was "a landmark in the history of the working class." But as soon as it became clear that the Federated Farmer-Labor Party was Communist-controlled, all the non-Communists jumped ship. Alfred Wagenknecht, the leader of the Workers' Party left wing, said that the FFLP "consisted of ourselves and our nearest relatives."

Blind to reality, Pepper insisted that the next move was to throw the

Communist-created FFLP behind the Wisconsin Progressive "Fighting Bob" La Follette, who in the fall of 1923 seemed to be a long shot for the 1924 presidential election. The outgoing and eloquent La Follette had been elected to the Senate in 1906, when that body was regarded as a sanctuary for millionaires. He was a new breed of senator, who embodied an ideology of "the people" against vested interests for control of the government. Like a New Dealer ahead of his time, he backed labor legislation and fought the power of the banks and railroads. In 1922, seeing no hope in the two major parties, he formed the Conference for Progressive Political Action, a federation that included the Farmer-Labor Party and the sixteen railroad brotherhoods. His aim was to get progressives, regardless of party, elected to Congress. In 1924, however, a certain amount of "labor party fever" was abroad in the land, and when La Follette was nominated at the Cleveland Progressive convention in July as a third-party candidate, he was endorsed by the Socialist Party as well as by the conservative AFL.

In the election year of 1924, both factions in the Workers' Party (Ruthenberg-Pepper-Lovestone and Foster-Cannon) agreed that a tactical alliance with La Follette would be desirable. The method of approach would be to latch on to another burgeoning Farmer-Labor party, the one in Minnesota, which in 1922 had elected both the state's senators and two out of its ten members of the House. In the summer of 1924, Lovestone, a strong backer of the strategy, returned to Minnesota to help organize the alliance. The stage seemed set for the Communists to give La Follette their backing, backing he had not asked for, knowing that Communist support was a poisoned gift.

This intriguing coalition, however, never came to pass. Not because of events in the United States but because of Lenin's death. After a series of strokes the Bolshevik leader died in January 1924. The opening bout of the five-year struggle for succession in the Soviet Union pitted Leon Trotsky against the triumvirate of Gregory Zinoviev (head of the Comintern), Lev Kamenev (head of the Moscow soviet), and Joseph Stalin (general secretary of the party).

In April 1924, Foster and Pepper arrived in Moscow for a meeting of the Executive Committee of the Communist International (ECCI). They wanted Comintern guidance in the projected backing of La Follette. Since Trotsky was against it, calling it "a senseless and infamous adventure," Zinoviev decided to preempt him, to avoid being outflanked. On May 6, at an American Commission meeting, he told Foster and Pepper to repudiate La Follette and break with the Minnesota Farmer-Labor

Party. The third-party alliance would only make the Workers' Party "a tail to the bourgeois kite."

Foster was at first astonished by the turnabout, which would once again isolate and marginalize the U.S. Communist Party, but upon reflection he decided that since it was useless to argue the issue, he would try to gain something in exchange. He agreed to adopt the new line in return for Pepper's recall. Much to the surprise of Ruthenberg and Lovestone back in Chicago, the Comintern gave Foster what he wanted. Pepper stayed in Moscow, and the Farmer-Labor front came crashing down.

On May 26, 1924, Lovestone wrote Bert Wolfe: "Things are wretched. We have just learned that the main office has . . . instructed us categorically against any alliance with or voting for La Follette. . . . None of us here can understand it. . . . It will prove disastrous for the party and will put us back years. We now have to smash agreements and arrangements we entered into months ago. . . . Ruthenberg, the rest of the boys and I have been having many sleepless nights over the fretfulness."

But on May 29, before the Communists could officially drop La Follette, he denounced them as "the mortal enemies of the progressive movement." The third-party alliance unraveled at both ends.

Lovestone did not think that the party could become a political force on its own. He believed it had to make tactical alliances such as the one with La Follette. He wrote Will Weinstone on July 28, 1924: "I am as convinced as ever of the correctness of our old policy. . . . I do not repudiate my views, though I am now strictly abiding by the Comintern decision." This was Lovestone's first break with the Comintern line, the seed of what would one day be called his "American exceptionalism." But in 1924 he was still an obedient servant of the Comintern.

Lovestone wrote Pepper on August 24 that "the decision of the Comintern coupled with the swift shift in tactics after St. Paul have made the party membership somewhat dizzy." There was a great deal of skepticism and cynicism, an absence of hope. "The I-don't-give-a-hang attitude dominates nearly all of us. The new policy seems to have checked our aggressiveness."

Still hoping to revive the Farmer-Labor strategy after the election, Lovestone threw himself into the faction fight against the Foster-Cannon camp, whom he saw as the scuttlers of third-party alliances. He carried the battle into each district, enlisting supporters, counting noses. He saw this as "a fight for our lives," and wrote the Wolfes in September that "we have never had factionalism as bitter and as intense."

The story was told of the pro-Foster Communist leader Jack Johnstone, who spent a number of months in Moscow, leaving his wife, Elizabeth, behind. When he returned she met his ship at the dock and confessed that she had lived with another comrade while he was away. Johnstone's only query was "Which faction?" When she told him that her lover belonged to the Foster faction, he breathed a sigh of relief.

While deeply engaged in the faction fights, Lovestone was also strident in his espousal of the class struggle and felt the need to denigrate bourgeois values, even within his own family. His sister Sarah's husband, Charles Gray, had given him a job making buttonholes during his City College years. But in September 1924, Jacob Hartman of Friends of Soviet Russia wrote Lovestone to ask, "Does your brother-in-law still run his silk-mill in Paterson? I would like to pick up some general information on textile processes." Lovestone replied, "My brother-in-law the Paterson cockroach capitalist was roasted out of business some time ago. In plain Sovietsky he is kaput—bankrupt—no more in business. That's the way of all the capitalist flesh."

This militancy, however, was a form of Communist posturing, for in fact Lovestone liked his brother-in-law, with whom he remained in close touch. The Gray family had moved to Detroit, where Max opened the Guarantee Toggery Shop at 519 Gratiot Avenue. In 1924 Jay complained to Max that he was being undermined by factional oppponents. Max responded with brotherly advice: "You did not expect that while you are away others will take advantage of your absence to promote plans which will suit them best. Everybody for himself and the devil take the hind one. That makes the world go round. . . . Get rid of the temporary discouragement and fight on. . . . If we would get discouraged so quick we would not live for even one day."

But a few months later Max admitted to his own discouragement, writing Jay: "I am broke. Busted. Things went against me and I must start something." His idea to recoup was to send four neckties in a package to four hundred businessmen and say "a friend suggested their name to buy them. . . . I want you to compose for me a forceful letter," he told Jay. "No, the idea is not new. There is a party in Philadelphia has made a nice piece of money in this game, why not me?"

And so Lovestone, vilifier of the merchant class and ardent young Communist revolutionary, composed a promotional message to help sell his brother-in-law's neckties: "Dear so and so, the holidays are with us! This is a season for happiness and bringing joy to friends! An alltime, oldtime friend of yours has had a happy idea. At his kind suggestion I thought of sending four handsome, high-class ties. Please send your remittance etc." In Jay's life there were party ties, family ties, and neckties. In spite of his promotional copy, the Guarantee Toggery Shop went under, and Sarah and Max moved to the Bronx and opened a candy store.

While the faction fight raged, Foster and Gitlow were on the hustings in their 1924 campaign for president and vice president. Moscow had supplied the party with fifty thousand dollars to get the Workers' Party ticket on the ballot in as many states as possible, and it succeeded in fourteen states. "Someday," Foster said in one of his speeches, "a Communist will lead the government that rules over America. When that time comes, the position will not be called president, it will be chairman of the All-American Soviet." The results in November showed 15,720,000 votes for the Republican Calvin Coolidge, 8,380,000 for the Democrat John W. Davis, 4,825,000 for La Follette (who died the following year, stopping the Progressive momentum), and 33,000 for Foster. This meager harvest seemed to confirm Lovestone's analysis that the party could not advance under its own steam, though Foster claimed it was "a great Communist victory."

After the failure of the Farmer-Labor policy, the failure in the election, and the failure of his affair with Crissie Ware, there was one bright spot in Lovestone's life in 1924—he was in love again, and this time it was reciprocated. Indeed it turned into the great love of his life, and it came about as the result of one of his clandestine party activities. American Communists going to Moscow had serious difficulties with travel documents. Since the United States did not recognize the Soviet regime, they could not use their American passports. Lovestone had a connection in Montreal who supplied him with Canadian passports made out in the names (or aliases) of traveling Communist leaders.

This contact was a customs broker named Nathan Mendelssohn, who according to the Communist leader Earl Browder was an agent for Soviet intelligence, the OGPU. Born in Romania in 1890, Nathan had come to Canada in 1900. He and his brother Samuel operated a customs brokerage and freight-forwarding business, the Mendelssohn Brothers, with offices in Montreal and Toronto. They handled the clearance of goods through customs, the warehousing of the goods, and the shipment from warehouse to customers. Nathan had excellent contacts with Canadian customs and passport officials.

It was evident from the correspondence between them that Nathan was supplying Jay with forged passports, which in the Comintern were known as boots. Without boots a man cannot travel. On March 11, 1924, Nathan wrote Jay: "How should shipment proceed? From Canada or the United States? To England or France?" Jay replied, "The shipment will be made thru an American port." On May 17 Nathan wired: "Am holding documents." On June 2 he wrote: "I have the necessary documents including the German endorsement which is good for six months, while the documents are good for three years." This meant a Canadian passport with a German visa for transit in Berlin en route to Moscow.

In the Comintern files in Moscow there is a memo from Lovestone to Ella Wolfe dated October 19, 1926, which says:

> Immediately go up to my brother [Morris, in the Bronx] and do the following:
>
> 1. Tell him he has my papers and that I have phoned you about them. . . . Take only the bare passport.
> 2. Please mail it to Nathan Mendelssohn, 111 Youville Square, Montreal, Canada, marked PERSONAL and REGISTERED. Make the return address not Ella or Bert but perhaps your mother's—Goldberg. Tell him to get a six months' German and a renewal of the passport for two or three years. Ask him to hold the renewed passport and visa until he hears from me. . . . Of course you must keep in the strictest confidence the whole transaction and every item and detail of it. Only you and Bert know about it.

Nathan's wife, Esther, was born Mendel (shortened from Mendelovitch), the same year as Nathan, 1890. Like Nathan she had come to Canada from Romania. When she was a child her beloved mother, Hanna, died of tuberculosis, and her father remarried. Esther disliked her stepmother, who wore her mother's jewelry. Although she was the product of an Orthodox Jewish family, she grew up an atheist and a political radical, saying, "How could there be a God that allows such suffering?"

Esther was a beauty, with large, expressive brown eyes, high cheekbones, an aquiline nose, sensual, bee-stung lips, and thick, lustrous, chestnut hair cut in a page boy. In her early twenties Esther became an actress and toured with a company that performed Shakespeare in Yiddish. She played Juliet at Pinski's New Little Art Theater in New York. In the Yiddish version, the Capulets and Montagues were turned into rival religious sects, the Hasidim and Mitnaggedim. The balcony scene was played in a synagogue with Raphael (Romeo) saying to Shaindele (Juliet), "The Jewish love of God is everlasting."

In 1920, when they were both thirty, Esther married Nathan, but the marriage was not a success. Over the years, however, time taught them to become companionable, so they never divorced. Nathan was a man-about-town, a skirt chaser, and, in Esther's words, "a bastard." Esther told her niece Anita Mendel Billick, "Sex is terrible. Don't ever get married. Don't make that mistake." Esther and Nathan had no children, and Esther told Anita, "I don't want a child with that man." Once, when she got pregnant, she had an abortion.

In April 1924 Jay went to Montreal to see Nathan on passport business, and he met the bored and unhappy Esther. There was a strong and immediate attraction between them. Back in Chicago, Jay wrote her a note: "I changed my mind quite a little about you. Here it is in black on white from one who wouldn't give most women a license to live, let alone conquer or marry." Coming from Jay Lovestone, this was practically a love letter. He followed up by sending an autographed copy of his book, *The Government Strikebreaker.*

Jay was seven years younger than Esther, who seemed to have concentrated upon him all her feelings, both passionate and maternal. The affair blossomed in 1924 and continued in one form or another for more than sixty years (though there were long periods of absence), until Esther's death in 1988.

At the time she met Jay, Esther was overcome by feelings of worthlessness and prone to allergic illnesses such as hives. She felt that her life was purposeless, wasted on a husband she could barely stand. She had thought of leaving Nathan, but her brother Charlie told her to "stay on the job" because she needed a "provider." This too disgusted her, though she had no alternative.

When Jay—this bundle of energy, this young man with a cause, not exactly a Valentino but incredibly alive—came into her life, she fell deeply in love. Here was a man she could believe in and admire, an authentic revolutionary working for the betterment of mankind. Jay the Communist leader and thinker seemed far superior to her cheating husband with his humdrum customs business.

Jay helped Esther lift herself out of her self-deprecation. When he told her that he faced a jail sentence on the Bridgman charge, she replied, "I know that if I had to stay in jail I'd die, perhaps that would be good riddance to a piece of useless flesh." But Jay gave her what she called "royal treatment," after she had been "treated as a second-class messenger all my adult life." Still, she was not sure she was "the type men would set Rome on fire for, but you know my shortcomings."

Her father's remarriage and her husband's philandering had made her wary of men, so at first she approached Jay a little gingerly, telling him, "You have a better mind than I gave you credit for and tremendous possibilities to develop, but you still need humanizing." Gradually she saw that her love for him was a way of validating her own life, telling him, "You are the most remarkable person I know, the greatest treasure life has offered." They became each other's mainstays, each the one person the other could truly count on, each basking in the unconditional love and admiration that neither had previously experienced.

Jay presented himself to Esther as the underdog in the faction fights, unfairly attacked. "It is only my sense of humor and unbounded faith that enables me to stand up and hit back," he wrote her. "From now on I will be the center of the attack—filthy, slimy, murderous . . . should they win they'll have my head. . . . You see dearest, its [*sic*] the ups and downs, the vicissitudes of life and not the pleasantries, that make us enjoy the even tone of our existence."

Esther began to see Jay not only as a lover but as her mission in life. It made her feel useful to help this splendid and unjustly bedeviled Communist leader in his political crusade. "If you need money, don't hesitate," she said. She kept a "Jay reserve fund" that he could draw on. "I want you to feel proud of having me for a lover," she said.

Far from objecting, Nathan was glad to have her involved, for he was busy with his girls. He and Jay remained friends, often vacationing together, and colleagues in party work. But Nathan drew the line at financial backing, saying, "If he got himself into this fix, let him get himself out." Esther insisted, saying, "You can't let a friend down."

Nathan didn't mind when Esther came to New York to see Jay that October, 1924. After meeting his sister Esther, she wrote: "Tell your sister there are now two Esthers who love you." She also sent him her photograph, inscribed on the back, "To a god among men." This sounds like a tribute to Jay's sexual prowess, to a physical compatibility that Esther had finally found at the age of thirty-four. But it was also an expression of deep and abiding devotion, not only to the man but to the ideals he believed in, which she shared. For both Nathan and Esther were members of the Canadian Communist Party.

After her time with Jay in New York, Esther's love letters began arriving with increasing regularity:

> You are in my blood. I feel a pride in the beauty of your soul
> and the beauty of your lovely blue eyes. Yes, Jay, there is a lot of
> beauty in you, don't suppress it.

Have dreamt of you two nights in succession. The first time you were asleep in the big bed here. . . . The next dream doesn't bear telling on paper.

I am knotted up and need you to untie me. . . . One thing I know, that is: I love you.

Jay kept up the correspondence, more guardedly with Esther, and also with Nathan, writing him on November 13, 1924, after the election: "When I think of the party in the elections and the results achieved, I remind myself of those first-class hotels where the bellhops get the change and the managers get the rest. We got nothing. I have my doubts whether we polled 20,000 votes, despite the reputation of our mass leader."

Esther took to calling Jay "my darling child," while he called her "mother." Like all mothers, she fretted. She sent him money when he was short. She worried when he had to make court appearances on long-standing charges—"criminal syndicalism" in St. Joseph, Michigan (for the Bridgman meeting), and "disorderly conduct" in McKeesport, Pennsylvania, as the result of his arrest on September 9, 1923, at a "free speech rally." She advised him, with her training on the stage, on correct breathing: "I started with a frail weak breathy voice but succeeded in rounding my tones so that my voice can carry in any theater."

Since they were apart most of the time, Esther was in a state of continuous longing. "I'd give half a life for a few days with you," she wrote. She did her best to keep the peace in her household, but wrote, "This is a messy world at times." Whenever she despaired of life with Nathan, she could summon up her idealized image of Jay. "I wish I could find a way to send you a chain of stars and moons and suns," she wrote him, "and oceans of love to keep you and bring you back to one for whom you know, or should know, that you are the whole of the world."

4

THE CHICAGO YEARS

The line for the American party, dictated by the Comintern in Moscow, depended on the twists and turns of the succession battle. Stalin, Zinoviev, and Kamenev, united against Trotsky, began to pick him apart through their control of decision-making committees. In January 1925 the Central Committee, which Stalin controlled, stripped Trotsky of the War Commissariat. Once he lost his operational base, it was only a matter of time before Trotsky's other positions were whittled away and he was sent into exile.

With Trotsky neutralized, the anti-Trotsky triumvirate fell apart; Zinoviev and Kamenev began to challenge Stalin. In 1925 Stalin formed a new alliance with the editor of *Pravda,* the leading Bolshevik theoretician Nikolai Bukharin. Together they built a majority in the Politburo against Kamenev and Zinoviev.

Into this nest of vipers stepped, in January 1925, a delegation of four unwary American Communist leaders representing the two competing factions—Ruthenberg and Lovestone, and Foster and Cannon. Actually, Ruthenberg did not arrive until February, for he had insisted on taking along his new girlfriend and assistant, Anna David. As Max Bedacht, who was in charge of party headquarters in their absence (and who in the thirties recruited Whittaker Chambers into the underground party), wrote Lovestone on January 28, "There is that damn female interfering with everything under the sun. Damned forever be the one who ever suggested to CE to take that *Weiberfleisch* [woman flesh] along. . . . The mere fact that he hid away with that damned female for a whole day made it impossible. The next boat will leave on the fourth. . . . He is hell bent on taking that encumbrance along." This was another indication of the party's male chauvinism, in which women were "encumbrances."

The four came to Moscow to discuss the strategy of the American party and find out what the Comintern line was, a business that kept them there until mid-April.

For Lovestone it was an exciting time, his first trip to Russia. When you reached the border and the train stopped for customs and you saw your first Red Army soldier, a young peasant in his teens, parading up and down with a rifle on his shoulder under the big arch that said "Proletariats of the World Unite" (in four languages), well . . . that was something you never forgot. You came from a country where Communists were a persecuted minority, hounded and jailed, to a country where the working class ruled and the Communist Party was in power. And when you got to Moscow, you didn't have to be furtive or secretive, for you were part of a global movement, not just Russian but German and British and Chinese and Mexican, actually working out the strategy to achieve a world revolution. It was heady stuff. And then to see the leaders, who up until then had been only names, up close, and to hear them speak . . . it was soul-stirring. You were not a stranger, you were not a visitor, you were not a tourist . . . you were home.

Lovestone was in a state of sustained excitement, face to face with the revolution, big as life. He watched Stalin, Zinoviev, and Bukharin closely, and discussed tactics with them. Bukharin told him, "Always make your political line clear. Then hold your conferences." With the frail, reddish-haired Bukharin, whom Lenin called "the favorite of the whole party," Lovestone formed a lasting friendship.

The four Americans stayed at the six-story Hotel Lux, the place for visiting foreign Communists, on Tverskaia Street. It was convenient for the political police to have these guests from distant lands, speaking different languages, all using false passports and aliases, in one place. The Lux was full of police informers, reporting on the goings-on, who was in whose room. They didn't have wiretaps then, but they had long ears. Oh, if those walls could speak, Ella Wolfe used to say. At the same time the Lux was a congenial place, a convention headquarters for revolutionaries, where friendships were quickly made, and conversations lasted through the night, and there was a great deal of sharing of razors, lipsticks, pens, coffee, and cigarettes.

The Comintern's American Commission began meeting in January

1925 to hear the factional grievances. Lovestone wrote Gitlow: "I will make the bastards [Foster and Cannon] show their true colors." He wrote Bert Wolfe that Zinoviev had called the sessions before the American Commission "the best-organized battle of any intra-party strife" he had ever seen. "You can rest assured I did my bit of battling," he added. On April 6, Zinoviev delivered a much-appreciated compliment to the American delegation, saying that he was glad to meet the new comrades, "outstanding figures who have stood the storm, men who have a great future in our movement." Lovestone, at age twenty-seven the youngest of the four Americans, felt that Zinoviev was speaking particularly to him.

A few days later the new Comintern line for the American party was announced. The previous instructions barring Farmer-Labor alliances were now modified. The American party should continue to work among the workers and farmers, and should not shun alliances with reform-minded parties. This about-face was dictated by Stalin, now that Trotsky was no longer a threat. It was part of his burgeoning alliance with Bukharin, intended to isolate Zinoviev and Kamenev. It seemed like a victory for the Ruthenberg-Lovestone wing, which had endorsed the third-party alliance while Foster had turned against it.

When the four American leaders went home in mid-April 1925, Lovestone had made a new friend. At the Hotel Lux he had met Lou (Louise) Geisler, an uncommonly pretty, blond German Communist, small and finely made, like a Meissen figurine. She was living with Heinz Neumann, another German, then chief of the Propaganda Commission of the Comintern, where he did Stalin's bidding. Lou and her sister Eva had been sent to Lenin in 1920 for their language skills and worked for him as translators. But Lou became better known as the femme fatale of the Hotel Lux. With her Bavarian charm and romantic temperament, she went through a procession of Comintern lovers.

While Jay was in Moscow, Lou Geisler fell for the charismatic American, who was refreshingly irreverent compared with all the Stalinist parrots. But she could not get away from the watchful eyes of Neumann or the Cerberuses (as she called them) at the Lux. Encouraged by Lovestone, she left Neumann and came to America, arriving in June 1925 at Montreal, where Jay entrusted her to the care of Nathan Mendelssohn. Jay wrote him on July 1: "Please rush the lady to Chicago as urgent work is awaiting her here. . . . This young lady was very helpful to us in Moscow. At least speaking for myself, politics do not always make strange bedfellows."

Esther, who missed Jay and was as usual fed up with Nathan—writing Jay that "Nathan gets my goat once in a while"—and who was offering to send Jay five hundred dollars, saying, "Take it, it will make me feel useful again," was not overjoyed by the arrival of Lou Geisler. In the petite and flirtatious blond she saw a rival, and she wrote Jay to tell him so. He replied with a cable on July 6: "You or anyone else is crazy with heat if you insinuate or infer my having slightest personal connections or intentions with Lou or anybody else."

Jay was in fact cheating on Esther (insofar as one can cheat on a married woman), but after a couple of passionate months with Lou he found it inconvenient to keep her in Chicago and sent her to New York, where he came regularly on party business. On October 27, 1925, Lou reported that she was taking English lessons at the Workers' School, adding: "I can hardly wait to see you. I am like a little girl, I count the days. Isn't it foolish? How long can you stay? Please, longer than a single one. You see, I am a very *bescheiden* [modest] woman."

Jay was not as attentive as Lou expected, and on March 20, 1926, she had a little jealous fit:

> What kind of a role do I play in your life if you don't tell me any more either your political troubles or your private affairs? . . . Why did you tell me you had a business appointment when I heard later from Ella [Wolfe] you bought a suit and called her to help you? . . . Why for heaven's sake have you to lie? . . . There was a time when you took me to every single meeting, why not any more? . . . There is something more between us than the distance between New York and Chicago. Maybe I lost already Heinz and now maybe I lost you too. . . . Answer me Jay, not with cheap phrases but clearly and openly. . . . I am ready for your death sentence or life-long imprisonment.

Jay's unspoken answer was that he was finding it burdensome to handle both Lou and Esther and that he wanted to avoid entanglements.

In May, Lou went back to Moscow, writing Jay: "I learned to love you during my stay." She would never forget that first time in Chicago. "But it bothers me not a little that I was untrue to you." Her infidelity was with Joe Freeman, the Communist intellectual and writer-editor. Jay concealed his private life so successfully that in the party the running joke was that he was still a virgin. Bill Kruse, a friend then in Moscow attending the Lenin School, wrote on May 14, 1926, "Latest reports are that your virginity is still intact." As for Lou, she later married one of the Comintern's birds of brightest plumage, the Indian Communist M. N. Roy.

　　　　The American party had been in existence six years and was stagnating—subjected to arbitrary changes in the line from Moscow and torn by incessant squabbling. Instead of being a vocation, Communism had become a cul-de-sac, a manufacturer of contentious and blinkered bickerers trapped inside their closed system, aeons away from the American mainstream.

Lovestone himself had become a divided being. The man of principle had joined the party because he believed in the example of the Bolshevik Revolution, which could, he thought, be adapted to the United States to form a classless, more equitable society. Industries would be in the hands of the workers instead of the fat cats. Farmers would receive price supports for their crops. The downtrodden, including the Negroes, would get a fair shake. All these fine notions were forgotten once he was in the party and caught up in its power struggles. Instead, circumstances made him develop into an adept infighter, changing him in ways that were not altogether pleasant. He became more conspiratorial, more suspicious of those around him. He had plenty of opportunity to employ his natural talent for sarcasm and invective and to hone his dialectical skills. The Communist faction fights of the twenties were not exactly character-building, though for the youthful Lovestone they proved to be formative.

Instead of resolving the quandary, the Comintern seemed to give the factions carte blanche to fight it out at the upcoming Fourth Workers' Party Convention in Chicago. Lovestone wrote Bert Wolfe in May that "we are doing nothing in the field of political and industrial work. . . . We are simply tearing each other to pieces."

To many of his colleagues, Lovestone appeared one-dimensional in his faction-oriented single-mindedness. He seemed to have no other interests, no friends, no hobbies, no romantic attachments. This was, of course, not the case, but he was able to compartmentalize his private life so that no one knew it was impinging on his deep absorption in party matters.

One young comrade who was attracted to Lovestone, Theresa Wolfeson of Brooklyn, wrote him on May 28, 1925: "All your passions, loves and hates are wedded to the Communist movement. . . . My own deep feeling about you is that you would be far more effective and have a greater following if you could make yourself be more human, less bitter (it's that deep-seated impersonal bitterness of yours that often frightens me)."

In the spring of 1925, the Comintern rep who was supposed to act as umpire at the Workers' Party convention arrived in Mexico City en route to Chicago. A short, jowly, potbellied man in his mid-forties introduced himself to Bert and Ella Wolfe as Sergei Gusev. He was in fact Yakov Drabkin, one of the twenty-two original Bolsheviks who had rallied around Lenin in 1904, the most senior Communist that the Comintern had ever sent to America. Now he was a loyal Stalinist, who spoke German to Bert, looking at him over his spectacles. "Ach," he said, "Trotsky is not a Bolshevik. We Bolsheviks always despised him for his vanity. . . . I myself have watched Trotsky stand before a mirror and deliver a speech to himself so that he could study his own expressions and motions."

Ella obtained an American passport for Gusev and spent many hours each day teaching him English. He became so fluent he told her, "You did magic." Bert briefed Gusev on the situation in the American party, telling him that "Jay Lovestone is the party's best political leader. But the party is torn by factionalism. If you can force them to work together, you will be performing a great service."

Bert came to realize that Gusev was not going to Chicago to settle the American faction fight but to spread the Russian faction fight into the American party. Stalin was now taking charge, and the American party had to be made a pro-Stalin party, which meant getting rid of suspected Trotsky sympathizers like Cannon, who was allied with Foster.

When Gusev got to Chicago, he told Lovestone: "Your friend Bertram Wolfe is very naive." Realizing that Gusev held the key to the forthcoming convention, Lovestone courted him assiduously, studied his tastes and habits, wined and dined him, and found him a "safe" apartment, for he was in the country illegally.

When the convention opened on August 21, 1925, Gusev set up a Parity Commission, with Ruthenberg, Max Bedacht, and Lovestone from one faction and Foster, Cannon, and Alexander Bittelman from the other. When the smoke lifted after a furious battle for delegates, Ruthenberg had twenty-one and Foster had forty, thanks largely to the pro-Foster Finnish federation, with its seven thousand members.

Foster was now in full control of the American party, or so he thought. But on August 28, a sweltering summer day, at an afternoon meeting of the Parity Commission, Gusev pulled out a cable from Moscow, which he casually handed to Ruthenberg. The cable stated that "it finally became clear that the Ruthenberg group is more loyal to the

Comintern and closer to its views" while the Foster group "employs excessively mechanical and ultrafactional methods." Thus, the cable went on, the new Central Executive Committee must have no fewer than four out of ten members from the Ruthenberg group, and Comrade Gusev would also have a vote. In addition, Ruthenberg must be renamed party secretary and Comrade Lovestone must be included on the CEC.

The cable offered Foster a sixty-forty majority on the Central Executive Committee while labeling the Ruthenberg group as more loyal. Foster knew enough Cominternspeak to realize at once that control without confidence was worthless. His victory had been snatched away by a decision in Moscow. "A more dramatic scene could not have been arranged," Bert Wolfe recalled. "Foster's jaw set; his eyes shifted back and forth from Gusev to Ruthenberg." Foster was so distraught that he asked to be relieved of his membership in the CEC. When Gusev said that was out of the question, Foster cursed and stomped out, saying, "I know who's responsible for this."

At this point the irrepressible Ella Wolfe danced into the room, and Gusev produced a bon mot for his English teacher: "Why are you dancing? Do you think this is a love affair? This is a Lovestone affair." "Thus he showed," Bert Wolfe recalled, "that he knew Lovestone was the real organizer of the Ruthenberg Caucus." Lovestone had been Gusev's adviser in the strategy that brought the cable from Moscow. Gusev had cabled Moscow, and Moscow had cabled back. The instructions could only have come from someone familiar with the workings of the convention. Gusev "felt right at home in our caucus and felt a benevolent sense of having done what was right with us," Bert Wolfe said.

A deal was worked out in the Parity Commission on August 29: The CEC would have ten members from each group, with Gusev casting the deciding vote. In this manner a sixty-forty Foster majority was converted into a Ruthenberg majority, for Gusev announced on September 1 that he had received special instructions to vote with the Ruthenberg group. What could Foster do? He could not attack Gusev, for the Comintern representative had the authority of a papal nuncio.

But in October the Ruthenberg camp learned that Foster had left for Moscow to appeal the Comintern decision. This was his second visit to Moscow that year, and each time it took about two months round-trip. But the habit was now ingrained that whenever the American party leaders had a problem they went to Mecca (as they called Moscow) to settle it. Foster was kept cooling his heels for several weeks, not a good sign. He finally saw Zinoviev, who was sick in bed in his house inside the

Kremlin. Foster said the American party was in turmoil, and there was a campaign of persecution against his group. But Zinoviev was noncommittal, ending the interview by telling Foster to "be cheerful." Foster had made the long pilgrimage to Moscow for nothing.

Zinoviev had more pressing matters on his mind. The American party troubles were a mirror image of the Russian faction fight between the Stalin-Bukharin camp and the Zinoviev-Kamenev camp. That December, Zinoviev was replaced as head of the Leningrad soviet by Sergei M. Kirov. Kamenev was downgraded in the Politburo to alternate. So that by early 1926 Stalin was halfway there. Lenin had conveniently died. Trotsky was no longer commissar for war. Zinoviev and Kamenev had been cut down to size. The cluster of heirs in the waiting room of the dead chieftain had been reduced to two—Stalin and Bukharin.

Alert to changes in the Soviet leadership, Lovestone wrote Herbert Benjamin, the Moscow envoy of the American party: "We have endorsed the Stalin Central Executive Committee." In the American party there was something approaching a truce. For the first time Lovestone could devote himself fully to party matters.

The initial order of business was the first major strike to be launched and organized by the Communist Party. Passaic, New Jersey, was then the biggest woolen and worsted center in the country, with six or seven important spinning mills surrounded by working-class communities. In 1925 there was a slump in the industry, and in September Botany Mills announced a 10 percent wage cut, which other mills also adopted.

The Workers' Party sent Albert Weisbord to organize the underpaid immigrant workers, half of them women, who were disdained by the AFL United Textile Workers. Weisbord, a twenty-six-year-old graduate of City College and Harvard Law School, intense and bookish, had joined the party and taken a job in a silk mill in Paterson, where he formed a shop nucleus. When the wage cut took effect, he moved to Passaic and set up a United Front Strike Committee with membership books and dues stamps. This smacked of dual unionism, but no matter, the situation was urgent. Botany Mills rejected all the strike committee's demands and fired the committee members.

On January 25, 1926, five thousand Botany Mills workers walked out. The strike spread to four other mills with eleven thousand workers. The dye workers from Lodi also struck. It turned out to be the longest textile strike in history, lasting more than a year. A cadre of Communists arrived from New York to man the midwinter picket lines, coffee wagons, and day-care centers. Weisbord was arrested and held on thirty thousand dollars bail. Press photographers caught scenes of cops clubbing women and children and hosing them with icy water in freezing weather. The New York liberal community, only half an hour away, was aroused, and notables such as Roger Baldwin and Norman Thomas joined the picket line.

Lovestone did not walk the picket line, but he masterminded the strike from his Chicago office without ever being publicly connected with Passaic. Here was an early example of his method as invisible puppeteer. The first thing he did was get in touch with his friend Frank Walsh, an establishment lawyer who was sympathetic to the Communists and who had defended Ruthenberg in the Bridgman trial. During World War I, Walsh was joint chairman of the War Labor Board with former president William Howard Taft. After the war he led a campaign that raised $6 million for the Irish Republican Army and defended some of the Communist leaders arrested in the Lusk raids. He was never a party member, but a document in the Comintern files describes him as "the most reliable friend of the Soviet government among the Americans."

Walsh agreed to act as lawyer for the Passaic strike committee. On March 8, 1926, Lovestone wrote Will Weinstone, the district organizer in New York, that he should see Walsh at his office at 55 Liberty Street and ask for his help in getting a congressional committee to investigate the textile industry. He should ask the well-connected Walsh to go with Weisbord to Washington and see William Borah, the progressive Idaho senator who was prolabor and in favor of recognizing the Soviet Union. Lovestone told Weinstone he had already fixed it with Walsh but added, "Keep Lovestone out of this. Lovestone never heard of Walsh. Walsh never spoke to Lovestone. This is coming out of the hearts and minds of the textile strikers themselves. No Communist has anything to do with it." On March 10, Lovestone wrote Ben Gitlow in New York, "I hope you have made the most of the Walsh matter. I have worked my head off trying to draw him into it. I think he is the best you can get."

Walsh got in touch with William Jett Lauck, considered the leading labor economist in the country. A Washington insider, Lauck was friendly toward the trade unions and thought the Russian Revolution was the greatest event since the French Revolution. He had known Frank Walsh since they both served on the War Labor Board, and he was also John L. Lewis's economist for the United Mine Workers.

Walsh told Lauck he was bringing Weisbord and other members of the strike committee to Washington to talk to members of Congress. Lauck wrote Lovestone on March 19, "The Passaic strikers committee arrived here and Walsh and I devoted four days to helping them raise all the commotion they could about the city."

With the help of Sen. Robert La Follette, Jr., Lauck and Walsh tried to get a Senate hearing going. Walsh reported to Lovestone on April 2 that he had seen Senator Edwards, "who is in the dark ages, imbued with the idea that the paramount issue is whether or not Weisbord is a Communist. . . . He is intensely interested in all the aspects of the Passaic strike except wages, hours, and conditions of labor in mills. He also takes a determined stand against 'Bolsheviks.' "

In April, thanks to the efforts of Lovestone, Walsh, and Lauck, La Follette introduced a Senate resolution calling for an investigation of the Passaic strike by the Committee on Education and Labor. With the support of Senators Borah and Burton K. Wheeler of Montana, La Follette tried to bring the resolution to the floor but failed. There was too much opposition from vested interests.

Then Lauck formed a committee that brought together Weisbord, Borah, and one of the vice presidents of Botany Mills, a Colonel Johnson, who said the mills were basically fighting against Communist influence and had no objection to negotiating with the AFL. On the basis of Johnson's statement, Borah and Lauck met with Thomas F. McMahon, the president of the United Textile Workers of America, who said he was willing to affiliate the Passaic workers if Weisbord withdrew. On August 13, Weisbord told Lauck he would pull out if a charter was issued to the Passaic strikers. On September 2, the Passaic strikers were brought into the United Textile Workers. There was a transfer of leadership from the Communists to the AFL.

But the mill owners reneged, refusing to negotiate with the AFL union, and the strike dragged on. On November 11 the Passaic Worsted Spinning Company broke ranks and recognized the United Textile Workers. One by one the other mills followed, and in February 1927 the strike ended. The strikers obtained almost nothing in terms of raises or better conditions. But at least they had stopped the wave of wage cuts and were now organized.

The whole episode was a lesson in the obstacles that the Communist Party was unable to overcome. A strike launched by the party was taken over by the AFL, which was able to benefit from employers' protests that they would not negotiate with Communists. The Communists, rather than sticking to bread-and-butter issues, were bound to politicize the strike, describing it as a struggle of "class against class" and citing it as the correct way to advance the revolution in America. In addition, they vilified the AFL as "a tool of the bosses" and "labor lieutenants of American imperialism." Lovestone, however, thought the Passaic strike was "a tremendous party achievement. . . . We have succeeded in winning over a number of influential trade unionists, either to join our party or at least to work closely with us."

In his second veiled endeavor that year, Lovestone was more successful. This was a classic Communist-front operation, under the direct order of the Comintern. In September 1925 the Comintern instructed the American party to organize a delegation of trade unionists to visit Soviet Russia. This was more than a friendly gesture; it was of vital importance to the Soviets. America, among the powerful nations of the world, was the major holdout on recognition of the Soviet regime. A visit from a delegation of non-Communist labor leaders was intended to move recognition along. They would come home with positive things to say about Russia, spread the word, and lobby for recognition. Once it came the trade agreements and foreign exchange would start flowing toward Russia. The American party was being told to assist the Soviet Union in one of its major foreign policy goals.

Ruthenberg turned the trade union delegation matter over to Lovestone, who admitted many years later to Sen. Paul H. Douglas of Illinois, a member of the 1927 delegation, "I was in charge of all the activities of the American trade union delegation to Russia." The front technique was to work through others who were not Communists. Lovestone became an expert at it, in this case working once again through Frank Walsh and Jett Lauck and through a third figurehead, Albert F. Coyle, editor of the *Journal of the Brotherhood of Locomotive Engineers,* based in Cleveland. The diminutive Coyle was disarmingly earnest, wore round-rimmed glasses, and didn't swear, smoke, or drink. He'd take a drink of water and say, "Ah, that steams me up." Outwardly, neither Lovestone nor any other Communist had anything to do with the trade delegation. In fact, Lovestone inspired every move that was made, slipping in and out of Coyle's Cleveland office, pale and secretive. Coyle's friend Len De Caux warned that "a jay is pugnacious and destructive of the eggs of other birds."

The plan was to get Walsh, Lauck, and Coyle to talk to some prominent labor leaders, who in turn would approach others. Once they had recruited the right people, they would form the National Committee for an American Trade Union Delegation to Soviet Russia. This committee would ask Lauck to serve as its chief economist. Walsh would be general counsel, and Coyle would be elected secretary. The committee would print stationery, establish an office in Chicago, and announce its existence. It would then inform the Russian trade unions of its intention to send a delegation and await an invitation.

On February 6, 1926, Lovestone wrote Walsh, "If I have to break my neck to put this proposition over, I will do it." Five days later he added, "I urgently recommend that you send letters to some of the prominent labor men who are genuine progressives but bona fide trade unionists, asking them to accept a place on a national committee. . . . Begin seriously thinking about the personnel. . . . We must make public the names . . . as soon as possible . . . in order to raise funds and get out the publicity." What Lovestone did not tell Walsh was that the American party had already received money from Moscow to subsidize the venture.

On February 12, Coyle wrote Walsh, "I feel we shall be making a very real contribution toward world understanding and peace if we can lay the facts about Russia before the organized workers of this country."

Lauck agreed to try to enlist his good friend John L. Lewis, who responded with a healthy dose of skepticism on April 16: "I am wondering who is to finance the expedition of trade unionists to Russia. On the face of it I scarcely like to identify myself with an expedition which might be believed by many to be the forerunner of an attempt to bring the Russian situation to the forefront in this country."

Another naysayer was William Green, president of the AFL, who blasted the whole delegation plan in May, pointing out that "such men as Coyle, Walsh, and Jerome Davis have already the reputation of being pro-Soviet." Lovestone wrote Lauck in June: "I am in despair over Green's tactics."

But Coyle kept plugging away, telling labor leaders that the Communist Party was not behind the delegation, that the money for expenses came from donations, and that the delegates would pay their own way. Among those who signed on were L. E. Sheppard, president of the Order of Railway Conductors; John Brophy, president of District 2, United Mine Workers; Frank L. Palmer, editor of the *Colorado Labor Advocate;* and James L. Maurer, president of the Pennsylvania State Federation of Labor, who was also the Socialist mayor of Reading, Pennsylvania.

Things were not going fast enough for Lovestone, who griped in June, "I am getting a little itchy on all these delays." In fact, the delegation, which was supposed to leave in the summer of 1926, did not leave until a year later. This was mainly because Walsh and Lauck were absorbed in the Passaic strike. Coyle in the meantime wired the All-Russian Central Trade Council, asking it "to ensure our free and unhampered right to make a complete investigation of that country."

When they finally left in July 1927, the delegation consisted of twice as many university professors (twelve) as bona fide trade union leaders (six). Among the former were Jerome Davis, professor of practical philanthropy at Yale; Paul H. Douglas, professor of industrial relations at the University of Chicago; and Rexford Tugwell, professor of economics at Columbia and soon-to-be member of FDR's brain trust. Neither Lauck nor Walsh went.

In Moscow the eighteen delegates had an interview with Stalin and then divided into three groups—one to the Ural mining area, one to the Donets Basin, and the third to the Caucasus. Tugwell and his group went down the Volga to the Caucasus. He found that their Russian guides insisted on telling them what the United States was like. "They quoted to us facts about wages and hours and factory conditions. They ignored our protests and corrections. I knew from then on how determined dictators learn to manage their people."

When their report came out in October 1927, only one member of the delegation, Silas B. Axtell, counsel for the International Maritime Union, branded it as a whitewash: "The whole report," he said, "was written with such an affectionate regard for the dominating group in Russia, whose guests we had been, and the impression from reading the report was so different from the one that I had received, that I could not possibly subscribe to it."

Whatever the merits of the report, the trip to Russia did not change the attitude of the Coolidge administration toward recognition. The president announced after the delegation's return: "I do not propose to barter away for the privilege of trade any of the cherished rights of humanity. I do not propose to make merchandise of any American principles."

Lovestone, however, remained convinced that the trade union delegation was an event of "paramount importance," although he denied having had any part in it. When Comrade William Dietrich of Denver wrote to ask him about Coyle's role, Lovestone replied that "we know nothing about Coyle and we have nothing to do with a labor delegation to Russia. If there is such a movement going on we have not heard of it."

In May 1926 Lovestone's party work was interrupted by a family crisis. Even though Barnet Liebstein had given up on his own children, who had defected into the hurly-burly of America, he was so distressed by the paganism of the new world that he resolved to migrate to Palestine, a land where the Sabbath was properly observed. At the Communist Party headquarters in Chicago, Jay received an urgent communication from his brother Morris: "In the name of Maimonides and induced by true brotherly love, I urge you my dear Jacob to come to New York. . . .

Our aged and sickly parents are sailing for Palestine early in June. Many important matters must be settled. I do not feel like assuming 100 percent responsibility for everything. I hope you will at least take 5 or 10 percent responsibility on your own shoulders. . . . Papa and Mama have begged me with tears in their eyes, that they must see you in May or at the very latest the first week in June."

Jay came to New York to see his parents off. His mother had a fear of automobiles—they made her carsick—nor could she abide the subway, so Jay accompanied her on foot from the Bronx to the pier in Manhattan where their ship was waiting. The Liebsteins remained less than a year in Tel Aviv. Barnet was shocked when he saw young men smoking on the Sabbath in cafés. "At least if I'm buried here," he said after he came home, "my children will visit my grave."

Emma died first, on May 1, 1938. Barnet moved into the third-floor apartment in Esther's home on Ditmas Avenue. He helped her son Bob, then in high school, with the passages of the Torah he had to learn for his bar mitzvah. In 1939 the Matises went to Atlantic City over New Year's and took Morris's son, Sidney. But Barnet, who wasn't feeling well, stayed behind. When they got back to Brooklyn on January 1, 1940, they found him dead in his bed. As they stood around the bed, Sidney said to Bob Matis: "Let me hold your hand."

"Working like hell is about the only way to make life worthwhile," Lovestone wrote Ella Wolfe from Chicago in 1926 as he grappled with his many assignments. In May he started seeing a young comrade called Nellie, who worked for the Lithuanian Women's Organization. She was such a diligent party member that she was reading Bukharin's *Historical Materialism.* Flattered and impressed by the attention being paid her by a party leader, a man of quick and incisive intelligence who in the eyes of many was the real boss while Ruthenberg traveled around and gave speeches, she responded with submissive ardor.

When Jay stood her up because of urgent party business, instead of expressing disappointment she wrote, "I feel like a counter-revolutionary, hindering you in the fight, bringing up my petty troubles." On May 6 she wrote, "Jay dearest, I wish I could just put my arms around your neck real tight and kiss you." Another time she wrote, "Gee honey, if I don't see you soon I'll become a candidate for the virginity club." After they did see each other, there was a moment of alarm when her period came three days late. She worried that he was working too hard and wanted him to get some rest, "even if I have to hold you down by physical force. . . . If I don't see you soon I'll scream or do something desperate."

But Jay was a perpetual-motion machine, around so seldom that she wrote, "I have been accused of having a phantom lover. If they only knew how real my phantom is! Real and Warm and Gorgeous!" And when he went away she wrote, "I'm going to sleep and I'll hold you, never to let you go and you'll be my captive." But Lovestone was elusive, avoiding capture.

Aside from his work as Ruthenberg's chief of staff, Lovestone kept up a brisk correspondence with Moscow. When the Central Committee backed Stalin and voted in July 1926 for Zinoviev's dismissal from the Politburo, Lovestone at once wrote Pepper, "We were shocked by the Zinoviev episode. Not even for a moment did any one of us doubt where we stood. We were without reservations for every disciplinary step taken by the Russian CC against Zinoviev. . . . I know that every one of our boys is solid with Stalin."

At the same time Lovestone was chafing under what he considered unwarranted Comintern interference in the internal affairs of the American party. The big argument at the time between the Ruthenberg and Foster factions was whether to move the party headquarters and the *Daily Worker* back to New York. The paper was having serious money problems, and Ruthenberg and Lovestone believed that moving to New York would increase the circulation and advertising. But Foster said he would fight the move tooth and nail, with an appeal to Moscow.

Just as Lovestone feared, a Comintern cable to suspend moving operations pending an investigation arrived in August 1926. Lovestone was furious, writing Pepper, "Since when is it the practice of the Comintern to mix into such petty affairs?" Ruthenberg was useless as usual. "He would consider it dangerous for somebody to place a mirror to his lips," Lovestone observed, "for then he would be compelled to indicate that he is alive."

On the larger issues, however, Lovestone was still a docile disciple of the Comintern. He reasoned that the Communist Party of each country was by definition the vanguard of the working class, and the Comintern was the union of all the Communist parties, and thus the vanguard of all the vanguards—so the Comintern could do no wrong. In 1926, aside from his work as Ruthenberg's chief of staff, Lovestone was absorbed in the Bolshevization of the American party, that is, making it a clone of the Russian party. In June he reported on his progress to Joseph Piatnitsky, the Comintern treasurer. The spine of the program, he said, was to dissolve the old language-federation branches and replace them with branches in factory shops called nuclei. The results in the factories were promising, Lovestone said. A model nucleus had been set up at the Ford plant in Detroit, and he noted "the admirable conduct of the shop nucleus in the Hays Durant Auto Plant," which had called a strike for shorter hours, while at the Bethlehem Steel plant the nucleus had spearheaded a union election, "which our comrades won by a vote of 700." Lovestone was hoping to "smash the dangerous barnacle of federationism."

Feeling burned out, he took a few days of vacation in August at Camp Tamiment, a spa for left-wingers in the Poconos. Esther Mendelssohn took a leave of absence from her husband and joined him. They swam and hiked in the mountains and rekindled a love affair that prolonged separation made more urgent. For Esther it was bliss to have Jay to herself, even though the accommodations were rustic. Back in Montreal she wrote, "Even a place full of bedbugs can be heaven to some." She also reported that a "miserable female Fosterite came this way and told Nathan you are a dirty politician. I told her you are a politician but never dirty."

In Moscow, at a plenary meeting of the Central Committee from October 23 to 26, Stalin dispatched the triumvirate. Trotsky accused Stalin of "offering his candidature for the post of gravedigger of the revolution." Stalin struck back, calling the trio a "union of eunuchs." When the smoke lifted Trotsky had been removed from his seat in the Politburo, Kamenev had been ousted as alternate, and Zinoviev had been dismissed from the Comintern, which he had chaired from 1920 to 1926.

On November 5, 1926, Lovestone left for Moscow for the Seventh Plenum of the Comintern Executive Committee; he sailed on a Cunard Line ship with a Canadian passport that described him as a businessman. "Being a native Canadian of many generations and very well connected in business," he wrote Bert Wolfe, "I have been given the best table in the dining room." His table companions were the purser, so perfectly British that Lovestone suspected his underwear and pajamas were made of Union Jacks, and a young Australian couple.

Lovestone spent the crossing listening to what he thought of as their bourgeois reactionary chitchat. In a typical dinner conversation, the wife said, "I caaan't see why the British don't turn out a good reasonable car to displace the American automobiles in New Zealand." "I can't eyether," the purser agreed. "It shouldn't be difficult. Why should we let the Americans have it all! I just caaan't understand it. . . . These Yanks even come to England and tell us what to do. The singer John McCormack said he would not brook our singing 'God Save the Queen' at his concerts. We soon showed him. We stood up and sang till the rafters shook." Lovestone got a kick out of pretending to be in agreement with all the nonsense they spouted.

The enlarged plenum of the ECCI opened on November 19, and the meetings went into December. On December 7, Lovestone wrote Bert Wolfe: "Zinny is wiped out. . . . Attacked from all sides most viciously." A few days later he went before the American Commission to deliver a progress report: "The party in September 1925 was in a totally broken-down condition insofar as work among the masses was concerned. We had specifically American difficulties. . . . First of all the language difficulty. I know of shop nuclei in the Pittsburgh district where of nine members there are seven languages spoken. . . . We went ahead and started English classes. . . . In the Bethlehem plant we had mostly Finnish comrades . . . then in Michigan more than forty workers were entombed for many hours in a mine. We had nine of our members there. While these fellows were entombed—they were in hell—they formed a nucleus and are now leaders in a movement against the steel trust to prevent the recurrence of such disasters."

His account had the commission members on the edges of their seats. Lovestone then took questions from the floor:

"How many real Yankees are there in the party?"

"I cannot answer that question."

"Do the factory papers reach the foreign-born workers also?"

"Here we have a serious problem. Many cannot read English, so we have special columns in different languages."

Piatnitsky, a member of the Comintern secretariat that had replaced Zinoviev, proposed that factory papers be distributed in the restaurants where the workers ate and in the streetcars they rode home. "For all to be compelled to speak English," he added, "is against our method of solving the problem of nationalities." He seemed to view America as made up of separate national groups, like the British and the French in Canada, each of which should be encouraged to maintain its ethnic composition.

Lovestone was back in the United States in January 1927, staying at the Hotel Albert in New York City. An FBI informant reported that on January 6, at a meeting in the hotel with other prominent Communists, he was overheard to say that in Russia grafters were shot but in America they were made senators and congressmen. During Lovestone's absence the *Daily Worker* had moved to New York, and the party was soon to follow. Lovestone reported to Stalin and Bukharin on January 23 that in the 1926 election for president of the United Mine Workers, John L. Lewis

had beaten John Brophy by 195,000 to 85,000 votes. The election, said
Lovestone, was "obviously fraudulent . . . President Lewis has faked and
padded his vote." Some years later Lovestone had occasion to ask Lewis:
"Who really won that 1926 election?" With a big smile, Lewis replied:
"John won it."

Charles Ruthenberg was not feeling well. Bittelman saw him on February 27 bent over in pain and told him to "go see a doctor." "Just a little
discomfort," Ruthenberg said. At a Political Committee meeting that day
he told Foster: "I'm kind of under the weather." That evening in his hotel
room, he was doubled up in pain and told Jay: "Oh, I've got that trouble
again."

Lovestone, accompanied by Ruthenberg's secretary-mistress, Anna
David, took him to the hospital, where he was operated on for a burst ap-
pendix. The next day, March 1, 1927, he was weak and said, "Anna dear,
will you deliver some messages to the comrades?" Anna and Jay stayed
with him through the night. His hands got colder and colder and on the
morning of March 2 he died of peritonitis. He was forty-six years old.

At a party meeting in Chicago on March 4, Anna David made a startling announcement. Ruthenberg on his deathbed had told her: "Of
course the party will have to move to New York immediately. Comrade
Lovestone, Jay, will have to be secretary. . . . Tell them to preserve their
unity." Lovestone had been named the new leader of the American party
by the dying Ruthenberg.

This was a shock to the Foster faction, but what could they do?
Ruthenberg was the hero of the party, and his deathbed wish carried considerable weight. The Comintern cabled: "At no time has his leadership
been more needed than today."

At the March 4 meeting, Lovestone declared war against all factions:
"There will be no more dilly-dallying with opposition to the Central Executive Committee. Some individuals in our party need cliques, they
need combinations, they need new alignments. . . . Now the party is facing a crisis. . . . But to me the corpse of Comrade Ruthenberg is not a life-
less corpse but a source of inspiration. A very fortunate heritage to me
has been my almost twelve years of close association with comrade
Ruthenberg. [It was more like eight years, since 1919.] Though I may
have lost him as a leader I have not lost the revolutionary personality. . . .
I say the time has come to stop factionalism." With those words, Lovestone took on the Ruthenberg mantle, presenting himself as the leader of
the party and calling for unity.

At a meeting of the Political Committee on March 5, Ben Gitlow nominated Lovestone as acting secretary of the party, and he was elected. Lovestone, not yet thirty, was in charge.

Ruthenberg's body lay in state in Ashland Auditorium amid a mass of flowers. To Gitlow, Charles Emil Ruthenberg was "the most ambitious of all, insufferably egotistical, resenting any challenge to his preeminence, seeing himself as the American Lenin." That was a harsh assessment, for Ruthenberg, while lacking in brilliance and perhaps in drive, had tried to rise above factionalism and create a mass party. He had not succeeded, however, remaining more the leader of a faction than the leader of a party. Ruthenberg was not inspiring or visionary. He was a capable company spokesman, pleased with the sound of his own voice, receptive to the attention of female admirers—the outside man, the greeter and the handshaker, while Lovestone was the inside man, doing the real work.

On March 6 the coffin was carried out of Ashland Auditorium by a bipartisan group of pallbearers—Lovestone, Gitlow, Bittelman, Bedacht, and Cannon—as women shrieked and fainted. Anna David cried all the way to the cemetery, where the body was cremated. The urn containing Ruthenberg's ashes then went to New York and was placed on display at the Manhattan Lyceum. J. Louis Engdahl, the editor of the *Daily Worker,* took the ashes to Moscow, where they were buried at the foot of the Kremlin Wall, next to John Reed's. At a memorial service in Red Square on April 26, one of the speakers was Bukharin, now with Stalin one of the two top Soviet leaders. "Ruthenberg was the leader of a comparatively small but energetic Communist party," he said. "Before his death he expressed the desire that his remains should be taken to our country of proletarian dictatorship, to the country which is incomparably much weaker than is his own 'Mother Country' . . . in which the hangmen of the working class are highly refined."

Meanwhile, in a letter to the *Daily Worker,* a party member, S. Richards, wondered about the incense burning, "the continual glorification of Ruthenberg. It would be all right for sob-sisters, a religious sect, Messiah peddlers and the like, but for non-hero-worshiping revolutionists it is absolutely the bunk. It's like the Socialist Party slop about Debs—'though jailed he speaketh.'"

LOVESTONE
SUPREME

At the age of twenty-nine, Jay Lovestone was now in charge of the American Communist Party—at least in theory. He had been named acting secretary three days after Ruthenberg's death. But the Foster-Cannon opposition immediately mobilized to challenge his leadership. They teamed up to propose William Weinstone, known as "Wobbly" for his frequent and opportunistic changes of position, as Ruthenberg's successor, with the matter to be thrashed out at a party plenum to be held in May 1927. Jay's old City College chum, now district organizer in New York, felt that his talent had been overlooked and was willing to accept a higher position. For years he had watched Jay's lightning ascent in the party hierarchy with barely concealed envy, and now came his chance to pass Lovestone's pawn.

There ensued a somewhat undignified scrambling for position, like that of boys playing in a sandbox. Lovestone wrote a friend: "Weinstone was saying one thing one day and another thing the next. If we gave him a bodyguard and a straight-jacket he would be all right."

As usual the solution was to send a cable to Moscow. In April, Moscow cabled back: "We categorically insist there be no change . . . in leadership positions in the party," which seemed to enshrine Lovestone as the leader. The Foster camp was crushed but planned to turn the plenum on May 4 into an anti-Lovestone putsch.

On the opening day of the American plenum, Weinstone went after

Lovestone for speaking of the "tremendous reserve powers of American capitalism." Lovestone responded that capitalism was not going to disappear by diktat from Moscow. On the second day of the plenum, Lovestone was nowhere to be seen. Was he sick, or smarting from the previous day's assault? As it turned out, he had left for Moscow with Gitlow, to argue his case, which Foster called "an unpardonable factional act." Foster soon went chasing after him.

Upon their arrival in late May, Lovestone and Gitlow went to the Kremlin Wall for a Ruthenberg memorial complete with a band and the Red Army cavalry. Their host was Bukharin, who told Gitlow: "When I die, I do not care what becomes of my *dreck*. They can throw it wherever they want to."

Lovestone found himself warmly greeted in Moscow. Bukharin accepted him as a friend and asked his advice on American matters. When the Foster-Cannon group arrived with Weinstone and Bittelman, Bukharin told them, "The Ruthenberg group is more consequential. . . . There is very little Marxism in the American party, but what there is tends to show itself in the ranks of those following Ruthenberg."

Stalin granted Lovestone a one-hour interview and treated him cordially, asking a great many questions. Lovestone's impression was that Stalin "talks little and does much. The difference between Stalin and Bukharin is that Bukharin is more of an abstract, philosophical polemist, while Stalin is sharp, concise." Jay by then knew a few words of Russian and recognized a word that Stalin used, *durak* (fool). Stalin told Lovestone that "anybody who thinks American imperialism can buy the whole working class is a *durak*." He also said: "Even with our fingers in front of our eyes we can see the political weakness of comrade Foster."

Bukharin formed an eleven-man American Commission and named as chairman a rising young German Communist, Arthur Ewert. Overfond of wurst and foaming steins of beer, Ewert was the cartoon German, with a bulging body and a face like a boiled ham. He soon made friends with Lovestone and Gitlow (they were all staying at the Lux) and spent the evenings with them drinking, telling jokes, and singing bawdy songs. When the Fosterites arrived, they seemed standoffish by comparison.

The American Commission met through June in an effort to resolve the inner party situation. Lovestone described it as "a very sharp fight." The Foster camp brought eighteen charges against the Lovestone camp. The first was that they were guilty of right deviation. Bittelman charged them with "moral corruption" and having "personal relationships." The commission eventually rejected all charges.

Though Ewert and Bukharin were partial to Lovestone, Foster still had powerful allies in the Comintern. On June 26, 1927, he saw the Finn Otto Kuusinen, a Stalin loyalist who told him: "Lovestone cannot take the place of Ruthenberg and collective leadership must now be established." This was heartening news, soon to be confirmed in an American Commission resolution: Lovestone and Foster would be joint secretaries until the party convention in August, at which, according to the wishes of the Comintern, a collective secretariat of three would be named. The Comintern was carrying water on both shoulders, though Lovestone did obtain from Bukharin one important concession: The Comintern representative at the convention in New York would be his new friend Arthur Ewert.

In the time remaining before the opening of the convention on August 31, the faction fight for delegates was at full throttle. Margaret Browder, Earl's sister, wrote that "Jay is feverishly building up fake party units in preparation for the convention." The battle extended to every aspect of party work. At that time along with "Hands Off China," there was a "Hands Off Nicaragua" campaign to protest the presence of United States Marines in the military campaigns against the guerrilla leader César Sandino. In charge of the anti-imperialist work in New York was the Fosterite Charles Shipman, aka Manuel Gomez, who came up with the slogan "Stop the Flow of Nicaraguan Blood," which Lovestone derided as "Gomez' Kotex campaign." At every meeting the insults flew: "labor fakers," "petty bourgeois intellectuals," "right deviationists," "clique leadership." This led to an admonitory Comintern cable on July 27 that such expressions "serve only to poison party life."

Lovestone's hard work in the districts paid off at the convention at Irving Plaza Hall, which lasted from August 31 to September 7. He won by a majority of twenty-five to thirteen in the Central Executive Committee, and of eight to three in the Political Committee. He had the backing of Arthur Ewert, whom Gitlow got so plastered one night that he threw up.

Lovestone was now firmly in control and announced "the last gasp of factionalism." He moved quickly to place his followers—Bert Wolfe as head of Agit-Prop and the up-and-coming Jack Stachel as head of the Organization Department—while he took the title of executive secretary.

Caught up in American party affairs, Lovestone failed to grasp what was happening in the Soviet leadership, where Stalin was consolidating his power. In November 1927, Trotsky and Zinoviev were expelled from the party. On January 19, 1928, Trotsky was deported to the forlorn oblast of Alma-Ata in Central Asia, where the Mongols used to roam.

Stalin was now working on the third panel of his succession triptych: in the first he had used Zinoviev and Kamenev to get rid of Trotsky; in the second, an alliance with Bukharin had helped him defeat Zinoviev and Kamenev; and now, in the third and final panel, he would destroy Bukharin and his two allies—A. I. Rykov, chairman of the Council of People's Commissars, and M. P. Tomsky, head of the Soviet trade unions.

Against Trotsky, Lovestone had jumped in early, for, as he later explained, if Trotsky had won out over Stalin, he would have been an even more cruel leader. Against Bukharin, with whose policies he was in close sympathy, he waited. In Moscow, Stalin made his spectacular turn to the left, ushering in the "Third Period" of revolutionary upheaval, extreme measures against the kulaks (the relatively well-to-do peasants), and a program of rapid industrial and agricultural collectivization.

The third period had more to do with isolating Bukharin than with conditions in the rest of the world. By doing away with the united-front tactics that he himself had only recently adopted, Stalin could accuse Bukharin of "right deviation." Bukharin was trapped, for though he did not believe that capitalist societies were on the verge of revolution, he had to pretend to go along with it—the alternative being a showdown with Stalin. So, at a Comintern plenum in Moscow in February 1928, the European parties were told to declare war on the non-Communist left, the Labour Party in Britain, the Social Democrats in Germany, and "the left petty bourgeoisie" in France. Electoral alliances of the Farmer-Labor variety were now banned.

In the Trade Union Commission of the February 1928 Plenum, Solomon Lozovsky called for dual unions. There would be no more burrowing from within. Bill Foster had to bite the bullet. Powers Hapgood, a Harvard graduate from an affluent family who had become a miner and a Communist, went to see Foster and said, "You denounced dual unionism, and now you come out for it, and frankly, Bill, I just don't understand it." "As a good Communist, I have to go along," Foster said.

Lovestone, however, who despised Lozovsky, was in no mood to go along, saying at the May plenum of the American party that he was "somewhat pessimistic . . . about building new unions." Lovestone did not yet see that these new policies were a loyalty test in the battle between Stalin and Bukharin.

In Moscow a sharp personal animosity was developing between the two men. Stalin called Bukharin "a liberal chatterer." Bukharin called Stalin "a neo-Trotskyite." In July 1928, in the Central Committee and the Politburo, the majority shifted to Stalin, leaving Bukharin in a minority with Rykov and Tomsky. Bukharin sensed in Stalin a ruthlessness and an unscrupulousness that his side could not match.

Meanwhile, 1928 was a presidential election year in the United States. At a convention in New York from May 25 to 27, Foster and Gitlow were once again nominated to run for president and vice president on the Workers' Party ticket. In a replica of the two major parties' gatherings, the convention was awash in foot stomping, snake dancing, and horn blowing. But when the fun was over Foster departed for Moscow and stayed until September, leaving Gitlow to campaign alone. Comintern intrigues had priority over running for president.

As Lovestone explained in a report to the Comintern, each of the forty-eight states had its own election laws, making it hard for small parties to get on the ballot. In Ohio you needed a petition signed by twenty-five thousand, in California by thirty thousand, and they were only valid if they came from all sections of the state. The Communists were hoping in 1928 to get on the ballot in thirty states, more than twice the fourteen states they'd been on in 1924.

To gather the signatures Lovestone spent thousands of dollars hiring professional canvassers, and one of the people in his office, Comrade Codkind, wrote a circular for the canvassers that said: "Remember that you are out to get signatures and not converts. This means no argument of any kind. . . . Don't ask for signatures in the name of the Communists. . . . If necessary you can explain that the signature is not an obligation to vote for the party. . . . See how many tricks you can work out and write your experience to the national office." The canvassers thus had permission from the party to misrepresent their mission and try every ploy they could think of, including taking names out of phone books.

The Fosterites leaked a copy of the circular to Moscow, and soon a cable from Bukharin arrived scolding Lovestone for his methods. Lovestone replied on July 1, 1928, that "the circular containing the silliest, non-Communist suggestions aiming to get signatures to place on the ballot through 'tricks,' was prepared by an office clerk without permission and in violation of instructions. It was withheld as soon as found." When questioned, however, Codkind said Lovestone had approved the circular. Lovestone denied it, but not very forcefully. His fingerprints were all over it.

Analyzing Communist hopes for the 1928 election in his report to the Comintern, Lovestone explained that the idea was not so much to elect candidates but to bring the Communist program before greater masses and introduce the party to thousands of workers they could not otherwise reach. By going house to house and factory to factory, they could turn the 1928 campaign into a membership drive.

On July 17, 1928, in Moscow's Great Hall of Columns of the Palace of Labor, the sixth Comintern Congress opened, the summit for all foreign parties and the first congress since 1924. Attending the forty-six sessions, which lasted until September 1, along with committee and subcommittee meetings, were 558 delegates representing fifty-eight parties, including twenty-nine American delegates. In fact, there were two American delegations, one representing the Lovestone leadership that was supposedly in control of the party, and the other the Foster opposition, which planned to use the congress to discredit Lovestone and take over the party.

On the surface Bukharin reigned supreme. He was chairman of the Comintern's Executive Committee, unanimously reelected to thunderous applause, and he delivered three major reports, which was without precedent. He was the shining star of the congress, attaining the apex of a brilliant career.

Behind the scenes, however, Stalin was at work to undermine Bukharin. For him the purpose of the congress was to bring the foreign parties around to his "Third Period" line. To do this, he had to subtly discredit Bukharin and make the mantra of the congress "the right-wing danger." His long-term goal was to prepare the purge in the Russian party and in foreign parties of "right deviationists," that is, those opposed to his policies.

The Americans arrived as innocents abroad. They were in a maze, not knowing which way to turn or that a wrong turn could lead to a dead end. As Bert Wolfe put it, "There we sat in the Sixth Congress like dummies, for Bukharin did not tell us of the losing battle he was fighting in the Politburo." The Foster opposition soon came to realize, however, that the best way to embarrass Lovestone was to attack him as a right deviationist. Secure in his friendship with Bukharin, and sure that the Comintern chairman would prevail, Lovestone did not see yet that, as Jim Cannon put it, "it was a guessing game, and those who guessed wrong ended up on the ash-heap."

The Stalin line, designed to outflank Bukharin, was to announce a capitalist breakdown. For Bukharin the evidence of such a breakdown was nowhere to be seen, so to him the thesis was "radically wrong, tactically harmful, and crudely mistaken theoretically."

Bukharin's first humiliation came when the Russian delegation told him to amend his report "The International Situation and the Tasks of the Comintern," including his definition of the Third Period. One by one Bukharin accepted almost all of Stalin's premises, confusing his supporters and adopting a policy he had no faith in. He ended up saying: "The Right Deviation now represents the central danger."

While the meetings rumbled on in the great hall, Stalin's spin doctors were in the corridors, enlisting support for the new line. They buttonholed delegates and whispered: "Bukharin is finished. He is a dangerous opportunist. If he isn't eliminated soon from the Russian leadership, there will be famine in the cities. In the Comintern, he works hand in glove with the renegades."

Lovestone was concerned enough about the damage being done in the "Corridor Congress" to send Bukharin a warning note. He said he had been approached by Heinz Neumann, "who made a very bitter attack on Comrade Pepper and yourself. In substance he said: 'Comrade Pepper must be destroyed. He is an adventurer, a petty bourgeois. People call him *Der Tripper*" [the gonorrhea].'" Then the bell rang, indicating that Bukharin was resuming his report, and Neumann said: "I must now listen to the 'Pepper' of the Russian party. I want to hear what the Russian *'Tripper'* has to say." Lovestone saw that Stalin was not yet strong enough to fight Bukharin openly, so he had his agents poisoning the atmosphere.

In the Anglo-American Secretariat hearings, where Lovestone was under attack, his sole ally was Bukharin, for the American question was about the only one left that Bukharin had not surrendered on. On July 31, Bukharin endorsed Lovestone's views: "I also say that there is no revolutionary situation in America and perhaps may be called a pessimist. . . . In no country is capitalism so strong as it is in the United States of America. . . . Is it a terrible thing to say that there is little likelihood of an immediate revolutionary situation?"

Apparently it was, for the Stalinist heavy artillery pounded Lovestone mercilessly. On August 17, Dmitri Manuilsky came up with the preposterous thesis that America was on the eve of revolution: "In the United States," he said, "there will open before our party such great perspectives as were opened for our Russian party after the first wave of political strikes in Russia." But, Manuilsky wondered, "would the American party in its present [Lovestone] phase rise to the occasion?"

The next day Lovestone's archenemy, Solomon Lozovsky, weighed in: "This party is sick, there is no mistake about it," he said. There were too many intellectuals. "You cannot have a successful leadership with comrades who come right from the university without a stop in the factory. . . . The only thing the American comrades do is quarrel about their own affairs. . . . The American party must elect at its next congress a Central Committee majority of proletarians and workers. . . . I confess I am not an admirer of the present leadership, but that is for the Comintern to judge."

An angry Lovestone responded that "Comrade Lozovsky has given his line to the Comintern for a long time and it has always gone straight into the wastebasket. . . . Lozovsky's office is the factional cable address for the opposition in Moscow. . . . With all our mistakes, we are the kernel and hope of the party . . . and I speak for the overwhelming majority." It was foolhardy to open a personal attack on a Soviet leader in Stalin's good graces, but Lovestone got carried away.

For him the Sixth Congress was one extended brawl, which served only to underline his refusal to jump on the Stalin bandwagon. He was outflanked by the Foster group, who quickly hopped aboard, even though Foster was not a Stalinist—he was a Fosterite. Observing the goings-on in the American party, Stalin made his move, granting Foster a two-hour interview as the congress was coming to a close. According to Foster, who immediately after the interview sent a jubilant cable to his faction in New York, Stalin said

> he was going on his vacation and was not very willing to go into a meeting, stating that he had been having only some four hours sleep a night; that Lovestone had been following him about for two weeks for an interview, he would also have to give Lovestone one. . . . On the inner party situation, he said he was opposed to our proposal for the removal of the Lovestone group from power at one blow; that this cannot be done from the top—meaning from Moscow—leaving the implication that it must be done from below—in New York. We proposed that the Comintern send an Open Letter to our party criticizing the Right line and the Lovestone group, and that a convention of the party be held two months after the presidential elections. He stated that no good could come out of the Lovestone group, that they simply liked to play with politics and mass work. . . . We feel that in him we have a very good friend and supporter . . . we were very satisfied with the interview. . . . Our conclusions from these

meetings were . . . that Stalin was decidedly against the Lovestone group and in favor of us.

Stalin did see Lovestone, on the morning after his meeting with Foster, in the interest of seeming fair, and asked, "Why does Foster shriek so much?" He advised Lovestone not to "press him too hard." But whatever credit Lovestone still had was further eroded in the meetings of the Senioren Konvent, or Council of Elders, the most prestigious Comintern subcommittee, upon which only the most trusted party members served. Stalin was on it, Bukharin was its chairman, and Lovestone was the only American member.

Here again Lovestone's confrontational style singled him out. At the Budget Commission of the Senioren Konvent, which met to consider American demands for funds, he said: "For our campaigns on issues that spring from American life, we ask no assistance. If our issues are properly chosen, we should be able to raise enough money. But whenever the American party is asked to carry on some campaign by the Comintern. . . . Then we may make a request for funds." This seemed to imply that the Comintern-ordered campaigns, such as Hands Off Nicaragua and Hands Off China, were an imposition that distracted the party from its main tasks, and that the American party could do with a little less guidance from Moscow. Bert Wolfe felt that Stalin saw Jay's request as a "Declaration of Independence." In Stalin's view the foreign parties should be completely subservient.

In a far worse blunder, Lovestone challenged Stalin directly, asking in a Senioren Konvent meeting: "Is there a fight brewing in the Russian Communist Party? If so, isn't a World Congress with a Special Russian subcommission the place to settle it?" It was heresy for an outsider to be inquiring into the affairs of the Russian party and proposing a special commission to settle Russian matters. At a secret session of the Senioren Konvent, Stalin presented a Politburo resolution: "The undersigned members of the Politburo . . . emphatically protest against the circulation of rumors that there are dissensions among the members of the Politburo." Though he betrayed no emotion, Stalin was furious with this American upstart who suggested that the shadowy struggle between himself and Bukharin be brought before the Congress.

One other member of the Senioren Konvent joined Lovestone in his proposal for a special commission, and that was Arthur Ewert. Like Lovestone, Ewert was tagged as a pro-Bukharin exaggerator of the strength of capitalism. Like Lovestone, he heard his analysis of capital-

ism castigated as pessimistic and incorrect. In his own party he was
called a saboteur of the "class against class" line and fought for his political life.

Another surprise in the American delegation was Jim Cannon's conversion to Trotskyism. When the Sixth Congress ended, he took up Trotsky's cause. On October 27, 1928, after a sort of heresy trial in New York,
he was expelled from the American party. According to Bittelman, his
parting words were "Stalin makes shit into leaders and leaders into shit."

Cannon was fed up with the American party as it then was. He detested playing "the Moscow game . . . going around to see one person
after another, like a petitioner." He said, "I always left Moscow with a
feeling of futility." He also detested Lovestone, writing in his memoirs
that he was

> unscrupulous in his ceaseless machinations and intrigues . . . down-
> right crooked. . . . The sinister stranger in our midst, who seemed to
> practice skullduggery maliciously for its own sake. . . . He was like
> an anarchist cancer cell running wild in the party organism. . . . He
> had an unnatural instinct to foul things up. . . . His chief enemy was
> always the factional opponent in the party rather than the capitalist
> class. . . . His methods were whispered gossip to set comrades
> against each other; misrepresentation and distortion of opponents'
> positions . . . and other tricks of the same order. . . . In intimate cir-
> cles, Foster remarked more than once that if Lovestone was not a
> Jew, he would be the most likely candidate for leadership of a fas-
> cist movement.

This is a harsh appraisal from a factional foe, and it omits saying that
what got Lovestone into hot water at the Sixth Congress was not intrigue
and duplicity but sticking to principle. While Foster was quick to switch
from burrowing from within to dual unionism, Lovestone refused to give
in to Third Period tactics. America was different, he kept saying, with
Bukharin's approval. As a follower and friend of Bukharin, Lovestone
self-destructed because he did not change horses fast enough. His offense
was not "machinations" but outmoded loyalty.

When Lovestone got back to New York that September, he told Gitlow: "I collaborated with Bukharin and aroused the enmity of Stalin."
But he did not yet realize that Stalin's enmity would be fatal, or that
Bukharin was on the way out. In fact, on September 27, he received
heartening news in a letter from the Bukharin-controlled Comintern,

which said: "The charge against the majority of the Central Committee of the United States party representing a Right Line is unfounded." This, however, had to be balanced against the demand that John Pepper, who had returned to New York after the congress with the American delegation, be recalled to Moscow. Pepper and Lovestone concocted an elaborate scheme to delay his recall. Pepper would say he was returning by way of Mexico because of his illegal status, while in reality he would stay in New York to help Lovestone with the preparations for the forthcoming party congress.

In the meantime, there was some last-minute campaigning in the presidential race, which Hoover won with 29 million votes, while Al Smith had 16 million and Norman Thomas had 267,000. The Foster-Gitlow ticket, which got on the ballot in thirty-three states, won 48,000 votes.

About two weeks after the election, on November 21, 1928, came a second letter from the Comintern. But this one was entirely different in tone, reprimanding the Lovestone leadership for "too much self-praise and too little self-criticism." The leadership, said the letter, seems to think it has continuing Comintern support, "but this is not so." The party convention, it added, should be postponed until February 1929.

Lovestone puzzled over the difference between the two letters within two months of each other, trying to figure out the hidden meaning. He had Louis Engdahl as his representative in Moscow, but Engdahl wasn't providing any inside information. He finally told Bert Wolfe: "Something is happening in Moscow that I don't understand. Our rep Engdahl doesn't seem to notice any change. He is a lightweight, a nitwit. He spends his time chasing girls. We need someone over there to see the top Russians and find out what's happening. You'll have to go."

Lovestone sensed that something had gone seriously wrong. He was right, for after the Comintern delegates went home in September, Stalin launched a frontal attack on Bukharin and his two cohorts. When Bukharin on September 30 wrote an important article in *Pravda* saying that the story of millions of tons of grain hoarded by the kulaks was a fairy tale, Stalin's Politburo majority reprimanded the "unauthorized" publication. In November came the first open clashes in the Politburo. Bukharin on one occasion called Stalin "an oriental despot" and walked out. On November 19, in a long harangue to the Central Committee, Stalin announced a new policy of rapid industrialization and collective agriculture, which was in effect a declaration of war on Bukharin.

Two days later came the letter to the American party reprimanding

the Lovestone majority, a portent that Bukharin was no longer in control
of the Comintern. In December a disgusted Bukharin quit the Comintern
as well as the editorship of *Pravda.* By the end of the year, the Bukharin-
Rykov-Tomsky trio was no longer a part of the Soviet leadership, but a
beleaguered opposition group inside the Politburo. To top things off, in
February 1929 Trotsky was sent to Constantinople for the start of a long
and peripatetic exile that would end with his murder in Mexico in 1940.

Bert Wolfe and his spirited wife, Ella, left for Moscow in mid-
December 1928 with forged Canadian passports, but Lovestone re-
mained in the dark. At the plenary session of the Central Committee in
New York from December 15 to 19, he hewed to the Comintern line as
expressed at the Sixth Congress by Bukharin, which was that American
imperialism and American capitalism were still in the ascendant. "What
did Comrade Bukharin say about this?" Lovestone asked. "I still quote
Comrade Bukharin. For me he does not represent the Right Wing of the
Communist International, although for some he does. For me Comrade
Bukharin represents the Communist line, the line of the Central Com-
mittee of the Communist Party of the Soviet Union. Therefore, Comrade
Bukharin is an authority—of the Comintern."

Alas, at the time Lovestone spoke these words, Bukharin was being
pushed out of the Comintern. In 1939, while testifying before the Dies
Committee, Lovestone explained the gravity of his decision to side with
Bukharin: "Everybody was rallying to endorse Stalin. I was not only a
personal friend of Bukharin, but I had fundamental agreement with him
on international questions. . . . I said, 'We will wear no Stalin buttons and
we will wear no Bukharin buttons, and we will not engage in gangsterism
against Stalin or Bukharin.' " Those words were relayed to Moscow by
the opposition in a cable, "and that pretty much served as . . . my political death certificate."

While Stalin and his minions were saying that capitalism was in crisis, Lovestone wrote an article that quoted the following comment from
the *Magazine of Wall Street:* "As Rome had its Augustinian Age and
Britain had its Victorian Age, so we are about to enter upon an epoch of
affluence and magnificence." Lovestone observed: "Translate 'we' into
Wall Street and the truth is here." Those words were to haunt him. They
were repeatedly attributed to him instead of to the magazine he was quot-
ing from, as evidence of his "American exceptionalism."

Bert and Ella Wolfe arrived in Moscow in January 1929. Responding
to requests from friends, they brought a five-pound jar of the original
brand of instant coffee, George Washington, and a suitcase filled with

rolls of toilet paper. At the border Russian customs officials opened their suitcases, took out the rolls one by one, and unrolled them on the floor, looking for hidden messages. The toilet paper was now unusable, so like everyone else at the Lux they used *Pravda* and *Izvestia.*

Bert Wolfe was unable to obtain an interview with Stalin. The two key men in the Comintern now were Stalinists—Otto Kuusinen, the Finn in the Political Secretariat, a workaholic mouse who scribbled over documents with pencils he wore down to stubs; and Joseph Piatnitsky, organization secretary of the ECCI, a bad-tempered bulldog of a man, short and stout with a hussar mustache, who took care (among other things) of the forged passports and secret service work.

When Wolfe asked Kuusinen if he could see Bukharin, he was told that Bukharin was too ill to come to Comintern meetings. Then Wolfe ran into Bukharin at the Lux, looking rosy-cheeked and fit, and asked: "Well, are you well or ill?" "By a vote of five to four [in the Politburo]," Bukharin replied, "I am too ill to function as chairman of the Comintern."

As Wolfe made his rounds, he saw that he was being treated as something of a pariah, except by a few old friends. Communicating with Lovestone in coded letters, he wrote on February 2, 1929: "The situation here is desperate . . . due to the attitude of Stalin towards us, especially Pepper and Lovestone, we stand on the brink of a precipice" (decoded version).

Even the once-friendly Gusev had turned against the Lovestone leadership, Wolfe reported. He had tried to bring Gusev around, but "he was as stubborn as 20-Mule-Team-Borax." He accused the Lovestone leadership of being against the Third Period and of accepting decisions with tongue in cheek. Wolfe warned Lovestone: "Be prepared to make the fight of your life" at the American party's Sixth Congress in March. The word was, Wolfe wrote, that two Comintern reps were on their way to New York to monitor the congress and summon Lovestone to Moscow.

Comintern representatives in the past—Pepper, Gusev, and Ewert—had been friendly to Lovestone, and he had cultivated them. But the two who arrived in New York in late February were anything but friendly. They were Philip Dengel, a former lieutenant in the German Army, a brusque and self-important Comintern functionary, and Harry Pollitt, a tractable boilermaker who had risen in the ranks of the British party. Both were Stalin yes-men.

They brought with them an Open Letter from the Comintern, an explosive document that ordered the dismissal of Lovestone as party leader and named Foster as his replacement. The open letter itself was window dressing; the real meat was in the secret "organizational proposals." They were not proposals but demands: Replace Lovestone with Foster, who would be named general secretary, the title that Stalin had just taken for himself. Remove Lovestone and Bittelman, the two worst factionalists, from the American party and place them at the disposal of the Comintern.

The organizational proposals would put an end to Lovestone's career in the American Communist Party, after ten years of fighting his way up the ladder. Being placed at the disposal of the Comintern, as Lovestone later told the Dies Committee, meant that "I would be sent to a very exciting place to start a revolution in the desert. . . . What it would have meant for me would have been a sort of living tomb . . . isolated from my country and my friends in the labor movement. . . . It might have meant that I could take a trip on the Volga and there would be an accident on the boat."

Whatever it meant, it was not an order that Lovestone was prepared to obey. He was in the paradoxical position of having taken full control of the American party, with a majority of 95 out of 104 convention delegates in his camp, with Cannon expelled, and the Foster-Bittelman opposition in disarray, while having lost the confidence of his Moscow bosses.

Thus, when Pollitt and Dengel arrived in New York on February 26, 1929, a few days before the convention's March 1 opening at the Irving Plaza Hall, they found a party in open rebellion. As Pollitt later wrote in his report to the Comintern: "For the past five weeks I have been wondering what sins I committed that this experience of being sent to America should have been placed on me. . . . When we arrived in New York we found an atmosphere of speculation, distrust, and hostility," because the Comintern instructions had been leaked by Bert Wolfe.

When the two representatives finally read the organizational proposals to the convention on March 3, Lovestone said: "They say the British House of Commons can do anything but change a person's sex. The Comintern is the same, it can do anything but change the leadership." Foster accepted the proposals without reservations, but Gitlow said, "This will throw the party into an open crisis, for Foster is thoroughly discredited."

"The whole fire of the majority," Pollitt said in his report, "was concentrated against the proposal that Foster should be General Secretary." The language became so violent that Dengel and Pollitt had to warn the Political Committee members that the convention was turning into an attack on the Comintern. The worst example was Lovestone, who said the proposals were "the result of a running sore in the Comintern apparatus." This expression, more than any other, was used to make the case that he was in open defiance of the Comintern.

Pollitt and Dengel squirmed in their seats as they heard delegate after delegate vilify the Comintern and attack Solomon Lozovsky as "the arch factionalist." For Dengel, it was "a frightful picture of the decline of a party that for too many years stagnated in the morass of factionalism. . . . Ours was an absolutely hopeless and impossible task."

In a clever tactical move, Lovestone offered his resignation, saying, "So long as there is anyone in the Comintern who doubts me, I cannot work." By a vote of eighty-seven to seventeen the convention rejected the resignation and the open letter.

At this point the Fosterites called for a condemnation of Bukharin by name. This put Lovestone on the spot. He knew by now that Bukharin was finished, and that it was pointless to defend him. He would be labeled a Bukharinite right-wing renegade, the final nail in his coffin. In an attempt to placate Stalin and obtain a reversal of the organizational proposals, he made a 180-degree turn, proposing an anti-Bukharin resolution and accepting the open letter. This was a complete abandonment of principle, a craven repudiation of his friend and ideological ally in order to remain in office.

And so it was that on March 9, the last day of the convention, the delegates voted to accept the open letter and repudiate Bukharin. The Fosterites threw their hats in the air and stamped on the ground and sang the Internationale. Gitlow thought it was sickening that they had all become Stalin's bootlickers.

But for the moment Lovestone had succeeded in preventing Foster's installation as general secretary. In his place, ignoring Pollitt and Dengel, the convention picked Gitlow. Lovestone dreamed up the idea of sending Stalin a petition from proletarian delegates asking him to reverse the organizational proposals and allow the convention to install a leadership of its own choosing. To his surprise Stalin sent back a cordial reply mixing praise—which Lovestone called "Flowers for Those About to Die"— with blame. Stalin insisted on Comintern assignments for Lovestone and Bittelman but agreed that the party could pick its own leaders. And he also demanded Pepper's immediate return to Moscow.

Where was Pepper? He was supposed to be in Mexico, on his way back to Moscow. In fact, he had secretly remained in New York to help Lovestone with the convention. Pepper was assigned a party stenographer, Lillian Gannes, to type up his harebrained convention resolutions, such as the one proposing a Negro Soviet Republic in the South. Bored in his hideout, he romanced her, telling her they would go to Mexico.

Gannes lived with a leader of the Young Communist League, Gilbert

Green, whom she later married and who became suspicious when she told him she was doing secret work for the party. Green went through Gannes's purse and found a New York Central timetable. He began to wonder whether Gannes was meeting a lover from the suburbs and decided to stake out the 125th Street station on March 3. At about 6:00 P.M. he saw Pepper exit the station and followed him to the apartment building at 404 West 124th Street. Soon he saw Lovestone and Stachel go into the building.

Motivated, as he put it, by the need to expose Pepper's defiance of Comintern instructions, Green revealed his whereabouts. This led to another cable asking for Pepper's immediate return to Moscow, to which Pepper replied on March 31: "The plans regarding my return trip to Moscow had to be modified. . . . I have a return attack of my old malaria illness causing serious heart trouble also. According to doctor's advice, I need medical treatment. Therefore I am forced to discontinue my journey for a few weeks."

But Pepper was in the country illegally, and when the Comintern asked the American party to prod him, the jig was up. He wrote the American Central Executive Committee on April 7: "In spite of very serious consequences to my health, I will return to Moscow immediately."

On May 12, 1929, Pepper was brought before the International Control Commission in Moscow. In a report dripping with sarcasm, Chairman Otto Kuusinen implicated Lovestone as Pepper's accomplice, saying that "for many months Pepper resorted to sabotage. . . . In February it was decided that he should depart. . . . Comrade Lovestone assures us that he had given him the money for the journey. Lovestone cabled that the decision of the Comintern was carried out. Pepper said he had left for Moscow . . . a boat came, but it was not found suitable. It was a slow going vessel, so he waited for a fast boat, but no fast boat came. But during the time he was supposed to be in Mexico, Gilbert Green saw Pepper with his own eyes."

On August 19, Pepper was expelled from the Comintern. Eventually he disappeared into the gulags. And so ended the career of one of the legendary Comintern figures, brought down by his own erratic behavior.

After the turbulent March convention, Lovestone formed a plan to bring a proletarian delegation to Moscow. He might get Stalin to relent if he was backed up by his handpicked delegation of ten, which included one woman: Mother Bloor; two Negroes, Edward Welsh and Otto Huiswood; William Miller, a machinist in a Detroit auto factory; Tom Myerscough, a coal miner; Alex Noral, a farm laborer; William J. White, a steelworker; and three nonproletarians, Lovestone, Gitlow, and Bedacht, the German-born onetime barber.

Why did Lovestone think he and his proletarians would get a fair shake from Stalin? He told the Dies Committee: "I was brought up in school, college, athletics, sports, to believe that if anybody wanted to fight me, and he wanted to fight on his own ground, I would say, 'Sure, let us go and fight it out.' I had the illusion that I could convince them not to declare war on us."

Lovestone was imbued with combativeness and a brash American optimism. For the first and last time in the history of the Comintern, the leader of a foreign party was coming to Moscow to fight it out with the leader of the parent party and chief of the Soviet state. It had all the earmarks of an epic battle, the thirty-one-year-old "City College kid" from the Lower East Side, who had been leader of his party for less than two years, and the fifty-year-old Georgian cobbler's son and professional revolutionary, who was in the process of establishing a police state over which he would rule until his death.

But the outcome of the battle had already been decided. Stalin's aim in allowing Lovestone to come to Moscow with his proletarians was not to give him a fair hearing but to teach him a lesson in obedience that would serve as an example for all the Communist parties around the world. Stalin was paying Lovestone the compliment of personally handling his funeral arrangements. In New York Harbor, it was in a spirit of unwary exhilaration of the "We'll show them!" variety that the Lovestone delegation set sail on March 23, 1929, into the jaws of the bear.

6

IN THE JAWS OF THE BEAR

When Lovestone left for Moscow in March 1929 with his proletarian delegation, he thought he held a winning hand. The delegation had behind it 90 percent of the American Communist rank and file. It had been chosen by the party convention. He was going to Moscow seeking to exercise the office he had been duly elected to, while thinking: "I have the party. It's my party." To mind the party while the top leaders—Lovestone, Gitlow, and Bedacht—were away, Lovestone chose his protégé Jack Stachel and the onetime cartoonist Robert Minor.

Lovestone left instructions for his stay-behinds: in case things went wrong and Stalin threw them out of the Comintern, they should be ready to transfer every piece of party property and every bank account to loyal members of the Lovestone group. They should start now, making a list of reliables and preparing deeds of transfer. Lovestone was prepared to take over the party and break with the Comintern. With his leadership at stake, he was willing to hold the party hostage.

When the delegation arrived in Moscow on April 7, 1929, Bert Wolfe met them at the station and told them that an American Commission had been formed to hear their case, under Stalin's supervision. Of its twelve members, eight were Russian, among them Stalin himself, Stalin's echo box Vyacheslav Molotov, Lovestone's archenemy Solomon Lozovsky, Lovestone's onetime friend Sergei Gusev, and the Stalin henchman Dmitri Manuilsky. The non-Communists were the Finn Otto Kuusinen, the Hungarian Béla Kun (a hard-line Stalinist), the German Walter Ulbricht (postwar ruler of East Germany for more than twenty years), and the Englishman Tom Bell, whom the Americans dubbed Dumb Bell. All in all, it was a hanging jury.

At the Hotel Lux, which Stalin referred to as the *lavotchka,* or den of thieves, Lovestone ran into Arthur Ewert, who was there with his wife, Szabo (Elise), awaiting a Comintern assignment to Latin America following his disgrace in the German party. Ewert invited Lovestone and Gitlow to his room for a drink. Lovestone was astonished to find the once jolly German tearful and discouraged. Jay said he would fight because he represented the majority of his party. "Don't," Ewert begged. "Learn from my example. I too was sure I was right, and then I realized I couldn't fight Stalin. You can see what I've become, a broken man about to be sent to some outlandish place, an outcast from my beloved party."

Gitlow asked Ewert why he didn't continue to resist outside the party, which was what he and Lovestone were considering. "Never will I be found guilty of formally breaking discipline," Ewert replied. "A Communist above every other consideration is a disciplined soldier. . . . My life is bound up with the movement and the Comintern. There is no other existence possible for me."

It may be that Ewert, now an obedient functionary of the Comintern, was instructed to seek Lovestone out and do a little missionary work. If so, he failed completely, for blind obedience was not in Lovestone's nature. There was a feisty show-me attitude in the American delegation. While Ewert pliantly accepted his Comintern duties, Lovestone adamantly refused to "start a revolution in the desert in Afghanistan."

What happened to Ewert offers an insight into what might have happened to Lovestone had he accepted a Comintern job. In 1935 Ewert and his wife were sent to Brazil to organize a revolution against the regime of the dictator Getúlio Vargas. In December they were arrested and tortured. The pro-Nazi Vargas regime sent Szabo Ewert back to Germany. After questioning by the Gestapo, she was interned in Ravensbrück, where she died in 1939. Arthur Ewert was sentenced to thirteen years in Brazil, but after his wife's death his mind snapped, and he was transferred to an insane asylum. Finally, in 1947 he was deported to East Germany, where he remained in a mental institution until his death in 1959. Such was the fate of a good Communist whose inflexible obedience took him to Brazil on a doomed assignment. Such was the kind of fate that Lovestone was determined to avoid.

On the morning of April 12, the ten American delegates plus Bert Wolfe filed into an auditorium in the Comintern headquarters on Mokhovaya Street for the first of nine sessions of the American Commission. The twelve commission members sat on a dais, and Lovestone seized on the fact of Stalin's presence to introduce his American proletarians, one by one, to the somewhat embarrassed Russian leader, for it was a little like introducing an executioner to his victims.

The first session was a skirmish between Lovestone and Foster, who had arrived with Weinstone and Bittelman to represent the pro-Stalin minority in the American party. Foster recounted the way he had been attacked at the March convention, saying: "I sat there and listened for several days to a stream of vituperation of the vilest kind. I was called a liar, traitor, thief, coward, faker, incompetent, for days and days. As for billingsgate and slime, the equal of it has never been seen in any American convention."

But then Lovestone placed Foster on the defensive over his boasting about his interviews with Stalin. "With regard to the statement that no good would come from a Lovestone leadership," Foster explained, "this remark I repeated to some other comrades here in Moscow. One of these wrote about it to a comrade in the United States. The letter containing this statement, the comrade had in a briefcase. Somebody took that briefcase and with it the letter."

"I would rather be the person who stole the briefcase than the one who wrote the letter," Lovestone exclaimed.

"It was wrong for me to have repeated this statement," Foster acknowledged, making his act of contrition to Stalin. "I am very sorry that I allowed these words of Comrade Stalin's to be repeated."

As a result of the Stalin interview, Lovestone said, the Fosterites were "crowing that they were in the Stalin camp . . . and if there was a Stalin group there had to be a Bukharin group. I think I once had some coffee and cake with Comrade Bukharin . . . we are speaking frankly here. . . . I once had coffee and cake with Trotsky . . . but don't call me a Trotskyite. . . . But after the interview between Comrade Stalin and Foster . . . the opposition were going around saying, 'We are the Stalin group.' "

White (the steelworker): "The report of handing over the party to Comrade Foster came from the rumor factory of Comrade Foster. I know Comrade Foster, I know his methods and I know that he would kill politically everything that stood in his way. He wants power."

Noral (the farmworker): "We could not accept the organizational proposals as they made Comrade Foster secretary of the party, and the delegates could not swallow this. That is why we came here. . . . Only when Foster knew he was to be secretary was he ready to swallow the open letter hook, line, and sinker."

The ensuing commission sessions saw the mounting of a three-pronged attack on Lovestone, for his convention tactics, for the Bukharin resolution, and for being a right deviationist. On this last point Ulbricht asked Lovestone to explain what the American party had done to fight the right danger.

"In America," Lovestone replied, "we are fighting Republican and Democratic parties for the majority of the working class, which has not moved forward to the socialist parties. They are still for capitalism. You can say what you like, but this is a fact. . . . In America, the bourgeois parties control the majority of the working class."

The first sharp attack came from the Comintern representative Philip Dengel, who said that "Lovestone's reaction to the open letter was: 'How are we going to get the majority of the delegates against the policies of the Comintern?' Never in the history of the Comintern was there such an unprincipled and demagogic convention. . . . Anyone who saw Lovestone's abusive attitude must declare that nothing more shameless and worse could happen. This was a nationalistic spirit, a spirit hostile to the Comintern."

Lovestone: "Tell the truth, Dengel."

Dengel: "The truth is that you are chiefly to blame."

Coming to Lovestone's defense, Eddie Welsh, an organizer in Harlem, said: "How can our party be right-wing, how can 90 percent of the membership support a right wing? . . . I have no time for factionalism, I am too busy doing party work. . . . Comrade Lovestone is our party, he has the respect of the membership. The American party wants Comrade Lovestone."

This was too much for James W. Ford, a pro-Foster American Negro in the audience, who jumped up to say the Negro comrades had been poisoned by the party leadership. At this the other Negro member of the Lovestone delegation, Otto Huiswood, an organizer of West Indian origin, exploded, saying, "If I want to go into the record of the opposition with regard to Negro work, I can begin with [William F.] Dunne [a Communist leader once active in Montana]. He once said that he could see Negroes in the army as soldiers, but for a Negro to be an officer was quite a different story."

"Don't take him seriously," Lovestone said. "He doesn't take himself seriously."

Ford: "You have nothing to say, Lovestone, nobody takes you seriously."

Lovestone: "You're badly mistaken; before this show is over, you'll be running on three wheels, Ford." Even when his survival in the party hung in the balance, Lovestone could not resist one-liners.

Then Weinstone weighed in, backing up Dengel: "Comrade Lovestone made the attack against me—that I was wearing a Stalin button . . . Who runs the Comintern, he asked—[Gregory] Petrovsky and [Solomon] Lozovsky? . . . What else was that but anti-Stalin talk? . . . They held meetings at three in the morning to prepare the next steps. . . . It was a war situation."

Now came the counterattack from five members of the proletarian delegation: Bill Miller, Bill White, Tom Myerscough, Alex Noral, and Bert Wolfe. "I have been working in Detroit since 1912 in the auto industry," said Miller. "Foster's record in the labor movement is one of continual passage from one movement to the other. . . . When he appeared before the Senate Committee, he admitted the leadership of Gompers and expressed admiration for this reactionary leader. . . . He boasted that he induced the workers to buy war bonds." As for Dengel, how could he say there were no shop units in Detroit after spending all of three hours there? He was "just a big liar."

The Americans were showing a style of plain speaking that no one had ever used in the Comintern before. They were pushing not only for Lovestone but for greater freedom in the American party, as White, the steelworker, made clear in his own homespun way. "I will tell you how I look at this," he said. "I once saw a working man planting a garden, and he had with him his little girl, who wanted a garden all to herself. So her father gave her a few little tomato plants and they began to grow, but she was tired of waiting, and every two or three days she went out and pulled up the tomato plants to see how they were growing. This is what you are doing to our party in the United States. We do not want you to come every four or five months and tear up our party to see how we are growing. . . . As for you, Comrade Dengel, did you investigate whether there were factory papers in Wheeling and Pittsburgh and McKeesport? Did you do this? You did not. You and Comrade Pollitt called the delegates to our convention 'low-down bastards,' you called us 'sabotaging reformists,' you charged us with every crime and every sin. . . . And you, Weinstone, why are you here? I have a suspicion that you think Comrade Foster will not be secretary of our party, and perhaps Wobbling Willie Weinstone, the savior of the world, will be secretary."

Then came the turn of Tom Myerscough, the miner, another blunt "member of the American army of invasion." He said, "I speak three kinds of English—plain English with a very limited vocabulary, dirty English with an unlimited vocabulary, and the third kind is turkey English, so I am going to talk turkey. . . . We have come here to fight the organizational proposals because we believe they would do an irreparable harm to the American party. . . . Some of you must think we are a bunch of marionettes that dance with strings. I am not a marionette because you would need a pretty strong rope to hold me, nearly as strong as you would need to lift Béla Kun [a man of great girth]. . . . I am neither a puppy nor a puppet, and I did not come here to see a Pope. . . . I come from a coal and steel district in Pittsburgh, where Foster came often, and one of the first things he would say was, 'Well, I have to catch an early train.' And once when he came to talk in a mining town he heard that John L. Lewis objected to the use of the hall, and the red standard-bearer showed a yellow streak and went to another hall."

Foster: "You are a goddamned liar and you know it."

Myerscough: "You are another one. . . . Comrades, the American party is sick and tired of this small and unprincipled opposition that is hampering the progress of our party. The American party wants to be allowed to do its work under the leadership that has built up the party, and that includes Comrade Lovestone."

Noral, the farmworker, said, "The opposition reminds me of a cow. A farmer had a cow, and every time he went to milk this cow it swished him in the eye with its tail. One morning he came into the house with a black eye, and his wife asked him what was the matter. He told her that to keep the cow from swishing him with its tail, 'I tied a brick to the end of it.' Comrades, we haven't come here to tie a brick on the cow's tail."

Thanks to Noral and the others, this was very probably the only time in the history of the Comintern that the authentic voice of the American working class was heard.

Then it was Wolfe's turn to speak. In Moscow since February, he had received such a cold shoulder that "there were times that I felt my role was reduced to that of snooper, or spy." Only once had he been invited to an ECCI meeting, and that was "when our Mongolian comrades were talking in Mongolian and everyone was walking out, so I was invited by telephone to go in and make an audience." As for Lovestone, Wolfe recalled that "Comrade Pollitt said here, 'Why make a fuss about one man?' . . . But this is not a personal matter. . . . Comrade Lovestone has been a driving force in America, a builder of the party, the bitterest foe of opportunism and unprincipled factionalism."

Wolfe also echoed the call for greater freedom: "Comrades, our party hasn't got time to wade through the flood of your cables and letters. . . . This is not the way to develop the work of the party; it causes high fever. We could not take a step without sending a cable to Moscow and without trembling in our boots that a cable would come back and our work would be undone. . . . We ask for an end to that system of cables and letters."

The next few days saw a running battle between Lovestone and Foster. Lovestone tried to make the point that an attack on him was an attack on the American party, mingling their destinies: "Whatever work is given me I will do. But we have a deep conviction that the proposal aiming to take me away from our party is not a personal matter but a slap and slam in the face of our entire leadership. . . . If you insist on taking these measures, you will create a situation in our party under which thousands of workers will be disgusted and totally demoralized. We say to you, Criticize, condemn, but don't pull our party up by its roots."

This statement was at once rebutted by an angry Lozovsky, who said it was "a monstrosity" for Lovestone to claim that he was speaking for the party, for that meant that the Comintern could not rebuke Lovestone without rebuking the party. Also, it was unheard of to try to discredit a Comintern delegation as Lovestone had done, and to call Dengel "a hysteric." "You treated them like hooligans," Lozovsky said. "Such a vicious campaign of discrediting a Comintern delegation as you conducted has never yet been witnessed in the international Communist movement. . . . All this was not double, triple, or quadruple bookkeeping," Lozovsky went on, "but Lovestone bookkeeping. . . . Toward the end of the convention you pulled the Bukharin resolution out of your pocket. . . . Is this not the most revolting type of politics? It was all done to deceive the party. . . . Comrade Lovestone said here humorously that matters cannot be corrected by sending one to Tibet and another to the Mediterranean . . . [however] such trips would have an invigorating effect, especially if the traveler would stay away some two or three years from America."

Lovestone was more than willing to match Lozovsky, the one Russian leader he truly despised, blow for blow. "Lozovsky's sole occupation is to misrepresent our party," he said. He quoted a letter from Lozovsky asking why an American party member had been removed for Trotskyism "without your having made any investigation of the matter." "Now how the hell do you know we made no investigation?" Lovestone thundered. "What and who the hell gives you the nerve to say this? I don't call this a running sore, I call this a cancer!"

"This is megalomania," Lozovsky exclaimed, "which will do you no good. . . . Your methods are bourgeois methods as practiced in Tammany Hall. If you continue you will destroy the American party."

There was a respite in the hearings from April 29 to May 6 as Stalin attended to the Soviet Party Plenum in the Throne Room of the Palace of the Tsars, which he used as a platform to further demolish Bukharin. In a long attack on his former ally, Stalin said Bukharin had headed "the most repulsive and the pettiest of all the factional groups that have ever existed in our party." Bukharin's "ill health" was now given as the reason for his removal from his posts at *Pravda* and in the Comintern, and that November he was expelled from the Politburo.

The demises of Bukharin and Lovestone took place simultaneously. In both the party plenum and the American Commission, Stalin had the same goal, to destroy an opponent, one in the Russian party, the other in the American party, by means of stage-managed hearings. Gitlow, the only member of the American delegation to attend the plenum, was all too aware of the connection, saying: "If Stalin can be so ruthless with his old companion in arms, what chance have I got?" But as it turned out the ornery Americans were harder to finish off than Bukharin, who meekly accepted his fate.

On April 27, Lovestone cabled Minor and Stachel in New York: "Disregard all rumors. No decision yet. All authority shattered. Bukharin openly branded as right-winger." Lovestone was now certain that no help could come from Bukharin's ruined camp. On May 2 he cabled: "Tomsky and Bukharin lost all posts except Politburo."

On May 6, 1929, the atmosphere was electric in the American Commission auditorium as Stalin prepared to make his first speech. He had never before been so personally involved in the affairs of a foreign party and never would be again, for it was not a sound practice to reveal how fiercely he cracked the whip.

Sixty-five years later, Ella Wolfe, who had been in the audience, vividly remembered his appearance: "Stalin was dressed in a tan tunic with leather boots. He was smaller than I expected, with a pockmarked face, a brutal mouth, and the yellow eyes of a mountain lion. His left arm was palsied. He was a hard-featured little man—all his photographs had to be retouched."

Instead of focusing his fire on Lovestone, as the other members of the commission had done, Stalin took an "above the fray" approach, expounding on the theories of American exceptionalism and right deviation. "It would be wrong to ignore the specific peculiarities of American capitalism," he magnanimously agreed. "But it would be still more wrong to base the activities of the Communist Party on these specific features . . . since every Communist Party must base itself on the general features of capitalism, which are the same for all countries." And there you had it, Stalin was saying, you could not have the tail wagging the dog. There was an American situation, which the Americans knew about, and there was a world situation, which Stalin knew about, based on the false premise that the "general features" of capitalism were the same in all countries. The American party was but a component of the Comintern and had to act accordingly. It did not have the deep knowledge of the world situation that Stalin and the other Comintern leaders pretended to have.

Thus the Americans had been led into right deviation. "They were infected with the disease of factionalism" and were conducting a policy "of rotten diplomacy . . . of diplomatic intrigue." And now Stalin berated both American factions. It was, he said, "a game of who can spit farthest." Foster and Bittelman had called themselves " 'Stalinites' . . . but that is disgraceful. Do you not know that there are no 'Stalinites,' that there must be no 'Stalinites'?" Here was a touch of becoming modesty on the part of the man who had waged a five-year struggle to succeed Lenin by building up a personal following. The Stalin cult was already launched, with his mustached and solemn countenance appearing on posters in every shop window and on the cover of every magazine.

But on this issue, Stalin went on, the Lovestone group's behavior was "even more disgraceful. . . . In order not to be outdone, the Lovestone group performed a hair-raising feat and carried through a decision calling for the removal of Comrade Bukharin from the Comintern [which Stalin had only a week before officially engineered]. . . . And so you get a game of rivalry and unprincipled speculation. . . . Comrades, the Comintern is not a stock market, it is the holy of holies of the working class."

Stalin then revealed that he and Lovestone had talked "just the other day. . . . It is characteristic that Comrade Lovestone has been spreading absurd rumors about this conversation. . . . What did he speak to me about? He asked that the Presidium of the ECCI should rescind the decision to withdraw him from America. . . . He promised to be a loyal soldier of the Comintern . . . if the Comintern would give him the necessary instructions. He was not looking for high positions in the American party but only begged to be tested and given the chance to prove his loyalty. What did I reply? I told him that experiments in testing his loyalty had been going on for three years, but no good had come of them. It would be better if Comrades Lovestone and Bittelman were kept in Moscow for a time. . . . This is one of the surest ways to cure the American party of factionalism and save it from disintegration." But Stalin had promised Lovestone to bring his request before "the comrades," as if anyone besides himself had the power to decide.

In fact, the decision had already been made, as Stalin now announced. A second open letter would be drafted, with six organizational proposals. Once again Lovestone and Bittelman would be placed at the service of the Comintern. But this time Foster was not mentioned as Lovestone's successor. Foster, too, as Stalin had emphasized in his speech, was a speculator, a maneuverer, an opportunist, guilty of "rotten diplomacy."

This might have been a good time for the American delegation to admit defeat, for it was a foregone conclusion that Stalin's proposals would be endorsed by the commission when it met on May 12 to read the new open letter. If Lovestone threw in the towel and agreed to remain in Moscow, some small advantages might be salvaged for the rest of the delegation. But this Lovestone could not do, and he was able for the moment to keep the delegation solidly behind him. They would go down fighting.

At Max Bedacht's instigation, the delegation decided to preempt the open letter with a statement of its own, on the theory that a forceful stand might make Stalin change his mind. After all, they had 90 percent of the party behind them back home. This statement, released on May 9, said that an unfavorable decision in the open letter would be ruinous for American Communism. If Stalin's proposals were adopted, the Americans would conclude that "the ECCI desires to destroy the American Central Committee." The Lovestone delegation was now in open defiance of the Comintern.

On May 12, Chairman Kuusinen proposed the adoption of the open letter, which was sharper than Stalin's speech, for it accused the Lovestone group of "misleading honest proletarian members." Kuusinen called the American statement of May 9 a veiled threat. The only question remaining, Kuusinen added, was "Does the Lovestone majority really wish to enter upon the path of splitting? Will you carry out unconditionally the decisions of the Comintern? Yes or no?"

The open letter and the proposals had been unanimously adopted by the twelve members of the American Commission. What could the Lovestone delegation do? They engaged in delaying tactics. Gitlow asked for a little more time so that he could prepare a statement. For the first time the usually poker-faced Molotov lost his temper. "This is no answer to Comrade Kuusinen's question," he said. "We must get a clear and concise answer to this question right here at this session."

Wolfe also asked for more time. Then Stalin also lost his temper, saying: "I think the statement of Wolfe is shameful. The leadership of the faction is so illiterate, so backward, that they don't understand the significance of the letter. You are asked in simple words: Do you recognize the discipline of the Comintern? Do you believe the part should obey the whole? If it is necessary for you to think this over, then who are you?"

But Wolfe stuck to his guns: "We will have our proposals ready tomorrow. This is not an abstention."

Kun: "We will ask the delegation one by one whether you will carry out the discipline of the Comintern without reservations."

Myerscough: "We have nothing to add to the statement of Comrade Gitlow."

Mother Bloor: "I have always obeyed the dictates of the Comintern. This letter makes very serious charges, and I ask as a Communist for time to consider our statement."

Bedacht: "I've always considered and do now consider myself a member of the Comintern and consider that I have a right to participate in the making of the decisions of the Comintern. Our statement will be ready tomorrow."

Lovestone: "I solidarize completely with Bedacht's declaration." Miller, Huiswood, Welsh, White, and Noral concurred.

Kuusinen: "No comrade gave a satisfactory answer. Meeting of the Presidium set for Tuesday evening."

The Americans were buying time, not only to prepare a statement but to make arrangements with New York for the transfer of party property to the Lovestone loyalists. They now realized that they were being railroaded into submission, and they took the perilous option of splitting from the Comintern. As soon as the May 12 meeting adjourned, Lovestone, Gitlow, and Bedacht joined Wolfe in his room at the Hotel Lux and drafted a cable to Minor and Stachel, telling them to take over the property of the party and its front organizations:

> Draft decision means destruction party. . . . Situation astounding, outrageous, can't be understood until arrival. Possibility entire delegation being forcibly detained. . . . Unless you hear from us within ten days that we are returning, start wide movement units and press for return complete convention inclusive Lovestone, Wolfe. . . . Carefully check all units all property all connections all mailing lists of auxiliaries, all sublists, district lists, removing same from offices and unreliables. . . . Instantly finish preparations sell buildings.

They could not send the wire from Moscow, but by luck they found an American OGPU agent who was leaving for Berlin and who promised to send it from there, which he did on May 15. It was just as naive to give a secret cable to one of Stalin's spies in the hope that it would remain unread as it was to take for granted that Minor and Stachel would blindly accept the enormity of a break with the Comintern. But the American delegation had no other way of getting their instructions out.

On May 14 the delegation came before the Presidium of the ECCI in a meeting that lasted from 9:00 P.M. to 3:00 the following morning. The meeting was held in the Hall of Columns, with Stalin in charge. Aside from the forty voting members of the Presidium (one of whom was Gitlow), the hall was packed with more than a hundred spectators who had come to witness the public humbling of the Americans.

But having already decided to break with Moscow, the American delegation had no further reason to comply with Comintern demands. To them, the soul of the American party, as well as Lovestone's continued leadership, was at stake. Kuusinen made the opening statement, telling them that their factionalism had been going on since 1925, despite warning after warning, violation after violation. Factionalism had spread to Korea, to Poland, to Yugoslavia, where the Comintern had removed the leadership of both groups and formed a new leadership from the rank and file. "It is clear that the ECCI must . . . put an end to this unheard-of situation."

Then Gitlow read a statement saying that although the delegation remained loyal to the Comintern, it could not accept the open letter, for "it would make it absolutely impossible for us to continue as effective workers in the Comintern movement." This led to outbursts from members of the Presidium:

Sen Katamaya: "Last Sunday you degraded yourselves. . . . And today you bring a statement against the proposals. . . . Comrades, you are breaking your necks. . . . As a friend of the American party—I love the American party—do not fight this platform."

Molotov: "Lovestone and his group have decided on a course of open war against the Comintern. . . . Why do these comrades so persist? Because they intend to form a separate group [apparently word of the secret cable to New York was already out]. . . . Unconditional subordination to the Comintern is their only chance."

Lozovsky: "They are already halfway down the road that leads out of the Comintern. . . . If you want to match your strength with the Comintern, we have seen greater heroes than Lovestone fall into the camp of our class enemies. . . . Think again, comrades. . . . There is a Russian proverb that says, 'Measure off seven times before you cut.' You have cut seven times without measuring."

And then it was Stalin's turn to slice up the Americans with the dialectics first learned from the monks at Tiflis Orthodox Theological Seminary: "For almost a month now we have been occupied with the problem of the American Communist Party. . . . And what do we find? Instead of a serious attitude . . . we have a fresh outburst of factionalism. . . . Extreme factionalism has driven them into the path of insubordination and warfare against the Comintern. This was an order from the Comintern, and they refused to submit." Their declaration of May 14 "was drawn up rather craftily . . . by some sly attorney, by some pettifogging lawyer. . . . It vows complete loyalty to the Comintern, and then says it cannot accept the Comintern decision. What is the reason for this duplicity? This hypocrisy?" It was, said Stalin, like Chamberlain promising arms reduction while increasing armaments. "The chatter about peace was necessary to cover up the preparations for a new war. . . . Comrade Lovestone of course is not Chamberlain . . . but his maneuver recalls the maneuvers of Chamberlain."

Then Stalin addressed "the vaunting manner in which the Lovestone group speaks in the name of ninety-nine percent of the Communist Party of America. . . . One would think they have that ninety-nine percent in their pockets. . . . Let me remind you that Zinoviev and Trotsky also at one time played trumps with percentages . . . and you know in what a farce the vainglory of Trotsky and Zinoviev ended. [It had not ended yet, though their endings were hardly farcical—execution for Zinoviev in 1936 and assassination for Trotsky in 1940.] You have a majority because the American party until now has regarded you as supporters of the Comintern. . . . Do you think the American workers will follow your lead against the Comintern? At present you have a majority. Tomorrow you will have no majority at all." By May 14, Minor and Stachel, who were playing a double game, were already communicating privately with the Comintern, so Stalin knew they were not going along with Lovestone. But beyond that he was telling the Lovestone delegation that majorities meant nothing and Comintern approval everything. No Communist party could exist outside the Comintern.

As for Lovestone, Stalin went on, "it is said that the American Communist Party cannot get along without Comrade Lovestone, that his removal may ruin the party. . . . But that is not true, comrades, the party is created by the working class and not by individual leaders. . . . And what is more, Comrade Lovestone is not such a great leader. . . . He is of course a capable and talented comrade . . . indisputably an adroit and talented factional wire puller. . . . But a party leader is one thing, a factional leader another. . . . I doubt very much at this stage that Comrade Lovestone can be a party leader." The solution, Stalin concluded, was simple: Either submit to the decision of the ECCI or make war against the Comintern.

When Stalin had finished, a sea of applause surrounded the marooned Americans, sitting all in a row on the prisoners' bench. Then Kuusinen said: "We shall now proceed with the vote on the draft of the open letter. I ask the American delegation to vote. . . . Bittelman, Weinstone, Foster in favor. Ten opposing." The Lovestone delegation was holding fast.

But the portly Béla Kun said: "I would like each majority comrade to vote." This meant that each one had to stand up, go to the dais before Stalin and the rest, and answer the question "Do you accept the decision of the Comintern?"

First came Mother Bloor, still feisty at sixty-seven: "Comrades," she said, "I cannot leave this place without a protest as a Communist. We have been charged with being unprincipled, dishonest, following the leadership of others, and not obeying our own convictions. . . . I shall be with the Comintern as long as I live, but I cannot sign a document that calls us diplomatists, calls us bourgeois politicians and a right-wing party. It is against my Communist honesty. . . . I stand by the letter of the delegation."

Welsh: "Comrades, this question involves more than just a yes or no answer. . . . I feel that if we go back to the party and tell the ninety percent majority that they have been following a group of petty bourgeois politicians, when we feel these charges are without foundation, I feel that is impossible."

Stalin had taken a liking to Welsh, a six-foot, fine-featured, burnished-skinned comrade known as "the bronze Adonis," and singled him out for special attention, hoping to find a breach in the delegation in one of its Negro members. "Does Comrade Welsh consider it permissible to carry on a fight against the open letter?" Stalin asked.

Taken aback, Welsh gave a muddled reply: "No, I do not propose to fight against the decisions of the Comintern. . . . But I cannot accept the proposals in their entirety, nor will I fight them."

Stalin: "Does Comrade Welsh intend to carry out the decisions embodied in the open letter?"

Welsh: "I cannot carry it through because I do not agree with the proposals."

White: "We have been characterized as opportunists, as right-wing, as anti-Comintern and other names. If we are that, we have no business in the Comintern. . . . I refuse to answer any questions concerning my loyalty to the Comintern."

Huiswood: "In spite of all the names hurled at us, we are as good Communists as anyone else. . . . Therefore I stand by our statement."

As for Gitlow, who had spent several years in jail for his Communist convictions, being called a petit-bourgeois speculator was just too much. By now he detested Stalin, and he said rather heatedly: "This is one of the most uncalled-for attacks upon the leadership of the party that I have seen. . . . The decision is so drawn up that some of the most active leaders in the founding and building of our movement will find it impossible to maintain the confidence of the workers. Such a decision I cannot accept."

Lovestone: "Comrades, in the course of my work in the Communist movement, I have stood for a lot of abuse. Comrade Stalin tonight gave me more abuse than I have ever got in my life. . . . I think Comrade Stalin could have found something better than to call me a businessman. . . . If I were a businessman I would not say what I am going to say. Comrade Stalin told us that he believed in speaking rough. . . . Well, I believe in speaking plain. I stand by the declaration of our delegation. . . . Comrade Stalin, we are not rotten diplomatists, we are not good businessmen. We do not want a test of strength with the Russian party. . . . We do not want to threaten anyone. . . . Communist persuasion, that is the method to use . . . the correction of our errors must not mean the destruction of those comrades who have made these errors." In this heartfelt plea, Lovestone was speaking not only for the party but for himself.

Then came Wolfe, Myerscough, Miller, and Noral, who all said basically the same thing: "I cannot accept this unjustified and incorrect decision."

The last to rise was Bedacht, who had been the most vehement in his defiance of the Comintern but was now having second thoughts. All day long he had been moaning and groaning about what to do. Now that the moment had come to break with the mother party, his nerve failed. With regret, he broke instead with the delegation, saying: "Why should Lovestone be torn from the American party while the lack of principle of Foster is rewarded? . . . I disagree with the characterization of our leaders as bourgeois politicians. . . . But now that the draft has become final, there can be no other way than to submit to the decision of the ECCI."

For the first time that night, there was applause for a member of the American delegation. As Lovestone later put it, Bedacht was a career Communist with a wife and four daughters to support. What else could he do, go back to being a barber? Lovestone composed the first line of a limerick: "Max Bedacht *mit Kinder acht* (with children to care for)." Back in his room at the Bristol Hotel after the meeting, Bedacht kept repeating, "Oh Mama, Mama [which is what he called his wife], I had to do it."

The delegates had been polled, and all but one had refused to submit. After so many meetings and so many speeches, after their repeated verbal bludgeoning, Stalin had expected obedience, but the mulish Americans refused to cave in. By now it was well past midnight, and Stalin rose again to deliver the coup de grâce. Starting out calmly, in a low monotone, he worked himself up into a fit of barely controlled rage.

"We ought to value the firmness and stubbornness displayed here by ten of the eleven American delegates," he began. "But true Bolshevik courage does not consist in placing one's individual will above the collective will of the Comintern. . . . Comrades Gitlow and Lovestone announced here with aplomb that their convictions do not permit them to submit to the decisions of the Presidium. . . . But only anarchists can talk like that, not Bolsheviks, not Leninists."

What if a majority of workers in a factory wanted to go on strike, Stalin asked, and a minority refused to walk out? What would those workers be called? "You know that such workers are usually called scabs," he said, "and for scabs, there is plenty of room in our cemeteries." Scab was perhaps the worst name that one Communist could call another, far worse than rotten diplomatist, speculator, or opportunist.

By now Stalin could not contain his anger; his voice rose almost to a shout in a passage that was deleted from the printed text of his speech: "And you, who are you? Who do you think you are? Trotsky defied me. Where is he? Zinoviev defied me. Where is he? Bukharin defied me. Where is he? And you! Who are you? Yes, you will go back to America. But when you get there, nobody will know you except your wives."

With this condemnation to anonymity, the show trial of the American delegation was over. Although they were told they would suffer the fate of Trotsky, Zinoviev, and Bukharin, the one phrase that Lovestone seized on was "You will go back to America." At least they would not be detained in Moscow, or so he hoped. When Stalin finished speaking, Kuusinen instructed the Political Secretariat "to carry out the line of the open letter."

Then Stalin rose from his seat on the dais, followed by his bodyguards, and marched down the aisle. When he came to the bench where the Americans were sitting, he stopped and extended his hand to Eddy Welsh, sitting between Wolfe and Lovestone, who was on the aisle. Welsh put his hand behind his back and said: "What the hell does this bastard single me out for?" It was a good thing that Stalin did not know English, though he understood the tone and the body language. His face reddened, and he strode briskly out of the auditorium.

On May 17 the Comintern's Political Secretariat met to determine the fate of the Americans: Lovestone and Gitlow were expelled from the American party. Wolfe was recalled from Moscow. The new American secretariat was to consist of Weinstone, Foster, Minor, and Bedacht, who was rewarded for his recantation. In addition, Lovestone would not be allowed to leave Moscow, and there would be a "campaign of enlightenment" (read purge) in the American party.

By this time it was clear that Minor and Stachel had betrayed Lovestone. As soon as they received the May 15 cable from Berlin telling them to transfer party property, they sent a copy back to Stalin. They saw the chance to show their obedience to the Comintern and take over the American party.

Looking for a way out of the pit he had dug for himself, Lovestone found a loophole in the Comintern regulations. Any Comintern agent sent on a foreign assignment had the right to go home for a period of up to two months. On May 22 he hand-delivered a letter to Kuusinen that said: "I hereby request permission to leave for the United States immediately. . . . I pledge myself to submit to the decision of the ECCI. . . . After a period of weeks I agree to put myself at the disposal of the ECCI for the assignment of work anywhere." He had no intention of carrying out any Comintern assignment. He was simply looking for a way to escape from Moscow and regroup his forces in the United States.

On May 24 three more—Noral, Huiswood, and Mother Bloor— defected from the Lovestone camp. It seemed a lost cause, and they decided they would rather stay in the party. Mother Bloor was known primarily as a public speaker and needed the platform the party could provide. They were allowed to go home.

As for the remaining six—Wolfe, Gitlow, Welsh, Miller, White, and Myerscough—three received offers from the Comintern. Gitlow turned down an assignment in the OGPU station in Mexico City. Wolfe was asked to go to Korea, which had been annexed by Japan and was swarming with Japanese intelligence agents hunting down Communists. It was a sure jail term, which he passed up. Welsh, Stalin's favorite, was offered a vacation on the Black Sea, followed by a stay at the Lenin School, but declined.

In reality the Comintern had no intention of keeping anyone besides Lovestone in Moscow, and by May 28 they were all told they could leave. This was the point when Lovestone got really worried, writing the Political Secretariat on May 30 to actually demand a Comintern assignment and listing his preferences as England, France, Germany, Argentina, and the Far East. He completed his prostration with this statement: "I condemn all resistance to the Comintern decisions." The Comintern was finally satisfied and cabled the American party that Lovestone would be allowed to leave if there was no objection to his return.

But the American party's new leaders did not want him back sabotaging the work of reorganization, and they replied on June 4 that they doubted the validity of his reasons. By then all the other Americans had gone. As Lovestone later told the Dies Committee, "When I was detained in Moscow and everybody was allowed to leave and I was not, I had the feeling of being in a locked trunk . . . the last sound of life you hear from the outside is the snapping of the lock."

On June 6, Lovestone wrote an agitated either-or letter to the Comintern: "Decide today to send me immediately to India or Latin America." If that was not granted, "I am compelled to ask that my passport be immediately given to me, so that I can return to America. . . . I feel . . . a complete lack of confidence in me. . . . I can no longer continue the never-ending postponements and delays."

Once again the American party rejected his plea, so Lovestone took matters into his own hands. By June 11 he was no longer in Moscow. How he got out has remained something of a mystery, for over the years he told the story ten different ways.

The key figure in Lovestone's escape was a legendary Comintern agent, Nicholas Dozenberg, alias Nicholas Dallant, alias Frank Kleges, alias Blumquist. This fair-haired, sallow-skinned, stoop-shouldered little man was an adventurer on the scale of John Pepper. Born in the Latvian capital of Riga in 1882, he came to the United States in 1904 and joined the Communist Party in 1919. In 1927 he dropped out of the party to go into illegal work for Soviet military intelligence. In 1929, as part of his training for setting up business ventures as a cover, he took a course in banking and finance at La Salle Extension University in Chicago, graduating with an A for the term.

Dozenberg's best friend in the party was Jay Lovestone, with whom he shared an attitude of jocular cynicism. In March 1929, when Lovestone and his delegation sailed from New York, Dozenberg was on the same boat, on his way to Moscow to get his marching orders from Gen. Ivan Pavlovich Berzin, the chief of military intelligence and a fellow Latvian.

In June, when Jay was frantic about leaving, he appealed to the well-connected Dozenberg for help. Dozenberg had a highly placed Latvian friend, Ian Rudzutack, a member of the Politburo in the Stalin camp who was also minister of railroad communications. Dozenberg used his good offices with Rudzutack to get Lovestone a passport. Friends in the Latvian embassy got him a plane ticket out of Moscow. The thread in his escape was the Latvian connection.

At the time the German-Russian airline Derluft was running a passenger service from Moscow to Smolensk to Danzig to Berlin. Armed with a one-way ticket and a passport, Lovestone fled on the June 11 Derluft flight. In Smolensk during the short layover, he lay facedown in a plot of grass near the plane, taking deep breaths and feeling the exhilaration of being free again. Suddenly he heard a band playing "The Star-Spangled Banner" and thought he was hallucinating. But it was a send-off for an American army engineer, Capt. Colby Bainbridge, who had been helping the Russians build a dam and was now boarding the plane. In Berlin, Lovestone was able to buy a steamship ticket to New York thanks to the two hundred dollars Esther Mendelssohn wired him. He felt that Dozenberg and Esther had quite literally saved his life. Both of them occupied a special place in his heart.

In the early thirties, out of gratitude to his rescuer, Lovestone on several occasions, though by then expelled from the party, assisted Dozenberg in his intelligence work. It was on the basis of these favors for a friend that the FBI, in February 1954, erroneously reported that "reliable sources have advised that Lovestone was active in the OGPU as late as 1935." On the contrary, in the thirties Lovestone moved to an extreme anti-Soviet and anti-Stalin position.

Lovestone and Dozenberg corresponded regularly. On March 13, 1931, while passing through India, Dozenberg wrote Jay: "It has appeared to me many times that you have missed a lot by declining the opportunity that was once offered to you to come to India. I think you would have liked it."

Lovestone replied on April 20: "There is a lot in what you say about my having missed India. But I certainly wouldn't have wanted to go there to sell that line of goods that the Rabbi [Bittelman] pushed. He made a horrible mess of a very favorable situation." He added: "Do not hesitate to ask me to do anything you want me to do which may be of help to you." Lovestone was not someone who routinely offered to help others. The offer made it clear that he was deeply in Dozenberg's debt.

By October 1931, Dozenberg was in Bucharest, where he planned to set up the American-Rumanian Film Company. "Rumania's not a country," Jay wrote him, "it's a nickname." Dozenberg wrote back that he was coming to America with a large sum of Comintern cash. If he was asked where he got it, he would say, "We made our money on stocks before the crash came and the wife inherited quite a fortune from her mother." He asked Lovestone to find him some contacts in the film business.

When Dozenberg arrived in New York in early 1932, Lovestone introduced him to an officer at the Irving Trust so he could establish a line of credit. He also arranged for him to see Sen. Burton Wheeler, whom he had known since the Passaic strike of 1926. Wheeler called the Department of Commerce, who put Dozenberg in touch with Bell & Howell, which sold him some movie equipment.

Dozenberg quit the party in 1937 and was lying low in Bend, Oregon, hoping he was forgotten, when in 1939 he was arrested for obtaining a passport under false pretense. He agreed to testify before the Dies Committee and relate his career as a spy in exchange for a one-year sentence. After his release he and his wife, Frances, moved to Florida, where they lived quietly in retirement.

The Comintern was slow to react to Lovestone's departure. Only on June 22, eleven days after he had said good-bye to Moscow, never to return, was a cable sent to New York announcing his escape and demanding the purge of all Lovestone adherents from the party.

On June 26 the American party cabled the Comintern: "Lovestone arrived two days ago . . . and immediately organized factional meetings. . . . The Pol Com [Political Committee] unanimously yesterday expelled Lovestone except vote Wolfe." Expelled on his heels were Wolfe and Gitlow. Gitlow's mother, Kate, known as a *verbissen* Communist, meaning dyed-in-the-wool, was present at the meeting that ousted her son and shouted: "Diamonds, diamonds, you are throwing out of the party!" By August 1929, according to a Comintern report, ninety-two Lovestoneites had been expelled, and sixty-one for other reasons. In addition, about two thousand party members jumped ship.

Lovestone, who had spent his entire adult life in the party, from 1919 to 1929, was out in the cold at the age of thirty-one. He was a career Communist, which was not unlike having had a career in General Motors or the Republican Party. Promotion depended upon pleasing the head office. Cliques competed for advantage. Management was recruited on the basis of dependability rather than brilliance.

Lovestone was not a good lackey. He balked at following a line that flew in the face of common sense and was charged with "American exceptionalism." He agreed with Bukharin's view that imminent world revolution was hogwash. He drew Stalin's ire not because he was a manipulator or a factionalist but because he held to his principles too long. He backed Bukharin to his disadvantage because Bukharin's policies conformed to the reality of the world situation. His biggest mistake

was that he thought the Comintern was a debating society, that he could
go to Moscow and deal with Stalin as an equal, as if they were the cap-
tains of rival debating teams. He learned the hard way that a branch office cannot dictate to headquarters, that a soldier in the field cannot
oppose his own high command, and that the Comintern was not a seminar but one of the levers of Stalin's rise to power. Now he was a pariah
cast out by his tribe. What would he do next?

7
STARTING FROM SCRATCH

Stalin had told the rebellious Americans that when they got home no one would know them but their wives. Although unmarried, Lovestone soon realized that Stalin was right. He had left New York in March 1929 with the backing of 90 percent of the party, but after his expulsion his majority evaporated. Those followers he had left consisted of a diaspora of the expelled; the bulk of the rank and file chose to stay with the mother party, under the protective Comintern umbrella.

Yet Lovestone, with a mixture of bravery and arrogance, decided to form an opposition Communist Party that (in his view) would represent the true Leninist line. All Communist parties, he believed, took on the worst aspects of the larger bourgeois society of the countries they were in, such as (in the American case) self-aggrandizement and greed, traits that he hoped to avoid. In August 1929, with his lieutenants Gitlow and Wolfe, he gathered a core of two hundred loyalists and pledged to continue the struggle against "the anti-Leninist party-wreckers."

He seemed, however, to be pursuing two contradictory objectives, for at the same time that he announced the birth of his own party in October, he appealed to the American party to be let back in, asking for the "reinstatement of all expelled comrades." This duality would characterize the Lovestone group, which according to Bert Wolfe never had more than five hundred members during its eleven-year existence, from 1929 to

1941. On the one hand Lovestone tried to put the American party in the worst possible light, to show its ineptness so that his group could shine by comparison. On the other hand, he kept knocking on the door and calling for unity negotiations.

Another kind of duality defined the positions Lovestone took with regard to Stalin. Secretly hoping that Stalin would reinstate him, Lovestone wrote glowing articles on the achievements of the Five-Year Plan in his group's organ, *Worker's Age*. At a time of widespread famine and the massacre of the kulaks, *Worker's Age* praised Soviet successes in agriculture. Lovestone also praised the Stalinist switch to piecework and speedup, which the American trade unions considered the worst kind of labor exploitation.

Even Stalin's rule by murder and purges in the thirties won Lovestone's endorsement. In the summer of 1936, when his onetime Comintern associates Zinoviev and Kamenev were on trial, Lovestone accepted the Stalin version. His strategy was to agree with Stalin on domestic policy so that he would be free to criticize him on Comintern policy. He thought of it as a trade-off. He could maintain his credibility as an orthodox Communist while continuing to argue for greater freedom in the foreign parties. He hoped to position himself as a farseeing leader whom Stalin would eventually be glad to bring back into the fold. This was wishful thinking. For Stalin, once a renegade, always a renegade.

The difficulties of forming an independent party with no outside support were primarily financial. As Lovestone wrote Bert Wolfe on December 30, 1929: "Now regarding finances. . . . We are absolutely up against it. . . . We have no Moscow and rich uncles today to support us. . . . You cannot imagine how broke we are."

On February 22 and 23, 1930, Lovestone held the second plenum of his National Council in New York. It was attended by sixty delegates, including such familiar faces as Bill Miller, the autoworker from Detroit, and Ed Welsh, chairman of the Harlem Tenants League. In a May 28 report on "right and left renegades," the Comintern, which closely monitored the Lovestoneites, observed that "the organizational strength in both the Lovestone and Trotsky groups is insignificant. Their mass meetings during the last few months had a smaller attendance. . . . Politically, the Lovestone group fights against 'Moscow interference.' . . . Every issue of its organ is replete with attacks on the Comintern leadership."

Lovestone, however, convinced himself that he was making great gains. After a trip to Detroit to recruit autoworkers, he wrote Gitlow: "You'd be amazed how the workers respond to our line. . . . We attract an excellent type to our meetings, good proletarians, many Anglo-Saxons. . . . Workers are asked to join, but not enuff cards are on hand for distribution and no one wants to come up front for signing up."

Lovestone thought his street demonstrations were far superior to those of the orthodox party, where the members "came in trucks from their summer camps as if they had come on an outing. You can imagine these everyday Jewesses in knickers with front porches, crowding Union Square, protesting against starvation and unemployment. Real Third Period fashion and fakery." In his comment about "everyday Jewesses," Lovestone revealed what his friend Gussie Kruse called his "anti-Semitic heart." But it was not so much anti-Semitism as non-Semitism. Lovestone felt that his Jewishness was irrelevant. He had changed his name and was as blond and blue-eyed as any goy. He defined himself not by religion or race but by political orientation. He was a Marxist-Leninist, with a system of beliefs upon which his Jewishness had no bearing. In this he was like Trotsky, who in 1903 had been asked, "You consider yourself, I take it, to be either a Russian or a Jew." "No!" Trotsky replied. "You are mistaken! I am a Social Democrat, and that's all."

To break out of his isolation, Lovestone made contact with opposition Communist groups in Europe. Perhaps they could form a Comintern of the expelled. In December 1930 he left for Berlin second class on the SS *Bremen* to attend the first convention of the opposition groups. The ever-loyal Esther Mendelssohn wired him a hundred dollars with the message "I picture your cabin full of red roses and each petal a thought from your sunnyside."

Lovestone worried that the opposition groups would be riddled with Comintern plants but was heartened to meet delegates from France, Sweden, Switzerland, Norway, and Czechoslovakia. They pledged to cooperate under the banner of an International Communist Opposition, but Lovestone did not expect too much.

He returned from Berlin in January 1931 having found a handful of European allies. But where could he find allies at home, when there were defections in his own tiny party? His friend Bill Kruse, who had remained in the orthodox party, arguing that a dual party was as bad as a dual union, sized up Lovestone's dilemma in a letter on May 12, 1931: "Your whole operation is that of a faction fighting a ruling faction, just as if you were still in the party. So every time the official leadership says yes, you have to say no. . . . This brings you into positions so impossible to justify that even some of your staunchest supporters are starting to waver."

Lovestone, however, still thought of himself as an orthodox Communist, which he demonstrated in November in a debate with the English philosopher Bertrand Russell at the Central Opera House. It was a fundraiser for the Lovestoneite New Workers School, and each debater had forty minutes to discuss and twenty minutes to rebut his opponent on the proposition that "the road to freedom is through the dictatorship of the proletariat."

Facing each other on the stage were the gaunt grandson of Lord John Russell, born to nobility and wealth, and the sharp-tongued radical immigrant who was perennially broke. One was a doctrinaire Communist and the other a tireless author and lecturer on every topic from logic to love, who would later win the Nobel Prize in literature. The only thing they had in common was that they had both been pacifists in World War I.

Taking the pro side, the thirty-three-year-old Lovestone said the ruling class was breaking down. Parliamentarism had outlived its usefulness. Democracy was democracy for the rich. The miners in Harlan, Kentucky, knew that clenched behind the Stars and Stripes was the iron fist of the ruling class. Look at what the Soviet Union had accomplished with its splendid proletarian society. Lovestone sounded very much like a man without a country, banished from the Soviet system he admired and living in the capitalist America he despised.

Taking the negative, the fifty-nine-year-old Russell said that he had recently visited a Russian village and asked if any Communists lived there. "Oh yes, there are two," he was told. Upon inquiring why they were Communists, the reply was, "They are both in the army and they have been guilty of offenses against discipline and they know that if they become Communists they will be let off." It was a pity, added Russell, that the word *proletarian* had been appropriated by the Communists.

Lovestone rebutted by describing capitalist violence against Communists and other radicals. In Council Bluffs, Iowa, a Communist was refused bail and the mayor said, "To hell with the Communist bastards." Russell replied that the methods of the Communist Party were self-defeating. The audience agreed that the debate was a standoff, but it gave Lovestone some much-needed exposure.

In June 1932, Lovestone went to Europe on a Canadian passport in the name of George Robin. While in Berlin attending the second Congress of the Communist Opposition, he happened to witness the tragedy of Hitler's rise to power. Given the strength of the Nazi vote in the Reichstag elections in March, Field Marshal Paul von Hindenburg, the eighty-five-year-old German president, was forced to make a deal with Adolf Hitler. On June 15 he lifted the ban on the storm troopers and dissolved the Reichstag. In the new election on July 31, the Nazis won an impressive 230 seats out of 608, while Nazis and Communists fought pitched battles in the streets.

Such was the Germany in turmoil that Lovestone saw, about five weeks before the Reichstag election. "Everything is being prepared for the government of Hitler," Lovestone wrote his people in New York on June 23, 1932. "I don't think the Nazis themselves will get a majority in the coming elections but I do believe they will take power thru some form of arrangement. . . . All steps are being taken to drive Communism underground. Workers are being murdered daily on the streets. 'Brown Shirts' march about in groups terrorizing them."

On July 6, Lovestone wrote Gitlow that the big question was whether the Catholic center parties would work with the Nazis. The leftist ranks were discouraged. The Nazis were making big gains, while the Socialists were going to the dogs. The Nazis controlled the streets through sheer violence, "but some of our [opposition] people in the united fronts are bearing the brunt of the heaviest street fighting and rendering real leadership."

Lovestone predicted a major disaster for the German Communist Party and the German trade unions. "Hundreds have been arrested and many hundreds will follow. . . . Martial law is already here. . . . It is already obvious that the Communist Party will be declared illegal after the elections. Hitler is more and more bossing the show in the open," while the Socialist conduct "is incredibly shameful and cowardly. . . . The masses are desperate and despondent."

It was a shaken Lovestone who left Berlin in the last week of July, having seen firsthand how a determined minority of fascist bullies could take over a great nation. As he had foreseen, Hitler became chancellor in January 1933. In March the Communist Party was banned and thousands of Communists were arrested. In June the Social Democrat Party was banned, its headquarters ransacked, its leaders arrested. It took Hitler only a few months to stamp out the German trade unions and the parties of the left.

Lovestone returned to New York by way of Canada. He imagined that Stalinist agents were waiting around every corner and wrote Gitlow concerning his homecoming: "A word of caution, no advertising of the date of my return, no tovarichi to hang around the piers, no gossip. . . . It is serious."

In Montreal he stayed with the Mendelssohns. Esther told him that a comrade had come to see Nathan, and when he saw Jay's photograph in the living room he asked, "Who is the follower of that renegade?" Esther replied, "I am the guilty party." When the comrade left she told Nathan: "I'm going to have it enlarged and put it in the center of the room, and any skunk who doesn't like it can go hang himself." Nathan laughed. As fond as he was of Jay, he had remained in the orthodox party, though there were about half a dozen Canadian Lovestoneites. "Muddled as he is," Esther told Jay, "his heart is drawn towards you, but he loves to be in the swing of things."

Esther had mood swings; she was at the same time overjoyed at seeing Jay and discouraged by the imbalance in her life. The man she loved she rarely saw, and the husband she saw daily she didn't love. She did her best to keep the peace in her household. It was a job, but it made her miserable when all she wanted was more time with Jay. To make him jealous, Esther said she had nearly been picked up by a flirtatious blond and blue-eyed Montreal policeman. "Had I been given to real promiscuity it might have been interesting, no?" she said. But Jay was not the jealous type and had no intention of disturbing the status quo.

Back in New York, Lovestone's loyal lieutenant, Ben Gitlow, who had fought for years at his side, was having qualms. He could no longer swallow Lovestone's uncritical defense of Soviet domestic policies. He was not prepared to describe the starvation that killed millions as a form of progress. In the fall of 1932, he left the Lovestone party and joined the Norman Thomas Socialists. Later he published an autobiography called *I Confess,* in which he did not treat his old friends kindly, and he became a professional witness for congressional committees.

But balancing Gitlow's defection came a stroke of luck that put Lovestone's little party on the map. This came about as a result of his friendship with Sasha Zimmerman of the International Ladies' Garment Workers' Union. Zimmerman had joined the Communist Party in 1920, and when Lovestone was purged in 1929, he bravely went to a Communist rally and presented a resolution for his reinstatement. "When I walked off that stage," he recalled, "going back to my seat, my coat was full of spit from all sides. The furriers were sitting there, they threw burning matches at me. . . . Never was it so bad." Expelled for his Lovestoneite leanings, Zimmerman told the Central Committee: "You're a party of robots, and robots don't make revolutions."

Zimmerman was gradually reintegrated into the leadership of the ILGWU, and in 1932 he was elected to the board of Local 22, a large dressmakers' local. In April 1933, Zimmerman ran for manager of Local 22 as head of a Lovestoneite slate and was elected by a narrow margin. Zimmerman and Lovestone now controlled that local, which gave Lovestone a mass base.

Then came the transfusion from FDR and the New Deal that revived the ailing labor movement, in the form of the National Industrial Recovery Act and its Section 7(a), which passed in June 1933 and gave workers the right to collective bargaining. Section 7(a) saved John L. Lewis and the United Mine Workers and killed the Communist dual unions. As Bill Foster put it, you didn't even have to organize the miners, all you had to say was "The President wants you to join the union," and all you needed were plenty of application blanks. The same was true in David Dubinsky's ILGWU, which had fought off the Communists and did not share the traditional AFL disdain for women and unskilled workers.

In August 1933, Zimmerman spearheaded a strike called by the Joint Board of Dressmakers, consisting of four locals, including Local 22. Seventy thousand dressmakers walked out, at a time when the National Recovery Administration was drafting industry codes. The class struggle went up in smoke, and the slogan was "Make Your Code on the Picket Line." They were out four days and won a thirty-five-hour week, a minimum wage scale, and job security, all of which were written into the NRA code that fall. Membership soared. Local 22 had thirty thousand members, and Local 89, the Italian local under Luigi Antonini, had forty thousand. They were the two biggest union locals in the country. When Antonini was asked if he would admit a Negro, he said, "Yes, if he speaks Italian." Zimmerman proved to be an outstanding leader and saw the success of the August strike as an example of the "correct course" of the Lovestone group, of working with the mass unions in a constructive manner. By 1934 the ILGWU had made stunning gains, to two hundred thousand members. Inside the union, Local 22 remained the fiefdom of Zimmerman and Lovestone.

David Dubinsky, the irrepressible head of the ILGWU, was not sure what to make of the Zimmerman-Lovestone partnership. Born Dobniesky in the Polish city of Lodz in 1892, Dubinsky had arrived in New York in 1911 and become a cutter; by 1922 he was a vice president of the ILGWU. He had a big, thick-haired, round-faced head on a five foot five body, hunched from years of bending over a cutting table. Volcanic in utterance, his English was laced with Yiddish and heavily accented, so that *sons of bitches* came out "sensapitches." Dubinsky was a *Kuechleffer* (stirring spoon), mixing up his syntax, but he was also a natural leader, displaying effortless authority without pretense.

All his life he fought the Communists, whom he saw as spoilers. But recognizing Lovestone's constructive role in the Local 22 August 1933 strike, Dubinsky invited him to speak at the union's 1934 convention. Lovestone did not soften his Communist line and asked those assembled:

"Why are you afraid of the dictatorship of the proletariat?" When he attacked the New Deal, Dubinsky told him they would have to agree to disagree. Lovestone, however, had gained his first foothold within a mainstream labor union and gradually moved closer to Dubinsky, who admired his analytical abilities. He was a good man to talk strategy with, bursting with ideas, some of them sound.

In 1934 the Soviet foreign policy line changed once again when Stalin sought to bring his country out of its isolation in an increasingly menacing world. One step in that direction was United States recognition, granted by the Roosevelt administration at the end of 1933. Then in September 1934, after years of scoffing at the League of Nations, Stalin joined it. This brought the Soviet Union into a compact of antifascist nations and helped to erase the impression that the Bolsheviks were out to subvert the rest of the world. The message was that the security of the Soviet Union now had priority over world revolution.

As a result of this and other changes, the American Communist Party gained a modicum of acceptance. First, the rise of fascism gave the Communists the appearance of fighting a common enemy. Then the Wagner Act of 1935, which maintained collective bargaining after the NRA had been invalidated by the Supreme Court, brought hundreds of thousands of new members, among them a number of Communists, into the unions. Finally, the purge of Lovestone ended factionalism in the American party, which was able to take advantage of a promising context under the leadership of the Kansas populist Earl Browder.

The American party grew in 1935 to a membership of thirty thousand. The party was now open and legal, trying hard to Americanize itself. If you hated Hitler, it was okay to like Stalin. The Soviet Union was pictured as a success. The planned economy eliminated unemployment. The Red Army was a bulwark against Hitler. The starry-eyed saw paradise in five-year slices. The thirties became known as the Red decade.

All this was not good news for Lovestone, whose group was increasingly marginalized. He sniffed the wind and tried to latch on to some of the Communist-run front groups and antifascist campaigns. But he remained an outcast. At an American League Against War rally on Columbus Day 1934, the league representative said, "The Socialists are dragging in these skunks [Lovestoneites] so that their stink will drive all others away."

Seeing there was no give with the Communists, Lovestone tried to infiltrate the Socialist Party, which in June 1934 was taken over by a group of Young Turks led by Norman Thomas. Lovestone had hope in Thomas, who saw Communists as "Socialists gone astray" and was receptive to a united front.

Resorting to his tested strategy, Lovestone planted one of his agents in the Socialist left wing, which called itself the Revolutionary Policy Committee. It was, said Lovestone, "stronger in revolutionary aspirations than in numbers and experience." His avowed goal was to stimulate factionalism inside the Socialist Party and eventually take it over.

On November 13, 1934, a Communist spy reported on a Lovestone membership meeting: "They spoke of Irving Brown as one of their men [in the Socialist Party]. . . . Lovestone told those assembled that they were not to go around bragging that the RPC was their baby. [They should say that] the Communist Party Opposition had nothing to do with it and will continue to have nothing to do with it. That the CPO had no plants in the Socialist Party. I really believe that Lovestone is getting worried that the Socialist Party is getting wise to his tactics. They also said that $500 was needed to continue their work in the Socialist Party and proceeded to collect money."

Irving Brown, Lovestone's plant in the RPC in 1934, was twenty-three years old and two years out of New York University. He would become Lovestone's alter ego, best known for his post–World War II activities in Europe with trade unions. Brown was always the outside man, while Lovestone was the unnoticed inside man. For thirty years they worked so closely together that they could anticipate each other's thoughts.

Brown was born in the Bronx in 1911. His father, Ralph, drove a milk wagon and was a minor official in the Milk Wagon Drivers Union. His Russian-born mother, Fannie, had thick, glossy, black hair, which Irving inherited. His first love was baseball. Yankee Stadium opened in 1923, and while Irving's body was in class at James Monroe High School, his mind wandered to Yankee Stadium with Babe Ruth and Lou Gehrig. Only at New York University did Irving give up his dream of wearing Yankee pinstripes and playing third base like Jumping Joe Dugan, the man with the slingshot arm. By then Lovestone was his mentor. Brown briefly joined the Communist Party in 1929, according to his FBI file, but left the party after Lovestone's expulsion. Lovestone found him a job as research director of Local 22. He also joined the Socialist Party as a secret Lovestoneite. At the 1934 Socialist Party convention in Detroit, with Jay hiding out in the Wolverine Hotel, Brown was accused on the convention floor of being "a Lovestone stooge." In 1936, however, the Revolutionary Policy Committee supported Norman Thomas in his showdown with the old guard, and Brown moved on.

Brown was five feet nine and stocky, with a pudding face often lit up by an ear-to-ear smile. His body language told you that whatever the activity—eating and drinking, discussion, office work, travel, disputes—he could wear you down, and drink, talk, or work you under the table. Brown was always in orbit, always collecting and storing information. It was easy to recognize Irving Brown. He was the fellow in the rumpled suit with the stained tie and the ring around the collar. No Depression-era hobo ever cared less about what he wore. But if you wanted to get a tough job done, Irving was your man, or rather your mensch.

In terms of Lovestone's future employment, the key event of 1935 was the AFL convention in Atlantic City that October. For it was there that the formidable John L. Lewis of the United Mine Workers took his union and seven others out of the AFL, which held to the craft model and disdained to organize industrywide unions. Lewis and his cohorts formed the Committee for Industrial Organization, which the AFL suspended in September 1936 as a renegade union.

Two years later the CIO was expelled and changed its name to Congress of Industrial Organizations, with Lewis as president, claiming thirty-two national unions and a membership of 4 million. Lewis had a friend in the Communist Party, Clarence Hathaway, the editor of the *Daily Worker,* who helped him hire Communist organizers. Lewis hired Reds for a very simple reason—he needed trained men fast. Membership in the CIO had gone from 1 million in 1935 to 4 million in 1938. The Communists were practiced organizers; they knew how to form shop nuclei, how to turn out a shop paper, how to speak in public, and how to start a riot. If they became a problem, you could get rid of them.

In his famous phrase Lewis asked: "Who gets the bird? The dog or the hunter?" The answer was that the Communists were not exactly retrievers. They had their own agenda. Lewis hired hundreds of Communists, some of them in key positions. Lee Pressman, who became general counsel of the CIO, later admitted belonging to a Communist cell. Len De Caux, a British Communist who had gone to Harrow and Oxford, was in charge of the CIO *News,* with a circulation of close to a million. Maurice Sugar, the counsel for the United Auto Workers, adhered to the party line.

In August 1935 the AFL had chartered the United Automobile Workers as an international union, unattached to any craft union. As Bill Green, the president of the AFL, wisely saw, the auto plants with their assembly lines were unsuited to craft distinctions. "They are mass minded," he said. "They ask me over and over again, are you going to divide us up? I cannot change their state of mind."

On April 27, 1936, in South Bend, Indiana, came the UAW's first convention. Homer Martin, a Baptist minister who had left the church to work for Chevrolet as a welder, was elected president, largely because of his stem-winding oratory. "Boy, can that baby talk," the workers said. Martin was an ardent admirer of the racist radio evangelist Father Charles E. Coughlin, then in his prolabor phase, to whom he wrote on April 25, 1935, in Royal Oak, Michigan: "I was formerly a Baptist minister and was thrown out of my own church because I believed that the Gospel should be applied to social and economic matters." He sent a dollar for a membership card in Coughlin's National Union for Social Justice.

In 1936 the popular front policy of the American Communist Party was in full bloom. The party was moving closer to the New Deal, spawning front groups like herring. On the labor front it was making headway in the CIO unions, particularly in the United Auto Workers, which had bolted to the CIO.

In the 1936 presidential campaign, Lovestone backed the Communist ticket, since he had no one else to support. He was in the position of constantly sniping at the party and then coming out at election time with the slogan "Vote Communist." This struck some of his supporters as muddled. In 1936, with FDR running for a second term against Alf Landon, Lovestone endorsed Earl Browder.

With Browder's campaign focused on beating the Republicans, the Communists multiplied their united front activities. At the New York May Day parade that year, Communists, Socialists, and Lovestoneites marched arm in arm. Never had the left seemed more united. Lovestone wrote his German friend August Thalheimer on May 19 that "the Communist Party officials have apparently passed the word around that we will soon be back in the party. . . . Of course there is nothing to it. The effect is to check the fighting ardor of certain sections of our membership."

In fact, lack of ardor and a dwindling membership were gnawing concerns at a time when the united front was siphoning off some of Lovestone's support. The liberals were drawn to the official party, "to atone for their past sins," Lovestone said, and his financial situation was more critical than ever. Even his faithful number-two man, Bert Wolfe, was showing signs of wanting to give up the struggle and devote himself to a biography of the Mexican muralist Diego Rivera. Stung by this threatened defection, Lovestone wrote him on June 8, 1936, that "you seem to have resigned yourself to the fate of a sort of wandering Jew or meandering literary hack, at best free lance. Don't kid yourself if you think you can eke out even the barest existence in writing. I am not trying to discourage you, I am simply trying to prevent you from suffering the pains of trouble and disillusionment. . . . I know of recent efforts in this direction that have proved disastrous." But Wolfe was not deterred, and the biography was published the following year. Wolfe opined, without false modesty, that it was "the best biography ever written about a living man."

That summer of 1936 two tremors in far-off places would have a lasting ripple effect in Lovestone's mind. In August came the first Moscow show trial, personally managed by Stalin. Less than twenty-four hours after their guilty verdicts were read on August 24, Stalin's bosom friends and collaborators Zinoviev and Kamenev were stood up against a wall and shot. In *Worker's Age* on September 5, 1936, Lovestone continued to defend Stalin: "We are convinced," he wrote in an editorial, "that there is no adequate reason to doubt the confessions made by the accused. We can see how there can be discussions as to . . . their groveling character, but we do not see any reason to doubt the genuineness of the confessions." Despite these assurances, Lovestone was troubled. A seed of doubt had been planted.

The second disturbing event took place in Spain in July, when army garrisons led by Francisco Franco rose up against the Popular Front government of Largo Caballero. By November 1936, Franco was laying siege to Madrid. The successful defense of the city, thanks in part to Soviet weapons and the international brigades, meant that the civil war would go on for two more years.

Lovestone was involved from the start. On October 6, 1936, he wrote the German Comintern agent Heinz Neumann, who had played a major part in shoring up the Spanish Communist Party in 1932–33 and was now back in Moscow under a cloud (he would be arrested and shot in 1937 for "deviation"):

> I do not minimize the critical military situation of the Madrid government. However, it is not the military situation, bad as it is, that troubles me most. What does is the chaos in its leadership, the conflict of purpose, the cross-currents leading to confusion. . . . The

military situation is in some respects no worse than that which confronted the Bolsheviks when Kolchak was at Gomel and Ydenick was at the gates of Petrograd. However in the Russian situation you had a Bolshevik party with sound policy and Lenin at the head; here we have nothing of the sort.

Lovestone's interest in Spain was that not of a sympathetic observer but of a leader in the international Communist Opposition. He had formed a friendly connection with the Catalan Communist leader Joaquin Maurin, whom he saw as his counterpart in Spain. Maurin had led the Catalonian Federation of the Spanish Communist Party, but like Lovestone, he was accused of right deviation and expelled in 1930. Then, again like Lovestone, he formed a Communist opposition party, which took part in Catalan elections and published a paper, *La Batalla,* with a circulation of seven thousand. In 1935 Maurin joined forces with another splinter group led by Andres Nin, a Trotskyite who had broken with Trotsky, and they formed the POUM (Partido Obrero de Unificación Marxista). The POUM briefly joined Largo Caballero's Popular Front government in January 1936, and Maurin was elected to the Cortes but pulled out in March. The Communists denounced him as an enemy of the Popular Front. The POUM policy was that the workers should take power. Maurin was anti-Stalin when Lovestone was still loyal. The POUM leaders didn't buy the show trials, the Stalin cult, and the systematic falsification.

In the wake of the July civil war, the POUM rose up in Catalonia to do battle against pro-Franco elements. But Maurin had a stroke of bad luck. Days after the war broke out, while on a speaking tour in Galicia, he was arrested in the northwest port city of Corunna. He spent the next ten years in Franco's jails, while his two chief aides, Andres Nin and Julian Gorkin, took over. As events developed Lovestone became intensely involved in the affairs of the POUM.

In the fall of 1936 came the American presidential election. Earl Browder ran the most successful campaign in the party's history. He spoke at the National Press Club and was covered in papers besides the *Daily Worker.* In November, FDR won, with 27 million votes, while Browder garnered a paltry 80,000. He hadn't campaigned to win but to help pull the party out of its pariah position. The new line did wonders, for after Browder's pro-Roosevelt cheerleading, membership soared. In 1935 it was stagnating around 30,000, a figure that doubled in 1937 to 62,000 and almost tripled in 1938 to 82,000. At last the Communists became a native American party, with less than 50 percent foreign-born members. By addressing popular issues like unemployment on the domestic scene and Spain on the foreign scene, it created a niche for itself in labor and politics.

At the second American Writers' Conference in the spring of 1937, Browder shared the speakers' platform with Archibald MacLeish and Ernest Hemingway. Someone from the audience said, "They're looking for pimples on the great smiling face of the Soviet Union." Amid all this effervescence, Lovestone was increasingly out in the cold. His speck of a party was going up against the global conglomerate of the Comintern— what gall, what pride before a fall. The acrobat takes a misstep on the high wire and tumbles from a great height, only to pick himself up and climb back to the swinging ladders. Even though Lovestone's tactics were opportunistic, in the sense of secretly hoping to return to the fold, his impulse was pure hubris, a refusal to admit defeat, an unshakable belief in his destiny.

8

LOVESTONE BREAKS WITH COMMUNISM

In 1937, after six years of struggle to establish his opposition party, Lovestone underwent a sea change. He broke with Stalin and stopped playing cat and mouse games with the official Communist Party. He awakened from the fond dream that he would one day be readmitted to the Comintern. He could no longer suspend disbelief concerning events in the Soviet Union.

This change occurred not all at once, as in a vision from above, but over the two years 1937 and 1938. On a practical level it had to do with the decline of his movement. The Communists, who had regularly sent out feelers, decided in 1937 that the Lovestoneites were now weak enough to ignore. On November 29 the party Central Committee wrote that the "Lovestoneites can no longer be considered a real trend in the labor and progressive movement . . . they end up in the camp of reaction and fascism."

Lovestone kept in his wallet a poem of indeterminate origin that expressed his stoic view of life. Even if you were getting nowhere, the daily effort had to be made:

> *Yonder see the morning blink*
> *The sun is up, and up must I*
> *To wash and dress and eat and drink*
> *And look at things and talk and think*

And Work, and God knows why.
Oh often have I washed and dressed
And what's to show for all my pain?
Let me lie abed and rest:
Ten thousand times I've done my best
And all's to do again.

On a deeper, visceral level, Lovestone's change of heart came from an inability to continue endorsing Stalinist tyranny. The two events that brought this home in a personal way were the execution of Bukharin and the destruction of the POUM in Spain.

Bukharin was the man Lovestone most admired in the Soviet party, the proponent of "Communism with a human face." Although divested of the emblems of office, he had remained a figure of some stature, with a minor job in the Commissariat of Heavy Industry. He made a modest political comeback in January 1934, when he addressed the Seventeenth Party Congress, endorsing Stalin's leadership.

In the summer of 1936 came the trial of Zinoviev and Kamenev, during which Bukharin's name and those of his two collaborators, Rykov and Tomsky, came up. Andrei Vyshinsky, the state prosecutor, announced that an investigation was under way. Knowing what that meant, Tomsky killed himself. *Pravda* commented: "Tomsky, hopelessly entangled in his ties with the Trotskyist-Zinovievite terrorists, has committed suicide at his dacha."

In February 1937, Bukharin and Rykov were arrested and thrown into Lubyanka prison. They spent a year in jail before their trial in March 1938. The procedure of Stalin's judicial system was first draw up the indictment, then obtain the confession. From prison Bukharin wrote forty-three letters to Stalin, not angry reproaches but professions of love, to salvage something from the wreckage, if only the devotion of the victim to his executioner. "I began to feel toward you as I felt toward Ilyich [Lenin] . . . a feeling of close kinship, of tremendous love, unbounded trust," Bukharin wrote. When Bukharin came to trial in the Hall of the Trade Union House, many could not believe that Stalin would dispatch the man who had been Lenin's favorite. But Stalin's ruthlessness had no bounds, and on March 15 Bukharin, along with Rykov, was shot.

For Lovestone, Bukharin's execution shook out all residual Stalinism. He unburdened himself to an old flame, Edna Mann, who had once written him when they were dating: "You need practice in persiflage more than in dialectics." She married Harvey Mann, who became Lovestone's friend and lawyer. In the thirties she was a Lovestoneite, sending Jay small sums of money, as well as this note: "My dear blond giant with Dante-esque profile. . . . In all the years I have known you—I have never known you to do a petty thing. Never known you to show false pride or conceit or any smallness of spirit."

But Edna did wonder how Jay could countenance Stalin's reign of terror. A friend wrote her: "Jay Lovestone himself was convinced of the authenticity of the 1936 Moscow trials until his own leader Bukharin was exposed and that made the difference." Indeed it did, as Jay told Edna himself, saying:

Stalin has been killing off his own closest associates and supporters. He has executed the general staff of the army, the heads of the navy and air force, 80 percent of the party secretaries, five out of seven of the presidents of the republics constituting the Soviet Union, a large part of the GPU, two heads of the Five-Year Plan, the heads of most of the heavy industries and collective farms, the press, the diplomatic corps, and the heads of the youth movements. Were all these people traitors because they were in charge of building Socialism in Russia? . . . The only explanation seems to be that there is great opposition to the Stalin regime inside the Russian party itself.

On April 9, 1938, three weeks after Bukharin's death, *Worker's Age* came out with Lovestone's *J'Accuse:* "Here is a bureaucratic clique which is trying to perpetuate itself by sheer brute force, barbaric terror, blackest frame-up, and wanton blood spilling. . . . The working-class movement outside the Soviet Union must leave nothing undone . . . to bring to an end a savage regime unworthy of a free working class and a socialist state."

Besides the situation in the Soviet party, Lovestone was profoundly affected by events in Spain. He saw the Barcelona-based POUM, the small workers' party, as a Spanish brother to his own party. After the successful defense of Madrid in the winter of 1936, Stalin began to think of Spain as a satellite, saying at a Politburo meeting that "it would be possible to create in Spain a regime controlled by Moscow." This meant eliminating groups that stood in the way of Communist control, and at the top of the list was the POUM.

Lovestone supported the POUM in its battle with the Stalinists, writing on January 9, 1937, in *Worker's Age:* "Only the POUM can be considered a leading revolutionary party." He decided to send a correspondent—Bert Wolfe, who spoke fluent Spanish—to cover the war. He financed this and other expenses with gifts from the Mendelssohns and other affluent friends.

Wolfe left in February, making his way to Valencia, which was jammed with half a million refugees. Signs everywhere said "Controlled by Workers." He proceeded to Madrid for an interview with the premier, Largo Caballero, who still hoped that the United States would lift its embargo on weapons. In the lobby of the Hotel Florida one morning he ran into Ernest Hemingway. "Come up to my room and I'll give you a drink," Hemingway said. "At ten A.M.?" Wolfe asked. "Don't be fussy," Hemingway said, "it's Black Label."

Wolfe then went to Barcelona and saw the POUM leader Andres Nin, whom he had met in the twenties at a Comintern congress. He told Nin that his life was in danger, but Nin contemptuously rejected the warning. He had always been arrogant, Wolfe thought.

At the end of April, Wolfe went to France and caught the *Normandie* to New York. Also on the ship, but in first class, was Hemingway, who came down to third class looking for his drinking buddy. "Did you see my name on the list?" Hemingway asked. "Yes, of course," Wolfe said. "Then why didn't you come up?" Hemingway asked. "I could not ascend," Wolfe replied, "but you could descend."

Wolfe had missed the action on the Madrid front and asked Hemingway to fill him in. "Do you think I would let you steal my stuff?" Hemingway asked. "Wait a minute," Wolfe said. "I want to tell you a story. In New York City there was a Jewish newspaper called the *Forward*. It had a weekly column called 'Pinya and Yenta.' One night Yenta was listening to Caruso on the Victrola. At about eleven, Pinya opened the door and told Yenta, 'Stop singing along with Caruso.' Yenta said, 'Do you know what he earns for one night at the Met? Five thousand dollars a night. Do you think that I would scab on Caruso?'"

The situation Wolfe observed in Barcelona was not favorable to the POUM, which had drawn Stalin's ire by proposing that the exiled Trotsky be given asylum in Catalonia. Stalin was quoted as saying, "We have a dangerous enemy in the POUM." Under Soviet pressure, a new Catalan government without the POUM was formed in Barcelona in December 1936. The reason given was "the unspeakable anti-Soviet campaign of the POUM. . . . To combat the USSR at this time is to commit treason."

In Barcelona, where workers had taken over the factories and public buildings, a three-day battle with police broke out in May 1937, with gunfights in the streets. The POUM was blamed, its organ, *La Batalla,* was closed on June 3, and on June 16 six members of the POUM Executive Council, including Andres Nin, were arrested. Nin's wife saw him in prison that afternoon. When she came back with a basket of food an hour later, he was gone.

Nin had been murdered, but it was only when a commission of members of the House of Commons came to Barcelona that summer that his body was found and his murder explained with a phony cover story. The leader of the British delegation was Fenner Brockway, a lifelong pacifist and a friend of Mohandas Gandhi. As one of the heads of the Independent Labour Party in England, an anti-Stalin Communist Opposition party that worked closely with Lovestone, Brockway was invited to write about the POUM in *Worker's Age.* "The suppression of the POUM," he wrote on July 31, 1937, "is the work of the Communist-controlled police force. . . . The Communist Party has concentrated on capturing control of the police and is applying in Spain the methods of the OGPU."

With the destruction of the POUM, the Stalinists had a free hand in running the war. Their generals gave the orders, and their commissars made the arrests. Lovestone was in close touch with the POUM agent in Paris, a man named Sogas, who reported that under the more pliable government of Juan Negrín, the Soviets had resumed their arms shipments. "One of the first acts of the new government," wrote Sogas, "was to shoot over twenty of our comrades at the front. . . . Another treachery was to leave behind, during the Aragon retreat, our comrades in the jails of Lérida. They were undoubtedly shot when the fascists came in." As for the POUM people left in Barcelona, they had gone underground.

Lovestone thought it was a tragic situation and asked his influential friends, such as Frank Walsh and Jett Lauck, to send Negrín the following cable: "Appeal to you to end persecution of loyal anti-fascists . . . Reports of shootings and imprisonments very disturbing." On October 7, 1938, Lovestone persuaded David Dubinsky to send a wire that said: "Strongly urge fair trial." The trial of the five POUM leaders on charges of espionage was set for October 22. The prosecutor was asking for thirty-year sentences. But all five refused to confess and were absolved, though they were given prison terms for taking part in the Barcelona uprising. Lovestone wrote Sogas in Paris on November 1 that "I am convinced they would have murdered our comrades had it not been for outside pressure." Sogas replied that hundreds of POUM refugees were crossing the border into France. "How are we to take care of them?" he asked. "Are they to live like hunted beasts abroad after what they have gone through in their own country? Who is to help the POUM?"

That question became irrelevant with the collapse of the Republic in the first three months of 1939. By the end of March, Franco had taken Madrid and the war was over. Half a million refugees streamed into France. For Lovestone it was yet another cause lost at the hands of Soviet tyranny. Just as the Spanish Civil War was a dress rehearsal for World War II it was a way for Lovestone to question his unconditional pacifism.

Lovestone was moving from anti-Stalinism to a more encompassing stance of anti-Communism. It wasn't only Bukharin, it wasn't only the POUM, it was the whole fossilization of the party and the slavish obedience required to avoid being purged. His own movement was getting nowhere, but he had gained a foothold in the ILGWU. He saw the growing Communist infiltration in the CIO, and thanks to his alliance with Sasha Zimmerman, he began to see himself as a crusader who could oust the Communists from the American labor movement.

In keeping with this confrontational line, Lovestone in 1937 found a way to direct his first frontal attack. This came about as the result of developments in the United Auto Workers, which, despite the efforts of its anti-Communist president, Homer Martin, was still under heavy Communist influence. In fact, it was Communist leaders like Wyndham Mortimer and Bob Travis who led a series of successful sit-down strikes that made General Motors a union shop. When an Episcopal priest resorted to the old homily that GM was one big family of 250,000, Martin showed his sense of repartee: "It's the kind of family where Father eats the bacon, Mother eats the gravy, and the kids can lick the skillet."

Sit-downs followed in swift succession at Chrysler, Hudson, Packard, and Studebaker. But Martin saw Communist influence increase with each victorious strike. Aside from strike leaders like Mortimer and Travis, there were open Communists in the tool and die locals, such as Nat Ganley and John Anderson, who were known as "twenty-minute-egg" Communists. The Communists were now considered the most powerful force in the UAW. Another up-and-coming group was led by the Reuther brothers, Walter, Victor, and Roy, whose parents had come to the United States from a village on the Rhine and who were then Socialists.

Martin's concern over spreading Communist influence was shared by David Dubinsky, whose union was then in the CIO, and Sasha Zimmerman, who recalled, "If we had not been on the job, the Communists would have taken over." They hit on the idea of delegating Lovestone to Martin as a *consigliere,* someone who knew the wiles and ways of the Communists and could help him regain control of his union. As Dubinsky recalled: "We gave [Lovestone] one hundred thousand dollars to help the autoworkers build their union."

For two years Lovestone served as Martin's chief of staff, masterminding the strategy to rid the UAW of Reds. Jay sent about thirty Lovestoneites to Detroit as an anti-Communist brigade to take the jobs held by Communists. In so doing he reverted to the role for which he seemed typecast, a factionalist. Victor Reuther described Lovestone as "one of the most Machiavellian union-splitters ever to prey on the American labor movement." This time, however, Lovestone was acting not alone but on orders from Dubinsky, with the estimable aim of preventing the UAW, the second-biggest union in the CIO, from being Communist-run.

It was a classic Lovestone operation, with Jay working behind the scenes, using surrogates, and coming to Detroit only in emergencies. The one person he confided in was Jett Lauck, still a close adviser to John L. Lewis. By going through Lauck, Lovestone was hoping to counteract the negative influence that he knew Lee Pressman, a covert Communist, had on Lewis. Lovestone wrote Lauck on April 28, 1937: "At the last board meeting [of the CIO], the Communist Party through Pressman must have done a lot of talking to John Lewis in denunciation of me. . . . He gave Lewis the notion that we are animated by some ulterior motive." Lovestone explained that he had the backing of Dubinsky. The aim was to oppose a political organization that was dominating a trade union.

By April, Lovestone's people in Detroit were in place. Francis Henson, a former minister, was executive secretary to Martin and wrote Zimmerman: "I am now in a position to check hourly with Homer on any matter." William Munger, a bright young instructor from Michigan State in Lansing, fired the Communist-leaning Henry Kraus as editor of the *Auto Worker* and took his place; and Alex Bail (George Miles), a Communist district organizer in Boston who was expelled in 1929 and became a leader of the Lovestone group, was in charge of operations and in daily contact with Lovestone. His wife, Eve Stone, was made national director of the UAW Women's Auxiliary. Irving Brown was not directly involved, having taken an assignment to organize the nonunion Ford South Chicago plant, where on May 16 he was so badly beaten up in the parking lot by company goons that he required surgery. His wife, Lillie, Lovestone's former secretary, asked Jay: "What do you think of Ford's tactics? I hope he kicks the bucket one of these days."

Lovestone's first move was to get rid of the Communist leadership in the powerful Flint local. Those targeted for the ax, aside from Kraus, were Bob Travis and Roy and Victor Reuther (who although not Communists worked closely with Travis). On April 7, 1937, Lovestone wrote Munger: "You might say, well you can't put these fellows out. Sometimes you not only can, but you must." He added: "If Travis and company should resist . . . then he and his cronies should be removed forthwith. . . . Now about the Kraus matter. I think it's suicidal for you to have him work as your assistant." In all, seventeen organizers were fired.

Lovestone's people in Detroit felt they were making progress, though they had grave misgivings about Homer. The book on Homer was that he never lived up to his promises and didn't show up at meetings. Lovestone privately called him the Jesus jazzer, writing Munger: "There is the additional danger that Homer will throw up the sponge and resign."

The UAW convention was coming up in August 1937 in Milwaukee. Lovestone's plan was to engineer the ouster of two Communist vice presidents, Wyndham Mortimer and Ed Hall. He also wanted to get rid of the Communist-leaning UAW treasurer, George Addes. Faced with a purge, the left wing of the UAW, combining the Mortimer-Hall-Addes forces and the Reuther brothers, also planned their convention strategy. The UAW was now split into two pugnacious factions.

The six-day convention opened on August 23, with two thousand delegates representing 256 locals. But on the fifth day the Lovestone-Martin plan was torpedoed with the surprise arrival of John L. Lewis. After a twenty-minute ovation the lion-maned CIO boss called for the re-election of the officers then serving, saying, "They are all good fellows." That meant the reelection of Martin as president but also of Mortimer and Hall as vice presidents and of Addes as treasurer. In addition, three vice presidents were added, presumably pro-Martin: Dick Frankensteen, head of the powerful Dodge-Chrysler local in Detroit; R. J. Thomas, a veteran UAW officer; and Walter Wells, who ran a small local at the Gemmer Gear Company. It was a stalemate, though fifteen of the twenty-four members of the new executive board were pro-Martin.

The UAW was now permanently split into pro- and anti-Martin camps, but after the convention Martin felt he had a mandate to continue the Lovestone-managed purge. Lovestone wrote Martin: "Your present Education Department should be overhauled from penthouse to subcellar. Not a cobweb of it should be left anywhere." Munger was cleaning house at the Flint *Auto Worker* as well as writing Martin's speeches.

In November, Martin was negotiating a new contract with GM, and Alex Bail reported to Lovestone: "Homer's attitude flows from two of his weaknesses, his keen thirst for applause and the ease with which he yields to last-minute pressure." In a time of depression and layoffs, Martin accepted wage cuts. When he asked John L. Lewis for advice, Lewis said, "Sign it and bring the boys in out of the rain." A thoroughly disheartened Bail wrote Lovestone: "Jay, you never saw such a yellow leadership. . . . They have laid the basis for a real calamity." Then, on November 29, Martin kept the executive board waiting for five hours. Some were threatening a break unless he mended his ways. The situation reminded Bail of Turgenev's story "Ward 13," in which a young doctor is posted to a ward for the insane and has some ideas on how to cure them but ends up going crazy himself.

In February 1938, Lovestone took a much-needed break from the Martin dilemma to attend a congress of nineteen small opposition parties in Paris. When the congress ended Lovestone was invited to Vienna by the Austrian group Der Funke.

As it happened Lovestone was in Vienna in March 1938, when the Nazis invaded Austria under the guise of putting down disorder. On the evening of March 11, the Germans crossed the border at Salzburg, and on March 12, Lovestone saw Austrian Nazis marching in the streets. At the Karlsplatz a mob swept toward the inner city, shouting, "Sieg Heil! Hitler! Hang Schuschnigg!" (referring to Kurt von Schuschnigg, the Austrian chancellor). In a letter to Jett Lauck, Lovestone wrote: "Hitler marched in after Chamberlain opened the door and Stalin paved the way."

Hitler followed his troops into the land of his birth and by the afternoon of March 12 was in the town of Linz, where he had spent his school days. On March 13, Himmler started arresting thousands of "unreliables." Hitler made a triumphant entry into Vienna on March 14, the day Lovestone left on a train to Paris. Lovestone did not stay for the Anschluss vote in April that made Austria a part of the Third Reich. Nor did he stay to see Jewish men and women scrubbing pro-Schuschnigg signs from city walls and cleaning the latrines of Nazi garrisons. But he did get a letter on May 7 from a member of the Austrian opposition group: "The terror here is great. The arrests amount to thousands and comprise Jews, Socialists, and Schuschnigg people. . . . They have a long list of all known opponents who will be arrested in the event of counterpropaganda. Thus we sit in the mousetrap and wait until it snaps shut. . . . Large parts of the working class are infected by Nazi demagogy and anti-Semitism. . . . The plebiscite was quite open, and under tremendous pressure even we have voted for Hitler. That will tell you everything."

Lovestone returned to New York in April 1938 to find that the situation in Detroit had not improved. Alex Bail reported on April 13 that Martin was "biologically incompetent," and there was a move by the board to take over. "Panicky I am not," Bail added, "but this is the worst situation we have faced." Then the opportunistic Dick Frankensteen was weaned away from Martin by the Communists. Martin's majority on the board had narrowed from fifteen to twelve plus Martin himself. Bail reported on May 18: "Homer feels depressed, ill, listless. The various crosscurrents have him in a whirr, hence he absents himself from board sessions and things get tangled up to the point of despair."

On June 18, in one of his episodic bursts of energy, Martin suspended five board members—Frankensteen, Addes, Mortimer, Hall, and Wells— on charges of conspiring to destroy the union. Six nonsuspended board members walked out, led by Walter Reuther, who said he wanted to "stop squabbling." Lovestone wrote Louis Stark of *The New York Times* on June 21 that "I was against the suspensions, not because I think they didn't deserve it, but because I didn't have enough confidence in the energy and vigor of the suspenders. . . . However my advice was thrown to the winds." Although Lovestone could no longer control Martin, he told Stark that he was still trying "to save the union from the Stalinist stranglehold. . . . Should the Communist Party win this fight and take control of the UAW, it would give them that springboard in the CIO they need so badly."

On July 17, 1938, the battle for control of the UAW escalated into criminal activity when Lovestone's apartment was burgled. Lovestone at that time was living with his sister Esther in Brooklyn, but he secretly rented an apartment in Manhattan at London Terrace, 410 West Twenty-fourth Street, under the alias George Thornton, using it as an office and keeping his papers there. Esther Mendelssohn helped out with the rent. His secretary, Ray Michael, an English girl who was the niece of his friend Jack Carney, came daily to the London Terrace flat, as did a few other aides.

July 17 was a Sunday, and Lovestone spent the day with friends in Nyack. He returned in the evening to find his apartment ransacked. Two briefcases and a gladstone bag filled with papers and correspondence were gone. His passport, a gold watch, and some hats and clothing were also taken to make it look like an ordinary burglary. To Jay it had the fingerprints of the GPU all over it. This impression was confirmed when a couple of weeks later the *Daily Worker* published photostat copies of a number of the stolen documents, exposing his role as the gray eminence behind Homer Martin, under the headline MARTIN PUPPET OF LOVESTONE IN DRIVE TO DISRUPT CIO.

Lovestone notified the police, but since the burglars had not been caught on the spot, nothing much was done. Conducting his own investigation, he determined that the burglary was the work of a veteran GPU agent operating in the United States, Leon Josephson. As he told the Dies Committee in 1939, "My home was not known to more than four or five people . . . because I had received in 1937 and 1938 quite a number of threats against my life—that I would be gotten, that I would be bumped off."

Later that year Lovestone applied to the State Department for a new passport. Because he was listed as a Communist, the FBI opened an investigation into the lost passport. Lovestone explained to the FBI man that the burglary was the work of Communist agents trying to expose his association with Homer Martin in the UAW crackdown on Communism. The FBI man interviewed the doorman at London Terrace, who said that all he had seen were two women coming in and out of Lovestone's apartment. The FBI man concluded that the burglary was a hoax staged by Lovestone to obtain a passport.

Only recently, when the Comintern files in Moscow were opened to researchers, has Lovestone's claim of a burglary been corroborated. In those files there is a letter from Pat Toohey, the Comintern representative in the United States, to George Dimitrov, the head of the Comintern, dated October 19, 1938:

> The entire archive of the notorious Jay Lovestone has come into the possession of our Central Committee. These archives are the complete records of Lovestone's letters, documents, and financial dealings for the past ten years. . . . Some of these documents indicate that Lovestone maintains very close connection with one Mendelssohn of Canada, whom Comrade Browder believes to be a Soviet employee of an important branch [OGPU]. Lovestone seems especially close to Mrs. Mendelssohn. . . . Lovestone maintains four bank accounts in four names, keeps four different homes with as many separate identities.

Years later, as part of another investigation, the FBI came across evidence that showed how the Lovestone burglary was arranged. The building employees at London Terrace belonged to a small Communist-controlled union. One of the maids reported to her union on the kind of correspondence Lovestone kept there. This report was passed on to agents in the party who rented one apartment across from Lovestone's and another on the floor above. One day when he was out, his apartment was burglarized and his papers taken to the apartment on the floor above, so that the doorman would not spot anyone taking out his bags.

Eight days after the Lovestone burglary, on July 25, the trial of the four suspended UAW officers (Addes had already been expelled) on charges of conspiracy got under way at the UAW headquarters in the Griswold Building on Detroit's Wall Street. Maurice Sugar, the lawyer for the ousted officers, offered in evidence some of the papers stolen from Lovestone's flat to show how he was manipulating Martin. Sugar had a field day with the letters, telling the press that the only conspiracy was between "Homer Martin and an irresponsible, disruptive political adventurer and meddler, Jay Lovestone."

Lovestone was in Montreal, where he had gone to store other documents with the Mendelssohns after the burglary. Bill Munger reached him there and said, "They really got the dope on us."

"Well, you know we can repudiate it," Lovestone replied.

"They've got too many original letters," Munger said.

"We can say they stole them and manipulated them," Lovestone suggested.

The trial lasted until August 6, when Frankensteen, Mortimer, and Hall were expelled from the union while Wells was suspended for three months. The winner in all this fracas, however, seemed to be Walter Reuther, who had positioned himself above the fray and who asked John L. Lewis to get the expelled officers reinstated.

Lewis, who was fed up with Martin and looked askance at Lovestone's meddling, sent a high-powered delegation to Detroit in the first week of September 1938, Philip Murray of the steelworkers and Sidney Hillman of the Amalgamated Clothiers. They presented Martin with an ultimatum—reinstate the expelled officers or lose the support of the CIO. Martin agreed, while furious at Lewis's interference, but he lost control of the board, which fired the Lovestoneites—their efforts had come to naught.

In January 1939, Martin suspended the board, which led to his being suspended by the CIO on January 22. The CIO charged him with conducting secret talks with Henry Ford to set up a huge Ford company union. Still fighting to retain control of his union, Martin called for a convention on March 1.

Things looked bad for Martin, and on February 8, Lovestone asked David Dubinsky, who had brought him into this mess, for support. "The high-water mark of Homer's support has already been reached," Lovestone said. "His big problem is to harness the rank and file. The argument of the other side is—Homer is alone—nobody is behind him." A Martin defeat, said Lovestone, would mean that "the Lewis dictatorship would become more arrogant than ever and the Stalinite stronghold would be strengthened in the CIO."

That March there were two UAW conventions, Homer Martin's in Detroit on March 4 and the CIO convention in Cleveland on March 27. Martin ended up with four hundred delegates representing about sixty thousand members, or less than one fifth of the UAW total. That June he took his followers into the AFL, whose president, William Green, was jubilant, thinking he now had a foothold in the auto industry. John Brophy said: "Martin now becomes the number-one problem child of the AFL." R. J. Thomas, a red-faced 250-pounder from East Palestine, Ohio, who always carried a packet of Mail Pouch in his jacket pocket, was now president of the UAW. All remnants of the Martin regime were ousted.

Martin in desperation called a strike in June at the Fisher body plant in Flint, which got nowhere. Local after local turned against him. Bargaining rights were determined in elections held by the National Labor Relations Board. That July in Baltimore, where he was in a Chevrolet plant trying to build the vote for Martin, Irving Brown reported to Lovestone that the situation was becoming impossible. He could not keep the workers behind Martin. "Frankly, I can no longer tell workers that our side is the real union," he informed Lovestone. When he talked about the AFL, the workers laughed at him. Brown was considering resigning and returning to the CIO autoworkers. "Can you offer any real alternative?" he asked. On April 21, 1940, Brown reported that the election at the Baltimore plant was over and Martin had taken a beating, 665 to 235.

At the end of 1940, when all the elections were over, Martin's union folded. He lost the backing of the AFL. One day at Ford headquarters, Henry Ford came into the office of his chief of staff, Harry Bennett, and said, "Harry, I guess this is our fault. Let's help Homer." Ford gave Martin an account buying paint for the company and set him up with a furnished house and a car. Martin later traded the house for a farm in Ann Arbor. Born on a farm, he died on a farm.

Lovestone could reflect that a jockey was no better than the horse he was riding, and Homer ran best on a muddy track. Jay had spent two years trying to throw the Communists out of the UAW, where they were more powerful than ever. As Bert Wolfe later wrote the poet Kenneth Rexroth, "Re Lovestone and the autoworkers, it is easy to condemn as wrong that which did not succeed . . . it failed because the Communist Party was too skilled and both Lewis and Browder put an army of paid organizers in the field to reverse the prevailing sentiment." Rexroth replied that it could be said of the Lovestoneites that "they were precious few and those few were precious." As for the power of the Communists, Rexroth remained a skeptic. "The world is full of very important fools," he opined, "and the fact that Carole Lombard is opposed to an open hearing for Trotsky does not mean that the old gentleman does eat babies." (This was a reference to a call for hearings on Trotsky after his 1940 assassination.)

The long-term damage of Lovestone's attempted coup was that he incurred the lasting enmity of the Reuther brothers, who saw him as a splitter and a spoiler. After World War II, when Walter Reuther became president of the UAW and then of the CIO and Lovestone was running the foreign department of the AFL for George Meany, Reuther continued to see Lovestone as the number-one enemy in the labor movement. Their mutual rancor poisoned the atmosphere between the two great federations for thirty years.

Having failed to take control of the UAW and incurred the wrath of the Reuther brothers, Lovestone turned his attention in 1939 to his own moribund party, which now called itself the Independent Labor League. The change of name indicated a change of position. Lovestone had completely broken with the Soviet Union. Stalin showed no inclination to make peace with Communist Opposition parties. Lovestone knew that he and his movement were Stalin's mortal enemies. At the same time he was disillusioned with the doctrines he had held since 1919. He admitted that "we have been wrong" and asked, "Where do we go from here?" Already in 1937 his publication, *Worker's Age,* said, "We must engage in some earnest soul-searching." To disassociate itself from Stalinism and Trotskyism, his movement reinvented itself as the Independent Labor League. It now stood for the abandonment of the Communist heritage and the search for a new Marxist vision, and it was against any "coercive cooperation" with Moscow. On December 16, 1938, Lovestone made this surprising announcement: "We stand for democratic socialism in the full meaning of the term."

In April 1939, Lovestone went to Europe to confer with the other Communist Opposition groups. On April 23 from London, he wrote Bert Wolfe, who had seen him off on the *Queen Mary* with a basket of fruit: "What a hellish world we are living in . . . a troop of soldiers in full attire just marched by my window! And girls in gas masks taking their Sunday stroll in rainy Paris weather . . . and the damned planes, they just don't even let the birds have their peace on earth."

Jay also wrote Sasha Zimmerman on April 18 that "while the date of the war cannot be pointed out in this letter, its immediacy is guaranteed and accepted by all. . . . The European labor movement is in a most desperate plight. Its leaders are being taken over by the war forces. . . . Have had good talks with the comrades going out of Spain." Zimmerman many years later reminisced that "Lovestone could analyze the international situation as very few people could. . . . He told me the war was coming. He predicted a year in advance that there will be a pact between Stalin and Hitler. He wrote it in *Worker's Age.* I remember an old Communist, a dressmaker, he saw the article in my office and he jumped at me: 'Look to what extent you are going! How you people have degenerated. The kind of slander you are spreading about Stalin!' "

The Nazi-Soviet pact in August 1939 created a crisis in the American Communist Party, where the line made a lightning change. When Hitler invaded Poland in September, George Dimitrov instructed Earl Browder: "This is not a war against fascism, this is a war of reactionary imperialist Germany against the reactionary imperialist states of England, France, and Poland. The question of who attacked first is of no importance." The party line was now to agitate against aid to Britain and France, and the *Daily Worker* announced that "The Yanks Aren't Coming." It became common practice to lump together the Russians and the Germans as "CommuNazis."

Lovestone's Independent Labor League, largely because of the inflexible pacifist Bert Wolfe, continued to work with such organizations as the Keep America out of War Committee. Wolfe's thinking was that whatever the evils of the fascist regimes, the British and the French were still basically fighting to preserve their empires. At its convention on Labor Day weekend 1939, the ILL proclaimed that "this second world war is neither more nor less than the continuation of the first. It represents the same imperialist conflicts. . . . THIS WAR IS NOT OUR WAR!"

Yet Lovestone began to question his group's position. In November he was stunned when Soviet forces invaded Finland and his old Comintern colleague Otto Kuusinen formed a puppet government. But the Soviets suffered a crushing defeat, and Kuusinen's regime was a dismal flop. Lovestone told a friend that Stalin was using Kuusinen in a sort of "educated Jew" role. "You see," he said, "Stalin is shrewd and not cultured. He has a wonderful sense of power. Harnessed to ruthlessness that is what makes him tick."

In 1940 experience and doctrine fought for control of Lovestone's mind. Doctrine told him that the war had been precipitated by the clash of two gigantic imperialist coalitions and that America should stay out of it. But experience told him that it would make a very real difference who won. He had seen the Nazis firsthand, when they took power in 1933 and when they invaded Austria in 1938. France and Britain were not to be compared with Germany and the Soviet Union.

On June 17, 1940, three days after German troops marched into Paris, Lovestone wrote Julian Gorkin of the POUM: "None of us foresaw the possibility of a lightning German victory. . . . Hitler had the choice last year of attacking in the East or in the West. Whatever you say about Hitler, it's clear that he isn't stupid. Hitler chose the West because it was easier for Blitzkrieg tactics and his western opponents were less prepared for him than were the Russians, with all their inefficiency and purges. . . . Stalin has learned much from his mistakes in the Finnish war and has strengthened his forces."

More practical matters also bedeviled Lovestone. With the war on people's minds, his little party was fading into oblivion. He could no longer find funding and was facing ruin. He owed the printer $417.38 and his landlord $412.50 in back rent. He owed back wages. People were working for nothing. He couldn't get a bank loan because his credit was no good. He'd reached the end of his rope.

By July he was in favor of aid to England, writing Bill Munger: "The entire debate about aid to England is really academic. It is here. It would be criminal to agitate against such a course and would simply be doing handy-work for Hitler. . . . I have in mind giving planes and technical assistance."

Seeing the change in Jay, Wolfe decided that his only course of action was to break with the Lovestone movement. He wrote Lovestone on July 4, 1940, that the movement was "sliding down. . . . We slowly diminish in number. . . . Nor is it amusing to sneer at each one lost and say there must have been something wrong with him. . . . I now realize I no longer represent the views of the majority on the war question."

Lovestone responded with his usual truculence on July 12: "You repeat my position is unintentional aid for Roosevelt. I could counter by saying yours is unintentional aid for Hitler. Are you prepared to write in the *Worker's Age* that you are against even conditional aid for Britain, now fighting to resist Nazi destruction? . . . Are you prepared to say, 'I am in favor of the appeasement of Hitler'? Why don't you say it? . . . I think you have been sliding into a position of sterile isolationism."

Wolfe did not back down, replying that Roosevelt's "war hysteria" showed that we "should fight harder than ever . . . exposing the frauds under aid and defense; believing that we can best help the world by keeping out . . . is not isolationism." True to his pacifism, Wolfe abandoned his comrade of twenty years and concentrated on his writing.

In the summer and fall of 1940, Lovestone was helped in resolving his own uncertainties by the contrasting attitudes of two of his English friends, the ex-Wobbly and working-class Communist Jack Carney and the upper-class intellectual Socialist Fenner Brockway. On July 25, 1940, Brockway wrote Jay: "My own expectation is that the war will develop into a long ding-dong affair, with increasingly severe bombing raids on both sides." In August, Brockway fell during a blackout and hurt his arm. "The pain is less," he wrote Jay, "but the progress is being delayed by sleepless nights in a damp, cold cellar under bombing conditions." He and his wife, Edith, moved to their country house in Lancashire to get away from the air raids.

Lovestone notified him on August 14: "I am absolutely against American appeasement of Hitler." To which Brockway replied on August 28: "The Socialist must not allow himself under temporary war circumstances to become committed to policies that will prevent him from independent action later on. . . . After some months of air warfare, a common desire among peoples will come to end not merely the war, but Nazism on the continent and imperialism here."

Impatient with Brockway's wishful thinking, Lovestone replied, a bit testily: "Would you like to be able to beat back the Hitler attack on you or not? . . . I assume that you welcome our assisting you via arms, tanks, and planes. . . . I would appreciate it if you would answer yes or no. . . . All talk of a British offensive against the Nazi army on the continent is putrid poppycock."

Bombs were raining on London, but Brockway maintained his lofty pacifism, to the point that Lovestone wrote him with some exasperation in October: "In the Battle of Britain, not only Hitler and Churchill have stakes. The world labor movement, crushed on the continent of Europe, has even more vital stakes. It will not have the barest existence if Hitler triumphs. . . . Imagine how much your British fascist movement would be stimulated. . . . It is far more to the interest of the international proletariat that Hitlerism should be defeated than it is even to the interest of the British and American bourgeoisie."

Lovestone lost patience with Brockway's specious reasoning that Hitler could not win and England could not lose, and therefore they must start planning for postwar Socialism. "I know nothing more suicidal," he wrote Brockway, "than to pretend that a Hitler victory is impossible. . . .

In order for social progress to have any future, the Nazis must be defeated. . . . The real worry is the terrible risk of a Nazi triumph." "You are
a bit of a Yankee tough!" Brockway replied. Jay said that he believed in
speaking straight from the shoulder.

While Brockway was on his country estate writing antiwar editorials
for Socialist journals, Jack Carney was in the factory with the workers
and wrote Lovestone on December 5: "Does anyone think for a single
moment that Hitler would be more merciful to the British than he has
been to the French? Can you imagine what would happen when the thousands of apelike little fuhrers of Germany arrive on these shores?

"When a trade union conference," Carney went on,

> as witness the Amalgamated Engineering Union last week, stands in
> silent tribute to its dead members—dead at the factory bench—
> surely there is something different in the nature of this war that
> ought to compel a revision of our ideas. . . . Think of a shop steward
> standing outside of the shop collecting trade union dues while the
> raids are on and know that the issues cannot be expressed in terms
> of capitalist aggrandizement. . . . In this war, the factory, the trans-
> port system, and the land are the front-line trenches. A man who
> joins the army is said to be seeking a safe berth.

Carney helped convince Lovestone that the Marxist analysis of class
against class did not operate in this case. Lovestone had seen Hitler crush
the trade union movement in Germany and was sure he would do the
same in the countries he occupied. Carney wrote: "Be proud of the
people of this island, battered from the sky, driven from their homes, their
families broken up, they still carry on. . . . The American Navy should
sail the Atlantic, the full power of American plane factories should be at
the beck and call of Britain—for if Britain dies, who else will live?"

Lovestone increasingly felt that his shrinking opposition movement
was out of kilter with the times. With Europe under fascism and England
facing invasion, with the Soviet Union occupying the Baltic states and
half of Poland, the relevance of his little group had ended. What mattered
now was to ensure the survival of the trade unions in Europe and England.

So Lovestone held a conference of the Independent Labor League on
December 28 and 29, 1940, and scuttled his own movement. "We have
decided to dissolve the league and release all members and officers from
any further obligation to the organization," said the final issue of the
Worker's Age on January 25, 1941. "Present-day American radicalism

finds itself in a hopeless blind alley from which there is no escape." The Communist Party was "nothing more than a foreign agency of the Stalin dictatorship of Russia. . . . A thoroughly alien and hostile element in the American labor movement." The Trotskyite sects were futile. The world was in turmoil. The tidy formulas of yesterday no longer served.

Lovestone had just turned forty-three. He did not have a dollar to his name and could look back only on a succession of failures. What had he done with his life? Ten years in the Communist Party, ending in expulsion. Another twelve years trying to get his own party off the ground, a failed attempt to take over the United Auto Workers, and now disbandment. Where could he go? What doors were open? How could he reinvent himself?

Once again David Dubinsky came to the rescue. Dubinsky played a leading role in the New York chapter of the Committee to Defend America by Aiding the Allies, which had been formed by William Allen White, the "maverick on Main Street" and editor of the *Emporia Gazette* in Kansas. The committee had a labor division, and in 1941 Dubinsky tapped Lovestone to run it. His job was to get labor behind FDR's efforts to help the British. From his desk at 8 West Fortieth Street, he sent releases to unions all over the country.

When Germany invaded the Soviet Union on June 22, 1941, Lovestone was told that the committee's new policy was to "back aid to Russia, which was delivering terrific blows to Hitler, but we will do nothing to advance Communism." Then came Pearl Harbor and America's entry into the war. The committee changed its name to Citizens for Victory. Lovestone continued to run the labor division, funneling funds to underground labor movements in occupied Europe, such as the CGT in France, which had joined the resistance.

But once the war was under way, Lovestone felt he was spinning his wheels with Citizens for Victory. He wanted to get into uniform but was deferred from the draft on the grounds that he was doing important defense work. He appealed the classification but to no avail. On August 24, 1942, he applied to the Office of Strategic Services, writing George K. Bowden, one of Gen. William J. Donovan's best staff officers, that "I have made a firsthand study of the Nazi movement and I have had practical experience in underground as well as open work in nearly fifteen countries. . . . I would like to see you soon for a real chat—unclocked."

But Lovestone's checkered past caught up with him. A most secret

OSS memo dated August 31, 1942, said that "Lovestone is engaged not only in a number of intrigues involving the Communist Party, from which he broke ostensibly in 1929 when he formed the Communist Party Opposition, but also in other activities which may render him useless as an impartial source of information." The irony was that the OSS, which hired a number of Communists, in this case turned down a man who had become an ardent anti-Communist.

Lovestone next applied to the Department of Labor for a job with the Wage and Hour Division and was again turned down. J. Edgar Hoover, who kept an open file on Lovestone, observed in the margin of a report dated September 9, 1942: "It is positively shocking that this man is even being considered for a government job."

The OSS and Labor Department rejections were not the only blows that Lovestone had to absorb that year. In February 1942, Esther and Nathan Mendelssohn decided to take a vacation. They were in Miami on February 12, aboard a Nassau-bound plane that was searched by customs inspectors. Nathan was seen to remove from his pocket a 35mm film negative, which he tore in half and threw on the ground. The customs people retrieved the negative but allowed the Mendelssohns to proceed on their flight while they developed the film. It was found to contain material in German, French, and English entitled "Immediate Peace, Socialist Peace," which had been printed by the Independent Labor League on January 1, 1940. This was obviously a release from the Communist Opposition movement, which in January 1940 was still in its antiwar phase. But in 1942 it looked suspicious, and when the Mendelssohns returned to Miami on March 2, they were arrested. Nathan was charged under the Trading with the Enemy Act, for failing to declare the negative. Bond was fixed at five thousand dollars, and he was held in the Coral Gables city jail. His arrest was reported in a Washington paper under the headline BROKER HELD IN PROPAGANDA PLOT.

Lovestone pulled out all the stops to help his friends. He asked the governor of New York, Herbert Lehman, to intervene. He wrote Judge Justine Wise Polier on March 6 that the Canadian police had raided Mendelssohn's home. "The problem now is to get them out on bail," he said. "All of this grows out of the general war hysteria and the stupidity of people." Lovestone asked the well-connected Justine Polier to inform Attorney General Francis Biddle about this "violation of constitutional rights."

Thanks to Lovestone's lobbying, the charges against Mendelssohn were dismissed on April 9 for insufficient evidence and he was allowed to go home. But as a result of his arrest, the FBI opened an investigation and discovered evidence of his forged passport activities. In addition, his name was found in the address book of a Soviet spy who had been arrested in Canada. Because of all this the Mendelssohns were barred from entering the United States. This was a major inconvenience, since they were in the habit of wintering in Florida. Again, Lovestone lobbied the State Department and the Immigration people, but not till 1951 was the ban lifted.

In 1943 Lovestone kept plugging away in his unsatisfying job with Citizens for Victory. He felt out of the loop, uninvolved. Taking stock of his life as he marked time, he realized that his destiny was bound up in his passage from Communist to ex-Communist.

Lovestone's conversion was based on the crumbling of his early beliefs. He had originally seen the 1917 Bolshevik Revolution as one of the greatest events in human history. But he had witnessed its degeneration into dictatorship, into a vicious system that did something terrible to the dictators as well as to the dictated.

At the same time he came to see that the Marxist analysis of the evils of capitalism did not apply to the American model. In fact, American free enterprise was the most powerful vehicle for the extension of democracy. He saw this firsthand in the ILGWU, which had, as part of its collective bargaining machinery, its own engineering department. Thus, when an employer did not produce efficiently, the union's engineering department had a right to examine his methods and to recommend improvements in the manufacture of garments. If the employer pleaded an inability to pay wages, the ILGWU accounting department had a right to examine the books. Meanwhile, in Russia, "the workers' paradise," labor was subjected to speedup systems and severely punished for infractions of factory discipline. You could go to jail if you were late for work.

Lovestone was now as committed an adversary of the Communist system as he had once been a fervent partisan. He was also part of a growing colony of "exes," men and women who had left the party in despair or disgust. Bolshevism had ruled in Russia for a quarter of a century, time enough in which to breed its share of apostates.

In Lovestone's entourage the exes included Ben Mandel (Bert Miller), a purged Communist and Lovestoneite who became a researcher for the House Un-American Activities Committee in the thirties; Ben Gitlow, who practically made a profession of testifying before congressional committees; and Whittaker Chambers, a Lovestone sympathizer who left the party in 1929 but was readmitted as an illegal until his final break in 1938.

By 1943, when Lovestone was wondering what to do next, there were so many exes that they formed a community of the disillusioned, a discrete subculture that might be put to use in the postwar years. They knew the pain of fire because they had been burned. They knew the workings and machinery of the system. They could pinpoint the operatives, legal and illegal. They knew the names on the membership lists and understood the levels of involvement in front groups.

At the same time they tended to be suspicious of those who had not been on the inside. As defectors they remained by habit and indoctrination the custodians of the body of dogma they had turned against. Almost without realizing it they clung to the rhetoric and tactics of their former faith. They continued to say, "We must be united as one man against the common danger," which was now Stalinism. They were useful because they were trained in Marxist-Leninist dialectics, on the grounds that "it takes one to know one," even though they continued to employ Communist tactics, as Lovestone had tried to clean up the UAW by instituting a purge. "I couldn't have been a good anti-Communist if I hadn't been a good Communist," he liked to say.

The exes, however, provided an effective antidote to the popular front mentality of the war years. In this view, now that the Russians were our allies, no price was too high to pay for their friendship. This was the mentality that held when Stalin gobbled up Eastern Europe, that he only wanted to protect his borders, or when Mao took over in China, that the Chinese Communists were "agrarian liberals."

For an ex like Lovestone, it was clear that the Soviet Union was bent on world domination. Once the war was over it would try to destabilize Europe. Not by military force but by taking over the unions through the local Communist parties. After Germany was defeated there would be another war for control of the trade unions of Europe. It was to this arena that Lovestone felt drawn, perhaps to fulfill the prophecy made by the Italian novelist and onetime Communist Ignazio Silone: "The final conflict will be between Communists and ex-Communists."

It was David Dubinsky, Lovestone's rabbi, who in 1941 introduced him to George Meany, saying, "The son of a bitch is okay, he's
been converted." Meany had just become secretary-treasurer of the AFL,
moving into the spacious corner office in the seven-story building on the
northeast corner of Massachusetts and Ninth in the nation's capital.

Meany was now number two in the largest trade union federation,
and its ruling force under the lackluster William Green. He would prove
to be the most powerful figure in the history of American labor. The saga
of the Bronx high school dropout who became the familiar of presidents
had nothing to do with chance and everything to do with ability. The
thick frame, the bald and speckled head, the horn-rimmed glasses, the
heavy jaw, and the cigar clenched between the teeth were like a Mr. Jiggs
cartoon, a crude disguise for a man with the intellect of a chess master.
Meany was a Derby winner who looked like a beer-wagon Percheron.

One of eight children of an Irish Catholic immigrant plumber, Meany
was born in 1894 at 125th Street and Madison Avenue, when Harlem was
still partly Irish. At sixteen he became a plumber's apprentice for $6.88 a
week. At twenty-two he took the oath of allegiance in his father's local.
Everyone knew Mike Meany's son, and at the age of twenty-seven he ran
for business agent. George was clean and ran against a man on the take
and won and never fixed a sink again. He worked hard, spoke well, and

had a knack for numbers. By 1934 he had risen to the head of the New York State Federation, which had eight hundred locals and represented 850,000 workers. He had the required mix of a keen mind and the common touch, and he spent three months a year in Albany lobbying the legislators to get prolabor bills passed. He had the phone number of every assemblyman and senator in the state and knew just where to put the pressure on—in the place the man was elected.

From his first days in Washington, Meany made his presence felt. Bill Green thought he was moving too fast. He had a natural authority, an inbred decisiveness. A week after Pearl Harbor, on December 15, 1941, FDR called a conference to prevent labor disputes in wartime. John L. Lewis was good with the oratory, calling the open shop "a harlot with a wig and artificial limbs." But Meany was the businesslike negotiator, and it was at this meeting that the crucial wartime transaction was forged— the no-strike pledge in exchange for maintenance of membership—all newly hired workers automatically became dues-paying members after fifteen days on the job. Membership soared. By the end of the war the AFL had seven million members and the CIO had four million.

The mild and plodding Green was fading, and Meany from the start looked for an area to call his own beyond the check signing and dues collecting of his official title. He shrewdly chose foreign affairs, which in the AFL had long been a matter of windy resolutions at convention time. But, with so much of the postwar world up for grabs, foreign affairs were, as Meany put it, "the meat of the thing," and he was at the carving table, even though he would not become president of the AFL until Green's death in 1952.

Once the war was over, Meany steered the AFL into the formation of what amounted to a foreign ministry, with a network of emissaries in a dozen countries from Indonesia to Italy. This foreign affairs division had a strongly anti-Communist ideology and assisted free trade unions everywhere to combat Communist influence. With an orientation and methods that were already those of the Cold War, with a political will and a vision as yet unshared by the government, the media, or big business, the AFL filled a void from 1945 until 1947, while the Truman administration was still wondering whether the Soviet Union was friend or foe.

The man Meany picked to run AFL foreign affairs was none other than Jay Lovestone, who at last found a task commensurate with his ability and experience. He had ten years of on-the-job training inside the Communist Party and ten years of leading his own movement. He had an understanding of the Soviet system matched by only a few State Department specialists, like George F. Kennan. He had no illusions about Soviet aims or Soviet friendship, which he called "hands across the caviar." He also brought the tactics and secretiveness he had learned in the Comintern into the AFL.

On the face of it, no two men were more dissimilar. The Irish Catholic plumber was the labor leader as capitalist, and proud of it. He boasted that he had never been on a picket line. His goal was to present labor as a responsible force in the nation, whose interests had to be negotiated like those of business and government. He sought to get labor out of its chip-on-the-shoulder ghetto mentality, by conveying the message to those high on the government and corporate ladders that "I am your equal in every way." Meany was in office long enough to work with nine presidents, from FDR to Ronald Reagan, and his favorite conceit was to say, "Tell them I'll call back," when his secretary, Virginia Tehas, informed him, "The White House is on the line." Eisenhower invited Meany to his monthly stag dinners, where he met the bosses of big business, like "Engine Charlie" Wilson of GM. Meany fit right in. They were the heads of corporations that made products. He was the head of an even bigger corporation that provided labor.

Lovestone, the Lithuanian Jew, was a former campus radical and zealous young Communist who spent twenty years trying to defeat the capitalist system. He had matured into an impassioned anti-Communist whose touchstone was a free labor movement. Like Meany, and in spite of his sometimes cynical and abrasive manner, Lovestone was a crusader. That is, he needed something larger than himself to believe in.

Ernest S. Lee, a decorated Marine veteran who married Meany's daughter Eileen and who worked for years with Lovestone in the AFL international department, recalled that "Meany saw people as they were and didn't like charlatans. Jay had some of the same qualities. He could not call a snake an Easter lily. His attitude to the Communists was 'those are the SOB's who tried to kill me.' Meany saw that he could be useful. He recognized the value of the man. Jay had been on both sides of the fence, his mind was like a road map, he knew the place names on the other side, he knew who was pulling the strings. Jay was invaluable, he had the background, he was organized, he read twenty newspapers a day, he listened to that little radio he carried around. Jay was always looking at what was behind something. He saw plots everywhere. If you argued with him, he'd say, 'I know them, I know how they operate.' And 90 percent of the time he'd be right."

Meany liked Lovestone, liked his encyclopedic knowledge of world affairs, his analytical acumen, his stand-up comic's sense of humor. He was dedicated, he had no family, and he thought about nothing but work. And Lovestone, who made caustic remarks about everyone else, never had anything but praise for Meany.

In 1944 Lovestone told Meany that once the war was over in Europe, the Soviets would use labor as an element of conquest by subversion. This would happen not only in Eastern Europe but in France and Italy, where the Communists controlled the unions and would start a wave of strikes to destabilize those countries. At that time three of the most powerful AFL leaders—Meany, Dubinsky, and Matthew Woll, the penguinlike head of the photoengravers' union—were anti-Communist internationalists. With the postwar clout of the labor movement, with the millions of new dues-paying members, they were in a position to act. At the 1944 convention in New Orleans that fall, a resolution drafted by Lovestone was passed creating the Free Trade Union Committee, with the mandate of assisting free unions abroad. Lovestone was named executive secretary.

For the next thirty years, until his forced retirement in 1974, Lovestone directed the foreign affairs activities of the AFL. Working behind the scenes and out of the limelight, in an office in the ILGWU headquarters in New York with only a couple of assistants, he played a board game on the map of the world that made him one of the masterminds of the Cold War. It did not seem possible that one man in a small, cluttered cubicle could get so much done. But he had the backing of the AFL triumvirate and the weapons of patronage and leverage.

In terms of patronage, Lovestone made the most of the new labor jobs being created in the government, particularly in the labor attaché program that the State Department had launched in 1943. The labor attachés were written up in a magazine article as "a new kind of emissary, more familiar with slums and sweatshops than with the salons of foreign capitals." One of the first, Sam Berger in London, was given high marks for predicting a Labour victory in 1945, when Churchill was voted out of office. Berger became the conduit to Britain's postwar labor leadership.

By 1946 the State Department had twenty-two labor attachés. For Lovestone, every opening became a battle royal to get an AFL man in the job over a CIO man. Meany had a virtual veto on the appointments, which he had to use judiciously. Behind Meany there was Lovestone, maneuvering to advance the men he considered reliable, like Joseph Godson in Canada and Herbert Weiner in Australia. By reliable Lovestone meant not only that they were sound on Communism but that they reported to him as well as to the State Department. This way they became "Jay's people," links in his global chain of informants. An FBI report at the time noted that "both Lovestone and Dubinsky have openly bragged that they have been successful in placing Lovestone's adherents in the majority of the Labor Attaché posts in the United States embassies in Europe. No explanation of how this was accomplished was given by the informant, but the opinion was expressed that 'Dubinsky has a pipeline to Truman or has one maybe to [George] Marshall.'"

But Lovestone's influence reached far beyond the labor attaché program. He forged alliances with a few trusted men in government, with whom he had in common that deep insider knowledge of the Soviet Communist Party. It was a brotherhood of the exes. Ben Mandel, the onetime Communist and Lovestoneite, was an investigator for the House Un-American Activities Committee and fed Lovestone classified information. He told Lovestone, before any arrests had been made, that Soviet spies had stolen atomic secrets. Lovestone responded on January 9, 1946, that "I am sure that Joe [Stalin] and Company have nearly everything we got through thievery. It will take only at most a couple of years before they can translate their knowledge into practical production."

Mandel and Lovestone monitored appointments in the government departments, looking for familiar names from their years in the party. Here was Harry Magdoff of the Young Communist League, now working in the Commerce Department for Henry Wallace. Here was Tom Constantino, who had been kicked out of the steelworkers as a Communist, now a labor adviser for General MacArthur in Tokyo. For Lovestone, there were three levels of guilt: party members, fellow travelers, and "nogoodniks," the ones they had no proof on.

Mandel told Lovestone to write the South Dakota Republican Karl Mundt about Communist influence in the War Department. The AFL, Mandel advised, "can either tie up with the non-Communist liberals who still have one buttock in the Communist orbit, or play ball with the Republicans, who . . . offer the most substantial guarantee against the Commie machine. . . . Why can't Woll or Meany be in touch with this crowd?"

Lovestone used Walter Winchell for an outlet, passing him items for his column though despairing that he would never see the light, writing Mandel on May 17, 1946, that "Winchell knows perfectly well that he is being used by the Commies in many ways. . . . Groups of wealthy fellow travelers hang around the Stork Club all week to pump him. . . . He complains that some of the stuff I gave him would make people believe Hitler was right about Stalin. The dope does not see that Hitler was right about Stalin in many ways."

Lovestone also worked closely with a little-known State Department veteran who ran a mysterious office called EUR/X, devoted to the study of worldwide Communist subversion. He was Raymond E. Murphy, and he had in common with Lovestone twenty years of day-to-day study of Communist activities and a prudent avoidance of publicity. His name never appeared in the papers, and he was not even that well known at State, for he cultivated anonymity.

Murphy was born in 1896 in Lewiston, Maine, the son of a mill worker. He went to Bates College in his hometown and joined the State Department as a clerk. Nights, he went to Georgetown University Law School and passed the bar exam. He was brought into the Eastern European Division by Robert Kelley, its sage head, in 1925. Murphy learned at Kelley's knee, studying the transcripts of Communist Party congresses, reading the Comintern periodical *Inprecor,* and building up his files.

Medium-sized and barrel-chested, Murphy had a reddish moon face that could turn purple when he was angry, or more frequently when he feigned anger. He suffered from poor eyesight but made up for it with total recall. His foes were the accepted wisdom and the inadequately documented accusation. His friends inside State were the members of the so-called Riga group, those Soviet specialists who had served in the capital of Latvia to report on the Soviet Union before the United States had diplomatic relations there. Among them were Loy Henderson, Elbridge Durbrow, Charles E. Bohlen, and George Kennan.

In 1937 Murphy's office was transferred to the European Affairs division under Assistant Secretary of State James Clement Dunn. When Communist defectors began arriving in the United States, it was Murphy who debriefed them. In 1938, Gen. Walter Krivitsky, the head of Soviet military intelligence in Western Europe, gave Murphy much valuable information on Soviet espionage operations. Murphy held regular meetings with Krivitsky until one day in February 1941 when Krivitsky failed to show up for an appointment. He was found in his room at the Bellevue Hotel with a bullet in his head, a revolver in his hand, and a suicide note next to him. Murphy agreed with Whittaker Chambers, who said, "Anyone can commit a murder, but it takes an artist to commit a suicide."

Murphy also debriefed Margaret Buber Neumann, daughter-in-law of the philosopher Martin Buber and widow of the German Comintern agent Heinz Neumann, who had led the disastrous Canton uprising and became a victim of Stalin's purges. She had the distinction of having been interned in both Russian and German prison camps. Sent to a Siberian gulag in 1936 after her husband's execution, she was released in 1939 in a prisoner exchange. She went back to Germany and was promptly reinterned by the Nazis. In 1945 she was liberated by the Allies, and Murphy arranged for her visa to the United States.

Margaret Neumann explained to Murphy the difference between the Soviet and the German camps. "The Germans only wanted to kill you," she said. "The Russians wanted to work you to death. In the Soviet camp I was attached to a wagon like a horse and I had to pull it." "How cold was it in Siberia?" Murphy asked. "When you spat," Neumann replied, "it clicked when it hit the ground." Neumann and Krivitsky were two of more than a hundred ex-Communists who passed through Murphy's hands.

Perhaps Murphy's greatest coup in terms of penetrating Soviet intentions was his analysis of the so-called Duclos article as the opening salvo in the Cold War. In May 1942, as a goodwill gesture during the visit of Soviet Foreign Minister Vyacheslav Molotov, FDR commuted the sentence of Earl Browder for passport fraud and Browder was released from prison. Browder, the head of the American Communist Party since the early 1930s, saw his release as an expression of the great wartime alliance of the United States and the Soviet Union and went overboard for the December 1943 Teheran agreement among Stalin, Churchill, and FDR for postwar cooperation.

These views became known as Browder's Teheran doctrine. He now believed that Stalin would abandon the campaign for world revolution after the war, which would make the class struggle in the United States irrelevant. Browder saw a long-term Soviet-American entente along the lines spelled out at Teheran. He wanted a restructuring of the American Communist Party so that it could join a coalition of other parties. In May 1944 he dissolved the CPUSA and created the Communist Political Association, of which he was the president and which he saw as the militant left wing of a broad coalition within the two-party system.

But then in the April 1945 issue of the French Communist journal *Cahiers du Communisme* came an attack on Browder from the number-two French Communist, Jacques Duclos, in an article entitled "On the Dissolution of the American Communist Party." One might well wonder why, in the midst of the turmoil in postwar France—when the Communists, brought into the government by General de Gaulle, had their hands full—Duclos would find the time to study the crisis in the distant American party. Today, thanks to the research of John Earl Haynes and Harvey Klehr in the Soviet archives, we know. The "Duclos" article was first secretly published in Russian in Moscow, then translated into French and sent to Duclos, the loyal company man, to be given open distribution under his name. The Russian text was published in the January 1945 issue of the top-secret "Bulletin of the Information Bureau of the Central Committee," which was circulated to a small number of high Soviet government officials.

The "Duclos" article pointed to Browder's "erroneous conclusions" and "notorious revisions of Marxism." It denied "the possibility of the suppression of the class struggle in the postwar period." Here was the word from Moscow, announcing a future confrontation with the West. Browder was stripped of power that June on orders from the Soviet Union and denounced as an "unreconstructed revisionist . . . a renegade . . . an apologist for American imperialism." In early 1946 he was expelled from the American party, and many years later he called the Duclos article "the first public declaration of the Cold War." To have published it openly in Moscow would have been too blatant a signal that Stalin was preparing for a fight with the West. It was thus arranged for the French party to release it.

Murphy of course did not know when he saw the Duclos article that it had originated in Moscow. But he was the only person in the State Department who recognized it for what it was, an announcement that the Communist world revolution would continue unabated in the postwar period. On June 2 he wrote an analysis of the article entitled "Possible Resurrection of the Communist International, Resumption of Extreme Leftist Activities, Possible Effect on United States." But since at that time the State Department was still hoping for postwar cooperation with the Soviet Union, with Truman about to meet Stalin in Potsdam, Murphy's memo was ignored.

Ray Murphy was also instrumental in having Whittaker Chambers testify before the House Un-American Activities Committee in 1948, which led to the two perjury trials and the eventual conviction of Alger Hiss. Murphy was a careful, lawyerly man who held to rules of evidence that were admissible in court. In March 1945 he went out to Chambers's Pipe Creek farm in Westminster, Maryland, and questioned him for two hours. He was struck by the amount of verifiable detail in Chambers's account and questioned him again in August 1946.

Murphy had long suspected Hiss, who had joined the State Department in 1936, of being a covert Communist, but his evidence was circumstantial. Hiss had warmly recommended his friend and colleague Noel Field for a key post in the Philippines, and Field turned out to be a Soviet agent who defected to the Eastern Bloc. Murphy also knew that, as head of the UN Desk, Hiss was trying to put over the thesis that the Panama Canal Zone was "occupied territory" and should be brought under UN trusteeship, which was also the Soviet line. Murphy recalled Hiss saying of Stalin, "He plays for keeps."

All this was far too feeble to pursue, but in talking to Chambers, Murphy began to think he had a case. He was further encouraged when a report he filed on Hiss led to a security investigation, which concluded in November 1946 that Hiss had taken home top-secret reports that he was not cleared to see. A few weeks later Hiss left his promising career at State to take a dead-end job as head of the Carnegie Endowment.

It was Murphy who in February 1947 brought the Chambers material to the attention of an unknown but ambitious freshman California congressman, Richard M. Nixon, who sat on the HUAC and was looking for information about Communists in government. Before his HUAC appearance in August 1948, Murphy coached Chambers on how to be an effective witness. Questioning him as a prosecutor would, Murphy asked about the color of the rugs and the curtains in the Hiss house, the furniture room by room, the pets and hobbies.

Nixon made his reputation in the HUAC hearings, and he had Ray Murphy to thank for it. In the late 1950s, when Murphy wanted to retire, perhaps with a small embassy, say Dublin or Reykjavík, he asked Nixon, then vice president, to put a word in, but only silence came back. Murphy retired in 1959, thinking that Nixon had shown his true colors.

Murphy saw himself as the lone professional anti-Communist in the State Department, working with a skeleton staff in a sometimes hostile environment, for some saw him as a Red-baiter. Thus he was drawn to Lovestone, another professional anti-Communist, with whom he could discuss the fine points of Soviet skulduggery, which so few understood. Murphy sometimes helped Lovestone get visas for his people coming to report from abroad, while Lovestone gave Murphy the papers he had stored in Canada and had Nathan Mendelssohn ferret out some information that Murphy wanted.

Murphy also shared his information with Lovestone. At a time when the United States did not yet have a peacetime intelligence service, he created an embryonic one within the State Department, arranging for a few loyal foreign service officers—Norris Chipman in France, Brewster Morris in Germany, Elbridge Durbrow in Rome—to report directly to him. Lovestone was privy to the classified reports that this sub-rosa group produced.

By 1948 the Central Intelligence Agency had been set up, and Norris

Chipman was in Paris working for its covert action arm, the Office of Policy Coordination. In 1950 he was transferred to Rome, and on January 18, 1951, he wrote Lovestone: "I am being very quiet here and am not working along the lines that I did in Paris and am no longer in any way connected with OPC." Lovestone replied: "I do hope that your pessimism is not definite nor frozen. . . . You know I am a great believer in Uncle Joe. Somehow or other, I feel that at the last moment he will make even bigger mistakes than our own dumb-bells will make."

In spite of Chipman's demurral, there were complaints from the CIA station in Rome that he was trying to run his own intelligence operations. When the matter of his transfer to Germany came up in early 1952, Elbridge Durbrow, then on the European Desk, told Murphy that the CIA objected to Chipman going to Germany because in Rome he had engaged in operations and "tried to be a sort of deputy on CIA operations and the CIA wanted no part of it."

Durbrow had talked the matter over with his friend Gen. Walter Bedell Smith, then director of the CIA, who told him, "The CIA desperately needs trained foreign service officers to keep the Park Avenue boys on the right track." Smith asked, "What happened to that young man in Paris who was sending such excellent reports to Moscow when I was ambassador there?" Durbrow said that was Norris Chipman, who might be available to help the CIA.

"I don't understand why Chipman can't fit in at an embassy somewhere doing political work," Murphy said, not wanting to lose him.

"Norris is so hepped up on the subject of Communism," Durbrow said, "that it affects his work and there is no opening."

"Why can't he be assigned to Egypt with [the former ambassador to Paris Jefferson] Caffery, who appreciated his work?" Murphy asked.

"The counselor has only been there one and a half years," Durbrow said. "It's too soon to ship him out."

Soon Chipman heard from the chief of personnel at the State Department, who asked if he wanted to go on loan to the CIA as a specialist. Chipman declined upon learning that he would go to Germany after all.

The days when Murphy was running his own intelligence operation inside the European embassies soon ended. With the coming of George Marshall and Dean Acheson as secretaries of state, his office was shunted aside. Acheson wanted to fire Murphy for collecting data on Alger Hiss, but his friends protected him, and none were more loyal than the AFL, thanks to Lovestone. Under attack, Murphy wrote Lovestone on February 1, 1951: "I am sick and tired and disgusted with being the pioneer . . . and bearing all the brunt of criticism."

Lovestone asked Matthew Woll to write President Truman urging that Murphy be assigned as liaison officer between State and the AFL. "In its dealings with the Department of State over a period of years," Woll wrote the president, "the AFL has found but one man in whom it has implicit faith and confidence—Ray Murphy. Yet he has been deliberately shunted to one side and ignored. The AFL desires that Murphy be given an adequate staff to carry on his studies, that he be recognized, that he be designated liaison officer with the AFL, that he be used in policy matters at the highest level involving the Soviet Union . . . as a special assistant to the Secretary."

This, however, was not to be. Acheson the patrician Wasp Episcopalian and Murphy the plebeian Irishman were like oil and water. Lovestone probably did save Murphy from the ax, but he was quarantined in his cubbyhole in the World War I building on Twenty-third Street, with the mice scurrying behind the filing cabinets, until his retirement. In 1963 Murphy died of colon cancer at the age of sixty-seven. Hardly anyone knew who he was or what he had done. Those few who did know thought that his contribution to American security had been impressive.

Lovestone felt that the State Department was caving in to the Russians and that he must make the Free Trade Union Committee an alternative State Department with steadfast and definite aims. He had the complete backing of the three men who ran the AFL and were all committed to aggressive intervention abroad: Dubinsky, with his ILGWU troops in the hundreds of thousands, who could be relied upon to raise money; Woll, an anti-Communist going back to the twenties and a lawyer with ties to big business; and Meany, with access to the highest reaches of government, thanks to the political clout of millions of labor votes.

Through Lovestone, their minister of foreign affairs, they articulated the AFL doctrine of free unions founded on collective bargaining in an open marketplace, and opposition to state-run unions on the Soviet model. Lovestone was the man with the emissaries and the listening posts, the octopus with a hundred tentacles, all run from his small office in New York.

The task facing the Free Trade Union Committee was best expressed by Varian Fry of the International Rescue Committee in a memo to Dubinsky on April 6, 1945: "The labor movement of the European countries will be divided geographically and ideologically into two main groups, in accordance with the division of Europe itself into two 'spheres of influence.' . . . The Communists will be represented in the governments of the individual countries. With the help of the Russian state and a powerful propaganda machine they will strive for the domination of the labor movement in every country." In the first postwar years, when American foreign policy had not yet jelled into an adversarial position, when there was no intelligence agency, when the government was still halfheartedly attempting accommodation with the Russians, the AFL assigned itself the role of preventing the Soviets from taking over the European trade unions.

This was a wondrous transformation for the federation, from a collection of parochial craft unions concerned only with bread-and-butter issues into an internationally minded movement with an aggressive foreign commitment. The AFL became active in a number of European countries, where it had to fight not only Communist attempts to subvert existing unions but the waffling policies of the American occupying powers. In taking on this significant task, the AFL was alone, for the CIO had embarked on an entirely different course by joining the World Federation of Trade Unions (WFTU), founded in Paris in October 1945 but based in Prague. For three years the CIO was trapped in a federation that turned out to be controlled by the Soviets, which also brought in the powerful British Trade Union Congress (TUC).

The founding conference of the WFTU was to take place in Paris from September 25 to October 8, 1945. In a last-minute effort to stem the tide, Meany flew to England in September to speak at the TUC convention in Blackpool. He pointed out that the AFL had supported every pro-British measure at the start of the war, from Bundles for Britain to Lend-Lease, while the CIO had opposed them. He then explained his reasons for not joining the WFTU and attacked the Soviet trade unions, not realizing that he was sharing the platform with a Russian "fraternal delegate."

"We do not recognize or concede that the Russian workers' groups are trade unions," he said in a speech written by Lovestone. "They are formally and actually instruments of the state. . . . These so-called trade unions support labor camps . . . that have enslaved millions. . . . The Russian trade movement is a government-controlled, government-fostered, and government-dominated labor front that denies to the workers the basic human freedoms." Shouts of "Shame!" and "Tommyrot!" interrupted Meany as he delivered the speech, for he seemed to be deliberately insulting the Russian on the platform. The chairman rang his bell and called for order, invoking the TUC tradition of free speech. Meany labored on and closed by saying, "I hope I have not offended anyone, but it would be silly to come thirty-four hundred miles and then go home without saying what was on my mind." With this he squeezed out a few cheers.

The WFTU was essentially an instrument for the dissemination of Soviet propaganda, but it was given validity as an international trade union federation by the membership of the CIO and the TUC. Its principal activity was sending delegations to countries occupied by the United States, such as Japan and Korea, or politically unstable countries, such as Iran and Indonesia, and writing reports stating that the Western powers were vile reactionaries oppressing the locals.

Its general secretary, the French Communist Louis Saillant, controlled the WFTU "Information Bulletin," which ran articles describing Western nations as "warmongers" and "servile instruments of the capitalist monopolies." As soon as a country fell into the Soviet orbit, its faults disappeared. For the sake of keeping the peace, the TUC and the CIO kept their mouths shut as the Red Army annexed Eastern Europe.

In the U.S. government the initial view of the WFTU was divided. The State and Labor Departments' reaction was at first positive, though George Kennan in a February 3, 1946, cable from Moscow described the union as an "instrument of Soviet foreign policy." The AFL at once denounced it as "a worldwide Fifth Column organization." The British kept saying, "This is an experiment. There are bound to be conflicting views." As for Jim Carey, the CIO representative in the WFTU, the labor attaché Herb Weiner recalled that if you told him, "They're making a fool of you," he would say, "We got it under control" or "We got our point of view across." He thought the CIO, by its presence, could reform the WFTU, swing it around. In fact, the CIO did not accomplish any meaningful work in foreign affairs until it extricated itself from the union in 1949.

Lovestone was all too conscious of Lenin's dictate "Postwar chaos offers opportunities for revolution that should never be ignored." In the summer of 1945, with the postwar labor situation in Europe appearing critical, and with the WFTU about to become an adjunct of the Soviets, Lovestone's Free Trade Union Committee made its move. By July 16 it had collected $186,393.59 in donations from AFL affiliates, including $50,000 from the ILGWU. Lovestone needed a man in Europe, and Irving Brown's name came up. "He's politically developed, he's enthusiastic," Dubinsky said. Meany approved, and so did Lovestone. Brown left for Paris in October 1945 to become the FTUC point man.

Lovestone also needed a man in Germany, where the first major battle of the Cold War would be fought, with the Soviets trying to impose their brand of trade unionism on all four zones before making all of Germany a Communist satellite. The man chosen was Henry Rutz, a German-speaking veteran of the Wisconsin labor movement, active in the Milwaukee Typographical Union. He had the advantage of already being in Germany as a captain in the occupation forces.

Thus, in the fall of 1945, as Lovestone launched his foreign opera-

tions against Soviet expansion in what seemed like one more of his futile
David-Goliath struggles, the FTUC was basically a three-man operation,
consisting of Lovestone, Brown, and Rutz. But over a period of thirty
years, Lovestone would turn his little committee into a veritable anti-
Cominform, working in many hidden ways. Lovestone and Brown remained teamed up as inside man and outside man. As the labor attaché
Dan Horowitz recalled, "Irving was the consummate field man, with an
enviable ability to connect with just about everybody. Jay was the consummate desk man, Rasputin-like, working behind the scenes. Irving had
the common touch. Jay wanted a tête-à-tête with Adenauer."

Lovestone was faced with a nebulous postwar international order.
The American priority was getting the boys back home. There seemed to
be only a dim awareness of Soviet intentions, although a de facto division
of Europe was being imposed by the Red Army's presence in Eastern Europe. But what would happen in countries like Greece, Italy, and France,
where, in the absence of the Red Army, powerful Communist parties
could organize subversion and insurrection?

Also, for Lovestone, Communism was not the only issue. He was opposed to all regimes that did not allow unions to operate freely, whether
they came from the left or the right. In his consistent opposition to
Franco's Spain, he broke with right-wing pro-Franco senators like Pat
McCarran. In Latin America he fought the Perón regime in Argentina
until its collapse in 1955 (though he waffled when Batista came to power
in Cuba in 1952).

In one of his more intriguing anti-Franco initiatives, in November
1945 Lovestone arranged a meeting in Washington between the papal
nuncio, Cardinal Cicognani, and the anti-Franco Socialist leader in exile,
Indelicio Prieto. "We met in the very private studio of the nuncio," Lovestone reported, "in the presence of none other than the book and candle."
Cicognani was very friendly and said he spoke with the full authorization
of Pope Pius XII. He told Prieto that if there was a revolution in Spain,
and if it was peaceful, the pope would do nothing to oppose a Republican
government. All the church wanted was a strong voice in the educational
system of the post-Franco government. Lovestone was astonished when
Prieto accepted this condition, saying: We realize that, particularly at the
outset, we could not have an educational system in Spain without the participation of the church. As Lovestone interpreted Cicognani's remarks,
the church would neither oppose nor assist an anti-Franco revolution.

However, nothing came of this meeting. Lovestone blamed the
British Foreign Office and the U.S. State Department, which at the time

were afraid of disposing of Franco. Also, Franco had a strong Catholic lobby in Congress. "I am a very strong man," Lovestone wrote a friend, "but I cannot drag an elephant up the trail to Mount Olympus." At the same time he never forgot the nuncio's astuteness.

The year ended for Lovestone with a dinner given by *The Nation* magazine on December 4, 1945. He was his usual suspicious and cranky self, writing the labor reporter Joe Shaplen: "I met Mrs. God (caretaker of Fala), and Harold Laski [the British professor and Labour Party guru], whose speech was a competent retract of the Communist Manifesto, plus a few sentences of lavish praise for Russia."

10

THE GERMAN COCKPIT

As World War II ended in August 1945, Lovestone saw the post-war period in terms of competing ideologies. This had nothing to do, as he put it, with small points of dogma, such as how many angels can dance on the head of a pin. It had to do with the democracies on one side, which lacked any sense of mission, had a live-and-let-live attitude, and did not clearly grasp the aims of the other side, the Soviet side, which planned to impose their single-party state, dominating every walk of life and every human activity, wherever they could. The difficulty for the West was that you could force men to be slaves but you could not force men to be free.

At home the danger came, as Lovestone told Ray Murphy on one of his weekly trips to Washington, in that "our government's agencies and our country's institutions are today at least as permeated by the Commies as those of France were by the Nazis in 1938." Murphy, who was at that very moment preparing a report on Alger Hiss, heartily agreed. Lovestone also worried about the rise of postwar Communist front groups, such as the Emergency Committee of Atomic Scientists, which had bamboozled Einstein. He warned Bill Green, the lackadaisical president of the AFL, that the Citizens' Committee to Defend Labor was also a front group, despite all the rabbis and reverends whose names were on its letterhead. It was hard to keep track of the camouflage, Lovestone told Green. Bishop Francis J. Connel was not a Communist, but he was on more front committees than there were fleas on a mangy dog. Nor was Rabbi J. X. Cohen, though he spread his blessings on Communist enterprises. Nor was Paul O'Dwyer, the brother of New York City's Mayor William O'Dwyer, though he was the attorney for Michael J. Quill's Communist-run union of subway workers. Although these men were not Communists, Lovestone said, they lent their names and prestige to Communist Party maneuvers.

Lovestone saw himself as an alarm bell, warning of the dangers of Communism at home and abroad at a time of "the Russians are our allies" and "bring the boys back home." As he sat in his New York office in the summer of 1945, his most urgent concern was Germany, now divided into four zones of Allied occupation. Everything depended on Germany, which the Soviets would try to take over by spreading their state-controlled unions to all four zones, while democracy would come only through a revived free labor movement.

But on this crucial postwar battlefield, a terrible mistake had already been made. The master plan for German occupation, Joint Chiefs of Staff Directive 1067, was inspired by the Morgenthau Plan, which mandated the return of Germany to a pastoral state. To ship out factories as reparations, to curb the production of coal and steel, Lovestone felt, were completely incompatible with German recovery, as well as the recovery of France and England, which desperately needed German steel and coal. The White House position, as expressed by President Truman in a letter to the UAW leader R. J. Thomas on December 4, 1945, was that "the chemical, metals, and machine-tool-using industries were very much expanded in the course of the war, as well as in preparation for it. It was evident to us that a substantial proportion of these industries was unnecessary if the German economy was to be truly disarmed. We propose to cause to be removed much industrial equipment from Germany by way of reparations and industrial disarmament."

This was folly, Lovestone thought. It would cause massive unemployment in German industries and allow the Russians to take advantage of the discontent in a weakened Germany. Through his agents in Europe, Irving Brown and Henry Rutz, Lovestone hoped to curtail the policies of dismantlement and to restore the unions of the pre-Nazi era. He knew that he would be bucking not only the official U.S. policy but also a nest of American officers well-positioned in the military government of the U.S. zone, who followed the Communist line and who would formulate policies to assist a Communist takeover of the German unions. The unmasking and elimination of this fifth column was the first order of business.

By June 1945 the headquarters staff of Military Government in the United States Zone of Germany (OMGUS) had been assembled in the IG Farben building in Hoechst, an industrial suburb of Frankfurt. Miraculously, the building was untouched, although the surrounding area had been flattened.

In charge of OMGUS's sixteen divisions was Gen. Lucius DuBignon Clay, at the same time a lowercase democrat, a civil libertarian, and a willful, thin-skinned, and authoritarian commander. Clay was an army engineer with a mind tooled to exact specifications. He had done a brilliant job running wartime military procurement, filling the needs of an 8-million-man army, and now he was running the three German provinces in the American zone: Hesse, Württemberg-Baden, and Bavaria.

In charge of the Manpower Division, which handled labor matters, was Brig. Gen. Frank McSherry, who had been Sidney Hillman's aide on the War Production Board. Thanks to his pull at the White House, Hillman, the influential CIO leader, had arranged for his loyal aide a double promotion—from lieutenant colonel to brigadier general. McSherry was forever in Hillman's debt, and Hillman told him not to trust the pre-Hitler German labor leaders but to find new ones "from the grass roots," starting with shop stewards in the plants. As David Dubinsky later put it, "McSherry was a patsy for the Communists, who almost persuaded him to write rules under which German labor would have to organize through workers' councils that would have been easy for the Communists to take over."

On McSherry's manpower team were two veterans of the National Labor Relations Board whom Lovestone and Rutz, his man in Germany, knew to be close followers of the Communist line: Mortimer Wolf, known as "Red" Wolf, in charge of the Labor Relations Branch, and George Shaw Wheeler, a covert Communist who had infiltrated the Socialist Party in the thirties and was now chief of the Denazification Branch.

Unions in Germany had been suppressed since 1933, when Hitler came to power; there was a whole generation of young people who did not know what a union was. In addition, while the Soviets were swiftly turning their zone into a Communist satellite, General Clay's attitude in 1945 was hands off—let the Germans work out their own system, so long as they got rid of the Nazis.

Inside the Manpower Division, two groups were battling it out. Wheeler and Wolf, assisted by two other officers—Capt. Joseph Gould, who came out of the Office Workers Union, one of the ten Communist-led unions purged by the CIO in 1949, and Lt. Ed Fruchtman, the labor officer for the province of Hesse—were manipulating General McSherry. The newly arrived Joseph Keenan, a veteran AFL man from Chicago, didn't quite get what was going on. Reinforcing Henry Rutz in the anti-Communist wing were Paul R. Porter, a onetime Norman Thomas Socialist now a labor officer in Frankfurt, and Louis Wiesner, a Harvard Ph.D. who was labor officer in the Political Affairs Section.

At a June meeting in Hoechst, Wheeler and Wolf presented a sixteen-page "procedure for organizing trade unions," which would ban the recognition of unions for two years. Instead, shop stewards would be elected for three-month terms on a plant-by-plant basis. This was presented as a from-the-bottom-up, grass-roots, democratic way of doing things, preferable to having the prewar Social Democrats organize from the top down.

Porter and Wiesner, who attended the meeting, saw that this proposal had concealed aims. It would remove trade union organization from the prewar anti-Communist labor people and put it into the hands of new groups in the plants. When Wiesner questioned Wolf, the explanation was: "This is grassroots democracy to eliminate the old trade unionists and put in younger, more aggressive ones." Who were they? Wiesner asked. "Communists and left-wing Socialists," Wolf said. When Wheeler said, "We'll elect them from the shop floor," it all seemed appealingly democratic, but Porter saw that it was a device to block the resurgence of the prewar unions. The longer Wolf and Wheeler could do that, the longer the Soviets would have to put their people in and prepare the takeover of the labor movement in the American zone. Porter wrote in his diary: "It is clear that he [Wolf] is pursuing what he regards to be the Communist line and is actively supported by Wheeler. They are fiercely determined to freeze out all the former leadership of the German trade unions."

Wiesner and Porter objected, but Keenan bought the "from the bottom up" explanation. Rutz wrote Lovestone: "Joe Keenan was the Communists' best friend. . . . McSherry could say he was influenced by Keenan and not by [the Communists] . . . who crowded the room and who were voluble in their denunciation of the non-Communist trade union leaders." McSherry decided to dissolve all unions that had already been approved by Rutz, a labor officer for the Twelfth Army Group.

Soon after this meeting Porter left for his new job in London, convinced that Wolf and Wheeler were "consistently and knowingly pursuing a policy designed to assist the Soviet Union to control the trade unions of all of Germany." Why the implacable hostility to the Social

Democrats, who had been Hitler's foes, suppressed and imprisoned and killed? Because their return would spoil the Soviet game. By August 1945, when unions in the American zone were still banned except for the election of shop stewards, the Soviet-zone federation, the FDGB (Freie Deutsche Gewerkschaftsbund), had a million members under strict Communist discipline.

Also in August, Keenan was brought back to Washington for consultations, and Lovestone explained to him the correct AFL position: "The FTUC is in favor of giving former German trade unionists an opportunity to resume their work in the trade union movement without any hindrance. We also favor the immediate return of the properties confiscated by Hitler to the trade unionists." When Keenan returned to Germany, he was no longer "go slow" or "no meetings." He was "full speed ahead."

By August 1945 the Manpower Division had moved to Berlin, to the Group Control Council headquarters on Kronprinzen Allee. Rusting tanks blocked the streets, and the walls were pockmarked from small-arms fire. The tail fins of unexploded incendiary bombs protruded from the asphalt. At the officers' mess on Hittoffstrasse, the men from Manpower could drown their cares with the bartenders' Atomic Special (Scotch and champagne).

Two newly arrived officers in the Manpower Division—Maj. Alfred Bingham, labor officer for the province of Württemberg-Baden and son of the Connecticut senator Hiram Bingham, and Newman Jeffrey, who came out of the Reuther wing of the United Auto Workers—were in open defiance of the Wheeler-Wolf camp. In Stuttgart, Major Bingham ignored the shop-steward order and recognized a trade union league. Giving in to protests from the anti-Wolf-Wheeler camp, General McSherry made Jeffrey chief of the Labor Relations Branch but kept Wolf on as special assistant. Jeffrey fought the shop-steward system and started organizing unions on the committee level. Like Porter before him, he believed that Wolf and Wheeler were trying to fragment the American zone unions so that the Soviet federation could take them over.

Wheeler and Wolf lobbied McSherry to get rid of the troublesome Jeffrey. When Jeffrey came down with hepatitis in September, McSherry took advantage of his illness to dismiss him and reinstated Wolf as chief of Labor Relations. Irving Brown got wind of the "German mess" and reported to Lovestone on "Newman Jeffrey's weird story on how the German situation is being bitched up by the dear comrades and how Hillman is the evil genius behind the whole works. Boy, if the AFL would stand up on this German situation and shriek to the high heavens they would not only topple Mr. Hillman but would influence the entire European picture."

Back in the States, Jeffrey reported to Lovestone that "the labor policy in the U.S. zone is being formulated by a group of Communists and fellow travelers in the army and civilian administration who are close to General McSherry [and who are] working with the KPD [German Communist Party] with the deliberate purpose of creating utter chaos and confusion in the American zone so that the German Communists can take over at an opportune time."

In October 1945, Wheeler left for Washington to appear before the Civil Service Commission Rating Board on his appeal after being declared ineligible for government employment because "Mr. Wheeler has followed the Communist line from before 1939." His savior at the hearing was David Morse, who had been head of the Manpower Division in London in early 1945 but was called back to Washington to take a high-ranking job with the Department of Labor. A protégé of Sidney Hillman, whose support he needed for the job he wanted as general counsel of the National Labor Relations Board, Morse came to Wheeler's rescue on orders from Hillman.

Appearing on the first day of the hearing, October 29, Morse testified that Wheeler's loyalty was "excellent and superb." If someone were to tell him that Wheeler was a Communist, Morse said, his reaction would be "one of absolute disbelief." When the hearing was over, the head of the rating board wrote Morse: "Based primarily on your testimony, the commission has concluded that Mr. Wheeler is suitable for federal employment."

Lovestone, who closely followed Wheeler's hearing, was horrified to see him cleared and on his way back to Germany to do more damage; he called Morse "a corkscrew on two legs." Back in the Manpower Division, Wheeler hounded the labor officers in all three provinces, particularly Major Bingham, for encouraging a "trade union league" rather than shop committees, but Bingham told him to "go jump in the lake." Wheeler also fought against measures that would have helped displaced persons from Central Europe, saying that DPs who refused to go back to Poland or Czechoslovakia were criminals afraid to face trial. "We are still in the Wheeler era at Manpower," Bingham wrote Lovestone, who put the pressure on General Clay, via the Defense and State Departments, to have Wheeler removed.

As Clay later described the situation to his biographer, Jean Edward Smith, "We had a fellow who had belonged to some book club or other back in Washington during the war who was supposedly a security risk." Clay called Wheeler in and said that because of all the flap he had to go. Wheeler said, "General, what do I have to do to prove myself a good citizen? I went into the Army. I got a battlefield promotion to captain. I think I performed my duties satisfactorily. Is this going to plague me all my life?" Clay said: "You've convinced me, and you're going to stay." Clay went on, "And that day when I told him it would be all right, he brought his wife and two young children to see me—charming little children—just to say thank you."

But the pressure from Washington did not let up, and "the cables back and forth got hot and heavy," Clay said. Then, in the spring of 1947, about six weeks after the visit from Wheeler's children, Clay got a telephone call from Ambassador Laurence A. Steinhardt in Czechoslovakia. "A fellow called Wheeler is in Prague consorting with all the Communist leaders," he said. "Do you know anything about it?" "Yes, I'm afraid I do," Clay said. "He went on a weekend leave and has not returned. He's a couple of days overdue."

That same day Wheeler called a press conference and said he was seeking political asylum and taking a job in a Communist indoctrination school. Clay was stunned. He had gone out on a limb for Wheeler—"I practically had to say, 'If he goes I go'"—and now Wheeler had defected with his entire family to a Communist satellite.

Lovestone, who was behind much of the pressure on Wheeler, informed Woll on April 8: "Wheeler, who was cleared by Morse, is now an instructor at the technical high school in Prague. He has been welcomed by the new Communist government of Czechoslovakia." Lovestone knew that Wheeler had while under surveillance by G-2 been observed in meetings with the East German leader Walter Ulbricht.

From time to time Wheeler's activities made the wire services. He turned up on November 24, 1950, on a lecture tour, at Bratislava University. His wife, Eleanor, spoke first and said she was glad their four children were being educated in the wonderful Czechoslovakian school system and were able to listen to the Czech radio, "because of its truthful news service." Wheeler was introduced as "an eminent economic expert." He said that U.S. imperialists were motivated in their warmongering by their hatred of Socialism and by their greed, which found outlets in the enormous profits from rearmament programs. "We are glad to disassociate ourselves from this policy and work for the camp of peace," he said.

After the Soviet invasion of Czechoslovakia in 1968, Wheeler left "the camp of peace" and came back to the United States. He got a teaching job at a university in his home state of Washington, with the help of his old friend Lucius Clay, who gave him a letter of recommendation. In 1990 Wheeler, ninety and ailing, returned to Czechoslovakia, where several of his children had stayed and could take care of him. He is there today.

Having dispensed with Wheeler, we can return to the situation in the Manpower Division in the fall of 1945. By the end of October, the Wolf-Wheeler policy was at full throttle, and shop stewards had been elected in three thousand plants in the U.S. zone. In Stuttgart, however, Major Bingham had gone ahead with his trade union league, which now had one hundred thousand members.

At the November 1945 meeting of labor officers in Heidelberg, the officers in the field, led by Rutz and Bingham, said they were already working with prewar labor leaders and that unions were functioning on an unofficial basis, in accord with the Potsdam declaration, which stated that "the formation of free trade unions in Germany shall be permitted." There was now a noticeable shift in the balance of power away from the Wheeler-Wolf camp, for McSherry was having second thoughts about their pro-Soviet agenda.

The Wheeler-Wolf forces fought one final battle. In December 1945, Wheeler sent Captain Gould to Stuttgart to break into Major Bingham's office while Bingham was in Berlin. Gould copied some of Bingham's files, which showed that he had made a deal with the Social Democrats to exclude the Communists from their labor league. Wheeler demanded that McSherry court-martial Bingham for "violating political neutrality and working for the exclusion of a group which furnished the lead in Germany's resistance movement." Instead, McSherry gently chided Bingham for not following the guidelines.

Seeing that his game plan had been repudiated, Wolf quit in January 1946, but not without a parting shot. In a self-serving memo to Gen. John Hilldring, the director of Civil Affairs in the War Department, Wolf named Bingham, Jeffrey, and Porter as "saboteurs . . . a small but strategically placed group of American officials who would not accept the non-political approach. . . . In a whispering campaign during and after the Heidelberg meeting, they characterized the [shop steward] process as a plot to assure Communist domination of the German labor movement. . . . These men were motivated by a violent anti-Soviet bias and conceived of Germany's future as dependent upon a split of the allies."

Rutz informed Lovestone on January 16: "Wolf has resigned. Joe Gould and several other Commies are gone too. . . . The American Communists in the Manpower Division overplayed their hand in attempting to remove Major Alfred Bingham."

During three weeks in January and February 1946, Irving Brown visited 159 German labor leaders in the British and U.S. zones. He wrote Lovestone that it had been "the most intense three weeks of my entire life . . . a mean dirty business . . . the pro-Communist group was greatly aided by none other than Sidney Hillman, who carried considerable weight with General McSherry. . . . Hillman was motivated by an emotional anti-German feeling and a deep-seated antagonism to the German labor movement, blaming them as much as any other section of German society."

On January 6, 1946, Lovestone wrote Brown that "the fight against Hillmanism in Europe must be made by the AFL." In the wake of Wolf's departure, McSherry was replaced. Brown had described him as "an overgrown boy and a fool." On February 23, Bingham wrote Lovestone from Stuttgart: "I had completely lost McSherry's confidence, but now I hear he's gone home. The influence of the Wolf crowd is almost gone, though they have moved over into OSS and dominate its labor relations there."

Wheeler hung on until his defection in 1947, but he no longer had any influence and complained in his pamphlet "Who Split Germany?" that "the staff meetings became a disgusting contest of ideas on 'how to fight the Ruskys.' . . . The labor officers going to four-power negotiations in Berlin would say: 'I'm off to fight the goddamned Ruskys.' "

At the start of 1946 Lovestone had a moment of what the foreign service fellows call guarded optimism. The American people seemed to be waking up. The clash over Iran, the pernicious situation in France, the forced merger of Socialists and Communists in the Soviet zone of Germany, the terrible depredations in Manchuria, the puppet regimes in Eastern Europe, all these indicators were alarming enough that there was no danger of isolationism in the old sense of paralyzing American initiative. Lovestone felt so lighthearted that he took the wife of his old friend Gen. Mark Clark to see Judy Holliday in the Broadway comedy *Born Yesterday*.

General Clark, the Allied commander in Italy, was now military governor of Austria and wrote Lovestone that he had been to Moscow and had dinner with Stalin and the whole Politburo. He looked around the room and thought: "Individuals will come and go, but more ruthless ones are echeloned in great depth to take their places." Lovestone felt that Clark in Austria was doing a better job than Clay in Germany, for Clark was both hated and respected by the Russians, while Clay still believed, in his own words, that "we can get to know them and they can get to know us."

For Lovestone, a strong trizonal and nondenominational labor federation (rather than a return to the prewar pattern of unions along religious lines) was the best defense against the western zones of Germany becoming a Soviet satellite. Now that Rutz, Porter, and the others had spearheaded the removal of the Wheeler-Wolf group, Lovestone and his people focused on enlisting the cooperation of General Clay in helping the non-Communist labor leaders.

There seemed to be a basic mistrust between the military and labor. Clay himself began to appear antilabor to Rutz and Brown as he blocked request after request. He saw no reason to give priority to the return of union property or bank accounts that had been seized by the Nazis in 1933. On the issue of scarce newsprint for labor papers, Clay promised to help but did not deliver. "Today in Germany," Lovestone griped, "magazines devoted to beauty culture and manicuring get a bigger proportion of paper than labor organs."

Brown warned Lovestone in February 1946 that "the Russians are moving with seven-league boots in Germany." To put pressure on Clay, George Meany went to see Secretary of State James F. Byrnes in March. It was Lovestone's job to dovetail the efforts of his men in the field and the AFL lobbying in Washington, where Meany and Woll had entrée to the top officials. Although removed from the action in Germany, Lovestone was the one who kept the threads together. It was a Tinker to Evers to Chance operation. A cable from Rutz to Lovestone led to a meeting between Meany and Byrnes or Woll and Defense Secretary Forrestal, which led to a cable to Clay from the Department of State or Defense. In this way, for instance, Lovestone was able to stop the dismantling of a ball-bearing plant. And on March 20, 1946, the State Department announced that "military government should permit proven anti-Nazis to organize primary trade unions" within the American zone as a whole. Brown reported to Lovestone on April 10 that the unions had begun to merge on a zonal basis, but "as usual the Russians are way ahead of us. The FDGB [Soviet-zone federation] is now beginning to seek the adherence of trade unions outside the Russian zone. The Russians have prepared an apparatus to take over Germany if and when the country is given a central government."

It was a victory for Lovestone and the AFL when on April 12, 1946, the zonewide conference took place in Frankfurt. Some of the labor leaders, in prison or in hiding until 1945, had not seen each other since 1933.

This meeting established thirteen unions and led to the eventual formation of the DGB (Deutsche Gewerkschaftsbund, or West German Labor Federation). The unions, however, still did not have permission to organize outside the American zone.

In October 1946, Henry Rutz was demobilized, but he remained in Germany as the AFL representative at forty-five hundred dollars a year, paid by Lovestone's Free Trade Union Committee. He had an office in Stuttgart, and Clay, as a gesture of goodwill, gave him a Volkswagen. In January 1947 the British and Americans formed Bi-zonia, a first move toward a West German republic and a shield against the Soviets. In February there was a bizonal union convention.

Pressing the demands of the German unions, Rutz saw Clay weekly and weekly made his case. Clay was always polite, but nothing was done. Rutz had the distinct impression that the West Point graduate and southern aristocrat was at bottom antilabor. Louis Wiesner, who after leaving Germany wrote a paper for the CIA on the occupation that remained classified top secret until only a few years ago, observed that "General Clay refused to acknowledge the real extent of the Communist menace during those desperately miserable years from 1946 to 1948 . . . and could not bring himself to give real aid to the non-Communist left in Germany."

It was left to Kurt Schumacher, the valiant leader of the Social Democrats, to mobilize not only his party but all the Germans in the western zones against the Communists. Lovestone's FTUC earmarked ten thousand dollars for Schumacher's party in April 1947 so that they could buy office equipment.

In early 1947 President Truman announced that he would oppose Communist probes wherever possible. Greece and Turkey were possible. China was not. Then in June came the Marshall Plan and Stalin's refusal to join, in the name of the Soviet Union and its satellites, which certified the division of Germany. After June 1947 it was only a matter of time before Bi-zonia became Tri-zonia and Tri-zonia became a federal republic.

In April 1947 the DGB was founded at a convention in Bielefeld, with 370 delegates representing thirteen American-zone unions. Membership had soared from 378,000 in January 1946 to 1,087,000 in January 1947.

In the fall of 1947, Lovestone asked Rutz to arrange for Schumacher to visit the 1947 AFL convention in San Francisco. To Lovestone, Schumacher was the outstanding hero of the German labor movement. Born in 1895, he had fought on the Russian front in 1914 and lost his right arm, which was amputated at the armpit. Before reaching the age of twenty he wore a prosthetic arm. Rising in the ranks of the Social Democrat Party, he became known, because of his aggressiveness, as "the man with one arm and a dozen elbows." Elected to the Reichstag in 1930, he was so outspokenly anti-Nazi that when Hitler came to power in 1933 he had Schumacher sent to Dachau. Released in 1943, Schumacher was a walking corpse, with an infected leg that eventually became gangrenous and had to be amputated.

In the fall of 1945, when the occupation authorities allowed the German parties to re-form, this Prussian Protestant with the gaunt frame and the jerky gestures, his face convulsed by nervous tics and his one valid hand fanning the air, took charge of the Social Democrats. When the party in the Soviet zone proposed unity, Schumacher said no. His flat refusal nipped the formation of a Communist-controlled unity party in the western zones. Lovestone firmly believed that Schumacher, more than any other individual, had kept the Soviets from advancing to the Atlantic. In 1947 he was the emblem of German opposition to Soviet expansion, the most prominent anti-Nazi in the western zone, and an ardent advocate of the Marshall Plan.

Lucius Clay and Robert Murphy, the head of the OMGUS political section, were in a dither over Schumacher's proposed visit and summoned Rutz in early September to express their misgivings. Why invite a political leader instead of a trade union leader, they asked, especially a radical who wanted to socialize the factories? Besides, the Communist press had launched a campaign of ridicule, telling the Social Democrats that this was their reward for having "become the lackeys of the AFL." The Communist paper in the Soviet zone reprinted an article from the *Manchester Guardian* describing Rutz as having "a powerful voice in German trade union policy as well as in the policy of OMGUS." Rutz replied that Schumacher had done more to stop Communism in Germany than any other individual. Clay and Murphy grudgingly cleared Schumacher's trip but warned Rutz that he would soon be seeing articles in the Communist-controlled press saying that the Social Democrats would do anything for their monthly CARE packages.

In fact, Schumacher's trip created a sensation in the western zones. It seemed phenomenal to the Germans that one of their political leaders was invited to an important American labor convention little more than two years after the end of the war, when they were still in history's doghouse. The visit made the Social Democrats more palatable to the American occupiers, and it gave Schumacher greater authority within his own party. In Washington, escorted everywhere by Lovestone, he saw J. Edgar

Hoover, Averell Harriman, then secretary of commerce, Defense Secretary Forrestal, and George Kennan, as well as half a dozen generals. He addressed a meeting of the National Security Council. In New York the leaders of the Jewish Labor Committee saw that this rigid and touchy Prussian was not an odious Nazi but a brave survivor of the camps. David Dubinsky, who had vowed never again to shake the hand of a German, embraced him.

At the AFL convention in early October, Schumacher warned that "Communist totalitarianism is now attempting to conquer the European continent. . . . The conquest of Germany would be the gravest menace to the peace of the world." Lovestone could not have agreed more heartily.

Schumacher told Lovestone: "There is no longer any difference between right and left in the old sense of the word. The only difference is between the right of the Elbe [the dividing line between East and West Germany] and the left of the Elbe." Lovestone thought that was the most profound evaluation he had heard of the period through which they were struggling. At a dinner in Washington, Schumacher and Lovestone sat with Kennan, with whom Jay clashed for disapproving of Schumacher's criticism of the German Catholics and their leader, the ex-mayor of Cologne, Konrad Adenauer. That was all beside the point, Lovestone said. What mattered was opposing the Soviets. Lovestone told Schumacher that Kennan was a "neurotic."

In November 1948, Schumacher's left leg was amputated. In 1949 Adenauer was elected chancellor of the German Federal Republic as the leader of the Christian Democrat coalition; he was seen as the "reasonable German" by comparison with Schumacher's "rabid nationalism." Schumacher sought German unification as fervently as he might have wished for the return of his lost limbs. He was suspended from the Reichstag for six months for calling Adenauer "the chancellor of the Allies" and was frowned on by the State Department for his opposition to West German rearmament.

In December 1951, Schumacher suffered a stroke. Lovestone urged him to come to the Mayo Clinic for treatment, but Schumacher replied that he could not accept because people would say he had sold out to the Americans to improve his health. Lovestone wrote Schumacher on January 9, 1952, that "too many of our enemies would welcome your being incapacitated at this moment . . . but they will be deeply disappointed." This time he was wrong. Schumacher's death on August 20, 1952, at the age of fifty-seven, ended his long struggle with physical and psychic pain.

One of the by-products of Schumacher's 1947 visit to the United

States was that Lovestone met James Forrestal, who was as keenly attuned to the Soviet menace as he was. Lovestone wrote Forrestal on October 28 that he wanted to show him some of the work he was doing with an underground network in the Soviet zone of Germany. Lovestone had an agent who handled workers in the German inland navigation system and who moved in and out of East Germany, providing information on conditions in the Soviet zone. The agent also distributed pamphlets on the order of "Germany Under the Hammer and Sickle." This was all part of the struggle against Soviet expansion in Germany and the rest of Europe.

In November 1947, Lovestone sent Meany and Woll a confidential report on the Free Trade Union Committee: "Our trade union programs," he said, "have penetrated every country of Europe. We have become, however, an army which is about a thousand miles from its supply bases. . . . The AFL has become a world force in the conflict with world Communism in every field affecting international labor . . . those in the Communist camp single out the AFL as the main target."

In Germany, however, General Clay's efforts to restore the property of German unions and provide them with newsprint progressed at a snail's pace. In February 1948, Lovestone appealed to his new friend the secretary of defense. Forrestal wrote Clay asking for a report on the paper shortage, with the result that the allocation for the unions was doubled. Clay stated that "the pleas for paper for trade unions have by no means been disregarded." Rutz informed Lovestone on March 3 that "this is a lot of nonsense" but that as a result of his prodding, "the unions not only have more paper but have received a new allocation of German automobiles."

In July 1948 came the first major crisis of the Cold War, with the Soviet blockade of Berlin. The tension was such that Clay came down with lumbago and could not move his neck. But in the end he scored a tremendous victory with the airlift, for Stalin backed down and the blockade was lifted in May 1949. "If we had withdrawn from Berlin," Clay later said, "I don't think we could have stayed in Europe. I doubt if there would have been a Marshall Plan."

Lovestone went to Berlin in August 1948, in the midst of the blockade, with David Dubinsky, to show AFL support for the anti-Communist union there. They flew from Frankfurt through the Russian air corridor, where their cargo plane was buzzed by Soviet fighters, and landed at Tempelhof. They met with eighteen Berlin trade unionists, who had among them 130 years in concentration camps. It was clear to Lovestone that the Russians were doing all they could to impose indignities and humiliations on the Berliners. At 9:00 P.M. they shut off the electric power, and the streets, lined with rubble and nightmarishly twisted steel girders, were plunged into darkness. The next morning Dubinsky and Lovestone were scheduled to fly back to Frankfurt at 6:30, but because of the blockade-busters' heavy traffic—a food-laden plane landing every eight minutes—there was no runway clear for takeoff until 11:30. Were it not for the airlift, as Lovestone reported, the Berliners would have starved to death.

In their first meeting with Clay, Lovestone and Dubinsky pleaded for the restoration of trade union property. Clay promised to speed up the process but said the unions were not vigorous enough in promoting their interests. But Willi Richter of the Hesse Federation of Labor told Lovestone that for Clay unions were a necessary evil. Clay was all on the side of the employers and big business, Richter said. The pro-Nazi trust magnates were coming back into the saddle. In Washington, Lovestone urged Undersecretary of the Army William H. Draper to "stop the improvisation" and "give the German unions all the property and all the assets stolen by the Nazis."

To Henry Rutz, having Clay become the hero of the Berlin blockade was a mixed blessing, as he reported to Lovestone and Meany: "Because everybody from the president on down has praised the general, he feels safe from criticism in his attempt to curb the powers of German labor." Clay was giving the unions the same paper allocation as the bee culture clubs and interior decorating weeklies. The "same treatment" principle had the effect of denying the unions their rightful role in reshaping Germany, Rutz said. Another reason for this hardening of Clay's bias, Rutz felt sure, was that "the general has been noting for the last half year that his commander in chief, President Truman, will probably not be his boss after the November elections and has changed his policy accordingly."

When Truman won in November 1948, with a hand up from the labor vote, Rutz was overjoyed though he reported that "my job will not be an easy one as long as General Clay and his antilabor advisers set German policies." Lovestone too was pleased at Truman's victory, having been shocked by Henry Wallace's third-party campaign. The Communist Party and all its stooges, agents, and termites, it seemed to Jay, were working overtime to put over Wallace in order to ensure the election of Robert A. Taft. The Communist strategy, according to Lovestone, was to engineer the election of a reactionary and isolationist president, which would facilitate the Soviet takeover of Western Europe. But Tom Dewey won the Republican nomination, Wallace faded, and Truman was reelected.

Back in Germany it seemed to Rutz that he was getting nowhere. He railed against Clay's "reactionary southern concept of 110 percent Americanism." Clay even had Army intelligence tapping the phones of veteran union leaders like Willi Richter and Fritz Tarnow. In January 1949, when Leo Werts, McSherry's successor as head of the Manpower Division, questioned one of his rulings, Clay exploded: "I don't give a damn what organized labor thinks of me, either in Germany or in the States." But because of the airlift, Clay was the fair-haired boy.

Just as Clay was spying on the German labor leaders, Lovestone was spying on Clay. He had in Clay's office a labor man, John Meskimen, who was tipping him off on the cable traffic. In January 1949, Meskimen forwarded a cable—"the principal subject is socialization of industry and the whole tenor of it reminds one of a petulant schoolboy. State has not yet replied. Will give you the dope when it is received. This exchange of cables is classified TOP SECRET." After a while Meskimen got worried and wrote Jay: "There is always the possibility of my being picked up for improper handling of classified material. If that should happen I must have unqualified support."

In 1949 the AFL turned up the heat on Clay. Woll in January accused him of pampering the Nazis and treating the unions in a petty and slighting manner. On February 14, Woll wrote Clay: "We have been deeply worried that the policies of the American Military Government have been characterized by a discriminatory attitude toward labor."

Rutz finally urged Lovestone and Meany to cash in some chips by asking Truman for Clay's removal. But that turned out to be unnecessary, for Clay had already applied to go home. Dean Acheson had succeeded George Marshall as secretary of state and told an off-the-record press briefing in May 1949: "Our fundamental attitude is to go ahead with the establishment of a Western government [in Germany] come hell or high water." Better a divided Germany than a Germany under Soviet control. Clay himself finally agreed with the AFL view that the Soviets were responsible for splitting Germany after having tried to subvert the western zones with their phony union.

Clay's successor, John J. McCloy, a Wall Street lawyer known as the Chairman, arrived in Frankfurt on July 1, 1949, with the civilian title of high commissioner. Lovestone knew that McCloy was being called "a cartel appointee," but with his penchant for seeing leftist conspiracies, he told Rutz that McCloy "was the same person who in the army made a ruling that officers who were Communists should have access to confidential material. Those were the days of rampant appeasement to Stalin." In this case, Lovestone had it all wrong. As an aide to Henry Stimson in the

War Department in 1943, McCloy had enforced a ruling that veterans of the Abraham Lincoln Brigade should be allowed to have commissions. But he also ruled that if a man openly advertised his Communist Party affiliation, he should be removed from officers' training school and sent overseas to a combat unit.

Lovestone added that "McCloy was the architect of Potsdam, which gave Russia everything." This too was off the mark. As an aide to President Truman at Potsdam in July 1945, McCloy negotiated with the Russians on reparations, finding them "difficult and stubborn, but not impossible." Molotov finally agreed to the American proposal that each power should take its reparations from its own zone of occupation, which saved the Western zones from wholesale dismantling and reflected the military positions of the Allied armies on the ground. Sometimes Lovestone's anti-Soviet fixation clouded his judgment.

McCloy's first job was to substitute an occupation statute for the military government and to preside over the formation of a West German federal government. The zonal military commanders were now an Allied High Commission. In September, Konrad Adenauer was elected chancellor at the age of seventy-three. The Federal Republic was divided into eleven provinces. Berlin had eight delegates to the Bundestag, among them Willy Brandt. In October 1949 the Soviets established the German Democratic Republic, a Communist police state.

But the most satisfying development for the AFL was the first congress of the West German Trade Union Federation (DGB) in Munich in October 1949. This was what Rutz and Lovestone had fought for since 1945, a trizonal federation of free unions. Hans Boeckler, its first president, was the head of the DGB in the British zone, the largest of the three. At its first congress the DGB already had 5 million members. It was an independent, industrywide, nonconfessional (that is to say, nonreligious), and nonpolitical federation consisting of sixteen autonomous unions. The success achieved in Germany was unique; it could not be repeated in either France or Italy.

Henry Rutz stayed on in Germany until 1952, but to his eternal disappointment, after spending seven years building up a free union as a bulwark against the Soviets, he saw the Social Democrats and the DGB tilt to the left. The crucial role the AFL had played in the birth of the DGB did not ensure its loyalty. In 1951 there was an article in the DGB newspaper, which had first gotten its newsprint thanks to Rutz, about the dynamism of Walter Reuther and the CIO and the stagnation of George Meany and the AFL.

In later years, when the DGB under its new leader Ludwig Rosenberg broke ranks and sought rapprochement with East German and Soviet trade unions, Rutz would recall a letter from Rosenberg dating back to 1947, when he complained bitterly that he had not received his CARE package for the month while others had gotten theirs. "But what the hell," he told Lovestone, "we did not go into the business expecting thanks."

On balance, however, as Louis Wiesner concluded in his report for the CIA, "We won the cold war in Germany purely by political action, except of course the Berlin airlift. . . . Ours was a 'people's war' without weapons." Much of the credit for that victory belongs to Jay Lovestone, Henry Rutz, Irving Brown, Paul Porter, Alfred Bingham, Matthew Woll, and George Meany, who were the first to conclude that Soviet strategy was designed to take over all of Germany, and that the counterstrategy was to establish free German unions.

One of the unintended consequences of the Marshall Plan was the breakup of the World Federation of Trade Unions, where the CIO and the British TUC were held hostage, unable to prevent or tone down its pro-Soviet and anti–Marshall Plan line.

In Britain, the TUC leaders began to waver a few months before the first Marshall Plan shipments arrived. The American ambassador, Lewis W. Douglas, reported to the State Department on February 21, 1948: "Certain TUC leaders have been maneuvering to extricate TUC from WFTU and form a bona fide trade union international. . . . But they must move in such a way that any responsibility for the split would be fastened on the Communists."

Jim Carey, the CIO wishful thinker, was in Moscow from February 24 to 26 to try to get the Russians to soften their stance on the Marshall Plan. Lovestone saw Carey's trip as a fatal blunder. He had played right into the Soviets' hands. The CIO was contributing sixty thousand dollars a year to a "Communist espionage agency." Irving Brown wrote Lovestone on May 14 that "Carey joined hands with the Russians to continue this monstrous quisling outfit. . . . Once again he got sucked in by the Commies." Lovestone, who saw conspiracies everywhere, wrote Ray Murphy on May 18, 1948: "I still don't believe that Carey behaved the way he did without someone in the State Department giving him the green light."

On July 29 and 30, Lovestone was in London to attend the second labor congress of Marshall Plan nations, with forty-five delegates from sixteen countries. London was dreary; there was a yellow fog in the streets, and they hadn't yet fixed the broken windowpanes three years after the end of the war.

Herbert Weiner, recently arrived as an assistant labor attaché, was assigned to find the American delegates hotel rooms. Because of the hotel shortage in the bombed-out city, some of these labor prima donnas had to double up, and Weiner had to make sure that Irving Brown and Jim Carey would not be sharing a room. "Of all the big shots," he recalled, "Lovestone was the only one who came to my tiny office to thank me. 'Take it easy, young fellow,' he said, 'the planet isn't going to stop turning.'" Lovestone was planting the seed of friendship with a labor attaché. And Weiner became a devoted friend; he saw Lovestone as the *Weltmensch,* the man with the worldview, who had stood up to Stalin. But Weiner's wife complained, "Why are you immediately available to Jay? Why do you do everything he asks you to do?"

As secretary of the AFL delegation, Lovestone told the TUC leaders that they could not support the Marshall Plan and remain within the WFTU. It was recovery or chaos, freedom or slavery. A TUC man told Herb Weiner, "You Americans have never had a Communist problem, but we've been living with these people all our lives. George Bernard Shaw is on the board of directors of the *Daily Worker.* Is he a Communist?"

Sam Berger, the labor attaché, complained that privately the British condemned the WFTU but publicly they defended it. Vincent Tewson, the general secretary of the TUC, was "a most indecisive character and incapable of moving directly on any problem," Berger said. The July meeting was also Berger's introduction to Lovestone, with whom he would shortly become better acquainted in Washington. Lovestone impressed him as "a man who could be utterly unscrupulous, so that one had to be cautious and guarded in working with him even when pursuing the same ends."

Lovestone described his strategy as "bringing pressure on the TUC for a collision with the Communists with all due allowance for British sensitivities." At the Executive Bureau meeting of the WFTU in Paris that October, the British said they were ready to walk out but had to wait for the CIO, which remained undecided. Irving Brown warned that "the British are double-crossers and anything can still happen."

The showdown came at a meeting of the Executive Bureau in Paris on January 17, 1949. Tewson said they had arrived at an impasse. Arthur Deakin, a TUC leader who was close to Ernest Bevin, the British foreign minister, said the WFTU was pursuing the Cominform line and "must completely cease its activities." The Italian Communist Giuseppe Di Vittorio then denounced the Marshall Plan as "a political and military pact being used to enslave a certain number of countries to the world domination of capitalist interests." Deakin, a man of impressive size, beadlelike and ruby-nosed, rose in indignation and called Di Vittorio's remarks "repulsive to all those who give value to the truth." The British walked out, accompanied by the CIO and the Dutch federation. Carey said: "It is no use pretending the WFTU is anything but a corpse. Let us bury it."

No sooner was the break accomplished than the AFL called for an international federation of non-Communist trade unions as a riposte to the WFTU and its use of labor to advance Soviet aims and sabotage the Marshall Plan. By manipulating sympathetic unions in non-Communist countries, the WFTU had engineered a coup in Czechoslovakia, tied up Canadian ships in English ports, shut down the coal mines of France with strikes, and launched guerrilla wars in colonial areas. An alliance of free unions could do much to thwart such moves.

It all happened remarkably fast—a conference in May 1949 to explore the formation of the new body, and two more meetings in June and July. In London for the July meeting, Irving Brown warned Lovestone that the British "lack any conception or imagination for the job to be done. . . . Outside of the Americans, there is no drive or real world-wide conception of this fight against the Cominform." The AFL should not give up its independent foreign activities, Brown said, such as the Free Trade Union Committee.

In mid-November 1949, Lovestone attended a preparatory meeting for the founding congress, to be held from November 28 to December 6. He saw at once that the British were trying to run the show by insisting that the headquarters be in London. When Lovestone and Brown proposed five vice presidents, including William Green of the AFL and Philip Murray of the CIO, Deakin jumped up and said, "I am absolutely against the proposal by the Americans. Talk about American domination! I believe in being frank. I am against the American domination. We will have none of it." Brown said they had no interest in holding offices but reported that "the entire incident created a deep and disturbing impression."

On November 28, in London County's labyrinthine Municipal Hall, across the Thames from the Parliament building, the founding congress opened with 261 delegates from fifty-three nations representing 48 million workers. In this same egg-shaped hall four years before, the WFTU had been triumphantly hatched. The new organization was called the International Confederation of Free Trade Unions (ICFTU). J. H. Oldenbroek, the Dutch-born head of the Transport Workers Federation, who had spent the war years in England and was as pro-British as you could get, was named general secretary. The AFL did not take any committee chairmanships, to deflect charges of domination, but British press accounts saw the Americans' polychromatic neckties as swaggering symbols of their pushiness.

Lovestone reported back to his New York office on December 3, 1949, that "the conference drags on, colorless, dull, stodgy. . . . European labor is in bad shape. . . . We will *not* accept London as headquarters. That would put us in a mausoleum." Brussels finally carried the day.

Some of those who attended rubbed their eyes in disbelief as they saw Walter Reuther agreeing with Matthew Woll. How startling it was to find the AFL and the CIO acting in concert to put forth an American labor position. Lovestone, however, did not have much faith in the CIO's abilities and wrote Henry Rutz on December 7: "CIO activities in Europe are divided in two parts: (1) Whining lackeys of the WFTU until the break. (2) A lot of cheap hot air boasting about what they do. . . . The CIO might send one or two people to knock around the cafes of Europe, but that's all there is to it."

The founding of the ICFTU, however, was seen as momentous. *The New York Times* in a December 1949 editorial observed that it was "an event of historic importance, in many respects the most significant development in the struggle for a free world." The ICFTU set up shop in Brussels thanks to sixty-five thousand dollars of AFL seed money. High hopes were riding on it, but it soon deteriorated through bureaucratic infighting, a do-nothing attitude, poor leadership, and hushed-up scandals, so that the AFL and George Meany became disaffected and eventually pulled out.

Lovestone came to regard the ICFTU as a nest of worthless anti-AFL intriguers and with his factionalist mentality fought it no less vigorously than he fought world Communism and the CIO.

11

IRVING IN ORBIT

In Germany, where Hitler had destroyed the unions, which had to be rebuilt from their foundations, Lovestone's strategy had been to root out the Communist faction in OMGUS and promote free unions among the hidebound antilabor generals of the Allied occupation. In France and Italy, an altogether different strategy was required, for in each of those countries the postwar situation presented a powerful Communist-controlled labor federation, backed by a mass-based Communist party, capable of destabilizing the government on Moscow's orders.

The strategy here was an international version of what Lovestone had tried to accomplish with Homer Martin's autoworkers in the 1930s—that is, to split the non-Communist branch from the Communist tree. In Detroit he had failed, primarily because Martin had self-destructed, but in France and Italy he succeeded, largely because he was working in tandem with Irving Brown, whom a *Reader's Digest* article described as "an entire diplomatic corps and a one-man OSS." Together, they were able to create viable alternatives to the Communist unions.

Although backed by the AFL, they acted on their own, at first on a shoestring, without the permission of the governments involved, in what was surely one of the most astounding private initiatives of the Cold War. While Brown rushed from capital to capital with a borrowed typewriter, churning out reports and attending to a million and one details, Lovestone acted as the headquarters staff, in charge of strategy, funding, and logistics. Lovestone was in charge also of Brown's morale, worrying about his hay fever and telling him that the work was vastly more important than any irritation or disappointment he might feel. Brown had to plug away and not worry about other people's antics and pettiness, Jay told him. Together they were like infantrymen who have moved ahead of the tanks, fighting the battle single-handed while waiting for the rest of the army to catch up.

In France the great trade union federation the Confédération Générale du Travail (CGT) was under Communist control. Gen. Charles de Gaulle had returned from London to form a provisional government but soon realized that to try to govern without the Communists would mean civil war. In Moscow on November 30, 1944, George Dimitrov briefed Stalin, saying: "De Gaulle is afraid of the French Communists and considers their activity a threat to his authority, but he is obliged to take into consideration their power established during the clandestine struggle." But de Gaulle soon grew disgusted with the parties and "their games of yesteryear" and resigned on January 20, 1946. The British ambassador, Duff Cooper, reported: "It looks as though the Communists are having everything their own way. They have the great advantage of knowing what they want."

It was in this context that Irving Brown landed in Paris in mid-November 1945, staying at the California Hotel on the rue de Berri. In his first report to Lovestone on November 27, Brown said that thanks to their record in the resistance and their constant bragging about their "75,000 martyrs," the Communists now controlled two thirds of the CGT's 5 million members. The capture of the confederation would lead to the capture of all European labor, Brown opined with some hyperbole, which would create "a Communist Party–controlled Frankenstein." Léon Jouhaux, the grand old man of the CGT, who had been deported to Germany in 1943, returning in 1945 to find his federation in the hands of the Communists, was the outstanding figure still. Around Jouhaux were other anti-Communists like Robert Bothereau of the metalworkers, who wanted to form a group of their own but did not have the resources.

Brown decided that his best shot was to work with the Jouhaux-Bothereau group. He realized that it was no use dealing directly with the CGT—that would be like handing money over to the Communist Party. Instead he had to cooperate surreptitiously with the dissidents, who called themselves Force Ouvrière. They were going to try to wrest control of the CGT at the next convention. Brown knew that was a pipe dream, but he was willing to help, for their attempt would crystallize the opposition.

On December 5, 1945, Brown asked Lovestone for three thousand dollars to help Bothereau prepare for the April 1946 CGT convention. The Bothereau people did not want it known that they were getting AFL dollars, which would lay them open to Communist attacks, so the whole deal had to be handled secretly. "We may have a split in the next convention," Brown wrote Lovestone, "and to the extent that the non-CPers can be assured of real financial backing, their will to resist the Communist Party can be reinforced."

Seeing the chance to mastermind a split in the biggest Communist union in Europe, Brown decided to go for broke and asked for a hundred thousand dollars to implement his plan. "I know this is a huge sum," he said, "but this is a desperate situation." Here was a lone AFL envoy, without even an office or a secretary, who spoke kitchen French and did not have the permission of the French or the endorsement of the American government, undertaking the task of splitting France's largest union.

At a meeting of the FTUC in January 1946, Lovestone endorsed Brown's plan, saying that "France is the number-one country in Europe from the point of view of saving the Western labor movement from totalitarian control." Brown's staggering budget was approved.

Brown crisscrossed France, visiting a dozen CGT bastions and secretly recruiting anti-Communist delegates and uniting the opposition so it could go into the April convention with a fighting bloc. Somehow he got himself invited as a speaker at the CGT congress in the northern industrial city of Lille on February 23. When he realized that his translator was distorting what he said, he gave his speech in his "lousy, halting French—and nobody laughed."

Brown, whose assignment in France was open-ended, wrote Matthew Woll on March 22, 1946, that "I should like to stay in Europe . . . the situation has gotten into my blood and although I am lonesome for home and country—as the saying goes—I would very much like to see this thing to the end." He stayed for seventeen years.

At the April convention the Communists had a four-to-one majority. The delegates whooped it up for Moscow, with speeches praising Stalin and the Red Army. All the convention decisions solidified Communist control. The special voting rights of small unions were eliminated. The ban on CGT officials serving as officials of a political party was repealed so that the Communist leader Benoît Frachon could be secretary general of the CGT as well as on the Communist Party Politburo.

Brown reported to Lovestone: "The CGT has become so thoroughly a Stalinist organ that there are grave doubts about any internal reform." He was coming around to the notion of creating an anti-CGT union with Force Ouvrière. But the split had to be carefully prepared so that it could not be portrayed as helping the employers. It would take time, because Jouhaux continued to oppose the move on the ground of "sacred labor unity."

In October 1946 Frachon wised up to Brown's activities and attacked him in the Communist press as an emissary of "American reactionaries," behaving as if "France is a conquered country." Frachon promised that "we will see to it that he does not establish his office here." Soon Irving received a couple of anonymous phone calls suggesting that Paris was detrimental to his health.

He thought of Geneva, but the workaholic Lovestone told him Switzerland was a playground. He didn't want Irving to pull out of Paris because to do so would look as if he was caving in to Communist threats. In addition, Brown had found a powerful ally in the American ambassador, Jefferson Caffery. But now there was talk of removing Caffery, who had offended a couple of senators on a junket to Paris.

On February 17, 1947, in an effort to save Caffery, Brown wrote Lovestone: "Please impress upon the AFL through Woll and Green that they should take every opportunity to let the new secretary of state [George Marshall] know that they would look with disfavor on any change in the American embassy in Paris. This would be a disaster at this time . . . and a victory for the Russians." Marshall was alerted, and Caffery remained in Paris.

In March, however, the threats against Brown were renewed, and he decided to move his base to Brussels, where his wife, Lillie, and small son, Bobby (fondly known as "belly-button"), joined him. Lillie wrote Lovestone on March 29 that "belly-button is having a good time with all the waiters and *femmes de chambre* at the hotel in spite of his vocabulary, limited to *oui oui* and *gâteau*."

In early 1947 the FTUC approved another fifty thousand dollars for Brown's Force Ouvrière budget. Although he remained in New York, Lovestone cast the lengthened shadow of the master strategist, plotting the moves that would stalemate the Communist unions of Western Europe, finding the funds, and keeping his agents in the field on the right track. Jay was Irving's facilitator; he knew the people in Washington, their moods and attitudes.

Brown was fed up with Jouhaux, who remained opposed to a split.

"I'm off Jouhaux," he wrote Lovestone. "Anyone who relies on him to fight the CP or stand up to the Russians is nuts. Thank God there are still some others in the ranks who will some day break through this fuzzy myth of unity in the CGT." Lovestone replied that "Jouhaux wants to live his last days without any disturbances. Besides, his war experiences and Communist corruption have sapped his former strength of character."

But in spite of Jouhaux, Brown was astonished at their success, writing Lovestone: "Between you and me, Jay, I never realized we could go so far as we have in some of our relationships with Americans and Britishers in government circles. . . . It seems to me to be a fantastic situation . . . we are trying to run an international business on a five and ten cent store basis."

In May 1947 the French premier, Paul Ramadier, went against the conventional wisdom that no government could survive without Communist participation. He dismissed the four Communist ministers in his cabinet. From one day to the next, the Communist slogan went from "work, don't make demands" to "make demands, don't work." Such was the price of having the Communists outside the government.

Then in June the Marshall Plan made history. The Soviet Union was invited, though the Americans privately hoped they would not come in. Ernest Bevin, the British foreign minister, said on June 19 that his country would go ahead with or without the Soviet Union. On June 27, Bevin and Molotov conferred in Paris with the French foreign minister, Georges Bidault. On the evening of June 28, Caffery saw Bevin and Duff Cooper and said: "If the Communists get back into the government, France won't get a dollar from America." It was already clear to Caffery that the Soviets would not take part in the plan and that the French Communist Party would try to gum up the works. On July 3, Molotov angrily left Paris, saying that the plan would divide Europe into two blocs. "Things are popping," Brown reported to Lovestone on July 23, 1947. The Marshall Plan was prompting the split in labor that Brown had hoped for.

In September 1947, at the founding meeting in Poland of the Cominform (created as a successor to the Comintern and in retaliation for the Marshall Plan), the French Communists were charged with "parliamentary cretinism" for letting themselves get kicked out of the government. They were also told to launch a wave of major strikes to sabotage the Marshall Plan.

In November, Ambassador Caffery forwarded Brown's assessment of the strikes to the State Department. This was not a genuine labor dispute, Brown said, but a political insurrection. Robert Lovett, then acting secre-

tary of state, cabled Paris on November 29 to "extend such assistance to
Brown as you deem proper," including secret funds to assist Force Ouvrière. The State Department now saw Brown and Lovestone as capable
of breaking the Communists' hold over the French labor movement.

On December 3, Communist miners sabotaged seventy-five feet of
track and derailed the express train on the run from Paris to the northern
city of Tourcoing, killing sixteen passengers. The newsreel footage of
railroad cars split open with mangled corpses inside incensed public
opinion and strengthened the government's hand.

The Communist-orchestrated violence finally pushed the Force Ouvrière group out of the CGT. The old trade unionists, like Jouhaux,
frowned on political strikes as the "path to adventurism." The younger
ones, like the dour Bothereau and the miner André Lafond, were glad of
the chance to bolt. Brown nudged them along, telling the leaders they
could count on AFL support.

On December 18, 1947, 250 Force Ouvrière delegates attended a national conference in Paris and passed a resolution to begin without delay
the organization of a new federation. When the younger FO leaders resigned from the CGT, Jouhaux went along. Force Ouvrière was formed
as a reaction to the Soviet takeover of the CGT and its obedience to the
Cominform. The FO militants left their offices, their desks, their files,
and their typewriters to start a union that represented the workers and not
the foreign policy of the Soviet Union. Lovestone and Brown were the
ushers who had led them toward the exits.

Jouhaux saw Caffery on December 26 and said: "It would be helpful
if the Americans did not claim they caused the split from the CGT." Apparently, Brown was making intemperate announcements of paternity.
On January 7, 1948, an ebullient Caffery cabled Lovett that the split was
"potentially the most important political event since the liberation of
France." Lovett made available twenty-eight thousand dollars from State
Department funds, and Caffery sent to the FO headquarters a truckload
of secondhand typewriters.

Lovestone thought Brown was doing a heroic job, though he confided to Herb Weiner: "Irving is a great field commander, but not a great
strategist." In the CIO, Brown was known as "the scholar pumpernickel,"
after the Scarlet Pimpernel, for his derring-do.

From his cubbyhole in New York, Jay acknowledged that "Irving
does enough work to exhaust six ordinary men." He was one of the six,
and the doctor ordered him to take two months off, but Jay said: "That I
cannot do." He took two weeks, after which he was going back to work

no matter what the doctor said, unless someone with more final authority intervened.

He went to Palm Beach to see Esther Mendelssohn, who had an apartment there with Nathan but was alone because of Nathan's contretemps with Customs and Immigration. With Esther, Jay could revert to a more playful and relaxed self, far from major events, as can be seen from a photograph where he is carrying her on his back into the ocean. Esther at fifty-eight was still attractive, though her body was thickening and her face was lined.

Jay was at that time in the midst of a rather stormy affair with a waif-like, mercurial woman named Natalie Davies. Natalie had independent means but a dependent nature, made unhappy by Jay's inconsistent attentiveness. Born in Czechoslovakia, she had moved to England and married a wealthy man named Davies, by whom she had two sons and a daughter. Widowed, she came to America at the end of the war and became a social worker in the pediatric ward of Roosevelt Hospital while living on Sullivan Street in Greenwich Village. In the summer of 1947, when Jay was in Toronto with Matt Woll and they had adjoining rooms, Natalie wrote: "Wish I were sharing your few leisure hours in the room next to Matthew Woll in a double bed. Memories of kisses and hopes of more to come."

The affair continued over four years, though kisses were in short supply. Jay told Natalie he was forced to be a workaholic because of the insecurity of his job. She replied: "I have now and always had enough money for any need we two might ever have, therefore the financial security of your job is necessary only for ego satisfaction. . . . However I do feel a burden to you emotionally in your important work."

Natalie oscillated between adoration and resentment. One day she wrote, "[I am] casting myself at your feet and on your mercy darling. I love you and so dare." The next she was "resenting having to compete with your job for your attention." She was seeing a therapist to help her analyze her moods and smoking too much and her nerves were in bad shape. "I am still infantile," she wrote Jay, "and need constant physical reminding of not being abandoned."

If such was the case, she made a poor choice of lover, for Jay was as undependable with women as he was dependable in his work. Natalie wrote: "I will be around when you want me between times and on ice the rest of the time. . . . Sometimes the bitterness wells up inside me . . . with weeks of sexual abstention I get insomnia. . . . I get cross and unhappy. . . . I must feel someone cares for me and only their physical presence keeps that feeling alive. . . . If you deeply desired me you could leave your job to be with me. . . . Failure! Failure! Failure!"

She finally realized, as other women had, that Lovestone was a lost cause. The temperature of her letters dropped: "I know you are busy with your work so I have made plans," she wrote. She complained that she never knew what alias he was using, so she could not get him on the phone when he was traveling. Soon her letters ended with "fondly" rather than "love," and one day she stopped writing and Lovestone became a memory. To him, she had been "kiddo," not to be taken seriously.

Early in 1948 Brown's work in France won recognition from the Soviet trade union paper *Trud,* which showed him in a cartoon wearing a business suit and carrying a large dollar checkbook in his coat pocket. He was depicted in a long article as an intelligence agent and a corrupter of labor. The American embassy in Moscow commented in a confidential report: "This is a further indication that the Soviets consider Brown a serious threat to their own operations in the European labor field."

Lovestone's job now was to get European labor behind the Marshall Plan. In Washington that April, he met with Paul Hoffman, the onetime chairman of Studebaker who was now running Marshall Plan operations, to tell him that he was the principal target of European Communists, since he was the head and face of the plan. The Communists were charging that big business was behind the European Recovery Program. For God's sake, Lovestone fumed, didn't they know that American labor was producing the goods to send abroad? Not even in the United States did tractors grow on trees. Lovestone wanted Hoffman to confirm that while head of Studebaker he had opened his books to the UAW during a business slump and the union had given him a loan to tide him over his difficulties. The story would help the AFL sell the Marshall Plan in Europe.

Lovestone was in a state of barely controlled fury over the February 1948 coup in Czechoslovakia, engineered with the help of the Communist-led unions and their so-called action committees. The probable suicide of the Czech foreign minister, Jan Masaryk, whose pajama-clad body was found on the pavement below an open window of his apartment, seemed to underline the hopelessness in Eastern Europe, where the Red Army imposed its will by force. Lovestone went to the State Department to advise Ray Murphy that, according to his sources in the exile community, the Czech Ministry of Education had sent an agent to New York who was threatening Czech exchange students at Columbia and other universities that if they did not come home, harm would come to their families. "How long must this lady stay in our country?" Lovestone asked. She was supported, he said, by the noted founder of structural linguistics, Roman Jakobson, who, ironically enough, occupied the Masaryk chair of Slavonic languages at Columbia. Should not Dwight Eisenhower, the president of Columbia, be informed of this financing by the Communist Czech regime of a chair that was filled by a man who had for years served as press attaché at the Soviet embassy in Prague? Lovestone also thanked Murphy for obtaining a visa for the German trade union leader Markus Schleicher. "With your help," he said, "our oxcart sometimes works like a sixteen-cylinder car." Lovestone wanted Murphy to find out why Hoffman had a CIO man as labor adviser in his Washington office. He did not like this "monkey business." Ray Murphy, Lovestone's staunch ally, was always on call.

There was also, as Lovestone informed Brown on April 6, a positive side to the Czech coup, in that it helped speed up Marshall Plan approval in Congress: "The ERP program has been enacted into law much faster and with a bigger majority than anyone expected." Soon Marshall Plan goods began arriving in French harbors and the Communist strategy switched to disrupting the unloading on the docks, where the CGT unions were under Communist control.

In May, Brown reported that "we are now working very hard to break the hold of the Communist Party in the ports and docks. If we can lick them there we can prevent the sabotage of the successful application of the ERP." The Communists succeeded at first in slowing down the flow of goods. At Dunkirk things got so bad that shipments had to be rerouted through the Belgian port of Antwerp. The Communists ran the hiring halls and froze out non-Communist longshoremen. Employers did not object as long as they got the work done.

To counter the Communist influence, Brown turned to a veteran union leader of the Marseilles docks, Pierre Ferri-Pisani. Born in 1901 of Corsican parents, Ferri-Pisani was a legendary figure in Marseilles, part hoodlum and part Renaissance man. He wrote poetry and had an encyclopedic knowledge of history, as well as a flair for mathematics. But being a son of Marseilles, which was gang-ridden and violent, he adapted to his environment. Ferri-Pisani grew up on the docks and signed on as a merchant seaman, becoming general secretary of the CGT Seamen's Union in the twenties, long before the CGT was Communist. During World War II, Ferri-Pisani started an underground seamen's union. In 1943 he was arrested and sent first to Buchenwald and then to the salt mines of Hadmersleben. His wife was told that he was dead, but he returned, a living skeleton who took several years to get back what was left of his health.

Brown started funding the fiery Corsican in early 1948, and Ferri-

Pisani set up FO offices in the major ports, Bordeaux, Le Havre, and Cherbourg. When the Communists used strong-arm tactics to keep him off the docks, he responded in kind. "In 1948," Brown told Ben Rathbun, "Ferri-Pisani's people were being beaten up and then shoved in the harbor, or left on the docks with knives in their backs." In March 1948, Ferri-Pisani walked into the CGT waterfront headquarters in Marseilles and declared: "If your goons beat up any more of our stevedores, we will not do a thing to them. But we will break the skulls of a number of you gentlemen."

To Ferri-Pisani's Marseilles office, with the bronze bust of Napoleon on the desk and the complete works of Victor Hugo on the shelves, came many Corsicans with *casiers judiciaires* (criminal records), armed with blackjacks, knives, and guns. "No ERP would have a ghost of a chance in France," Brown wrote Lovestone, "if the Communist Party had been successful in closing the French ports and docks."

Jean Lapeyrade of the Bordeaux Dockers' Union wrote Lovestone on May 20: "The first Marshall Plan shipments arrived in Bordeaux and were unloaded by Force Ouvrière, in spite of Communist efforts at sabotage." Lovestone replied: "I was glad that you succeeded in checking their destructive work. . . . As soon as possible we will transmit more aid."

The Communist press called Ferri-Pisani a gangster in the pay of the Americans. His connection with Brown and Lovestone was ceaselessly proclaimed. Lovestone wrote him on February 12, 1951: "Let me congratulate you on your splendid victory in the port of Marseilles. The crushing defeat you imposed on the Communist saboteurs is an event of the greatest significance." The sad truth, however, was that Ferri-Pisani had never recovered from the camps, either mentally or physically. His health declined, and in 1961 he put a bullet in his brain at his home in Marseilles.

In July 1948, Lovestone came to Paris and found an exhausted Brown, his allergies in full bloom. Lillie too was worn out from serving as his secretary, and Bobby had the grippe. Irving was never too tired to talk, however, and gave Jay the rundown. There were leaks at the heart of the French government to the Communists, who had published some confidential memos from the papers of the former U.S. ambassador David Bruce. Brown's biggest worry was the return of de Gaulle, still the strongman of France, who had the army with him and could sweep the country. Taking stock, Irving told Jay that there was not a single country in Europe where the AFL did not have contacts, legal or illegal. He was working with underground groups in Prague and Berlin. "We have the basis for the finest labor network in Europe," he said, "but our lines are overextended."

Lovestone said he was glad to see that the Commies had taken a shellacking in the Paris Teachers' Union. Brown agreed that the problem with Force Ouvrière was Jouhaux, who was hesitant, weak, and nostalgic, and could never provide aggressive leadership against the Communists. In addition, Lovestone was furious with David Schoenbrun of CBS, who had reported that Brown was supposed to have $2 million. "I sure wish we had that much," he said. Brown wanted affidavits from the AFL to help some of the exiled Central Europeans he was handling get to the United States. "If God's first wife wanted to come," Jay said, "I couldn't get her an affidavit."

Back in New York in November 1948, Lovestone wrote Brown that he would vote for Truman "with one nostril closed." He would not have voted for Henry Wallace, he said, "unless my hands were tied and my eyes were shut and my head was off. . . . Truman is inept but he is not dishonest. He inherited a tough situation."

In France there was a new wave of strikes to sabotage the Marshall Plan. On November 21, Jules Moch, the minister of the interior, said in the National Assembly that the miners' strike had been ordered by the Cominform and the Soviet Union, which helped finance it. He stated that the Cominform had contributed more than 270 million francs (about $50 million) so far, distributed to the CGT by Czech and Polish nationals. David Bruce, chief of a special mission in Paris, told Paul Hoffman on November 23 in a secret cable that "both the Communist Party and the CGT have publicly declared their strong opposition to the Marshall Plan. . . . Their new tactic is the rolling strike, that is, the commencement of a strike in one key industry, and then the commencement of a strike in another key industry. The CGT will stop at nothing, and uses tactics of desperation and terror without regard to cost in order to defeat ECA aid."

Brown wrote Lovestone that "the Communist Party machinery is terrific and during the strike they were reinforced to the tune of 600 million francs from the trade unions of Russia and Eastern Europe as stated on the front page of *l'Humanité*." But Force Ouvrière stood fast as the leading anti-Communist union, with half a million members, and the CGT strikers went back to work.

As the year ended, Bill Donovan, who had met Lovestone through Ray Murphy, recommended him to Secretary of Defense Forrestal, who was looking for an adviser familiar with the methods of subversion and fifth columns. Lovestone, said Donovan, was "uniquely equipped for the task. . . . He is better informed on the subject of Communist theory as well as its activities than anyone I know. . . . He is a man of high and forceful character. His loyalty and devotion to his country is unquestioned." This was the same man that Donovan's OSS had turned down in 1943 on the grounds of vicious and unfounded rumors. Lovestone, however, was far too busy with his own activities to take the job, though he became a close friend of Donovan.

In 1949, Lovestone looked askance when Dean Acheson replaced George Marshall as secretary of state. Acheson was able, good-looking, and a real diplomat in appearance, he said, but some of his friends at State still thought Russia was a great experiment and a new type of democracy. Lovestone would have preferred Averell Harriman, but Truman had a way of doing things all his own, without listening to those who knew better. One of Lovestone's informants told him that in 1944 Donald Hiss, Alger's brother, had been made a partner in Acheson's law firm in the expectation that he would bring in the legal business connected to an $80 million loan to Poland, which he did.

Irving provided some comic relief by informing Jay that Marcel Cachin, the fourth-ranking French Communist, had hailed "Comrade Taft" (the right-wing Ohio senator) for his opposition to NATO. "We find his declarations virtuous, pertinent, and full of wisdom," Cachin was quoted as saying. So now "Mr. Republican," the cosigner of the antilabor Taft-Hartley legislation, was a hero to the French Communists.

In April 1950 the CIA, in a paper for President Truman, cited labor unrest, with the CGT promoting political strikes on orders from Moscow, as France's principal handicap. In 1951, Léon Jouhaux won the Nobel Peace Prize "for giving strength to the free labor forces that are helping to restore Europe." The prize went to his head, and he began to see himself as the leader of a Third Force, which could promote nonalignment in the midst of the Cold War. Brown turned against him, but in April 1954 Jouhaux died of a heart attack at the age of seventy-five, ending their dispute.

Force Ouvrière continued without Jouhaux under Bothereau and Lafond, but once again, as with the German unions, the AFL was unable to make it conform to its Cold War orthodoxy. The heresy in this case was that Force Ouvrière supported the Yugoslav unions in their bid to join the International Confederation of Free Trade Unions. Lovestone, acting as an anti-Communist political commissar, wrote Lafond on November 15, 1951, that the AFL "does not endorse the domestic regime of Tito, nor do we close our eyes, dull our minds, and forget the fact that what you have in Yugoslavia are not bona fide free trade unions but state company unions like the ones in Russia, Argentina, and Spain. I think Tito is impudent even to apply to the ICFTU for affiliation. . . . Frankly, Lafond, I felt very shocked by your approach and your false estimate of the Tito situation." As far as the FO was concerned, Tito had broken with Stalin, and his unions might be brought into the Western camp.

The dilemma was, as Lovestone would have to learn again and again, that you could assist free unions and fund free unions, but you could not control free unions. Once established, they went their own way. Even so, Lovestone remained the proud if sometimes disenchanted godfather of Force Ouvrière, writing George Meany from Paris on June 19, 1951, that "the prestige of the FO is great and has been rising, altho it does not translate itself into organizational growth. Those who leave the CGT are too disgusted to join others right away. At the same time the masses of workers will not join full force in any strike unless it has the approval of the FO." Lovestone claimed that in 1951, the Force Ouvrière had six hundred thousand dues-paying members, including not only white-collar workers but coal miners, railroad men, and workers in metal trades and docks and harbors.

Following its success in France, the Lovestone-Brown technique of splitting off a rival to a dominant Communist union was tried in Italy. The Communists in Italy, like those in France, had burst into prominence as a result of their resistance activities. From a small, underground party under Mussolini, they had grown into an open party of 2.5 million.

In June 1944 the Pact of Rome had created a federation of Italian workers (CGIL) representing the three main parties (Communists, Socialists, and Christian Democrats) as well as a number of smaller parties. The "membership card" tradition in Italy was that each union had strong links to a single party. The Communist program, in Italy as in France, was to take part in the government (which they did from April 1944 to May 1947) and to push for control of the CGIL, with the ultimate aim of making Italy a "People's Democracy."

The situation in Italy in 1945 was alarming. Adm. Ellery Stone, chief of the Allied Control Commission, sounded the warning bell when he wrote in June that Italy was "a fertile ground for the rapid growth of the seeds of an anarchical movement fostered by Moscow to bring Italy within the sphere of Russian influence."

In the November 1946 election, the Communists formed a voting bloc with the Socialists. The AFL strategy was to shore up the anti-Communist forces in the CGIL. Although tied up in France with Force Ouvrière, Irving Brown began working with the embassy in Rome to identify groups in the CGIL who might eventually split off. One likely candidate was the leader of the Catholic union, Giulio Pastore.

At the same time the State Department awoke to the need to become more active in Italy when Walter Dowling, the Italian desk officer, warned that food shortages and worker dissatisfaction would strengthen the left. "The wops do feel we have let them down," Dowling wrote in an influential memo in November 1946. Aid would show that the United States was "so god-damned pro-Italian that even the dumbest wop would get the drift." Dowling recommended as a first step that Italy's Christian Democrat premier, Alcide De Gasperi, be invited to the United States.

De Gasperi spent ten days in Washington and New York in January 1947, and Italy was awarded a $100 million Export-Import Bank loan. The main result of his visit, however, was that a high-level government committee recommended that the United States support Italy with economic and military aid to prevent a Communist takeover. This new interventionist policy fitted in with the Truman Doctrine, which involved the United States in Greece and Turkey and required a friendly Italy in the Mediterranean. As in France, the way to pressure Italy was to make American aid contingent on the removal of the Communists from the government.

From Rome, Ambassador James Dunn sent alarming reports that the Communists intended to paralyze the Italian government. On May 5, 1947, Dunn saw De Gasperi and told him that the price of American aid was expelling Communists from his governing coalition. De Gasperi resigned on May 12 and formed a minority government without the Communists.

Once the Communists were out of the government, they acted as a disloyal opposition. In the AFL leadership, as well as in the State Department, fears arose that the Communists would use the CGIL to take control of the country. But would the non-Communist unions follow? When the Communist leadership of the CGIL called for a general strike in Rome on December 11, the Catholic leader, Pastore, told his people to stay on the job. The Communists charged that he was doing the bidding of the Christian Democrat Party.

The Lovestone-Brown policy of splitting Communist-dominated unions now jibed with the U.S. foreign policy of supporting the democratic left in Italy, as enunciated by Secretary of State George Marshall. Brown reported to Lovestone in November 1947 that "trade union opposition [in Italy] is weak and is just beginning to develop. This situation is less favorable than the French one." But one man to watch, said Brown, was Pastore, a forty-five-year-old Piedmontese peasant with nine children and a stubborn hatred of Communism.

The Lovestone-Brown strategy for Italy in 1948 was to stimulate a split in the CGIL, where the non-Communist unions felt smothered under the weight of the Communists and their Socialist cohorts. The split became urgent when the Communist leader Giuseppe Di Vittorio declared that "participation in any Marshall Plan organization is incompatible with membership in the CGIL."

Also, Italy's crucial parliamentary elections were coming up on April 18, 1948. A Communist victory would be a serious loss of prestige for the United States and might trigger the collapse of democracy elsewhere in Europe. In January, when polls showed that the left was in the lead, millions of dollars were secretly funneled to the Christian Democrats. On March 9, Lovestone saw Ray Murphy and told him the Italian situation was desperate. Murphy sent fifty thousand dollars, which he had collected from private donors, to his old friend Ambassador Dunn. The CIA, created in 1947 and still in its infancy, earmarked $10 million to help fund covert campaign operations. When the smoke of battle lifted, De Gasperi had scored a stunning victory, with 48.5 percent of the vote. *The Economist* wrote: "America took off the gloves for the first time."

Irving Brown saw opportunity in the results. "They will have to repeat the French experience," he wrote Lovestone. "All those who are fighting Di Vittorio and his gang should be supported and aided to prepare for the eventual split." Brown looked for hopeful signs that the election had broken the unified CGIL labor front. He was glad to see that the Catholics in the CGIL did not join in the traditional May Day rally, which was pretty much a hammer-and-sickle affair.

In early June 1948, Lovestone and David Dubinsky came to Rome to prod the split along. The Socialist paper *Avanti* noted that "the American specialists in splits have arrived." The two "specialists" were granted an audience with Pope Pius XII in the Sistine Chapel. Lovestone was not overly awed, taking advantage of the opportunity to lecture the pope on the need for a united democratic trade union movement in Italy. "We are anti-Communists without any reservations or hesitations," he said. "The Communists seek only to exploit labor to disrupt social and economic functions and weaken other nations and strengthen Russia, whose venal tools they are." The perplexed pontiff could only reply: "But, Mr. Lovestone, I too am anti-Communist."

Lovestone's plan was to bring together the leaders of the three non-

Communist groups in the CGIL—the Catholic Christian Democrats, the centrist Republicans, and the Saragat Socialists or PSLI—and promise to fund them if they broke away as a unit. Dubinsky even went to Giuseppe Saragat's trade-union conference and displayed a ten-thousand-dollar letter of credit, which would be theirs if they went along.

On July 14, 1948, as the Communist boss Palmiro Togliatti walked down the steps of the National Assembly, a disturbed right-wing student shot and wounded him. The CGIL called a general strike. Fighting broke out in the streets, leaving 16 dead and 206 wounded. Pastore and his Catholic workers refused to join the strike. On July 24, Di Vittorio expelled the Catholics from the CGIL. They took about 800,000 members with them, but the failure of the Republicans and the Saragat Socialists to follow spoiled the prospect of a mighty nonconfessional free trade union federation.

Lovestone hoped that Pastore would have some company, but for the moment he stood alone. He and Brown were not overjoyed at having to back a Catholic union, but in Italy it was the Catholics or nothing, at least to begin with.

The State Department adopted the Lovestone-Brown plan, predicated on the pullout of the non-Communists from the CGIL and the establishment of a nonsectarian federation. Secretary Marshall wired Dunn that such a group might be found worthy of financial aid. Pastore gladly fell into the arms of the Americans, telling the labor attaché Tom Lane that he would need $1.5 million for operating expenses for the first nine months, which the State Department approved.

On October 16, 1948, with the promise of funding, Pastore created a rival federation, the Free Italian Confederation of Labor (LCGIL). He invited the Republicans and the Saragat Socialists with open arms to join him, but neither responded. Lane said they stayed in the Communist federation out of an "opportunistic desire to ride the fastest-moving and largest bandwagon." Another reason was their distrust of a Catholic-controlled union. Brown kept telling the Saragat people that he had "suitcases of money" for them if they agreed to leave the CGIL. But one of the Saragat Party leaders, Giuseppe Favarelli, said they were not about to become "sextons and bell-ringers for Pastore in a confessional organization . . . dominated by a clerical spirit that is no more compatible with us than the Bolshevik spirit."

A disgusted Lovestone told Brown that "as long as organizations stay the size of insects, they will multiply like insects. The Saragat Socialists are afraid of being raped by the College of Cardinals."

But even worse than the smell of the sacristy was the absence of money. Pastore was getting all the U.S. dollars. In 1949 Lane won a commitment from the Republicans and the Saragat Socialists that they would merge with Pastore by November. When and if they did, the Pastore federation membership would reach the million mark. Lovestone and Brown wanted a quick merger so that the Pastore federation could attend the founding meeting of the newly created ICFTU, at the end of November in London. If the Italians were represented, along with the German DGB and the Force Ouvrière, it would be the high-water mark of AFL strategy.

This was not to be, however, for after much wrangling, the Republicans and the Saragat Socialists left the Communist federation (CGIL) but only to form their own Italian Federation of Labor, or FIL. An exasperated Lovestone wrote Brown: "These fellows don't know the difference between an undertaker and a midwife." He was the midwife. As for Giuseppe Saragat, Lovestone said, "We have tried to put cement in his backbone but he prefers Rome sewage. . . . We all tried but there is an organic relationship between a hydrant and a dog. No matter how much you train the hydrant or teach the dog, you can't change it, you have to work with both animals as they are." Saragat was the dog and Lovestone the hydrant.

Brown also lost faith in the Italians, submerged in their petty political calculations. They failed to see the big picture of blocking the Soviets in Italy and supporting the Marshall Plan. On September 4, 1949, he wrote Lovestone that they would get "not another penny" until a firm agreement was reached.

Thanksgiving passed, and no merger was achieved. A nauseated Lovestone said he was ready to wash his hands of the situation and take the AFL out of the Italian labor mess. But in November, when Pastore went to the ICFTU conference, his LCGIL was admitted without being designated as a religious federation, and he was elected to the Executive Council. These developments greatly increased his prestige at home, and in December the Saragat Socialists and the Republicans, who made up the FIL, hopped on the Pastore bandwagon. On May Day 1950, in Rome's Adriana Theater, the merger was sealed with the birth of the Italian Federation of Trade Unions (CISL, or "sizzle" to the Americans). It had a membership of close to a million, 800,000 from Pastore's group and the rest from the two others.

It had been a long uphill road with many hairpin turns, but now the merger seemed like a brilliant success. The Communist hold on the Italian trade unions was broken, and most of the non-Communists were integrated into one federation. Brown visited various locals and reported approvingly that the CISL believed in collective bargaining rather than the class struggle.

The Marshall Plan wound up its affairs on December 30, 1951. It had lasted three years and nine months, with a staff of twenty-four hundred in Washington and twenty-five missions around the world. With the help of the AFL, the spread of Communism to Western Europe was checked, inasmuch as Stalin had been counting on the Communist-run labor federations in France and Italy to disturb and perhaps upset the status quo. Lovestone found himself countering "the fallacious approach" of those who argued that the Marshall Plan, while stimulating production, had made things worse for the workers of Europe in a number of countries by freezing wages.

In the final analysis the Brown-Lovestone-orchestrated splitting of the united-front unions in France and Italy, and the sponsorship of the German DGB against the wishes of the U.S. military government, contributed substantially to the political stabilization of Western Europe at a time when fear of a Communist takeover had to be taken seriously. Irving Brown found it hard to believe that a private labor group, the AFL, had succeeded in a sweeping foreign policy endeavor that in more normal times would have been the purview of government.

This may have been Lovestone's finest hour. From November 1945, when Irving Brown arrived in Paris, until the first Marshall Plan goods were unloaded in Europe in the spring of 1948, he and his Free Trade Union Committee stood alone in acting against Soviet expansion via the trade unions. The Truman administration was slow to move, and there was no CIA until September 1947. Lovestone sounded the trumpet and led the charge, and it took a while for those at embassy desks or in executive offices to catch up. And the best part was that most of the funding during the early period came from the AFL and its affiliates—that is, from the pockets of American working men and women, who were informed, via Lovestone's *Free Trade Union News,* of the AFL's exploits in the foreign field and who supported those efforts through resolutions at the annual conventions.

LOVESTONE
JOINS
THE CIA

On April 12, 1945, Franklin Delano Roosevelt died at the start of his fourth term as president. His vice president, Harry S Truman, replaced him. On May 14, Truman called in William J. "Wild Bill" Donovan, head of the wartime OSS, and told him: "The OSS belongs to a nation at war. It can have no place in an America at peace. I am completely opposed to international spying on the part of the United States. It is un-American." The OSS was dismantled on September 20, 1945, but the United States remained for only four months without a distinct intelligence agency. For Truman, who was inexperienced in foreign affairs, had been thrown into the foreign policy pond that July at the Potsdam Conference with Churchill and Stalin. His first brush with the Soviets changed his outlook; he realized that he needed to know Stalin's intentions. By the end of the year he was yelling at his advisers, "I want someone to tell me what's going on around the world! Damn it, different people are telling me different things."

In January 1946, Truman created a Central Intelligence Group. His chief of staff, Adm. William D. Leahy, recommended Sidney W. Souers —a Missouri businessman and rear admiral in the reserves who had been deputy chief of naval intelligence during the war and in civilian life ran the Piggly Wiggly grocery chain—to head it.

On January 24 at the White House there took place a mock ceremony that showed Truman's continued disdain for espionage even while he realized its necessity. The president stuck a black mustache above Leahy's lip, gave him a wooden dagger, and said: "By virtue of the authority vested in me as Top Dog, I require and charge that Fleet Admiral William D. Leahy and Rear Admiral Sidney W. Souers receive and accept the vestments and appurtenances of their respective positions, namely as Personal Snooper and Director of Centralized Snooping."

It took another year and a half to move to the next step, under the pressure of events. For in January 1946 the Communists took over Poland in fraudulent elections; in March 1947 Truman warned about the danger of Greece and Turkey going Communist; and in May a Communist coup made Hungary a Soviet satellite. The objections to reading other people's mail were now more muted.

On July 26, 1947, Truman signed the National Security Act, which provided for a National Security Council, a secretary of defense, and a Central Intelligence Agency. On September 18, the Central Intelligence Group became the Central Intelligence Agency, headed by another admiral from Missouri and friend of Leahy, Rear Admiral Roscoe H. Hillenkoetter. Fifty years old, tall, and athletic-looking with brush-cut hair, "Hilly" was soon derided by intelligence professionals as an inept old sea dog, an "amiable Dutchman" worse than "Piggly Wiggly Souers."

As William R. Johnson, a twenty-eight-year veteran of the CIA, once put it, "The new CIA . . . was a little like the Baltimore Orioles when they were first admitted to the American League. All the old minor league enthusiasm was there," but the talent had to be updated and a certain savvy had to be acquired to play in the majors. Under Hillenkoetter, who was not a Washington infighter, and who maintained an old-fashioned preference for analysis over covert operations, the CIA made a slow start.

It was in this context that George Kennan, now head of the Policy Planning Staff, a sort of State Department think tank, recommended an organization to handle covert operations. On June 18, 1948, a month before the Berlin blockade, the National Security Council authorized an Office of Policy Coordination to conduct secret operations.

To run it, Kennan picked Frank Gardner Wisner, a former OSS man who had witnessed the Soviet takeover of Romania in early 1945, which had made a lasting impression. Although from Mississippi, where his father was a lumber baron, Wisner did not conform to the laid-back, homespun, drawling, Deep South stereotype. If anything, he was hyperactive. He attacked everything he did with enormous energy and gusto, whether it was the low hurdles at the University of Virginia or seducing a Romanian princess in Bucharest.

Once installed in his own building, at Twenty-first Street and Virginia Avenue, Wisner was ready to pounce. Covert operations sprang up like crocuses in May. Agents were parachuted into the Ukraine. Ex-Nazis were retrieved for duties in the United States. Wisner was mission-oriented to the point of recklessness, but he enjoyed wide latitude and plenty of money. The OPC grew exponentially, from a staff of 302 and seven overseas stations in 1949 to a staff of 2,812 and forty-seven stations in 1952; it came to be known as Wisner's Mighty Wurlitzer. Wisner saw intelligence gathering as "a bunch of old washerwomen exchanging gossip while they rinse through the dirty linen." As for Admiral Hillenkoetter, "he didn't have the wickedness" to deal with the Soviets, Wisner declared. While complaining that the OPC was practically a rogue outfit, Hilly left Wisner pretty much to his own devices.

Wisner's biggest booster was Jim Forrestal, who had been promoted in 1947 from secretary of the Navy to secretary of defense. High-strung, humorless, unrelentingly driven, Forrestal was the administration's champion cold warrior, one of the first to have recognized the Soviet threat. In that role he was a major force in favor of covert action.

Lovestone had met the secretary of defense in the fall of 1947 during Kurt Schumacher's visit, placing himself at Forrestal's service. Soon Lovestone was briefing Forrestal on AFL activities in France and Italy. Forrestal introduced Lovestone to Hillenkoetter, and the two became friends, keeping up long after Hilly had left the CIA. Forrestal informed Wisner that the AFL had been working with European unions since late 1945 and had developed a network of valuable contacts. This was right in line with Wisner's program of "support of anti-Communists in free countries."

Wisner saw the chance to enlist labor in his anti-Soviet operations, just as Donovan had set up an OSS labor desk during World War II. He got in touch with Matthew Woll, who told him about the Free Trade Union Committee and the activities of Lovestone and Brown. Wisner expressed interest, and on December 10, 1948, Woll wrote him: "This is to introduce Mr. Jay Lovestone. . . . He is duly authorized to cooperate with you in behalf of our organization and to arrange for close contact and reciprocal assistance in all matters."

With this letter began a period of collaboration between the AFL and the CIA that lasted for more than twenty years. Despite their vociferous denials, the collaboration involved, as will be seen, not only Jay Lovestone and Irving Brown but George Meany, Matthew Woll, and David Dubinsky. Many millions of dollars changed hands. To those tempted to say that the AFL became an instrument of American foreign policy, the obvious answer is that, in spite of the collaboration, the organizations' policies often diverged. Sometimes it seemed that American foreign policy was an instrument of the AFL.

The marriage was not harmonious; indeed it was quarrelsome and recriminatory. Lovestone came to detest the arrangement, not realizing at first the extent to which the CIA would try to control him, but he saw it as a necessary evil—it was that or shut down. He wanted to expand the FTUC—an office in India, one in Japan, more people in Europe, someone to cover the Arab world. He saw himself as the mastermind of a worldwide organization assisting free labor and checking Soviet expansion.

But at the time Lovestone first connected with Wisner, the FTUC's activities had outpaced its funding. From 1945 until 1949 the money had come from the contributions of affiliates. Unions with deep pockets, like the ILGWU, gave handsomely. But with Brown spreading himself all over Europe, disbursements soon exceeded receipts. The FTUC needed a new source of funding, which Wisner's timely appearance provided.

Lovestone used a simple device to cook the FTUC books. Before the CIA funding he had itemized the contributions of affiliates union by union. In 1949, when Wisner started paying, contributions from "individuals" were also listed, with numbered receipts giving the amounts and the made-up names of the supposed donors. Thus, that year contributions from affiliates amounted to $56,000, while contributions from "individuals" were $203,000. The individual's real name was Frank Wisner.

Disbursements for that year included $50,000 for French and Italian unions. In 1950 total receipts were $252,000 and contributions from affiliates were $50,000, leaving $202,000 from "individuals." That year the biggest expenses were $145,000 for China and $27,000 for Finland. In 1951 contributions from affiliates fell to $24,000, perhaps because less effort was being made to collect them, given the new source of funds. In 1952, however, funds from affiliates were back up to $54,000, out of total receipts of $175,000. This accounting did not include the counterpart funds that Irving Brown received directly for his European operations, via the Marshall Plan people or the American embassies. Tom Lane in Rome also had access to counterpart funds, that 5 percent of the total Marshall Plan package held back in each country to cover U.S. administrative expenses and also, as it turned out, to finance covert operations.

Lovestone received his first payment from Wisner—$35,000—on January 7, 1949, and wrote him: "Rest assured that these funds will be spent entirely in line with your request to meet urgent needs in France." Lovestone was feeling his way in his new role as CIA agent, reporting to Wisner on relevant activities. In January he saw some Polish leaders in exile and obtained valuable information on conditions behind the iron curtain.

He also urgently needed funding to produce a pamphlet on slave labor in the Soviet Union, which would include maps pinpointing the locations of the gulags. With Wisner's money Lovestone hired Toni Sender, a German Social Democrat who had been a member of the Reichstag in pre-Hitler times, to collect affidavits from survivors of the gulags. In 1949, after a year of strenuous lobbying, Sender succeeded in placing the "Survey of Forced Labor and Measures for Its Abolition" on the agenda of the UN Economic and Social Council. The Soviets boycotted the council when she spoke, giving eyewitness accounts of conditions in the gulags and demonstrating that the Soviet economy was built on "millions of the enslaved."

Lovestone printed his pamphlet in eleven languages, including an edition on thin paper that was smuggled into Eastern Europe. When a copy of the map was handed to Andrei Gromyko, the "Mr. Nyet" of the Security Council, he threw it on the floor in horror. In Vienna the Russians raided the bookbinder who was binding the pamphlets and threw him in jail. In East Germany they confiscated thousands of copies. Matthew Woll asked Secretary of State Acheson to protest these high-handed Soviet actions, which gave the pamphlet some unasked-for publicity.

While Wisner was quick to fund obviously worthwhile projects such as the slave labor pamphlet, he had reservations about Lovestone opening new offices. His reaction was chilly when Jay proposed a Tokyo office with an annual budget of twenty thousand dollars and a Bombay office at thirty thousand a year. Lovestone explained that Irving Brown had been to India and was anxious to have a man there, while in Japan they could "undo much of the damage done by the fellow-travelers who infested MacArthur's apparatus." The budget for six months in Japan was less than one month in France, but, as Lovestone wrote Brown, "we get a very cold response. It is incredible."

Wisner also proposed some assignments for the FTUC that Lovestone was less than enthusiastic about. The state of Israel was proclaimed on May 14, 1948, and the British pulled out of Palestine. The seventy-five-year-old Zionist leader Chaim Weizmann, now president of Israel, was in Washington in April 1949 and briefed Wisner's OPC people, telling them that the Communists were making inroads in the Israeli labor movement. Wisner asked Lovestone on April 26 to send a man there, "a real go-getter." Lovestone was already funding the Israeli union, the Histadrut, in a modest way, but he thought of Israeli labor as a sideshow, not worth sending an agent under AFL cover.

On May 9, 1949, Wisner raised the issue again: "Continued reports on Communist infiltration of the Israeli labor organization confirm more strongly than ever the fears I expressed the last time I talked to you." Lovestone replied that the Israelis did not want an AFL representative, but Wisner urged him "to pursue the matter vigorously with a view to compelling them to accept your representative even if you have to threaten curtailment of funds."

Lovestone did not pursue it. This was the sort of interference that he found maddening. What did Wisner and his people know about labor? What did Israel matter with France and Italy hanging in the balance? In June, when he saw the budget for Italy, Lovestone was furious at how chintzy it was. "Are we such big fools really?" he asked Wisner. "Why do these people over there [in Italy] think we are such idiots?"

The French and Italian operations were well under way, however, with the money going to the Force Ouvrière and the CISL. With Brown on the spot to take care of things, Lovestone turned to two major problem areas for which he had big plans. The first was China, where the Communist victory over Chiang Kai-shek in 1949 shocked him as had few other postwar events. Chiang evacuated the mainland and moved his forces to the island of Formosa. On October 1 the People's Republic of China was proclaimed in Peking, with Mao Tse-tung as chairman and Chou En-lai as premier and foreign minister. Leo Borochowicz, the German ex-Communist whom Lovestone had brought to New York as his assistant in the FTUC office, told him that the corrupt Chiang regime had made collapse in China inevitable. But that did not make Jay feel any better about what he surmised was the loss of Asia to Communism. The second problem area was Finland, which had a border with Russia and was under intense Soviet pressure. In both these countries Lovestone planned major CIA-funded operations.

In Finland the Communists had not been able to seize the trade unions as they had in Czechoslovakia. The Finnish unions remained the major barrier to a Communist takeover. The trade union federation, the SAK, had a Socialist majority, but it was touch and go. The strong Communist element, funded by Moscow, was probing and pushing in the hope that a Communist victory in the SAK elections would force the Finnish government to form a coalition that included the Communists. In addition, the SAK was the only non-Communist union left in the Soviet-controlled WFTU, which the CIO and the British TUC, along with the Dutch, had bolted in January 1949. The SAK was now the fig leaf that allowed the WFTU to claim that it was not completely Communist. Thus, Lovestone had two objectives—the first was to get enough CIA funding to put a hundred organizers on the payroll of the Socialists in the SAK, so that they could build up their forces in every factory and mill. The second was to wean the SAK away from the WFTU.

Lovestone did not try to engineer a split as he and Brown had done in France and Italy. The Finnish Socialists feared that a split would squeeze them between the employers and the Communists. They felt that their strategy should be to reduce the Communist elements in the SAK. In 1949 the Socialists held a 60–40 majority, but the Communists controlled important unions and remained a constant danger.

In October 1949, Brown went to Helsinki and reported that Finland was on a tightrope. That it was still free was impressive, with the bear breathing down its neck. The Finns were tough and brave and had a clandestine army of partisans 200,000 strong, ready to take to the woods against any Soviet military incursion. Vaini Leskinen, one of the top SAK Socialists, told Brown that because of their relatively small membership—300,000 for the entire SAK—money was tight. The Communists were well funded, but the Socialists were broke. They needed cash for cars and outboard motors so they could go door to door all over Finland. With $500,000, Brown said, they could deal the Communists a final blow. But as the year ended Lovestone still had no reply from Wisner on his proposals for China or Finland.

The Finnish situation improved in the spring of 1950, when Wisner opened the money pipeline. Olavi Lindblom, the SAK secretary general, wrote Lovestone on May 4: "To fight back requires a lot of money. The means of the SAK are not enough. Now we would need 50 million Finnish marks, equivalent to 200,000 dollars." They did not get it all right away, but they got enough to push through a vote on May 26 that the SAK would stop paying dues to the WFTU, waiting until the June 1951 congress to decide whether to sever relations.

Lovestone bridled at having to wait for the rest of the "Finnish lumber." He did not make promises lightly, he told Brown, but he began to realize that when someone in Wisner's outfit said, "Fine, everything is okay, we will do it," it didn't mean a darned thing. Those people glibly said, "oh, sure," which then turned into "so what?" In addition, Brown was laid low by asthma, which Lovestone thought was mostly psychosomatic. Brown was running around too much, and Lovestone told him to take a vacation and get a little rest.

The "Finnish lumber" finally came through, and at the SAK congress on June 28, 1951, the Socialists outnumbered the Communists 152 to 65 and seceded from the WFTU. Without the SAK, the WFTU was exposed for what it was, a federation of Communist unions. The CIA continued to fund the SAK to the tune of about $160,000 a year.

Matters also improved for Lovestone's ambitious China operation. His agent in Formosa was a young man from Monroe, Wisconsin, Willis R. Etter, who before the war had been an organizer with Irving Brown in Homer Martin's United Auto Workers. Etter then joined the State Department, which posted him to the American consulate in Shanghai in 1947. But when he tried to blow the whistle on a nest of Communists he said he had uncovered in the consulate, he was accused of insubordination and sent home in 1948.

Back in the States, after the fall of China, Etter got in touch with Lovestone, who decided to send him to Formosa. Etter had kept his contacts with anti-Communist labor people there, who were starting up a Free China Labor League. He and Lovestone devised a plan to train them as a secret insurgency force that would conduct guerrilla and sabotage operations in mainland China. They made a proposal to Wisner, whose covert action experts drafted a detailed blueprint. This secret document called for six units to be sent to mainland China, with personnel including radio operators, saboteurs, and intelligence agents. Each unit would be provided with a large receiver-transmitter, twelve small receiver-transmitters using eight batteries each, fifty revolvers at eighty dollars each, and one hundred pistols at fifty dollars each, with fifty shots for each weapon and ten kilos of TNT.

Etter would run the show. Some seed money, enough to send Etter on his way, arrived from Wisner in November 1949. Etter was waiting in Riverdale, Maryland, with his wife, Joyce, and their two children, who would stay behind. Lovestone wrote him on November 3, 1949: "Here is the check. That is the best I can do. I am sure it is a good beginning." Etter arrived in Formosa in December, ostensibly as the adviser to the Free China Labor League. Using the code name Earle T. Overland, he wrote Lovestone on January 12, 1950, that he had been in Taipei a month trying to see what could be salvaged from the tragedy. Chiang had brought his corrupt system with him from the mainland, Etter said. Within his party, the Kuomintang, there were cliques, subcliques, and subsubcliques, all rigidly hierarchical, with the leader commanding complete loyalty. At the head of all the cliques was Chiang, the Gimo, whom the GI's called Chancre Jack. Those around him kept him from bad news in order to win his favor and cover up their own corrupt activities. Thus, Chiang never got the true picture.

Yet Etter thought that China could still be saved from Communism by a free labor movement. On the mainland the Communists had taken over the Chinese Federation of Labor. In Shanghai, for instance, there were more than four hundred industrial and occupational unions, all taken over by the Communists. Turning the unions Red was called "crossing the bridge." Workers who failed to attend indoctrination meetings had to wear tall paper hats on which was written: "I am a Kuomintang diehard and secret agent." They had to slap their own faces with both hands and read statements of repentance. A thousand union leaders had been thrown into three Shanghai jails as "class rebels." Many others were sent to border regions to work as slaves.

Funded by Etter, the Free China Labor League was inaugurated on January 15, 1950, combining elements from a number of groups intent on continuing the struggle against the Communists. Its guiding spirit was Liu Ching-lih, a former minister of agriculture and labor, whom Etter considered "a political and organizational genius." He had been a postal worker, active in the Chinese labor movement for many years. Etter saw the Free China Labor League as "the sole hope of eventually salvaging China from Communism."

All this looked rather promising and fit into Wisner's general strategy of mounting multiple operations to destabilize the mainland China regime. Gen. Richard Giles Stilwell (not to be confused with "Vinegar Joe" Stilwell), a scholarly-looking West Pointer who had seen combat in World War II, was on special assignment as chief of the OPC Far East operations. Stilwell, who had a good analytical mind, later acknowledged that the OPC started more operations than it could handle. The Far East seemed to be going up in flames, he told the writer Burton Hersh, and "I had a hell of a budget."

In February 1950 the Etter operation was approved, and on February 27 Wisner sent Lovestone the first installment for the FCLL with this note: "Here's your laundry budget." Some laundry! The grand total for the first six months of 1950 was $145,472. The itemized budget included a fund "for rescuing or saving comrades in danger or under arrest." The money was transferred in installments via the Munsey Trust Co. in Washington to Etter's account in Taipei. Lovestone wired: "All your requests assured favorable action."

By mid-March, Etter had his first teams on the mainland. Intelligence arrived over his radio transmitters by bits and pieces. In Shanghai the inmates had been cleared out of the Ward Road Gaol and sent to the northern province of Kiangsu for hard labor. There were signs that the Communists were planning an invasion of Formosa; the military authorities had ordered 700,000 life belts from the Cheng Tai Rubber Works in Shanghai.

Impressed by Etter's quick start, Wisner asked Lovestone to bring him back for consultations. At the end of April 1950, Etter arrived in Washington, where General Stilwell and Frank Lindsay, Wisner's chief of staff and an OSS veteran who had served with Tito's partisans, tried to enlist him into the CIA. They preferred to run the China operation without Lovestone as an intermediary. Etter declined and informed Lovestone, who protested to Wisner on May 1, 1950, that Stilwell and Lindsay had offered Etter "a contract at a very high salary to take him out of the field of labor as an employee of the CIA. . . . Such conduct on the part of your colleagues is dishonest and stupid. . . . To put him on your payroll would undermine everything worthwhile."

Etter went back to Formosa to resume his activities. Lovestone warned him to "watch out for the idiots who offered you a seat to paradise while you were in Washington last." On May 11, 1950, Liu Ching-lih wrote Lovestone that "though we are exposed to danger we are not in the least frightened. Though we are suffering from financial pinches, we are still sending workers to the mainland and giving some kind of assistance to workers there. . . . A great deal of work has also been done in regard to the seamen of North China in Tsingtau."

In June 1950, North Korea invaded South Korea, turning the Cold War in Europe into a hot war in Asia and giving a fresh urgency to the CIA's China operations. Envoys from Wisner came to Taipei to ask Etter to extend his radio network on the mainland and step up his activities. Etter sent a sabotage team to Shanghai led by the FCLL team leader Pan Tung-chen, who found a likely target in a hundred tons of aviation gasoline stored on one of the docks. Three bombs were made, and the storage tanks were blown up on November 8, but one of the locally recruited men was hurt in the explosion and captured by Communist agents, who also arrested his two sons and his wife. Pan reported that the fire burned for fifteen hours. It was a major catastrophe, with many civilian houses destroyed and a number of people killed. His last radio message before he was captured said: "We have been in Shanghai for some time and are at our wits' end for material support."

Etter was having trouble supplying his teams with funds once they were on the mainland. With this in mind, he gave notice in the fall of 1950 that Wisner's radio mission to Shanghai was ready to go, but they needed six months' expenses for the salaries of the personnel. Smuggling monthly paychecks to the mainland was not possible. But the urgently needed extra money did not arrive. In fact, even the basic monthly stipend was inexplicably cut off. After asking for expanded operations, the CIA now balked at financing them, for Wisner's OPC was shifting from operations on the Chinese mainland to North Korea.

No help was sent to the operatives on the mainland, and on December 5, 1950, the leader of the team, Chou Yun-kiang, was arrested by the Communists. On January 18, 1951, he was shot. "Perhaps this would not have happened if help had come to the boys there in a state of mobility," Etter wrote. At the request of General Stilwell, another man had been sent to Tientsin (about sixty miles southeast of Peking) to lay the groundwork for a radio team there. He too sat and waited, and on March 31 he was arrested and shot.

Etter also had a small operation going in a Shanghai textile mill where he had planted a female agent, Chen Tau-pao. The idea was to get the workers in the plant to demand a year-end bonus. When the demand was made, it created the desired unrest, which was traced to Chen; she was arrested on New Year's Day and shot in the factory courtyard before the other workers. In another Shanghai operation, Etter funded three men to launch an anticonscription movement, since so many Chinese were being sent to fight in Korea. The three—Liang Chu-huan, Chih Lung-chi, and Chu Teh-san—worked in one of the plants of the China Textile Corporation. The movement was touched off in January 1951. A month later all three men were arrested and shot.

Etter's operations on the mainland were a disaster. With his nerves frayed and his asthma kicking up, he wrote Lovestone in February 1951: "I tell you all these tragic things because the people mentioned who have sacrificed their lives for their nation are dead and gone. . . . Many of these men were personal friends of mine. Some of them I bid good luck to from this very place."

Etter's news shocked Lovestone, who blamed Wisner and his minions. "I curse the day I ever introduced you to that pack of bribers and corrupters in Washington," he replied. "They have gone back on every agreement. They have lied. Please cut all relations with them. . . . I do not want to be responsible for so many broken hopes. . . . You know what I think of them. They make big promises but flatten out."

The irregularity of CIA payments had less to do with developments in Formosa than with changes in the CIA itself, as we shall see. From being the top recipient of Wisner's largesse among Lovestone's programs, the Free China Labor League in 1951 was increasingly cut off.

The closing of the faucet was documented in Lovestone's letters to Etter.

November 14: "We simply have to stop our contribution. I hope our friends do not think we are a mint or a cash register."

November 20: "Our lush days are over. No blood out of stone nor cash out of the undersigned. Believe me I have also learned a little."

Etter returned to the United States in January 1952, ill with worms. He had to go to the Tropical Diseases Hospital "to eliminate the insect world." Later that year he went back to Formosa as part of the Mutual Security Administration labor mission. He found that the Free China Labor League had folded as the Chiang regime stifled all trade unions. Formosa was now a police state, Etter wrote Lovestone, under military domination.

To go from the tragic to the comic, news that the AFL was funding anti-Communist movements in the China theater led to strange offers, one of them reminiscent of the spy in Graham Greene's *Our Man in Havana,* who sent his British spymasters a diagram of a vacuum cleaner purported to be a secret weapon. As Lovestone was soon to learn, all an aspiring recipient of funds needed was a letterhead and a tongue to lick stamps with.

In January 1953, Lovestone received a communication under the impressive letterhead DEMOCRATIC REVOLUTIONARY LEAGUE OF CHINESE PEOPLE, signed by one Wei Ming, who did not supply a curriculum vitae. He resided at the Hotel Homo in the Portuguese colony of Macao, on the coast of southeast China, and offered to send Lovestone material on POW camps in mainland China. Lovestone sent him two hundred dollars. You never knew.

Wei Ming reported in February that his number-two man, Fuchill Sun, had absconded with the two hundred dollars. "Re the fraudulency of Mr. Sun," he wrote, "I am not convenient to expose my political standing to strike him in the face of the law. It is not advisable to treat such a small potato with the military punishment. Therefore I let the matter to be laid aside."

On February 18, Wei Ming sent Lovestone the flag of the party he had founded. "It has a yellow background," he wrote, "a pentagonal red star, and a branch of green olive leaves under the star." Lovestone thanked him, writing that "I treasure the flag as a precious souvenir." The flag was followed by the verses of Wei's party anthem, "Emancipation in the Iron Curtain."

Wei Ming was a man after Lovestone's heart, for he used as many aliases as his correspondent once had. The first was Po Pin, which he described as "my pseudonym." The second was Op Lu, which he said was "the name on my ID card." The third, Wei Ming, was "the name I use in political circles." All three names were employed, he added, "to produce many clues and revelations."

In March 1953, Wei Ming sent Lovestone a report on the Chinese army and wrote: "I am looking forward to have a long discussion with you about the situation in China as well as the whole world." Lovestone sent him a hundred dollars but observed that he had shown the report to some of his friends in the intelligence community. "They challenged the accuracy of quite a number of your statements," he wrote, "but we have vouched for the accuracy and truth of your findings." Wei replied that he was launching a "New Truth Service." His first item was that the Red Chinese were preparing for war by digging long corridors of trenches.

Lovestone took the bait and asked Wei Ming to come to the United States to work out all the technical details. Wei replied that he could not come until he obtained a Portuguese passport. "We need a chance to go over things in person," Lovestone wrote. Wei replied that he could get a passport on the black market for $5,000 Macao (about $900 U.S.). Lovestone sent him some money via the San Francisco office of the Bank of Canton, which had a branch in Macao. But Wei did not arrive. Instead, he proposed writing an open letter to Chinese soldiers in Korea, urging them to desert. The letter, to be smuggled by his agents on the mainland to the Korean front, would say: "While you are fighting in the front lines under the piercing wind, while you are struggling in the miry trenches, Mao Tse-tung and Chou En-lai are comfortable in gorgeous palaces, enjoying extravagant feasts." Again, Lovestone sent him some money to support this effort. Pushing his luck, Wei asked for funds to start a "Liberal Asia University." Lovestone replied that he would take it up with the Rockefeller Foundation, but he began to have doubts about his man in Macao. Wei's pronouncements grew more cryptic. What did it mean, Lovestone wondered, when he wrote that "the flames of Communism shoot high into the heavens"? Then Wei wrote: "Death will at any moment occur to a politician. I send you herewith my photo as a remembrance." In the margin of this paragraph, Lovestone jotted three question marks. There the correspondence ended.

The Wei Ming episode had cost Lovestone a couple of thousand dollars. In exchange, he had a flag, an anthem, and a snapshot.

On June 27, 1950, a UN Security Council resolution called the North Korean invasion a breach of the peace and committed UN members to furnish assistance to the Republic of Korea. Lovestone was incensed that India's response was one field ambulance and four hundred thousand jute bags. In July he saw Wisner and presented an analysis of the war that left Wisner "white as a sheet." Lovestone believed that the UN forces were fighting not only North Korea but Communist China, and that for Stalin the attack was a good way to get the West to waste its resources at little cost to himself.

When the Chinese joined the fray in November, proving him right, Lovestone wrote Matt Woll that he had received reports from Etter on troop movements from Manchuria southward into North Korea. "This information was sent by our Chinese friends at great sacrifice," he said. "Some of our best people have been killed by the Communists in their desperate attempts to stop our people from learning what goes on."

In June 1951 an armistice was proposed, but negotiations dragged on. The thorniest issue, more than boundary lines or troop removals, was prisoners of war. The UN forces held 171,000 Chinese and North Koreans, many of whom were unwilling to go back to their countries of origin. The Communists, not wanting to lose face, insisted on their return. Negotiations were deadlocked over their repatriation.

In New York City in May 1952, in the cramped office of the Free Trade Union Committee in the ILGWU building at 1710 Broadway, Lovestone's assistant Leo Borochowicz was browsing through one of the scholarly Russian tomes he collected, a symposium published by the Soviet Institute of Law. Chapter 2 was entitled "Methods of Solving International Conflicts by Compulsion: The Laws and Customs of War." One section caught Borochowicz's eye: "Treatment of German Prisoners by the Soviet Army." This was said to be diametrically opposed to the Nazi treatment of Soviet prisoners. Comrade Stalin, said the text, had pointed out in Order 55 of the People's Commissariat for Defense that "the Red Army takes German soldiers and officers as prisoners if they surrender and leaves them alive." Thus, on January 8, 1943, the Soviet Army Command addressed an ultimatum to the commander of the German troops near Stalingrad, guaranteeing to all officers and soldiers that if they surrendered they would be returned to Germany *or to any country of their choice*. This offer was made again to German and Hungarian troops during the siege of Budapest in 1945.

Borochowicz pointed out to Lovestone that, by these two examples, the Soviets had set the precedent that prisoners of war had the right to decide where they wanted to go after their release. "The attitude of the Communist negotiators in Korea regarding the repatriation problem," he noted, "is not supported but implicitly repudiated by an official Soviet text on international law," he said.

This information was passed from Lovestone to Matthew Woll to the State Department to the American negotiators at Panmunjom. The chief Communist negotiator, Gen. Nam Il, expressed contempt for the position that POWs should be allowed to choose the place of their repatriation. All prisoners must be returned, he insisted, if necessary at the point of a bayonet. In reply, the senior American negotiator, Maj. Gen. William K. Harrison, said that "your side has violently opposed the humanitarian principle of no forced repatriation. . . . It may come as a surprise to you that this principle has been utilized by the Union of Soviet Socialist Republics, a nation for whom your government has expressed great admiration. This was granted at Stalingrad on January 8, 1943, and at the siege of Budapest in 1945."

Harrison's argument had a dramatic effect, and he later wrote that "the stunning blow struck on June 21, 1952, against Communist opposition to voluntary repatriation of war prisoners in Korea was based on evidence produced by the historians of the AFL." On June 27, David Bruce, the acting secretary of state, wrote Woll that "the White House has asked me to thank you. . . . I am free to tell you that your documentation was very useful in our negotiations on the repatriation issue."

Still, it took a while before the negotiations bore fruit. Lovestone did not think the North Koreans would ever concede on the POWs, for "if it was made a practice the Russians could not hold an army intact. There would be many desertions because the soldiers would feel this was the best way to get out of the trap." The armistice was finally signed on July 27, 1953. A neutral Commission for Repatriation processed the POWs, who were given the right to choose: 7,852 North Koreans and 14,277 Chinese elected to stay in South Korea or to go to Taiwan.

By that time Eisenhower was president, and the man who had set the precedent, Joseph Stalin, had died, in March 1953. So had the man who had done the brilliant bit of research, Leo Borochowicz, in February 1953, of a heart attack. Lovestone was grief-stricken and paid for his burial. Leo's wife, Ellie, continued to work in the FTUC office.

Lovestone's position was that nothing would change in the Kremlin as the result of Stalin's death. But in his own shop there was a big change in June 1950, when Frank Wisner was forced to get rid of one of his most valued agents and passed him on to Jay.

This nonpareil was Carmel Offie, known to his enemies as Carmie Awful. Wisner said he was "sui generis"—a species of his own. His was one of the most remarkable careers in the Foreign Service, where he got his start. Offie was born in 1909 in the coal-mining country of Sharon, Pennsylvania, of Italian parents who came from Caserta, north of Naples. Mediterranean in appearance, he was short and swarthy, with a face that seemed to have bumps instead of features. But sunk in that face, above his Neapolitan mustache and his rubbery nose, were two gleaming eyes that astutely appraised what they saw.

Offie entered the Foreign Service as a clerk, and his chance came when he was posted to Moscow in 1934, to serve under the impetuous and mentally untidy ambassador William C. Bullitt. Offie soon displayed an astonishing faculty for making himself useful. When Bullitt had insomnia he rang for Offie and they played chess. When he rose at five he took Offie for a dawn stroll.

Bullitt sang Offie's praises as the best stenographer and typist in Moscow. When he was transferred to France in 1936, he took Offie with him. Bullitt reported to his old friend FDR that Offie was a great success in Paris. In 1937 he played bridge with the duchess of Windsor. In 1938 he entertained the young Jack Kennedy and his brother Joe, and got them invited to parties where they could meet young ladies. "Jack came to my office," Offie said, "and read various things which were none of his business, but since he was who he was I didn't throw him out."

After the 1940 armistice Bullitt went back to Washington for reassignment, and Offie was transferred to London. Bullitt was expecting to be appointed as ambassador to the new French government in Vichy under Marshal Pétain. But in November 1940, Undersecretary of State Sumner Welles announced that Admiral Leahy would go to Vichy. Convinced that Welles had sabotaged his chances, Bullitt went home to Philadelphia, nursing his humiliation and plotting his revenge.

In 1943 Offie was back in Washington. Bullitt decided to use his devoted assistant to spread some evidence of Sumner Welles's homosexuality on Capitol Hill. Cordell Hull, the secretary of state, who complained that Welles routinely went behind his back or over his head, was only too glad to cooperate.

Offie leaked the evidence to the Republican senator from Maine, R. Owen Brewster, who threatened a Senate investigation. Roosevelt had tried to protect Welles, who had been a page boy at his wedding, but now saw him as a liability in the 1944 campaign. Welles presented his resignation on August 16, 1943, but FDR never forgave Bullitt for snitching on him.

The irony was that Offie, who had done Bullitt's and Hull's dirty work on Capitol Hill, was himself a homosexual. At night in Washington he went cruising gay haunts such as David's Bar and Mickey's Grill and other known hangouts such as the men's room in Lafayette Park, across the street from the White House. On September 8, 1943, less than a month after Welles's resignation, Offie was arrested by Washington police at 12:40 A.M. near the Lafayette Park men's room and charged with "perversion—disorderly conduct." He had solicited an undercover cop. According to a memo from the State Department Security Office, "He was arrested as he talked to a police officer about his perversion and the manner in which he preferred to conduct his perverted act."

Offie spent the night in jail, amid cockroaches and the stench of urine. His offense was listed in the police blotter. On September 9 he was released on twenty-five dollars bond to await a court appearance. But Offie's case never came up, thanks to an intervention from on high. Cordell Hull, the Tennessee mountaineer, prized loyalty above all. Hull had his protégé and special assistant, James Clement Dunn, visit the jailed Carmel. After expressing his outrage at the conditions, Dunn made arrangements for Offie's release. On September 10, 1943, Dunn wrote a note to the court, initialed by Hull, stating that Offie had been in Lafayette Park on "official business," having been asked to meet an informant there. "I consider Mr. Offie a highly effective and loyal servant of the United States," the note said. "It would be unjust to penalize him for carrying out his mission." Thus Hull saved Offie from punishment for the same offense for which he had helped ruin the career of Sumner Welles.

Scrambling to get out of Washington and resume his career abroad, Offie made the rounds of his contacts and latched on to Robert Murphy, who had been in the Paris embassy in the gloomy days in 1940, when Offie had impressed him as Bullitt's "indispensable personal assistant." In March 1944, Murphy was with the Allied Advisory Council in Italy, where Offie joined him. In 1945, when Murphy was named Gen. Lucius Clay's top civilian adviser, Offie tagged along as his passe-partout. While Murphy was in Berlin with Clay, Offie was in Frankfurt, acting like a minor potentate. He made friends with the higher-ups in OMGUS by holding soirees where he produced normally unobtainable delicacies— lobsters and champagne from France, Gorgonzola from Italy, and Russian caviar.

Eventually Offie's wheeling and dealing got him into hot water. In 1947, in a routine check, State Department Chief Inspector Merle Cochran turned up four thousand dollars in cash sent by Offie in the diplomatic pouch from Frankfurt to Paris. This was a violation of the ban on using the pouch for private transactions. Offie was in fact only doing a favor for a friend, Anthony Drexel Biddle, an army colonel in Germany who was trying to get some cash to his ex-wife in Paris.

Offie was removed from the list of middle-level officers eligible for promotion, which in effect ended his foreign service career. He resigned in April 1948 and went back to Washington. But in his German stint Offie had done extensive work with refugee groups from Eastern Europe. When Frank Wisner set up his Office of Policy Coordination, Offie fit right in, even though he had detractors from the security side who were privy to his 1943 arrest. In September 1948, Offie joined OPC as a special deputy and troubleshooter, working mainly with émigré groups, Radio Free Europe, and Lovestone's labor operation.

Inside the OPC, Offie was openly homosexual, referring to his bedroom as "the playing fields of Eton." According to a recently declassified top-secret report, he made advances in October 1949 to an agent of the U.S. Army Counterintelligence Corps. The agent, James H. Paul, reported that on October 15 he went to Offie's OPC office, Room 1702, Temporary Building L, Seventeenth Street and Constitution Avenue, to obtain a character reference for a Central European émigré. Offie said the émigré was a family man, "not like you or me, who have to chase around for our pussy. I'll bet that if all the time you spent chasing pussy was computed at the end of the year, it would amount to a tremendous figure."

Then Offie walked over to a wall map with Paul, who continued the account: "And he stood in such a position that a positive body contact was made . . . with his right arm hanging down and his palm outward so that it came in direct contact with my thigh. I backed off a bit, and Mr. Offie attempted to close the gap. . . . When I was leaving . . . Mr. Offie stated in an intimate voice that if he could help me in any way or do anything for me, to be sure and get in touch with him." On October 23, a CIC officer reported these "unusual advances" to Col. Sheffield Edwards, chief of security for the CIA, "who requested that an official report be made to him so that action could be taken against Mr. Offie."

The action taken in the spring of 1950 by CIA security staff was to leak a copy of the police blotter with Offie's 1943 arrest to Sen. Joseph McCarthy, then making his reputation as a Red-baiter. The senator's charges were being investigated at the time by a subcommittee of the Senate Foreign Relations Committee, chaired by Millard E. Tydings of Maryland.

On the first day of the hearings, March 8, Tydings asked McCarthy to identify Number 14 on his famous list, the State Department official who

Jacob Liebstein's parents: Emma and Barnet Liebstein
in the Old World became Minnie and Barney in the New.

A HAPPY NEW YEAR

לשנה טובה
תכתבו
ותחתמו

Jacob Liebstein at Hebrew school, New York City.

Jacob and his sisters, Sarah and Esther, in their homemade dresses.

Jacob, the proud graduate of City College, New York, class of 1918.

Jay Lovestone with Willi Muenzenberg, the most gifted Soviet propagandist and the inventor of the front group. This photo was probably taken in Moscow.

The leading lights of the American Communist movement in the 1920s: Jay Lovestone, William Foster, Charles Ruthenberg, Anna Damon (foreground), and Max Bedacht.

Bert and Ella Wolfe:
two lovebirds and
Lovestone's closest
friends in the Party.

Esther Mendelssohn:
The back of the
picture is inscribed
"To Jay Lovestone,
not a man, but a god."

Matt Woll (center), an AFL leader and ardent anti-Communist,
receiving a union delegation. Lovestone stands second from the right.

Lovestone and his rabbi, David Dubinsky of the ILGWU,
at a mass meeting in the 1930s.

Louise Page Morris, the American Mata Hari, as a Powers model, 1929.
"Every Strike a Lucky Strike," read the caption.

The last photograph of James Jesus Angleton,
taken by his wife, Cicely, in 1987.

The Lovestone Intelligence Service

A rare photograph of Raymond Murphy, Lovestone's man in the State Department, with Pagie Morris.

Pagie Morris and Jay Lovestone working the United Nations, here with Mohammed Yazid of the Algerian delegation.

The inimitable Irving Brown (left), Lovestone's man in Europe, with AFL
president George Meany and Arthur Deakin of the TUC.

Richard Deverall (extreme left) and Mohan Das (third from the right),
two Lovestone operatives, at work in India.

Harry Goldberg (center), Lovestone's man in Italy,
delivering a CARE package.

Maida Springer,
Lovestone's agent in Africa.

The Zelig-like Lovestone

Lovestone (extreme right), getting spiritual advice from
"the Red Dean" of Canterbury, Hewlett Johnson.

More spiritual advice: from Pope Pius XII.

Lovestone (extreme right) in Berlin, May 1, 1962, with (from left) Theodor Heuss, the first president of the Federal Republic of Germany; Willy Brandt, then the mayor of Berlin; and General Lucius DuBignon Clay.

Konrad Adenauer (extreme left) presents medals to
George Meany and Jay Lovestone.

Lovestone with President Habib Bourguiba of Tunisia.

Lovestone speaks; Norman Thomas, whose Socialist Party Lovestone tried to infiltrate, is in the foreground.

President Nixon greets Lovestone, Labor Day, 1969.
Lovestone later repudiated Nixon for the opening of China.

Lovestone peers over
Secretary of State
Dean Rusk's shoulder.

Jay carrying Esther
Mendelssohn into the
Florida surf, 1970s.

Jay Lovestone in the 1970s.

had blocked the dismissal of a homosexual employee. McCarthy said he didn't have the name right there, but on March 14 he again raised the case of the "convicted homosexual," who had resigned from the State Department in 1948 and was currently enjoying a "top-salaried important position" with the CIA. In this case McCarthy's information was accurate, for the CIA man was Carmel Offie, and the tip had come from those inside Wisner's shop who saw Offie as a self-aggrandizing promoter with the scruples of a black marketeer and the fawning manner of an Oriental bazaar manager.

On April 25 the senator from Wisconsin raised the matter once again, asking Tydings: "Is the senator aware that I gave the complete police record of this man to the senator from Maryland, this man who was a homosexual . . . [who] spent his time hanging around in the men's room in Lafayette Park? This man is still in an extremely sensitive position . . . and yet, so far as I know, the senator from Maryland has not done one single thing to get him off the government payroll."

Later that day McCarthy's chief supporter on the subcommittee, Kenneth S. Wherry of Nebraska, announced: "Within the last thirty minutes, I have been informed by the head of a government agency that the man against whom the senator from Wisconsin made a charge on the Senate floor this afternoon has finally resigned."

With Offie's name about to be disclosed, which would have smeared the OPC and the CIA, Wisner was forced to get rid of him. He steered his valuable aide into a safe harbor by placing him with Lovestone's Free Trade Union Committee. On June 14, 1950, Lovestone wrote Offie to say, "how pleased I was to learn that you decided to join our staff. . . . Your unusual background and experience will be invaluable in building up this long neglected service. . . . Incidentally, your title will be that of Director of International Labor Information Services of the Free Trade Union Committee, AFL."

In fact, Offie acted as liaison between Lovestone's FTUC and Wisner's OPC. Lovestone gave him an office on Dupont Circle, a secretary, and the code name Monk, since Mount Carmel was the place where a famous monastery had been founded. Lovestone soon came to appreciate his new director's abilities, writing Irving Brown: "Monk grasps quickly. He is intelligent. He is far superior in other ways to his associates, who act like Park Avenue book-keepers and frustrated socialites. I have three drawers crowded with broken promises."

Lovestone was completely disenchanted with the CIA partnership and its on-again, off-again enthusiasms, and wrote Wisner on October

24: "I am getting discouraged with the constant dragging and dragging in the handling of our work . . . words, words, words! . . . I don't cherish being deluged with verbiage." Not being privy to the inner workings of the CIA, Lovestone did not realize that a changing of the guard was taking place, which would have a drastic effect on Wisner's clout and Lovestone's operations.

Having dumped Hillenkoetter for failing to predict Korea, President Truman had brought in Gen. Walter Bedell Smith, Eisenhower's chief of staff during Operation Overlord and the Battle for Europe. Smith had joined the Army right out of high school and was a first sergeant at the age of eighteen. He continued to cultivate the left, right, do-the-drill, cuss-the-raw-recruits topkick style. He saw that the CIA was a tangle of warring baronies that had to be brought under control. Smith took a close look at the Mighty Wurlitzer and realized that Wisner had to be reined in. It was a traumatic time for the agency. Even the genial, pipe-smoking, avuncular Allen Dulles, whom Smith had brought in as a consultant in November 1950, was the victim of his wrath. Smith would be sitting in his office drinking herbal tea for his ulcer and suddenly bark at Dulles, "Goddamn it, get in here." Dulles took it in stride, saying, "The general was in fine form this morning, wasn't he? Ha, ha, ha!" But the tightly wound and stressed-out Wisner griped that an hour with Smith was like an hour on the squash court.

When General Smith took charge in October 1950, the funding for Lovestone and Brown's activities—in France, Italy, Finland, and Formosa—was put on hold. Expressing his disgust to Brown on November 20, 1950, Lovestone wrote: "Nothing has come through on any questions we agreed upon. . . . Some people are taking us too much for granted and use our name as if they own us." He was even annoyed with the ingratiating Offie, adding that "the Monk who is the best of them is very loose and has an inadequate concept of labor."

To remedy the situation a summit meeting of AFL and CIA leaders was held in General Smith's office at 10:30 A.M. on November 24, 1950, to introduce the new CIA director to the labor chiefs. Carmel Offie was present to keep the minutes, using transparent code names for those who attended: the Plumber (George Meany), the Photographer (Matthew Woll), the Garment Worker (David Dubinsky), the Intellectual (Lovestone), the Soldier (Smith), and the Lawyer (Frank Wisner).

Wisner opened by saying that General Smith in his new capacity wished to meet the labor gentlemen and review the conditions that had been established in May 1949 by Hillenkoetter and Lovestone for cooperation between their organizations in international work.

Woll said he thought the work served a very useful purpose.

Smith agreed that the work should continue.

Meany said it had been far more successful than he had dared hope.

Dubinsky said it had been effective in most places but inadequate in others.

Lovestone said the AFL had plunged into international work some time before the CIA had been created. The cooperation with the agency was less than two years old, and CIA assistance had enabled the FTUC to handle certain strategic emergencies. He was entirely satisfied, but now the arrangement had to be improved. He wished to make certain specific proposals, which were in a memo he had given to Wisner. Lovestone pointed out that the CIA aid was "a small fraction" of the total disbursement by the FTUC. In fact, by the end of 1950, CIA contributions were greater than funds collected from affiliates.

Smith asked how much the CIA had contributed in the last year. Lovestone said about $200,000.

Dubinsky said that sounded right. He added that the FTUC since its creation in 1944 had spent over $2 million. On Italy alone they had spent $750,000. The program in France had been a heavy one too.

Woll said the funds had been raised from the contributions of the AFL trade unions, which was gratifying.

Wisner added that a substantial amount above the $200,000 mentioned by Lovestone had been made available through the sugar funds (Marshall Plan counterpart funds)* in Italy and France.

Smith touched on bringing the CIO into the work.

Woll said he would be loath to do this, because of the CIO's inexperience and penetration by unreliable elements.

Lovestone concurred, saying that all their work would be placed in jeopardy if the CIO was brought in.

Smith asked Wisner if he had received any requests from the CIO.

Wisner said that certain conversations had taken place on the topic.

Meany said that his great fear was that the CIO, which had friends in high places, would get one of their friends to recommend that they share equally in the conduct of international work. He spoke in great detail on the Communist penetration in the CIO, mentioning dates, names, and

---

*Each country receiving Marshall Plan aid was obliged to deposit an equal amount in its central bank. These deposits in the national currency were called counterpart funds, of which 95 percent were to be used by the country's government in Marshall Plan programs, while the remaining 5 percent were turned over to the United States to cover the administrative costs of the plan in that country, or, as it turned out, to pay for covert operations.

places. (There was in fact a purge of Communist elements in the CIO as Meany spoke. By mid-1950 Communist-dominated unions claiming to represent over one million members had been drummed out.) Meany said that he for one did not want to be involved with the CIO. He would prefer to withdraw entirely from the present arrangement. He would rather stop work than jeopardize it by bringing in the CIO.

Lovestone mentioned the haphazard CIO effort in Italy and France.

When questioned by Smith, Wisner admitted that the CIA had funded some of the CIO efforts. (These concerned a rising Socialist union in Italy, the UIL, which was outside the AFL-backed federation.)

At this point Smith was called out of the room. In his absence Wisner explained the conditions under which the CIO might be brought in. Any trade union organization wanting to engage in this type of work would have to have a small group of men sworn under oath (as those present had been). It would also need an experienced foreign service in the field with its own funds for this type of work. When the CIO met those conditions, they would be advised that the CIA would be glad to deal with them on a project-by-project basis.

The AFL men said that was satisfactory.

Smith returned and said he was impressed by the opinions of his guests regarding the CIO and agreed with most of what had been said. The general said he knew the CIO men better than he did those in the room, but he was dubious about utilizing the CIO and did not feel he would have to submit to pressure from the president.

Wisner said the main source of the security troubles was the disposers of the sugar account. The matter was now straightened out. (The Marshall Plan people in Europe talked too much about their disbursements to Irving Brown.)

Smith repeated that he wanted as much information as possible from the AFL field people. He told Wisner to pass it on directly to him.

Lovestone said he could be of help in Germany because of his relationship with Kurt Schumacher and the Social Democrat Ostbureau.

Smith said he was glad that they now had a Charter of Operations that clarified their positions. He did not for one moment regard CIA funds as a subsidy for the labor movement.

Woll said the chief value of labor in foreign operations was its independence from government influence.

As the meeting broke up, Dubinsky observed that the French Socialist leader Daniel Mayer had come to New York seeking seventy-five thousand dollars for the Socialist newspaper *Le Populaire*. Dubinsky said he had given him sixty thousand. Mayer had promised to sever the paper from the party and make it a publication for all forward-thinking Frenchmen.

Smith said that a recommendation had been made to FDR that part of his unvouchered funds left over from the conduct of the war be used to buy up French newspapers, which would be placed in reliable hands and could be counted on to follow the right line. But then FDR died and nothing had come of it.

This meeting confirms the collaboration at the highest level between the CIA and the AFL. The three AFL leaders, Meany, Woll, and Dubinsky, were deeply involved, though they went to their graves denying it, having been sworn to secrecy. The propriety of a labor movement becoming an instrument or partner of American intelligence never came up at the meeting. Woll's remark that labor was useful because of its independence from government was jejune to say the least. Once funded by the CIA, the AFL foreign programs became accountable to the CIA. The AFL rationale, as Lovestone noted, was that they were simply carrying on what they had started before the CIA existed.

The only concern of the AFL leaders was that the CIO not be brought in, so they could keep the foreign field to themselves. The old animosity against the CIO was stronger than any scruples about government funding. For their part, Smith and Wisner felt that it was impolitic to leave out the CIO. Why alienate one wing of labor, which might resent the incumbent president for freezing them out and turn against him or his party at election time? In addition, given Lovestone's stubborn prejudices, the CIO could prove useful in working with unions that Lovestone refused to help, such as the UIL in Italy and the Christian unions in France. By funding both the AFL and the CIO, the CIA could cover all the bases. Its function was not to take sides but to plant agents on all sides.

Lovestone wrote Brown on December 4, 1950, that "we got together [with the CIA] two weeks ago with Meany, Dubinsky, Woll, and myself present and worked out a fairly sound agreement. The Monk hastily volunteered to prepare a draft." Lovestone heard from Offie that General Smith had described him as "uppity." "Frankly, Irving, I will not be a doorknob for anybody," Lovestone wrote. "I am going to speak out about inefficiency and incompetence no matter where I find such evils." In addition, Wisner told Offie that Lovestone was "a hard man to work with." Offie repeated the comment to Jay, who said: "Maybe he better try the other crowd."

In spite of the November agreement, Lovestone did not see any improvement. Wisner continued to work behind his back, trying to deal separately with Brown, who loyally informed Lovestone about the double cross, saying, "I am completely nonplused about what goes on in Washington. We should pull out, even at the risk of giving them the other wing to fly on." Lovestone responded in December 1950 that "these people are purely socialites whose names appear in the Social Register, who look for excitement and who confuse thrills with results. . . . I have not minded being a janitor of the firm, but Irving I do not want to be a janitor whose functions are increasingly devoted to carrying out strange tenants' garbage." There was continued dillydallying on the Finnish matter, as well as on China, where, Lovestone wrote, "some of our boys have lost their lives . . . due to double-crossing and stupidities."

Lovestone went to Washington to meet Allen Dulles, the new deputy director for plans, who now had oversight of his operations and whom Lovestone code-named Gouty (because he suffered from gout and was often in his office in carpet slippers) and Squinty (he was nearsighted).

Having just been promoted, Dulles was in a magnanimous mood and promised $25,000 for the Finns. Lovestone at once wrote Vaino Leskinen: "I am arranging with Irving about shipping the proper support. You are in the meanwhile perfectly at liberty to go into expenditures of $15,000." Lovestone also obtained $3,500 so that his agent Harry Goldberg (Ella Wolfe's brother) could go to Indonesia. He wanted $35,000 to start a labor training school there, but that was on hold. Lovestone took the occasion of his meeting with Dulles to gripe about the accounting practices of the agency, which had made a thousand-dollar mistake in its favor. He told Dulles that he had once been dressed down for a one-dollar mistake by the CIA bookkeeper. He also deplored "the piecemeal hand-out of funds," which was "not conducive to the building up of confidence."

But Lovestone liked Dulles, who was a great improvement over the man he had been assigned to under Wisner, Pinky Thompson, an affluent Philadelphia clubman with a plantation in Georgia where Wisner went shooting each year. Thompson was a large man, heavy in the chest, with curly hair and a big, friendly face, a boozer like so many of the men in the OPC, which was also known as the FOW (Friends of Wisner). Wisner used Thompson as a utility outfielder. Jay called him Stinky, for his habit of getting drunk to the point of incoherence at lunch. Thompson represented the society-boy dilettantism that Lovestone detested, while in Dulles he found a real pro, well-informed, experienced, and balanced in his judgment, though as devious as the others.

Lovestone also had Carmel Offie on his team now, which was a mixed blessing. Offie was an intriguer at heart, always pulling strings and working angles. He held a grudge against the CIA for firing him. Playing to Lovestone's disgruntlement, he was only too glad to run down Wisner, Dulles, and the rest. It was an odd situation: Offie was the liaison between the FTUC and the former employer he had come to despise.

Offie told Lovestone that at a dinner attended by Allen Dulles and Maynard Barnes, an old friend of Offie's from the Paris embassy days who had also been minister to Bulgaria, the status of the refugees from Eastern Europe had come up. "By Gawd," Dulles said, "these refugees have never lived so well in all their lives as they are living here, but they are getting too big for their britches, and they'd better do what we tell them to do or else." Barnes said they were men of principle who should not be bought with good living conditions. Dulles said, "Dimitrov [the Bulgarian] has gone practically wild, Mikolajczyk [the ex–prime minister of Poland] never did have any brains, and Nagy [the Hungarian] is saying terrible things about us. I know it because we intercept his mail." Offie told Jay that it was indiscreet of Dulles to say at a dinner party that he was opening the mail of the refugee leaders.

At another dinner, Offie reported, he had seen John Paton Davies, the China hand who was to be suspended from the State Department that June of 1951 as the result of Senator McCarthy's charges. Davies had said of the CIA: "That outfit isn't second-rate, as I used to think, it's fourth-rate," a judgment with which Lovestone heartily concurred. (Davies was cleared of all charges. However, he was fired by John Foster Dulles in November 1954 on the ground of "lack of judgment, discretion, and reliability.")

Offie also reported that Wisner had said, "Poor Carmel, as a result of the persecution he's been through, he has become positively nihilistic." "My crime," Offie told Lovestone, "an unpardonable one, was that I had been too intimate and honest with you." Thus, Offie became an Iago-like figure, dripping poison about the CIA into Lovestone's receptive ear. Lovestone and Offie began to refer to the CIA as the Fizz Kids, effervescent but producing only bubbles.

In March 1951 the situation deteriorated once again. Lovestone came down with viral pneumonia resulting from overwork. Offie wrote Brown that there was still no French budget. "There is confusion here about it all, with the Fizz Kids denying they promised to produce, while Jay was told that the necessary would be done. . . . There should be no difficulty about the increased maritime budget of our Corsican friend [Ferri-Pisani,

who had just scored a big success by taking over the Dockers' Union in
Le Havre]."

It seemed to Offie that he and Lovestone had done everything to
make the system work, but it simply didn't work. He urged Lovestone
to see "the super-duper Fizz Kid" (General Smith) and recommend
that only one person deal with the FTUC, so that they would not have
to go to Stinky and two or three others, then to an area desk, then to a
project committee, then to a special funds committee, then to a coordination committee, then to a security committee, and then to an implemen-
tation committee, ad infinitum. The red tape was mind-boggling. Offie
thought the CIA under Smith was changing for the worse. One of his
friends told him that Smith was being severely criticized "for bringing in
a lot of deadbeat generals who don't know their ass from a hole in the
ground." Wisner now had less authority than ever, Offie thought, and
Lovestone should deal with someone else.

As if in reply to Offie's hopes, in April 1951 Dulles brought in his
protégé Thomas Wardell Braden to handle labor matters. Braden was an
immensely likable, bright, and nonthreatening fellow. After talking to
him for fifteen minutes, you wanted to offer him a job or ask him to
marry your daughter. Born in 1918 in Dubuque, Iowa, he was known as
the man with the Marlboro cowboy face. After graduating from Dart-
mouth, he enlisted in the British Army in 1941, serving in the Royal Rifle
Corps in North Africa, then transferred to OSS. After the war, through an
acquaintance with Nelson Rockefeller, he became executive secretary of
the Museum of Modern Art, where he met his ebullient wife, Joan, with
whom he had eight children. "I was way over my head," he recalled. "I
didn't know enough about modern art."

In 1949 Dulles hired Braden away to be executive director of the
American Committee for a United Europe, one of those high-minded
Cold War outfits where former OSS men like Chairman Wild Bill Donovan and Vice Chairman Allen Dulles waited in the wings to be recalled to
active service. It was there that Braden met Lovestone, who was on the
board, and when he made his lateral move into the CIA in April 1951, he
wrote his new acquaintance: "I am down here on a short assignment as
Allen Dulles' assistant. I hope we shall not lose touch with each other.
My address is Central Intelligence Agency, 2430 E. Street, N.W."

Perhaps Braden was the man Lovestone and Offie were looking for,
who would be more understanding of the FTUC position, and who would
create a separate labor division. Then again, perhaps not. For, according
to the Monk, the Fizz Kids were planning to circumvent Lovestone as

often as they could: "There will be a more concentrated effort to allow people in the field [Brown, Etter] to work independently of the home office.... Seeds and ideas would be gotten around you by working with the boys in the field who would be glad to receive approaches. This is the party line as conceived by our 'friends.'"

Acting on Offie's advice, Lovestone asked to see "the super-duper Fizz Kid," and he and Dubinsky were given an appointment on April 9, 1951. Offie wrote Brown: "I'm afraid it's going to be rough and heavy but we have made up our minds that we don't care." Lovestone went down his list of grievances, telling General Smith that the CIA people had rejected his request for a blanket sum for operations in the field. They had listed Irving Brown as "insecure" and himself as an ex-Communist, which had killed mutual confidence.

Everything had to be reorganized, Lovestone said. Every project had to be put in writing, with at least 50 percent of the funding advanced upon approval. The FTUC would no longer submit to the method of the carrot and the club—that is, to threats of cutting off financial support unless satisfaction was received on some minor or unrelated item. The conversation grew quite heated, with Smith barking at them, but Lovestone barked back: "You may be a general, but you talk like a sergeant."

After his talk with Smith, Lovestone wrote Dulles to congratulate him on his daughter Toddie's wedding and asked about China. "Unless I get an answer, I shall be compelled to cable all our field men to return," he said. Dulles replied on April 26 that they were going over the projects one by one. The full French budget had finally been approved, and Brown was operating under it.

Under the new system, "Memorandums of Understanding and Agreement" were now drawn up for each project between "Mr. George" (Lovestone) and "Mr. Welsh" (Welsh was Allen Dulles's middle name). In May a memorandum on India pledged $30,050 for the 1951 budget for Lovestone's man there, Richard Deverall.

For the Finnish SAK, the agreement provided $50,000. Lovestone sent $15,000 to Brown for "the northern lumber people." For China, Lovestone felt the offer of $1,500 a month was inadequate. "Mass labor activities when conducted on an underground basis in the face of Communist Chinese terror cannot be operated on a push-button basis at somebody's whim and will," he wrote Dulles. "We do not want to be held responsible for any further loss of life in this struggle as a result of negligence and incompetence."

To Lovestone's surprise, Bill Etter was back in the States in June

1951, without having warned him. His wife was distraught because one of their children had tuberculosis, contracted, he thought, when they were in China. Etter himself was fed up, telling Lovestone that "these lousy characters who claimed to be our friends could never get around to understanding our position. . . . The monthly help has all gone into operations. . . . Living conditions are tough." The China operation, as has been seen, thereafter went downhill. On November 9, 1951, Lovestone sent Dulles an itemized report that showed a deficit of $2,435.97, and China was closed down. Lovestone was shocked by the senseless loss of life and the CIA's cavalier attitude.

His worst nightmare was that the Fizz Kids would bring the CIO under the umbrella. In May 1951, Squinty was in a New York hospital for a week getting a full checkup. When Lovestone paid him a call, Dulles told him in passing that he was using Braden as his contact man with Mike Ross, the genial Britisher who was running the CIO's newly formed International Committee. "This is a disgusting situation," Lovestone wrote Brown on May 26.

As Braden recalled, "Allen would ask me, 'Have you seen Mike Ross lately? You ought to go and see him, Tom, maybe he needs ten thousand dollars.' The fact that the CIA was funding the AFL was known in inner circles. Walter Reuther knew it, and Dulles didn't want to make enemies out of the CIO, so he cut them in. From time to time Allen would tell me to help Mike Ross and give him a few thousand in cash."

In May 1949, Victor Reuther had been shot in the face by Detroit gangsters. As he recalled, "I lost my right eye, my teeth were shattered into my skull, my right arm was paralyzed. I had bodyguards in my apartment, sleeping on the floor on the goddamned rug. They made my children nervous." So when Philip Murray in the spring of 1951 asked Reuther if he wanted to become CIO European director, he was glad to leave with his wife, Sophie, and his two sons, John and Eric. "I wanted to get the hell away from my bodyguards," he said.

Ancient enmities were revived, going back to the Homer Martin fight in Detroit in the late thirties. Victor Reuther still despised Lovestone, saying, "If Jay could cut a deal with Harry Bennett and Ford, I wasn't surprised he cut a deal with the Corsican mobsters in Marseilles. The net result was to bring the Mafia into the international labor movement. Jay was divisive. If you had three people in a room and he was one of them, you had three caucuses. If Jay was invited somewhere, he would come in through the transom even if the front door was open. He loved to be conspiratorial. The greater tragedy was that George Meany used him as a gray eminence."

Lovestone didn't like Victor much either, saying that "with Victor it is not enthusiasm and innocence but petrified clichés and a Messianic complex." Victor left for Paris in May 1951 and set up an office in the rue du Temple, a proletarian neighborhood near the Hôtel de Ville (City Hall), in contrast to Irving Brown's fancy address on the rue de la Paix. "I did not go to France to compete with Irving," Reuther recalled. "I hoped we were on the same side. But I disagreed with Irving's appraisal of who was reliable. He dismissed the Catholic trade unions and backed the Force Ouvrière."

By assisting the CIO, Lovestone figured, the Fizz Kids were protecting their flank in case Adlai Stevenson, who was likely to gain the support of the CIO, won the 1952 Democratic presidential nomination. Dulles was courting the liberal wing of the Democratic Party by funding the CIO.

One day Braden flew to Detroit carrying fifty thousand dollars in cash, took a cab from the airport to the UAW headquarters, and gave the money to Walter Reuther. "There was no congressional oversight of the CIA then," Braden recalled. "I could hand over fifty thousand dollars and never account to anybody. The CIA could do exactly as it pleased. It could hire armies. It could buy bombs. It was one of the first multinationals."

According to Victor Reuther, however, Braden gave the money to one of Walter's aides, Jack Conway, who sent it to him in Paris. Victor gave it to Paul Vignaux, the head of a reform group in the Christian Federation of Trade Unions.

Lovestone went to Europe in June and July of 1951 to block the CIO inroads and reported to George Meany on June 19 that "Victor and Co. are very busy here. . . . What is new and dangerous is that the Fizz Kids have entered the picture and are collaborating in silly projects with Victor," one of which was backing the Socialist UIL in Italy. "Does the right hand know what the left is doing?" Lovestone wondered.

When Lovestone got back in August, Offie had a backlog of gossip. There had been a blowup with Stinky Thompson, whose "drunken parodies" dealt with Jay's sabotage of the Fizz Kids' activities in helping the CIO. One day Lovestone would be called to account, Thompson warned. He was going to get word to high AFL officials that Jay was using his position to vent his personal prejudices. Offie told Lovestone that "Stinky gets everything twisted because he can't think straight." He got so drunk that he threatened to physically attack Offie, who commented: "I am well able to take care of myself in fisticuffs or rough-and-tumble."

Offie also had another disparaging story about Allen Dulles. During World War II the Romanian industrialist Nicholas Malaxa had been a business partner of Albert Goering, the field marshal's brother, and a supporter of the pro-Nazi Iron Guard, which in 1941 conducted a pogrom in Bucharest, murdering seven thousand Jews. Later Malaxa served the Communist leadership in Romania and was rewarded with the return of $2.4 million in frozen funds.

In 1946 Malaxa came to the United States on a trade mission and stayed. His lawyer in his efforts to obtain citizenship was Allen Dulles, who, according to Offie, managed to transfer his "ill-gotten gains" to American banks before joining the CIA. An immigration hearing for Malaxa was held in September 1951. Malaxa's lawyer was the prominent New Dealer and State Department man Adolf A. Berle. Before the hearing Malaxa had been given three-month renewable residence permits. But now, Offie thought, he would probably get his permanent permit. "Malaxa stinks to high heaven," Offie told Lovestone, "and the whole thing was engineered by our gouty friend."

In 1951 Malaxa set up the Western Tube Company, supposedly for oil drilling, which planned to build a factory in Whittier, California, the hometown of Sen. Richard Nixon, Eisenhower's running mate in the 1952 election. Nixon asked the Immigration Service to give Malaxa a "first preference quota" for permanent residence on the ground that he was essential for the construction of the plant. Western Tube was in fact a dummy company created for the single purpose of obtaining citizenship for Malaxa. According to Seymour Hersh, Nixon received from Malaxa a check for one hundred thousand dollars. A copy of the check came into the hands of the CIA, but Smith sat on the information, which would have hurt the Eisenhower campaign.

In the fall of 1951, Allen Dulles was in Europe "to set up a few more of his little empires," as Lovestone put it. In October both Lovestone and Brown had their minds on the World Series. Their passion for baseball was a strong bond. Lovestone was like the radio announcer Mel Allen. He could give you the play-by-play with all the fine points. He could tell you which foot Willie Mays landed on after jumping to catch the ball against the wall, in order to pivot and throw. It was an all–New York World Series, with the Yankees beating the Giants. In Paris, Brown rocked with laughter as he told his wife, "I wish I could see Jay's face when he sat at the game and watched the Giants go up in smoke." Rubbing it in, he wrote Lovestone on October 13 that "it just goes to prove that when one plays baseball, one should not mix categories, as we used to say in the old Hegelian days, by bringing in the strategy and tactics of football." Jay replied that "the Bronx Yankees are a special breed, which makes them neither Bronxites nor Yankees."

In November tragic news brought Lovestone back to reality. Dulles's twenty-two-year-old son, Allen Macy, a Marine lieutenant in Korea, was critically wounded by shell fragments. He had volunteered for assignment as a forward artillery observer and was in the wrong place when mortar shells began to fall. Lovestone wrote on November 28: "I hope you are getting encouraging news re your son's condition." The news, alas, was not encouraging. Allen Macy, a promising young man who had graduated from Exeter and Princeton, suffered brain injuries. In and out of medical care, he finally had to be placed in a Swiss sanitarium near Lake Constance.

It had been a difficult year for Lovestone. The CIA connection was proving to be a terrible encumbrance. The Fizz Kids had fostered divisiveness, trying to hire his people behind his back and nitpicking him to death with their dollar-by-dollar accounting. They had killed the promising Formosa operation and left Etter's agents on the mainland twisting in the wind. Lovestone had never imagined that he would be responsible for sending people to their deaths, and it weighed on his conscience. In Italy the CIA was subverting his policy by backing the Socialist UIL while he fought to maintain one powerful anti-Communist federation.

Lovestone never fully grasped that he and the CIA had different agendas. His aim was to promote free trade unions as a way of checking Soviet expansion. The CIA agenda was to infiltrate all the significant groups in a given country. The agency wanted footholds in all camps, which was one reason it backed the CIO, because it had access to different camps. As Sam Halpern, an analyst in the Far Eastern Division, put it: "I was collecting intelligence. I was not involved in nation-building."

To cheer Lovestone up, Offie organized a dinner for him with Chip Bohlen, Dick Bissel (the Marshall Plan strategist about to join the CIA), and Alice Longworth, the daughter of Theodore Roosevelt. "She asked me if I could get Joe Alsop," Offie said, "and I said certainly not—he always likes to dominate the conversation."

Carmel Offie's contract with the FTUC expired in June 1952, and he went looking for greener pastures. In his work for Lovestone, Offie had become familiar with the ins and outs of offshore procurement, under which the Mutual Security Administration (successor to the Marshall Plan) handed out hundreds of millions of dollars a year to foreign companies. Lovestone monitored those contracts, trying to see to it that they did not go to companies employing Communist workers.

Thanks to this know-how, Offie landed a job as consultant with the high-powered Washington law firm Cummings, Stanley, Truitt and Cross. Homer Cummings had been attorney general under FDR, and Max Truitt was the son-in-law of Vice President Alben Barkley. With Offie on board, the firm could obtain lucrative fees from foreign companies needing a little help in obtaining MSA contracts. At the same time Offie continued to work as a consultant to Lovestone.

Unknown to Offie, the FBI had been investigating him since 1950, when his homosexuality was publicized on the floor of the Senate and he was forced to leave his job with Wisner. Agents tailing Offie saw him on several occasions in the company of Lovestone. On August 22, 1950, FBI Director J. Edgar Hoover added this comment to a report on Offie: "Shouldn't we keep an eye on Lovestone?" The FBI had a file on Lovestone going back to 1922, which was periodically updated. On December 31, 1943, a bureau report stated that "Lovestone cannot be completely trusted. Informants have stated that he continued working for the OGPU after being expelled from the Communist Party. . . . He may still be a Communist and a very dangerous one." (The informant was probably Nicholas Dozenberg, for whom Lovestone had done a favor in the early thirties.)

In September 1950 the FBI opened an espionage investigation of Lovestone, on the grounds that "he may be engaged in activity on behalf of the Communists, having at one time been alleged to be employed by Red Army intelligence." It was part of the FBI reporting system to keep updating unsubstantiated accusations. The bureau of course did not know that Lovestone was now a fervent anti-Communist covertly working for the CIA. This investigation, which lasted until 1957, used the following methods:

- Physical surveillance: Lovestone was followed wherever he went.
- Continuous mail cover: His mail was opened.
- Confidential informants, at least one of whom was privy to his conversations with George Meany in the Washington headquarters of the AFL.
- "Technical coverage" on his home phone, which was authorized by Hoover on October 23, 1950.

The FBI phone tap soon revealed that Lovestone had a lady friend and associate, Louise Page Morris (of whom more later). A November 1950 phone tap recorded a conversation between them concerning the CIA director.

According to Morris, General Smith, Eisenhower's chief of staff during World War II, when he was acclaimed as the war's "general manager," was building up an art collection by helping himself to some of the paintings looted by the Nazis during the war. Morris called this "looting the looters." When the American army moved into Germany and Austria in 1945, they found that both countries had been turned into warehouses of stolen art. Anticipating the division of their country into zones of occupation, the rulers of the Reich had moved the art to hiding places in what they thought would be the American zone.

Racing across southern Germany, General Patton's Third Army took the small town of Merker-on-the-Werra on April 6. Outside the town, in the dark, damp tunnels of the Kaiseroda mine, Patton's men found not only four hundred tons of art but one hundred tons of gold bars and thousands of bags of currency, stored there by the Reichsbank in Berlin to keep the Russians from taking it.

Patton had seven hundred men guarding the mine when he showed the gold horde a few days later to an astonished Eisenhower, who was accompanied by his chief of staff, "Beetle" Smith; his political adviser, Robert Murphy; and the First Army chief, Omar Bradley. Over dinner that evening, Smith suggested that part of the captured German gold be distributed among the American generals chiefly responsible for defeating Germany. "Can't some of us quietly arrange some of our own bonuses?" he asked. He may have said it in jest, but Murphy was "horrified," according to Secretary of War Henry L. Stimson, who recorded the incident in his diary. This remark was one of the factors that led FDR to appoint Gen. Lucius Clay as commander of the U.S. zone in Germany, rather than Beetle Smith, who wanted the job. Clay observed that "the president has told me several times he has lost confidence in Smith," who seemed to have a limited understanding of civilian values.

Smith remained as chief of staff of the U.S. Army there, based in Frankfurt, until January 1946, when he went back to Washington and was appointed ambassador to the Soviet Union by President Truman, who liked him. While in Germany, Smith had enlisted the services of an American soldier who was knowledgeable about art, the Polish-born sculptor Nisan Trigor, a close friend of Louise Page Morris (he had done a head of her in 1941). Trigor told Morris that in occupied Germany in 1945, in the shadowy world of black marketeering, an Old Master could be had for a carton of Lucky Strikes. Looting was commonplace, and there was leakage from the American collection points in Marburg (north of Frankfurt), Munich, and Wiesbaden (west of Frankfurt). Trigor's job, he told Morris, was to find some paintings for Beetle Smith. The trick was, he said, not to take any paintings that would attract attention, the loss of which would be investigated. Five years later, in 1950, the collection points had still not been cleared, and there was still art for the taking. Smith sent Trigor on another mission, which was the topic of the following phone tap:

> MORRIS: Trigor is full of stories about Washington and he is coming to dinner tonight. But don't lose your temper and don't make any cracks about Bedell.
>
> LOVESTONE: I tell you, it's gonna be a tough time restraining myself.
>
> MORRIS: Don't say anything because then he'll stop talking. . . . Bedell is sending him to Germany on a particular project.
>
> LOVESTONE: To steal more stuff for him?
>
> MORRIS: It's the funniest story in the world. I think you are going to collapse, and Bedell just apparently laps up everything Trigor says. This is the answer to the whole thing. I of course cannot wait. When I get it all I'll write it down quickly. . . . But any person of Bedell's, you know—position—to take a person like that into his confidence or to give him a mission is just insane. I mean, it's just as though you gave a newborn baby a gun.
>
> LOVESTONE: Yes, yes.
>
> MORRIS: Now, there you are, and the irresponsibility of Bedell is something appalling in my mind because of this, and by God it is going to be written down word for word as soon as I get home tonight.
>
> LOVESTONE: Well, as a matter of fact you don't need to. Take a little pad and pencil in your bag and in between go into the ladies' room and make notes.
>
> MORRIS: Darling, I don't need to, 'cause I'm pretty good even remembering words that he used.
>
> LOVESTONE: Okay.
>
> MORRIS: I'm perfectly horrified.
>
> LOVESTONE: You are?
>
> MORRIS: I could scream.

Lovestone's dislike of Smith was shared by his friend "Wild Bill" Donovan, now reduced to the rank of elder statesman without portfolio while hoping to be summoned as director of the CIA. But Truman, who had no use for Donovan, had brought in Smith. Donovan pretended cordiality toward "Beetle," sending him policy papers and making personnel recommendations. Behind Smith's back, however, Donovan undermined him, going as far as taking his gripes to Capitol Hill, as can be seen in the following tapped conversation of March 21, 1951, between Lovestone and Donovan.

Lovestone was in one of his bilious moods and told Donovan that the CIA boys were "Park Avenue socialites and incompetents and degenerates."

LOVESTONE: I'm just about to start a fight with your friends.

DONOVAN: Who? . . . Mr. and Mrs. Smith? . . . I'm glad to hear it.

LOVESTONE: Oh, and it will be a fight that may have repercussions on the Hill.

DONOVAN: Good work.

LOVESTONE: You see . . . I'm nobody's stooge, or agent, or lackey.

DONOVAN: What's the basis of it, Jay?

LOVESTONE: The basis of it is that . . . they're trying to tie me down to certain things I won't accept. . . . They can go plump to hell. . . . The old man [Smith] is sick, you know. He is very ill. He's not around much. This is strictly entre nous.

DONOVAN: I told you that some of these Republican senators asked me to appear before them, which I did. I thought I'd have a fight with Taft and the others, but I didn't. This fellow from Wisconsin, Wiley, he said we got to get rid of Smith.

LOVESTONE: This fellow they brought in, Allen Dulles, they can have him for my half-penny. . . . I had a session with him and—

DONOVAN: Of course. He just is overruled by his subordinates. That's the damndest thing I've ever seen.

LOVESTONE: Well, I don't think so. . . . You know, he's a better intriguer than you think. . . . But as far as that goes, General, you have no conception of intrigue, that's your weakness . . . but that whole organization is thoroughly mismanaged, thoroughly inefficient, thoroughly irresponsible.

DONOVAN: Well, I agree with that.

LOVESTONE: They have lost the goodwill of all the refugees whom they thought they could corrupt for $375 a month.

DONOVAN: Well, they're very foolish, Jay. You can be one of the greatest assets they have, as I told them.

LOVESTONE: . . . If you ask me, that Smith doesn't know what the hell goes on even.

DONOVAN: As you know, three of them on top, Jay . . . and the three are at one another's throats.

LOVESTONE: If they don't accept my proposal . . . then I will go to the Hill. I like Senator McCarran, see?

DONOVAN: It's a very sad loss for our country that they haven't been able to work things out.

LOVESTONE: They got people out of China who came for appointments and never kept them, and they double-crossed them.

DONOVAN: Oh Christ.

LOVESTONE: I have never seen any public administration at a lower point than what we've got in Washington now.

DONOVAN: I was three and a half hours with these congressmen, some of the boys from the House in there, Tabor, Wigglesworth, those fellows. Their greatest hate is Acheson. They say Acheson has been given control of the whole government.

LOVESTONE: Acheson is a much overestimated hero, pretentious, pompous, shallow, with no principles for or against. But what is your relationship with Bedell?

DONOVAN: Oh, well, my relationship with Bedell is a very frank one. I told him to his face that what he was doing was destroying everything that I've ever undertaken to build up in intelligence. Because he surrendered to State. He dismantled that whole political intelligence. He has no comprehension of what it's about. . . . And one fight he is having with Dulles, is that he promised Dulles he won't bring in any other military men, and then the next minute they're in.

LOVESTONE: You know, by the way, they have turned down my friend Carmel. They criticized him that he is too communicative to outsiders, so he asked them which outsiders and they mentioned Irving and me.

DONOVAN: Oh Christ.

By January 10, 1951, Hoover was urging that "a very thorough and searching investigation of Lovestone should be made." By then the FBI had figured out that "Offie may be employed in a covert capacity or on a special project by the Army." On May 8, as part of its normal distribution, an FBI memo was sent to Smith describing Lovestone as "a proficient con-man capable of intrigue and assuming any role . . . the type of operative relied upon by Russia to assume an inactive and anti-Communist role for a number of years. . . . It was this informant's opinion that Lovestone is still a Communist and a very dangerous individual."

Of course, the informant might have gone back thirty years, or had an ancient grudge against Lovestone. Or it might have been the informant described this way: "While entirely honest and very highly motivated, is inclined to be somewhat eccentric and erratic . . . and to see things that may not have happened." By June the FBI realized that Offie and Lovestone worked for the AFL. On June 13, Agent S. J. Tracy recommended that Offie be investigated "with a view to eliminating him from his present employment in the AF of L." Hoover, personally keen to nail him, commented in the margin that "Offie is dangerous to the security of this country." In the margin of another memo, on January 16, 1952, he scrawled, "We should be alert to Lovestone, Offie, and Brown, as I have grave doubts about this trio."

In his research Offie sometimes obtained classified information about where the offshore contracts were going. It came to the attention of Col. Thomas C. Murray in the office of the secretary of defense that Offie had quoted verbatim the entire proposed Italian offshore procurement program for the fiscal year 1953. Murray passed the information on to Hoover, and on December 9, 1952, two FBI agents interviewed Offie in his office at the Cummings law firm on K Street. Offie said that in his work with Lovestone and the FTUC he had followed the Italian program closely, discussing it with the U.S. ambassador in Rome, Ellsworth Bunker. It was part of his job to spread the contracts where they could combat Communist influence.

In December the Defense Department ruled that Offie was entitled to the information, and the case was closed. But Hoover maintained an interest in Lovestone and Offie. When Offie was quoted by the columnist Westbrook Pegler as saying that he had been framed in the Lafayette Park arrest, Hoover commented in a handwritten note: "It seems to be an inherent part of a pervert's makeup to be also a pathological liar."

Offie did so well with offshore procurement that he started his own company, Global Enterprises. By 1955 he had a house on Woodley Road with an excellent wine cellar, and a farm in Markham, Virginia, to both of which Lovestone was often invited.

Offie was known no longer as the Monk but as the Grasshopper, always hopping around the globe. In 1972, on a British Airways flight from London to Brussels, he took his last hop. His plane crashed on takeoff at Heathrow, as his friend the American ambassador to Belgium, Douglas MacArthur II, nephew of the general, waited for him at the Brussels airport. Offie was sixty-three.

Lovestone was having dinner at home in New York with Louise Page

Morris when the phone rang with the news that Offie had died. Morris said it was the only time she ever saw Lovestone cry. "Carmel looked like a monkey, but his drollness made up for his ugliness," she recalled. "He had more lines out than the phone company."

The memos from the FBI director regarding the watch on Lovestone kept coming. On January 28, 1952: "It is imperative that this investigation fully develop his . . . possible connections with any Communist underground movement to be doubly sure that he is not a sleeper-type agent." Every conversation, every activity was reported. In January, Lovestone discussed the Harriman-for-president movement. "Don't take it seriously," he told Morris. "It's bad enough that Harriman takes it seriously. Although Harriman would be a good candidate since he has deserted his class like Roosevelt. However, he lacks the guts and is not as dynamic as Roosevelt."

By July 1952, Hoover seems to have figured out that Lovestone had some connection with the CIA, noting: "This CIA operation is certainly a mess of confusion." By October the FBI had its "first indication that Lovestone's activities in the international field have developed to the point of sending roving ambassadors through countries in the [Latin American] hemisphere. As you are aware, he has representatives stationed in Europe and the Far East."

On October 7, Lovestone told Morris that the CIA had bugged the Soviet embassy. "If I were Acheson," he said, "one fine morning I'd swoop down on the Russian ambassador and confront him with some stenographic records we have of what goes on in there and declare the ambassador a spy and give him forty-eight hours to leave." The FBI was astonished by this information, since it was supposed to handle domestic spying.

> MORRIS: But you never give your hand away, that you know.
> LOVESTONE: They could do it without giving their hand away.

In November, after Eisenhower's election as president, Morris told Lovestone she had heard that Allen Dulles would head CIA. Lovestone disagreed. He was furious with "Frankie boy" [Wisner] and said, "This section is going to be exploded if it's the last thing I do."

On December 30, Lovestone called George Meany and reported that Dubinsky was upset over Julius and Ethel Rosenberg being sentenced to death for espionage.

LOVESTONE: He's in a state or peculiar mood.

MEANY: Was he in his wavering mood?

LOVESTONE: Yes. This is for yourself, you don't know. This Rosenberg business, you know. There is a big drive on, particularly amongst the Jewish people.

MEANY: Sure.

LOVESTONE: I want you to know he's wavering on that.

MEANY: Oh, no!

LOVESTONE: Yes, he hasn't issued any statements yet.

MEANY: Oh my God.

LOVESTONE: He said, you know, they tell me there are two children involved. So I told him there are a million children involved in the United States who might be destroyed because of what these fellows have done and they can help themselves if they gave away some information. If they are so loyal to the other side that they wouldn't give information, why worry for them?

The conversation then turned to the newly elected administration.

LOVESTONE: Next thing—as to undersecretary of state—there's a proposal that they bring in somebody from the Quaker Oats Company. Somebody who knows nothing about the whole business.

MEANY: Well, he's made money.

LOVESTONE: Yeah, well, sure, that's your answer.

MEANY: Prerequisite, you got to show that you know how to make money.

LOVESTONE: Well, you know what the story here is. The cabinet is eight millionaires and one plumber. [Martin Durkin, Eisenhower's secretary of labor, came from the plumbers' union.]

MEANY: And they'll add more millionaires to it.

LOVESTONE: One fellow makes a crack that if they keep it going the plumber won't be able to fix it. . . . Now the next proposal is that John Foster Dulles wants his brother to be the head of the CIA so as to coordinate things. Woll is up in arms because he said that's nepotism, and the family and the law firm. Because he's a very poor administrator, he knows nothing about it.

MEANY: He can make his son ambassador to Spain.

The phone taps continued in 1953. In a January conversation, Lovestone and Bill Donovan discussed the nomination of Charles Bohlen as ambassador to Russia. Lovestone said Senator McCarthy was going to quote from the security investigation and denounce Bohlen as an alcoholic. Donovan exclaimed, "My God, that is true, too." But McCarthy did not make that accusation, and Bohlen was confirmed.

To another one of his close contacts, the chief labor writer for *The New York Times,* Louis Stark, Lovestone worried that the House Un-American Activities Committee, under its new chairman, Harold Velde, was on a lower level even than it had been under William Jenner. Lovestone said that Hoover was bitter about HUAC—"they buy some of his people to steal information and this unevaluated." Lovestone had sat in on some State Department meetings, and, he said, "You never had such a low state of morale in political relations." Stark blamed McCarthy. Lovestone agreed and said Ike and Dulles had capitulated to Joe. In September 1953, Stark was with the president in Denver and told Lovestone that "he never consults anyone except big businessmen, whom he worships." Lovestone agreed that "Ike never sees anyone in the academic or labor world—it is all big business."

In November, Eisenhower's attorney general, Herbert Brownell, in an ill-conceived attempt to exploit the politics of anti-Communism, delivered a speech accusing President Truman of having knowingly appointed a Communist agent, Harry Dexter White, to the International Monetary Fund. Lovestone was beside himself. In a tapped conversation on November 10 with his friend Ernest Cuneo, a New Dealer and syndicated columnist, he said: "This could be the beginning of fascism." Cuneo suggested that the AFL and the CIO declare a one-hour protest strike. But Lovestone felt any such strike would have a very bad effect. Cuneo said: "The FBI will suffer heavily on this as it will knock them off their pedestal." Lovestone then said: "This is a gang of vulgar and ignorant desperadoes headed by Ike himself, who is a damned fool politically, you know." Thereafter, whenever anyone mentioned McCarthyism to Lovestone, he would say, "The proper term is Brownellism."

In 1954, however, the most dangerous attack ever mounted against Lovestone came from the administration he had grown to detest—from the unlikely quarter of the office of the secretary of labor. The assistant secretary for international labor affairs, Spencer Miller, nursed a hatred of Lovestone so pronounced that the FBI at once suspected some grudge was involved, writing in a memo that "Lovestone's long connection with the AF of L . . . may have resulted in Lovestone's stepping on Miller's toes at some time . . . and it is possible that Miller may be quite vindictive toward Lovestone." The odd thing was that Lovestone did not even know Miller, a sort of jack-of-all-trades who switched from job to job. He started out in the twenties as the assistant warden of Sing Sing prison.

From there he went into the labor movement, spending twenty years as director of the AFL Workers' Education Bureau. He then served as New Jersey highway commissioner and president of the American International College in Springfield, Massachusetts. He had been named assistant secretary of labor in July 1953 thanks to the backing of Lovestone's friend and colleague Matthew Woll.

Martin Durkin, the Illinois Democrat whom Eisenhower had named secretary of labor, tangled with the president over the antilabor Taft-Hartley law. Ike told him to represent the government and not the AFL. Durkin resigned in September 1953 and was replaced by James P. Mitchell, a vice president of Bloomingdale's department store in charge of labor relations. When Durkin left, Miller stayed on.

The FBI had investigated Miller in connection with his appointment and reported to the president's chief of staff, Sherman Adams, that he was said to be indecisive, insincere, and a "parlor pink." As president of the college in Springfield he was said to have mingled personal and college expenses and to have no administrative sense. On January 14, 1953, Adams returned the bureau report, stating that Miller would not be employed. But with Woll's endorsement, he was appointed in July.

On January 7, 1954, Miller went to the FBI with charges that Lovestone was still a Communist and an active agent. When asked for evidence, he said, "Once a Communist, always a Communist." The FBI interviewer noted that "it was clear from the beginning that Miller had an ax to grind with Lovestone and that he had no pertinent information." But Miller stirred up a tempest that spread to the White House. The incident is instructive in terms of the chaos accusations can create, and also how one government department knows nothing about what others are doing.

Carmel Offie was another target of Miller's shotgun blast on January 7. Miller described him as "a tax evader, a homosexual, a blackmailer, and an extortionist. . . . He has used CIA funds to build some cabins in Warrenton, Virginia, where he furnishes women for immoral purposes. He allegedly has these cabins rigged with sound recordings and photographing devices for recording compromising situations for blackmailing purposes. . . . He brought into this country illegally a former member of the German storm troopers, whose wife was a prostitute for Offie in Warrenton." Miller added that Lovestone "probably procures people to stay in Offie's cabins."

On January 20, Miller returned with more charges. He said that Harold Stassen's deputy (unnamed) in the Foreign Operations Administration had told him that "Lovestone was responsible for sending a group of Communists to Europe who spent money wildly and caused a break in the labor movement in France." Miller also claimed that of the thirty-two labor attachés in American embassies abroad, sixteen were Lovestone men.

In early February 1954, under pressure from George Meany, Mitchell asked for Miller's resignation. To save his job Miller went to the Senate Internal Security Subcommittee, known as the Jenner Committee. Agent L. B. Nichols of the FBI reported on February 8 that a member of the committee staff had told him, "We are firmly convinced that Jay Lovestone is no good." Nichols advised: "My curbstone opinion is that we [the FBI] should stay out of this."

On February 16, Miller called FBI Agent Bartlett to tell him that the storm trooper who had lived on Offie's farm was now working in a defense plant in Milwaukee. Bartlett observed that Miller "appears to be playing cops and robbers in that he speaks in very hushed tones and is sometimes almost incoherent in his conversation."

On February 19, Miller made a third visit to the FBI offices. He said he had been to see Sherman Adams, who told him, "We want to catch this fellow [Lovestone] this time." While at the FBI, Miller received a call from the White House and a call from the New Jersey senator H. Alexander Smith. Miller said, "Jay Lovestone is the kind of fellow who wears gloves and leaves no fingerprints." Miller offered to do research on Lovestone for the Criminal Division of the Justice Department. Hoover observed, "We do not need his services. He is not to get any impression he is working for us. We will handle our investigation our own way and with our own staff."

The FBI report following Miller's February 19 visit stated that "Dr. Miller considers himself a 'living history' of the labor movement. He has followed Lovestone's activities since the twenties." Miller described Lovestone as "a shrewd, brilliant Jew with an overwhelming ambition to be one of the big shots." Miller seemed bent on seeing the Lovestone case as part of a Jewish conspiracy. He said that the International Monetary Fund "had been headed by a Jew, Harry Dexter White," and that "Dumbarton Oaks was headed by a German Jew, Alger Hiss. Few people realize that Hiss has a Jewish background." Miller said that the Oxford historian H.A.L. Fisher had written a book proving that every subversive movement of the nineteenth century had been headed by Jews.

Today, Miller said, Lovestone was "a Rasputin-type character who desires to dominate the labor picture throughout the world." The CIA, he went on, "gave Lovestone $2 million for operations behind the iron curtain, and some of it stuck to his fingers."

Miller also charged that Irving Brown had used thirty thousand dollars of the CIA's money to buy gold on the black market in Greece. He added that Matthew Woll, the man thanks to whom he had obtained his job, "poses as a great anti-Communist fighter but is working with Jay Lovestone."

On February 19, Adams called Hoover from the White House to ask him what he thought of Miller. Hoover said that Miller had just been in to see him, that Secretary of Labor Mitchell had asked him to resign, and that Miller had asked Hoover to intervene on his behalf with the White House. Hoover said he told Miller that was highly improper. "It is my impression," Hoover said, "that Mr. Miller is a gentleman who boasts quite a bit and throws a lot of names around, which always makes me suspicious."

Hoover told Adams that Senator McCarthy had been in to advise him that he was having some spadework done on Lovestone and Offie. "I cautioned Senator McCarthy," he went on, "not to jump off in deep water unless he had facts, because he could do irreparable harm." Hoover told Adams that he had said to Miller, "There is no question but that Lovestone is a rather sinister character, and it is a fact that he is being paid by the government in a kind of third-party activity to carry on certain intelligence work through the labor situation for the CIA."

Adams said that the CIA deliberately had Communists in its employ for a specific purpose, and of course that could look bad. Adams then asked how long the Lovestone investigation would take. Hoover said, "We have been working on the case for some years; he is a very astute and clever individual, and I personally have always gravely doubted his reformation. . . . He has terrific power and has boasted as to how he can get labor attachés appointed, and of his control in the AFL." Hoover added that "Lovestone has been very critical of the president personally. . . . His tie-ins with various newspaper columnists make him able to plant stories."

One of Lovestone's plants was aired on a February 23 radio broadcast when Walter Winchell said that "Assistant Secretary of Labor Spencer Miller is in the White House doghouse." Also on February 23, the agent in charge of the Lovestone investigation, C. E. Hennrich, reported that Miller "will probably continue to deluge us with miscellaneous trivia. . . . I would suggest that we ask him to submit his information in writing, except that he would spread the word around that he is being requested to submit investigative reports to the FBI."

On February 25, Adams called Hoover to say that Allen Dulles had been in touch with him concerning Miller's allegations about Lovestone and the CIA. Adams said that "inasmuch as Jay Lovestone is reported to be on the CIA payroll, Dulles must be paying for his information, and I thought I should talk to him about it." Dulles said he would give the matter his personal attention. Adams also said that Senator Smith had called him on behalf of Miller. Hoover replied that "Miller is probably going around to see as many people as he can to bring pressure to bear to be retained."

On March 4 the phone tap recorded a conversation between Lovestone and Woll:

> LOVESTONE: Spencer Miller is on the warpath.
> WOLL: Is he out yet?
> LOVESTONE: He is blaming you for his plight. . . . He says Irving and I poisoned your mind.
> WOLL: He went to see Meany, and Meany told him if he was asked to resign he better resign. . . . I told him I was through with him. When he needed me he was after me right along, but when he got the job he didn't even thank me.

On March 9, Westbrook Pegler, who had been waging war on Lovestone and Brown in his column for years, announced that "Spencer Miller, Assistant Secretary of Labor for International Affairs, has been fired because he protested against the radical background of labor attachés and other useless and pestiferous parasites. . . . Miller was fired by James P. Mitchell, a stranger who was tagged for the office of Secretary of Labor after Martin Durkin, a Democrat and the president of the Plumbers' Union, called Ike, in effect, a double-crossing liar and resigned." Miller and Lovestone were slugging it out through surrogates in the press.

As part of his counteroffensive, Lovestone wrote Hoover on March 9 that "it has just come to my attention that numerous slanderous statements have been made against me in many quarters of Washington which challenge my personal integrity, my political conviction, my motivations for breaking with the Communist Party and its world movement and masters about twenty-five years ago." He asked for a chance to answer the charges, and the FBI replied on March 11 that they would be glad to hear what he had to say.

On March 10 the phone tap recorded a conversation between Lovestone and Louis Stark.

LOVESTONE: Miller brought in the Jewish angle.

STARK: Has Ben [Mandel, a friend of Lovestone who was now on the staff of the Senate Internal Security Subcommittee] got any in with Joe?

LOVESTONE: He told me I was going to be called. My past is an open book, they can ask anything they want.

STARK: If Joe doesn't prepare this thing any better than some of these other things, he will make a damn fool of himself.

LOVESTONE: I've got at least a dozen letters from admirals and generals about my lectures on Communism at the National War College.

STARK: Joe might have a rush of brains and see the danger in this thing.

LOVESTONE: There is a terrific pressure on him. The real aim is to knock out labor as a force in foreign policy. The isolationists want a free road to fight Communism in the United States, but they want to appease the Russians to do business.

On March 14, Lovestone informed Woll that Miller's resignation had not silenced him.

LOVESTONE: Miller went to the Jenner Committee to denounce us. He was trying to create a situation whereby he would not have to resign. You see his scheme?

WOLL: He can't get it through.

LOVESTONE: If he made a scandal, some committee would look into it and Mitchell would hesitate to have him removed and President Eisenhower wouldn't want to become involved in any more arguments with senators.

On March 16, CIA Director Dulles conferred with Attorney General Brownell and his staff on problems that might arise over the Miller charges. Brownell was concerned about the CIA connection, and about Senator McCarthy airing the Lovestone matter in a public hearing. Dulles assured Brownell that none of the labor attachés were in any way connected with the CIA. Dulles also brought up Miller's allegation that Irving Brown had used CIA money to buy black market gold in Greece. Dulles said he had had inquiries made and they had turned up nothing. Miller had told the FBI that he had been given the information by a woman employee of the CIA, but when the FBI asked him to identify the woman, he declined to do so.

On March 18, James Angleton, the CIA liaison with the FBI, informed his FBI contact Sam Papich that the State Department had contacted Dulles on March 12 concerning the Lovestone matter. This was, Angleton said, at the instigation of Undersecretary Walter Bedell Smith, and Angleton underlined that it was significant that Smith was getting into the act. It would be well to bear in mind, he said, that when he was director of the CIA, Smith had developed an intense dislike for Lovestone. Smith had been perturbed that Lovestone was repeating derogatory information about Smith's alleged "commandeering" of stolen Nazi artworks.

By March of 1954, the FBI, the CIA, the State Department, and the White House all had their noses in the Lovestone goulash. Congress was about to jump in, for on March 24, jobless and bent on vengeance, Miller appeared before the House Un-American Activities Committee. In a closed-door executive session, he denounced Lovestone as a Trotskyite and a Tito Communist.

In a tapped conversation on March 26 with his friend Robert Morris, who had been Sen. Pat McCarran's chief counsel on the Internal Security Subcommittee, Lovestone said: "They are trying to spread a rumor, you know, that I was working with Russian agents a number of years after I split. I'm twenty-five years out of the racket; I was only in ten years." The last Soviet agent he had seen, he said, was Whittaker Chambers, just before Chambers defected from the party in 1938. Chambers had asked his advice about traveling to the Soviet Union to receive a decoration. Lovestone said he told Chambers: "You've been decorated twice before. This is one decoration you don't want."

Jay said it was ridiculous for Miller to call him a Titoite, for in the recent fight against Milovan Djilas, who was removed as a leader because he was too democratic, Tito had warned Djilas that if he kept it up he would land where Lovestone had landed. "I'm being held up by Tito as the model ogre," Lovestone said. Morris, who was privy to some of the HUAC testimony, said, "Only one thing they asked, if Lovestone ever renounced Marxism." "These formulas have lost their meaning," Lovestone replied. "Marx analyzed eighteenth- and nineteenth-century capitalism brilliantly, but he didn't know a thing about the United States. And don't forget that Marx made the most powerful criticism of Russia. He warned against Russian reaction sweeping the world."

On April 15, Lovestone's labor columnist friend Victor Riesel called with a juicy item: "Mitchell brought Miller into cabinet meetings, and Miller made long speeches and on one occasion fell asleep. Ike told Mitchell, 'Don't have this man here on any more occasions. Don't bring that stupid man in here anymore.' I got it from way up. It couldn't go much higher."

The Miller tempest seemed to peter out. Miller found a job with the Office of Defense Mobilization. McCarthy stayed out of it after Lovestone explained the situation to Roy Cohn on May 4. Cohn told Lovestone, "We have no interest in causing you trouble in any way."

But under the ashes of the Miller case some embers still glowed, and they flared up in December 1954. A lame-duck Republican congressman from Michigan, Kit Clardy, who was serving on a HUAC subcommittee, was badly in need of publicity. On December 15, Clardy held a press conference to reveal that his subcommittee was working on a gigantic Communist conspiracy in government departments, the "kingpin" of which was none other than Jay Lovestone.

Clardy based his information on the Spencer Miller testimony in executive session and on another source, an FBI report dated December 2, 1952, and entitled "Espionage: Lovestone and Aliases." As usual the report had been sent to the intelligence arms of the Army, Navy, and Air Force, as well as to the CIA, State Department, and White House. Someone among the recipients had leaked it to HUAC, to the acute embarrassment of the FBI. For, in the words of an FBI memo, the document contained "considerable information developed through the use of a wiretap on Lovestone's residence and developed through 'surreptitious entry.'" The disclosure of wiretap information would make the FBI look bad.

On December 16, 1954, Victor Riesel called Lovestone and said, "Hi ya, kingpin." Riesel said he would print a story that Clardy was part of a plot to smear Jay. "That way, you don't issue a statement. You don't know from nothing."

LOVESTONE: Velde has been doing this before, and this is the parting shot of the committee before it dies.

RIESEL: It's the parting shot of a lame duck. He has only ten days [before the next session of Congress].

LOVESTONE: You should talk to [Francis E.] Walter [the incoming HUAC chairman], and tell him the whole thing is fantastic, that it is just too silly for words, it is part of the Spencer Miller stuff.

RIESEL: I'll write a piece. I'll say how you worked in Italy against contracts to Communist plants and in France when I walked in on Irving.

LOVESTONE: It should have to do with AF of L foreign policy, which is

the most consistently effective anti-Communist policy in the
world, barring none.

RIESEL: I'm willing to do that and put that on the record on Monday.

LOVESTONE: I would not center the piece around me, do you understand?

RIESEL: I'll talk to Walter.

LOVESTONE: There's only one thing to do, call Walter and say that this
destroys the last vestige of respect the committee had, or print a
story that this is part of the plot to smear Lovestone.

The FBI had known since July that its report had been leaked to HUAC,
whose chairman, Harold Velde, kept it in his safe. Hoover, who was said
to be "boiling mad," launched a widespread investigation. An examina-
tion of the Velde copy showed that it had originated with the Air Force
Office of Special Investigation (OSI). An FBI agent went to see Gen.
Joseph F. Carroll, director of OSI, on July 14, 1954. General Carroll said,
"This is the most disturbing thing that has ever happened in OSI." The
agent said the bureau wanted vigorous action.

General Carroll's investigators found the "access sheet" giving the
names of those who had access to the report; it had been wadded and
thrown into a wastebasket. The hunt narrowed to a highly decorated
World War II tail gunner who had flown thirty-three missions against the
Germans, Capt. Rea Van Nassan, who lived in Silver Springs, Maryland,
with his wife and two children. When questioned he admitted that he had
an interest in Lovestone and that he had received a copy of the transcript
of Miller's HUAC testimony. He refused to take a lie detector test and
would not allow agents to search his premises.

Van Nassan was relieved of his duties pending a resolution of the situation. Four latent fingerprints, found on the back of the last page of
Velde's copy, matched the captain's. Under further grilling Van Nassan
confessed on August 22, 1954. On September 1, Secretary of the Air
Force Harold E. Talbott discussed the case with President Eisenhower at
his summer headquarters in Denver. On November 4, General Carroll
recommended that Van Nassan be court-martialed. Talbott's failure to act
quickly, General Carroll said, had created a ridiculous situation. On November 23, Van Nassan was summarily court-martialed and stripped of
his reserve captain's commission. On November 24, he was hired by
HUAC.

The question now was whether there should be a criminal prosecu-
tion of Van Nassan. On April 21, 1955, Attorney General Brownell

pointed out to Hoover that the FBI report would have to be produced in court. Since the phone tap was still operative, Lovestone would become aware of it. Hoover agreed, adding that public knowledge that his agency was tapping the phone of a high AFL official "might have repercussions in labor circles."

On August 12, 1955, Van Nassan was indicted on eight felony counts. But in a plea bargain made to avoid a trial, the felony counts were dropped and he was allowed to plead guilty to a single misdemeanor—unlawfully removing 113 sheets of paper owned by the government. Van Nassan's lawyer, Edward Bennett Williams, noted that the captain had been awarded the Distinguished Flying Cross, the Air Medal with three oak-leaf clusters, the Purple Heart, and four bronze combat stars. He had acted, Williams said, out of misguided patriotism. Van Nassan received a six-month suspended sentence. By this time, after being fired by HUAC when Walter became committee chairman in January 1955, he was a salesman for a frozen-food company.

13

JAY
AND JIM

In August 1952, in a private chat with a member of the Eisenhower camp, Lovestone was told: "Well, we think we are going to win because in 1948 everybody said Truman was going to lose and he won. Therefore, in 1952, when so many people say Ike is going to lose, he will win." Lovestone was not impressed with this reasoning and bet on Adlai Stevenson, whom he didn't particularly like. He thought of Stevenson as a Calvinist preacher, able and a hard worker, who could coin good phrases for counterfeit ideas. He had played his cards shrewdly at the convention but then had surrounded himself with CIO Boy Scouts and Americans for Democratic Action crackpots like Anna Rosenberg, the liberal New Dealer active in New York City politics. What a menagerie!

Of course, the Eisenhower-Nixon ticket carried thirty-nine states and collected more than 33 million popular votes. Lovestone had been all wrong about the popular vote. As expected, the trade union members' vote had gone to Stevenson, but that did not mean that their sons, wives, and daughters voted for him. At the same time, Ike did not carry Congress decisively; he had only a slim margin in both houses. Nobody could tell who would be the new secretary of state. If it was John Foster Dulles, Lovestone said, "I might be tempted to join a monastery. . . . If it is Chet Bowles [Truman's ambassador to India], I will join a convent." It turned out to be Dulles. As for the new head of the CIA, the front-runner was Allen Dulles, though Lovestone's friend "Wild Bill" Donovan was making his availability known.

When Allen Dulles was told that the job was his, he left it to Tom Braden to break the news to Donovan, who was visibly upset and said: "Tom, Allen has never run a big organization. He'd make a very good second in command, but he has no executive authority." Dulles ran the agency for nine years as its first civilian director.

Lovestone's unhappiness with the Fizz Kids overflowed. In terms of inefficiency, changing their minds, and backstabbing, they were as rotten as the Comintern, bad paymasters, and some of their people, like the drunken clubman Pinky Thompson, were substandard. Others, like Frank Wisner, were as underhanded as any apparatchik. Carmel Offie agreed 100 percent. When Offie came down with jaundice, the doctor told him, "This as you know is due to exhaustion, fatigue, and an association with dirt. Have you had any contact with rats?" "Yes," Offie said, "the two-legged kind."

In 1951, when Lovestone's operation came under the tutelage of Tom Braden and his International Organizations Division, Braden wanted a strict accounting of funds spent. The scrupulous young men whom Braden called the Ivy League Indians came to him and said, "The people from Radio Free Europe make acceptable reports, but from Lovestone you don't hear a damn word."

In 1953 Braden went to the newly appointed Allen Dulles about the Lovestone problem, and Dulles agreed to talk to George Meany. One evening in March, Meany arrived at the stately Dulles home on Wisconsin Avenue and was offered a cigar. After Braden detailed his problems with Lovestone, Meany said heartily: "Lovestone and his bunch? Those boys do a good job." And that was it.

In 1954, Braden, always the rover, left the CIA to start a new career in California, as publisher-editor of a small newspaper, the Oceanside *Blade Tribune.* His replacement was Cord Meyer, a Marine hero who had lost an eye in the 1944 landing on Guam.

At about the same time, James Angleton was made head of counter-intelligence (CI), a position he would occupy for the next twenty years. His appointment came on the heels of the Doolittle report. In July 1954, Eisenhower had commissioned the Air Force hero Gen. James Doolittle to report on the CIA's covert activities. On August 18, Angleton gave the group a briefing. According to a top-secret FBI report, he

> was subjected to several questions which led to his open criticism of many of CIA's operations. . . . He was highly critical of Gen. Walter Bedell Smith's administration at CIA. When Angleton finished his briefing he was asked numerous questions by the Doolittle group.

Nearly all the questions were predicated on what was wrong with CIA and how it could be improved. Angleton "opened up" and said exactly how he felt about his agency. The present setup which allows for joint operations has led to confusion, duplication, and waste of manpower and money. Angleton placed great emphasis on the fact that his agency has suffered because of the many directors and the inevitable changes in policy and thinking. The changes in leadership had led to one revolution after another, which had affected production and morale. Angleton was openly and strongly critical of Gen. Walter Bedell Smith's administration and claimed that Smith had been hoodwinked by the psychological warfare experts like Frank Wisner. Smith forgot espionage and counterespionage operations and devoted his time and attention to psychological warfare projects, many of which failed miserably.

The Doolittle report established the CIA as the foremost Cold War agency and validated its espionage functions. Under Allen Dulles, Angleton found the continuity he so desired, as well as a greater understanding of the counterintelligence function. The two men had a close relationship. They both appreciated the sophistication and subtlety of counterintelligence, which consists of preventing the enemy from penetrating one's own operations. Dulles also confided to Angleton two "accounts" that had nothing to do with counterintelligence. The first was the Israeli account and the second was the Lovestone account.

Lovestone's role in the CIA had changed direction. In the early days he ran his own operations, such as with Bill Etter in Formosa. But now Lovestone's main job was collecting intelligence. He had Irving Brown in Europe and agents in India, Japan, and Africa sending in their reports, which were turned over to Angleton, who labeled them the JX files. In exchange for the reports, the agency financed Lovestone's foreign operations.

Angleton disguised the source of the JX files so that when the material was passed on to "customers," no one could tell it came from Lovestone or one of his people. This once caused a certain amount of friction between British and American intelligence services, according to a CIA man who was in the London station at the time. A wartime agreement between Bill Donovan and Sir Stewart Menzies, the head of British intelligence known as C, had been kept going after the war. This agreement, "cast in concrete and scrupulously observed," according to the London station man, called for the sharing of information and pledged that the two services would not poach on each other's turf or recruit each other's subjects.

The JX reports were distributed to the British, and on one occasion included a thirty-two-page dispatch on the inner workings of a British Trade Union Congress convention. This had in fact come from Lovestone's man in London, Jack Carney, who was an official in the TUC. But since the source was disguised, the British were sure that the CIA had recruited an agent in their labor movement, in violation of the agreement. "The Brits were aghast," the London CIA man recalled, "and my station chief said, 'God, this looks like we've got an agent in the TUC.' The Brits wanted to know who the agent was, but Jim kept mum."

Angleton had a Special Projects Section to run his two outside accounts, which he entrusted to his right-hand man, Stephen Millet, a blue blood from Bristol, Rhode Island, whose family went back to colonial America. According to someone familiar with the Angleton outfit, "Ninety-nine out of a hundred guys at the agency didn't know what Millet did. He kept to himself, though he cut quite a figure in Washington social circles."

In passing Lovestone on to Angleton, Allen Dulles made an inspired personnel decision. In Angleton, Jay finally found a CIA man he truly liked. Jim Angleton was not only a colleague but a best friend and kindred spirit. Each found in the other a deeply compatible mirror image. Lovestone, who had no family and spent three days a week in Washington, found himself practically living at the Angleton house. He was made welcome by Angleton's spirited and attractive wife, Cicely, who recalled that "Jim was devoted to Jay. He thought that Jay had struggled all his life to make his ideas prevail. Many were the times when Jay came to dinner and he and Jim sat up talking into the night. Jay was the only person Jim didn't call a cab for. Even in the driving rain or snow he would drive Jay back to the Statler."

Lovestone was accepted as a member of the Angleton family. This intense worker who had no hobbies found himself immersed in those of his friend, learning about the pollination of orchids or how to tie a fly. He drew the line at going fishing in Canada but was often invited to dinner to partake of the catch. Jay's running joke was "I hope you spared the lives of some salmon."

With the Angletons' children, Helen (known as Truffy), Jim Jr., and Lucy, Lovestone was like an attentive uncle, remembering birthdays and keeping up with progress at school. In 1968, while Truffy was at Antioch, Lovestone gave her a wallet for Christmas and congratulated her on working as a salesgirl at Macy's over the vacation. She told him that sell-ing was not her calling and that she didn't like New York because it was dirty. He replied that "if one is to live in any big city, there is no nicer place than New York. You can escape from everybody. You can even es-cape rats despite the refusal of Congress to get rid of them."

The bond between Jim and Jay was founded on the conviction that they had a higher understanding of the Soviet threat. They were the guardians at the gate, with access to information others did not have. As Cicely Angleton put it: "They saw what others did not see. They knew the enemy and how he operated. They could put the pieces together, draw the inferences. Their judgment was based on long experience."

Lovestone's experience came from leadership in the American Com-munist Party, attendance at Comintern congresses, and acquaintance with the Soviet leadership. Angleton's perspective came from his intellectual formation and an adult life spent entirely in intelligence.

Like many of the orchids he cultivated, Angleton was a hybrid. His father was from Idaho, and while riding with Gen. John Pershing in 1916 in pursuit of Pancho Villa, he had met and married a lovely Mexican girl still in her teens. Jim was born on December 9, 1917. In 1933 Angleton Senior obtained the National Cash Register franchise for Italy and moved his family there. Jim lived in Rome under Mussolini before being sent to Yale, where he founded a poetry magazine, *Furioso*. As Jim explained to Jay in their endless conversations, poetry is a good introduction to espi-onage, for in both one hunts for clues to meaning, one tries to decipher the hermetic and establish a connection between seemingly disparate motifs. In fact, when Angleton was drafted in 1943 and inducted into the OSS, he listed as his special aptitude "training in literary criticism."

As Angleton recounted to Lovestone, his friendship with poets also led to his first brush with the FBI. Having published Ezra Pound in *Fu-rioso*, Angleton went to Italy to see the author of *The Cantos* in the sum-mer of 1939, as war broke out over Europe. He wrote one of his other poet friends, e. e. cummings, that "the old fellow has got plenty on his balls and every time I get the least bit worried, he lifts me up to the point that I feel like murdering professors or at least cutting off their dung-dragging beards."

Absorbed by the myriad predicaments of launching a periodical pub-lication, Angleton was barely aware that a war was on. His one concern was what Italy would do. "I guess the crapwriters in America have been telling you that Italy wants war," he wrote cummings. "Frankly I have never seen any country that wants peace so much as do the Italians. . . . A friend of mine who has just been called tells me that after a week he and a thousand others haven't even received uniforms." And he signed off, "As ever the furious man who smoked your cigarettes and drank your brandy." As for Italy, in spite of the lack of uniforms, Mussolini invaded France in June 1940.

In August 1940, Angleton heard from Pound, who by then was broadcasting anti-Semitic and anti-American diatribes over the Mussolini-controlled radio: "If the American people *still* want [Walter] Lippman[n] and Shittery [Dorothy] Thompson and can't yet print me then they better go die. Something is diseased in the nation and no therapy will save them." Angleton commented to cummings, "Ezra . . . has a habit of placing people in his Inferno; a helluva lot of people have fallen through the hole of his outhouse."

One day in the early months of 1943, when Angleton was still at Harvard Law School, an FBI man came to ask him about Pound, whose conduct in wartime was considered close to treason. "Tell me all," the man said. "If I tell you all," Angleton replied, "it will take a long time." The FBI man insisted, so Angleton took him through the years in London and Paris and the move to Rapallo in 1925, until the FBI man had filled several notebooks. Angleton offered an exegesis of each book of *The Cantos,* speaking not of fascism and Jews but of Jefferson and social credit, until the FBI man had filled several more. "I only wanted to give you both sides of the picture," Angleton said. "Poets are funny," the FBI man replied.

That was Angleton's version. According to his FBI file, "Angleton advised bureau agents in 1943 that he was intimately acquainted with Pound . . . and subscribed to most of Pound's political theories. . . . Angleton said that Pound was irrational in his theories due to strong anti-Semitic feelings and hatred of the international banking class."

Angleton, like Lovestone, was primarily a strategist and a thinker rather than a warrior, and he did not take to the OSS training in hand-to-hand combat, writing cummings that he was "listening to a number of officers inform me . . . of the porcine ways and mechanics of kill or be killed." He preferred the lectures on methods of security to avoid detection and volunteered for the counterintelligence unit being started up in London in December 1943, known as X-2.

X-2, the only unit in OSS that was cleared for ULTRA, the British deciphering of the German military codes, shaped Angleton. It became for him a way of life and a method of thought, in which everything was subordinated to guarding exclusive access to a superior source. X-2 was a closed system and corresponded in that sense to the Marxist dialectics that formed Lovestone. Angleton, habitually secretive and fond of intricate poetic forms such as sestinas, had a nature that conformed to its requirements.

William Hood, who was with Angleton in X-2 in London, and again thirty years later in CI in Washington, after a long career on the covert side in Europe, recalled that X-2 "created a band of brothers mentality; an obsession with secrecy, with watertight compartments, was formed at an early age. Once Jim was head of CI, there was no more ULTRA to protect, but the mentality lingered, and in many cases, it was a good one to have."

Angleton stayed less than a year in London. In October 1944, a twenty-six-year-old second lieutenant with the code name Artifice, he arrived in liberated Rome to head the seventeen-man X-2 field unit. ULTRA reports told Angleton that as the Germans were pushed northward, they left Italian stay-behinds to spy on Allied troop movements. With the Germans losing the war, some of these people could be turned.

His X-2 bosses called Angleton's work with the Italians "the most spectacularly productive" of X-2's liaison efforts. In April 1945 he was made chief of X-2 for all of Italy, at twenty-seven the youngest X-2 branch chief in the OSS. He was later awarded the Legion of Merit for his "performance of outstanding services" in directing operations that led to the capture of over one thousand enemy intelligence agents.

One of the correlatives of the X-2 mentality was that you cannot have too much information. There was always a second source to be checked against the first source. And no matter how esoteric, the information was worthwhile. Lovestone and Angleton both had this obsessive curiosity. Their ultimate though unattainable purpose was to know everything about everybody.

James Dolan, Angleton's FBI liaison, recalled that when they had lunch, "he would know the life history of the waitress who had served him. The second time she served him he would be inquiring about her children and what each one was doing. It was probably all recorded in his tiny handwriting on the back of a matchbook."

As chief of CI from 1954 to 1974, Angleton had to decide whether Soviet defectors were genuine or plants; whether their information was true or false; whether, when one of them said there was a mole inside the CIA, he was telling the truth or trying to sow discord. The lesson of X-2 was that it's preferable to have unfounded suspicions than to be duped by a bogus source. Over the years Angleton was seen as having become skeptical to the point of paranoia, as having shut down perfectly good operations that he suspected were penetrated, and as having spent fruitless years hunting for a nonexistent mole. He came to be seen, unfairly, Hood thought, as "Angleton the mad mole hunter, Angleton the daffy paranoid."

But in Angleton's mind, as he explained before the Senate's Church Committee in September 1975, what others called paranoia was in reality having all the facts. When Angleton testified, Sen. Walter Mondale pointed out that President Nixon believed that the thousands of young anti–Vietnam War protesters of the early seventies were out to destroy the society and were reaching out to revolutionary movements in Cuba, China, and the Soviet Union. Angleton responded that "the depth of the president's feelings were in part justified because of the ignorance in the West regarding these matters. In other words, the quality of the intelligence going to him he found totally unsatisfactory."

Mondale replied: "That's right. Because it did not square with his paranoia that the American people were trying to destroy the country." But Angleton begged to differ: "Anyone who was receiving in-depth, around-the-clock reports from all over the United States of bombings and civil unrest and murders—and I can go all the way down the long grisly list . . . it was not in my view paranoia."

Angleton saw himself as one of the few—along with Lovestone— who did have the available facts concerning national security, in particular the Soviet threat. This gave him the arrogance of omniscience, which he let slip before the Church Committee with this observation: "And I do not base this on reading information at the corner drugstore." He had convinced himself that his information was so superior, so ULTRA-like and cosmically applicable, that it gave him a savant-like level of enlightenment. It came from debriefing Soviet defectors and from the mail-intercept program he directed for twenty years—reading the letters of Americans (including those of Frank Church to his mother) and their Soviet correspondents.

In 1955, Angleton explained, he began to read the mail traffic to and from the Soviet Union that went through the port of New York. This program was called HT/LINGUAL and lasted for eighteen years. The systematic reading of the mail of a large number of American citizens was illegal. The rationale was that sometimes you have to break the law in the interest of national security.

HT/LINGUAL was approved on December 7, 1955, and Angleton was allotted $86,722.50 for its 1956 budget. He rented a room at New York's La Guardia Airport that was off limits to postal employees to house his staff and equipment. In 1960 he added a lab to look for secret

writing and microdots. In 1962 he moved the operation to Idlewild Airport. His "flap and seal" people, as they were called, processed two to six
bags of mail a day, from five thousand to fifteen thousand items. The letters were opened with the old-fashioned "kettle and stick" method. The
glue on the envelope was softened by the steam from a tea kettle and the
letter was pried open. "You could do it with your own teapot at home,"
one agent said.

The letters were photographed and resealed, then reinserted into the
mail stream. The photographs went to Angleton's CI offices, where a
group of six "very sophisticated technicians and analysts," according to
Angleton, fluent in languages, went over them. During the eighteen years
the program was in effect, from 1955 to 1973, a total of 215,820 letters
were opened. Was the effort worth it? A 1961 review by the CIA Inspector General's Office said: "No tangible benefits have accrued to the Soviet Union Division as a result of this project."

A second review in 1969 said: "The material is of very little value.
The positive intelligence from this source is meager." Howard Osborn,
the CIA director of security from 1964 to 1974, told the Church Committee: "We got no benefit from it at all. The product was worthless." Angleton, however, believed that the project "was probably the most
important overview [of Soviet intelligence activities] that counterintelligence had."

Whether or not it was worth the risk of conducting an illegal activity
on a large scale over a long period of time, the program went ahead quite
smoothly. In 1969, however, William Cotter, an ex-CIA man, became
chief postal inspector. He of course knew about HT/LINGUAL, so that,
in case of a flap, he could not testify under oath (as his predecessor had)
that "the seal on a piece of first-class mail is sacred."

The flap came in January 1971 with a letter from Dr. Jeremy J. Stone
of the Federation of American Scientists, asking Cotter if the post office
permitted any federal agency to open first-class mail. Cotter was in a
dilemma. He had signed a secrecy oath when he was in the CIA. "If I had
responded accurately to Mr. Stone," he told the Church Committee, "it
would have blown the whole operation for the CIA." But the lie bothered
him. As he testified, "We arrest people every day for . . . opening mail,
stealing it and so forth, and so I was very, very uncomfortable with
[knowledge of] this project."

In the meantime, the Stone letter occasioned a flurry of meetings in
the agency. On May 9, 1971, CIA Director Richard Helms asked Angleton who outside the agency knew about the program. Only the FBI, An-

gleton said, "and the little gray man," the postal clerk who brought the bags to the room where the mail was screened for the "take." He was paid fifty dollars a month to perform this service. Helms wanted to give up the project or turn it over to the FBI, but Angleton said they could live with the risks.

Cotter continued to ask himself to whom he owed allegiance, the CIA or the post office. He finally told Osborn at the start of 1973 that "unless I receive some indication that this project has been approved at an exceedingly high level [meaning presidential], I am going to withdraw post office support." He gave the CIA security director a deadline of February 15.

The Watergate burglary in June 1972, with a trail that led straight to the White House, had created a new climate. The ensuing brouhaha was a sign of the trouble that could come with the exposure of the mail intercepts done with post office collusion. Osborn agreed that the intercepts "were illegal and in the Watergate climate we had absolutely no business doing this." The project was effectively terminated that month.

On the basis of his information (not from the corner drugstore), Angleton formed a worldview that was identical with Lovestone's: The Soviet system was bent on spreading Communism through the world and destroying America. Jay and Jim saw themselves as partners in vigilance, overseers of the Cold War. They shared the credo that every Soviet thaw was a feint, every overture a trap. Anyone who disagreed with them was not cleared to have all the facts.

Angleton tried to clarify for the senators the difference between those who had the facts and those who did not, as he had once tried to explain *The Cantos* to an FBI agent. People were not aware of the threat, he said, because of the policies of détente and peaceful coexistence. But détente was a ruse, and peaceful coexistence was a tactic to make America lower its guard. "It is a complete illusion," he said, "to believe that on the operative, clandestine side—which is in a sense a secret war that has continued since World War II—that the Soviets or the Soviet bloc have changed their objectives." Only those with privileged information, like Angleton and Lovestone, were not fooled.

The mail-intercept program was illegal, since spying on Americans was outside the mandate of the CIA, but Angleton, rather than apologize for it, insisted on its necessity. It was an "indispensable means of collecting foreign intelligence on the Soviets, who regard this country as the main enemy. . . . I come back again to the nature of the threat." This was followed by a lecture on the evolution of the Soviet intelligence services, based on "some thousands of pages of interrogation of high-level Soviet intelligence officers."

In fact, even as he tried to explain matters to the senators, Angleton operated from the conviction that there was an unspannable chasm between those who were "witting" and those who were not. This came out when he was asked why the CIA had ignored a presidential order to destroy the shellfish toxins that the agency had stored following one of its James Bondish attempts to assassinate Fidel Castro. Angleton replied: "It is inconceivable that a secret intelligence arm of the government has to comply with all the overt orders of the government."

This was taken to mean that the CIA had the right to disobey presidential orders. Sen. Richard Schweiker of Pennsylvania asked: "You feel, or the intelligence community feels, that they are removed from even a direct order of the president?"

"I withdraw the statement," Angleton said.

Why try to render the arcane reasoning of the intelligence mind? As Angleton later explained it to Lovestone, his reply had several levels of meaning. On one level, if a high government official named in a presidential order was thought to be a Soviet mole, the agency would be right in refusing to comply. On another, the government might give an overt order so that it could be leaked to the press while simultaneously giving a countermanding covert order to the agency. But all that was tradecraft, which Angleton did not deign to share with the senators.

Only with those who approached his level of knowledge was Angleton completely at ease. As a result, Jim and Jay were "peas in a pod," a friend said, always on red alert, seeing significance in small matters, from the vantage point of "the nature of the threat." In addition, Lovestone was Angleton's paid informant, whose reports piled up in his office under the cryptic JX label. The two communicated on a daily basis, in writing on Lovestone's part and by phone on Angleton's. Their collaboration was in effect an alliance between the CIA and the AFL. They were agreed on the need for vigilance at a time after Stalin's death when the Eisenhower administration might be letting its guard down. Between them, with their respective influence in the labor movement and the intelligence community, they formed a hidden power center bent on advancing a hard anti-Soviet line. This was particularly effective from 1953 to 1959, when John Foster Dulles was secretary of state and Lovestone could work the quadruple play from himself to Angleton to Allen Dulles to John Foster to Ike.

Lovestone kept Angleton informed on efforts to subvert their anti-

Soviet line. On May 21, 1956, he reported that Walter Reuther, unable to see Ike, had gone to see his brother Milton, to complain about "the machinations of Jay Lovestone," who had sent a list of Social Democrats in Russian gulags to Hugh Gaitskell, leader of the Labour Party in England. When Nikita Khrushchev came to England, Gaitskell presented him with the list, which conferred an "unfriendly spirit" on the visit. Reuther told Milton Eisenhower that "Lovestone is working to disrupt the efforts of President Eisenhower to establish good relations with the new Russian government." Lovestone told Angleton that Reuther's theme song was "George Meany continues the Cold War when nobody else does. He doesn't know that the Cold War is over." Jim and Jay developed an "us and them" mentality. Both of them felt they were being sniped at by the "détente-mongers" in their backyards.

Sometimes Lovestone asked for Angleton's help in lobbying for appointments for high-ranking AFL people. On March 27, 1959, he wrote that Meany was hoping to be named to the next U.S. delegation to the UN General Assembly. "Please make sure that Squinty puts in his two cents of strongest support for GM. It is most urgent that it be done now and no time lost." Jim, who was known as No-Knock Angleton for his easy access to Allen Dulles, put in a good word, and Meany was appointed.

On December 6, 1960, Lovestone wrote that David Dubinsky "would very much like to be designated as ambassador to the Soviet Union. I am all for it. I think he would do a far better job than experts like Chip Bohlen. He not only knows the language but he knows the gang and the gangsters. He is a good bargainer and he can take off two shoes in half the time that Khrushchev can take off one." (Khrushchev had banged his shoe on the table at the UN.) In a Republican administration, however, Dubinsky was a long shot who didn't place.

In the fifties, with Europe stabilized, Lovestone turned increasingly to third world countries emerging from colonial rule, where free trade unions could block the advance of Communism. Since the State Department supported the colonial powers who were NATO allies, Lovestone turned to Angleton and the CIA for help in backing the nationalist movements in Africa and Asia. Thanks to Lovestone, Angleton was provided with a second opinion on world affairs.

In 1954 a nationalist rebellion broke out in Algeria. The AFL supported the Algerian rebels, who obtained observer status at the UN. On August 6, 1956, Lovestone wrote Angleton: "For heavens' sake, can't something be done before we lose the last opportunity in this part of the world? As you know, the French have been trying to merge their Algerian mess with the Suez crisis. This is exactly what Moscow would like to see happen. How stupid can even a French diplomat be? We here have tried our best to have our Algerian friends refuse to merge their struggle for freedom with the arrogance of Nasser."

Lovestone was also deeply involved in Tunisia, which won its independence in 1956. In September 1957 he went to Tunis and met President Habib Bourguiba, who asked him, as Jay reported to Jim, "Must I become a Nasser in order to get the support that the United States gave Nasser during the Suez crisis? Must I emulate Tito? Must I do business with the Russians in order to survive?" "The situation is desperate," Lovestone told Angleton. "We have to give them certain types of military assistance to enable them to maintain order at home. The Russians are making systematic efforts to provide Bourguiba with military aid. . . . Unless we stop letting the French government dictate to us . . . we might as well kiss North Africa goodbye." Lovestone was hoping that via Angleton he could get his message across to John Foster Dulles.

Lovestone also monitored black Africa, warning Angleton on October 6, 1958, that General de Gaulle, now president of France, had given its independence to former French Guinea, which had a Communist leader, Sékou Touré. "Here is a Communist puppet, to be well-heeled, greased, and well-financed by Moscow as a model and rallying force amongst the black Africans." Guinea had already recognized East Germany and appointed an ambassador there. Lovestone urged a large CIA effort in Nigeria, which was becoming independent in 1960.

While focusing on Africa and Asia, Lovestone remained alert to developments in Europe and the Kremlin. On May 15, 1961, he argued against a Kennedy-Khrushchev summit, telling Angleton that "the most dangerous impact is that it drives home to the American people that our country is so much on the defensive that the President is going to kneel to Khrushchev in Vienna or Stockholm."

In November 1961, Lovestone reported that Khrushchev was putting military pressure on the Finns and the Austrians in a pincer movement against West Germany. "Combine this with the explosion of the fifty-plus-megaton bomb," he wrote, "and you have an entirely new situation in the cold war. It is not so cold and it is getting much hotter." Such was the leitmotiv—things were always bad and getting worse, which justified a permanent state of alarm.

In more news from behind the iron curtain, Lovestone told Angleton on June 11, 1962, that "recently Czechoslovakia in exchange for some of its spies apprehended by Bonn, sent back to Germany several former

German generals. Upon their return to Germany, these generals reported that in 1955–56 there was a heavy influx of prisoners into their jail. These prisoners were largely Social Democrats and trade unionists."

Another fertile foreign policy field that Lovestone plowed for Angleton was the United Nations. On November 10, 1959, he wrote that UN Secretary General Dag Hammarskjöld was "quite a factor in getting the Swedish crowd to award Boris Pasternak the Nobel Prize [for his novel *Dr. Zhivago;* Soviet pressure forced him to refuse]. It seems that Hammarskjöld has cooled off a bit in his ardor for the Kremlin."

On November 16, 1962, Lovestone reported a conversation with a member of the Indian delegation at the UN who said the prime minister, Jawaharlal Nehru, was getting senile in his expressions and contradictory in his utterances. The country was headed in the direction of a military takeover. At a time of Chinese border incursions, the takeover would be greatly speeded up by the first Chinese Communist bombing of any Indian city. (This was useful information, though there was no military coup, for Nehru suffered a stroke in 1963 and died in office in 1964 at the age of seventy-five. The medical conditions of world leaders were part of the CIA's stock-in-trade.)

Lovestone also wrote right after the missile crisis that November that the Cubans were spreading reports in the UN that they had shot down fourteen American planes. They promised to provide within a few days the names of the American pilots killed. The Cubans said they expected direct military action from the United States within a fortnight (it did not come).

The final link in Lovestone's chain of information to Angleton consisted of gossip, which Angleton was eager to pass on to Allen Dulles, who liked to chuckle over the foibles of the mighty and not so mighty. One item had to do with a third world ambassador to the United States, a woman, who had just been recalled because soon after her arrival she had married a man who had forgotten to divorce his wife. "When the wife threatened to make a big scandal," Lovestone reported, "out went the Lady Ambassadress."

In 1961 Lovestone reported that his friend the Spanish philosopher living in London, Salvador de Madariaga, had been discontinued as a lecturer for the BBC and as a columnist for the London *Observer* because of his "too friendly" attitude toward the United States. Madariaga had told Lovestone, "Something is radically wrong in England," and had shown him a cartoon in the *Observer* of an American spaceship on the moon. "In this spaceship," Jay wrote, "the Negroes are seated in the rear, segregated from the whites in front. Only an 'ally' can be that stinking dirty." Love-stone was always looking for examples that showed England up as an un-dependable ally.

No matter how slight or seemingly insignificant the data, Lovestone passed it on, knowing that Angleton's appetite for detail was insatiable. Thus, he reported that at the Belgrade Conference of unaligned countries in November 1961, Nasser had made special arrangements for an expert masseur for his wife. Also, in preparation for his visit to the UN Fifteenth General Assembly, Tito had ordered eight pairs of shoes.

The correspondence continued after Angleton's resignation in 1974. On July 9, 1977, Lovestone sent Angleton a photograph of the CIA defector Philip Agee giving the Communist clenched-fist salute, with the comment: "Even Soviet Marshals don't do this any more." On December 3, 1981, Lovestone wondered why Angleton was not communicating. "I am going to call you silent Jim," he said. On May 6, 1982, there was this item: "Tovarich Hiss [Alger] was paid by the University of Colorado [in Boulder] $4500 for his innocence and his very coy remarks."

By the mid-eighties neither Lovestone nor Angleton was in the best of shape, but they could look back on twenty years of daily cooperation, of sharing the same gospel and joining in its propagation. Lovestone's information was a potpourri, ranging from the momentous to the marginal. His motto was better feast than famine, for one never knew what might be of value in Angleton's planetary scheme of things. Information on Tito's shoes might develop into a prognosis of fallen arches.

14

THE AMERICAN MATA HARI

Lovestone's romantic life during this time was somewhat perfunctory. He had too much on his mind to let a woman occupy his thoughts. The world hung in the balance. When he met a woman he liked, he saw her for a while, then vanished. He traveled constantly, and his schedule in New York did not allow for candlelit evenings. The one exception was Esther Mendelssohn, who had vowed eternal love and to whom he remained devoted, though he didn't see her that often—maybe once or twice during the winter when she and Nathan came to Palm Beach, or on his occasional visits to Montreal. In any case, with Esther, the fires were banked.

In the early 1950s, however, at about the same time Lovestone found in Jim Angleton a CIA man he could admire unconditionally, he also found a woman he did not discard. Indeed, they lived practically like man and wife for more than thirty years, though keeping separate apartments. For the first time since Crissie Ware, Jay felt the aches and pains of a romantic relationship—the anger, the jealousy, and the resentment, as well as the pleasure of a strong attachment.

To compound the perplexities of their long affair, Lovestone's beloved was also a spy, known in certain circles as the American Mata Hari. Louise Page Morris, this Boston debutante who erred into espionage, this onetime Powers model–turned–secret agent, joined the OSS in 1942. After the war she worked for Wild Bill Donovan and Ray Murphy. In 1949 Angleton recruited her as his personal spy. Her cover was that she worked for Jay Lovestone's Free Trade Union Committee. She operated the "Gompers Research Library" at 406 East Fifty-eighth Street, which Angleton paid for and stocked with books, though its small reading room was rarely attended and Mrs. Morris, known as Pagie, was seldom there.

Being Angleton's roving agent for a quarter of a century was not your usual nine-to-five job. If Jim said, "Go to Baghdad tomorrow and get a line on the new regime," she went. If he said, "Find out if the Algerians are getting funds from Peking," she did. If he said, "Turn the Chinese ambassador at the UN," she tried. This was a job where she spent weeks with the marsh Arabs of southern Iraq to gauge the support of the tribes. (Once she was awakened in her tent by a large wet nose nuzzling her cheek. It turned out to be a camel. She gave the tribesmen postcards of New York City skyscrapers, which they pinned to the walls of their tents, asking, "Is it true? How many tents high?") She traveled by night to reach the bombed-out villages of liberated Algeria, helping the overwhelmed doctors care for wounded children. On an overnight train to Pakistan, she was saved from being raped by a Muslim porter by assiduously reading the Koran. She was shot at, run off the road, and almost thrown overboard on a Soviet ship, aside from minor affronts.

Why did she do it? Because her main enemy was routine—she preferred to live in a way that was improvised daily. Because she wanted to be useful. Because by any quantitative measure she would rather be terrified than bored. And why did Angleton need to go outside the CIA hierarchy to establish a private arrangement paid for with unvouchered funds? Because in his aim of attaining global knowledge, Pagie could supply a small piece here and a small piece there. Because he wanted his own pawn on the chessboard. Because she was removed from the agency jargon, the agency bureaucracy, and the agency vested interests. And because he trusted her. Besides, compared with his other expenses, she was a drop in the bucket.

Jay Lovestone and Pagie Morris came from opposite ends of the class struggle. At Lovestone's end were the teeming Lower East Side, stickball in the streets, boxing on tenement rooftops, City College, and a career as a Communist. At Pagie's end stood the family home in West Newton, near Boston, a sturdy house with a broad terrace, well-kept grounds, and half a dozen servants that spoke of unostentatious wealth. In the living room hung the portrait of an Adams ancestor. "That one goes," Mother said, "he has wooden teeth." "By marriage," Father observed, "we are related to the second president of the United States." "They were no more than farmers," Mother said. It was an ongoing dispute.

Father, Edward K. Page, was president of the New England Coal & Coke Company, which owned mines in West Virginia. He had risen in the coal business because he always did what should be done. He wore a pearl stickpin in his necktie, he called Pullman porters "Mister," and he removed his glove before shaking hands.

As for Mother, she was born Olga von Bendler. Despite the German name, her family was Polish. She met Father when she was a student nurse, and they married in 1903. Louise was born a year later. Mother was a beauty, with her mass of auburn hair and skin like honey. Wasp-waisted and full-lipped, she could have been a Gibson girl.

Louise went to Miss Winsor's finishing school in Brookline but spent part of the year touring Europe with her mother. The spring of 1922 found them in Florence, where Louise met an ardent young nobleman, Fabrizio Gonzaga, who had the chiseled features and cold blue eyes that one sees in the portraits of the early dukes of Mantua. Louise at eighteen offered proof positive of the benefits of outbreeding between a Slav and a Wasp. Her large and luminous eyes were slightly catlike, observant but wary. Her perfectly oval face, with its hint of cheekbones and turned-up nose, appeared through a tangle of bronze hair. Her cupid's-bow mouth was quick to smile and quick to say what was on her mind. Louise was the American beauty, gloriously high-complexioned and high-spirited.

The attraction was immediate and powerful. By the time Louise left Florence, there was talk of an engagement. Louise and Fabrizio pledged to love each other in absentia and write often. But when she got home, Father was beside himself. He said that Fabrizio was a fortune hunter and that he hadn't raised his daughter to "marry a Gorgonzola."

Louise nonetheless left a letter each morning in the front hall for James the chauffeur to mail. Weeks passed, then months, and not a single letter arrived from Fabrizio. She eventually stopped writing. Only later did she discover that her father had instructed James not to post her letters and to intercept those Fabrizio wrote her. Louise learned the sobering lesson of self-reliance—those closest to you can betray you, supposedly for your own good. Furthermore, this was the first time her mail was tampered with, an experience that would often be repeated when she was on assignment for Angleton.

Marriage seemed to be the thing to do, and in 1925, at the age of twenty-one, Louise married John Boucher Morris, known as Koko, a clean-cut Yale man who excelled at polo, golf, tennis, and backgammon. Koko turned out to be a drunk, who started the day with a tumbler of prohibition gin and went on from there. Louise divorced him in 1932. After her divorce she worked occasionally as a Powers model. One day her father opened a magazine and saw a full-page photograph of a young woman in an evening dress holding a lit cigarette in her left hand, over the caption: "Every Strike a Lucky Strike." "Doesn't that look like Louise?" Father asked. Then he saw another Louise look-alike sitting at a Remington typewriter. "Why," he said, "she's never been near a typewriter in her life." Threatened with having her allowance cut off, Pagie gave up modeling.

In the thirties Pagie lived a café society life of men and late nights. When she went to Larue's for dinner and dancing, the band played her special song, "Stay As Sweet As You Are." All the men had money and multiple ex-wives. Pagie came close to marriage more than once. She was engaged to Ned Post, the son of Emily Post. Ned was old New York and knew everybody. "He didn't mean to be boring," Pagie said, "but he couldn't help it. I want a man who can make me laugh every five minutes."

Then she took up with Freddie, marquess of Queensberry, grandson of the man who introduced gloves to boxing. Freddie was fun, though cross-eyed, but he was such a gambler that he'd bet on a cockroach running across the carpet. He'd bet on which of two raindrops sliding down a window would hit the pane first. Though flattered by his attentiveness, Pagie decided that "I couldn't have an affair with a cross-eyed man—you never know when he's looking at you."

It was the war that changed Pagie, giving her the chance to do something useful. In December 1942 she was in love with a White Russian, and to further the romance she took Russian classes at Columbia University. One day in Boston her father was playing golf with General Egan, who was involved in something hush-hush. They were looking for people who knew some Russian. "Why don't you try my daughter?" Page asked.

Soon she was in the OSS, in the Russian division of Research and Analysis. In mid-1943 she was sent to London as deputy chief of the USSR R & A section, located in a handsome Georgian mansion at 68 Brook Street. "I spent most of my time trying to outwit the British, who saw us as a bunch of amateurs," she recalled.

At the time she was seeing a dashing RAF Group Captain, Hubert "Dixie" Dean, who was part of Overlord. In early June of 1944, he told her, "We're going to land in Normandy. What do you want me to bring back?" So much for security, she thought, but as a joke she said, "Cheese." He brought her back a Camembert, but it was high.

Hers was a curious war, fought mainly against the British, who refused to share information. Thanks to Dixie, she found out about a secret
factory near Whitfield where the RAF was working on an ejection seat
for fighter pilots and a recoilless machine gun so the fighter wing
wouldn't wobble when it was fired. Wilfred "Biffie" Dunderdale, the
number two in British intelligence, who became a close friend, told her:
"We had to put three men on you—one to follow you, one to read your
mail, and one to tap your phone."

By the time Pagie was back in New York in the fall of 1945, the OSS
had been disbanded and she wondered what to do next. One day she got
a call from Ned Buxton, one of Donovan's principal OSS deputies, who
said, "Bill wants to meet you." Donovan was by now a semiretired elder
statesman, hoping to get back into intelligence work if Truman ever decided to start an agency. He saw a large number of people and asked
Pagie to work with him and serve as his hostess when he gave dinners,
since his wife, Ruth, spent most of her time at the farm in Virginia,
Chapel Hill.

Donovan was a seducer by instinct, and Pagie started an affair with
him. At the same time she became great friends with his wife, whose passion was riding. Ruth came on one of her rare visits to New York to see
Pagie and asked, "You're not in love with him, are you?" "Certainly not,"
Pagie said. To tell the truth, she wasn't even attracted to him physically,
though she kept that to herself. "You and I know certain things that we
don't talk about," Ruth said. "I hate New York, but Bill needs a hostess.
He has to give dinners and see people. I want you to do it, because if you
don't you know who will."

The "certain thing" that Ruth did not want to talk about was her
daughter-in-law Mary, née Pinchot, married to their son David. Mary was
so obviously in love with Donovan that Pagie had noticed it on weekends
at the farm, when Mary would say, "Mother, don't interrupt Father," and
"Mother, Father wants some coffee." "I was ready to kick her," Pagie
said. Mary wanted Donovan to divorce Ruth and marry her. Ruth now felt
that in Pagie she had found a surrogate who could protect her husband
from Mary. It was a happy faculty of Pagie's to stay on good terms with
everyone, and she also befriended Mary, who confided in her. Mary was
a devout Catholic, and Pagie asked: "What has your confessor told you?"
"He told me I'd be absolved," Mary said. Pagie replied: "Bill will never
leave his wife."

Pagie came to the conclusion that Donovan was at bottom a weak
man. He continued to take trips with Mary to see clients while asking
Pagie, "What am I going to do about Mary?" It seemed to Pagie that

Donovan, by sleeping with his daughter-in-law instead of his wife, was breaking up the marriage of his own son, and then who would take care of the children?

After Donovan's sixty-ninth birthday party in 1951, when Mary's youngest child, five-year-old Sheila, died from drinking silver polish, she started taking barbiturates. One day in July 1955, Pagie got a call from Mary saying that she was briefly in New York on her way to the Donovan house in Nonquitt, Massachusetts, and wanted to see her. Pagie was busy that day but said, "The change will do you good. Call me when you get back." The next day, July 25, Mary died in Nonquitt from an overdose of barbiturates. Donovan asked Pagie to go to the church and sit by her body. Pagie looked into the open coffin and thought, Even in death she doesn't look peaceful. She looked mad as a hornet, as if the morticians had captured her mood.

To get back to 1946, when Pagie started working for Donovan, he introduced her to Ray Murphy, the Communist expert at the State Department. Donovan was alert to subversion at home and the techniques of front groups. One such group that he had discussed with Murphy was the Congress of American Women. Why couldn't Pagie, with her OSS experience, infiltrate this outfit and find out what it was up to? Murphy asked to meet Pagie, who went to see him in the spring of 1948. The florid-faced man in the small, book-lined office in Foggy Bottom explained the situation: "The Communist Party is not strong in the United States," he said. "But they are adept at infiltrating organized groups and taking them over." The Congress of American Women was launched on March 8, 1946, at the City Center Casino in New York. The guests of honor were the French Communist Irène Joliot-Curie and the Spanish Communist Dolores Ibárruri, better-known as La Pasionaria, who had delivered the famous "No pasarán!" speech in Madrid in 1936. Among the CAW's activities, Murphy went on, was lobbying in 1947 against the Truman Doctrine (aid to Turkey and Greece), which was denounced as warmongering; protesting the outlawing of the Communist Party in 1947; and coming out for Henry Wallace in 1948.

Murphy asked Pagie to infiltrate the congress and "find out all you can." She should go to meetings and gain access to their files. Nothing could have been easier, for one of the officers of the CAW was her friend Zelma Corning Brandt, one of those rich society women who love to see their names on letterheads and who belonged to half a dozen Communist front groups. Pagie had met her in 1942 at Columbia, where they both took Russian classes.

Pagie joined the CAW and attended meetings but wrote in her first report: "I have yet to meet a Communist. These are just muddle-headed women taken in by slogans." Murphy asked her to persevere. In 1949 Pagie took a more active part, attending a meeting to support the Comintern agent Gerhart Eisler, who in May jumped bail in New York and escaped aboard the Polish ship *Batory,* and who was described by the CAW as an innocent victim hounded by government agencies. She attended "women fight back" rallies in support of indicted Communist leaders. In February 1949 a CAW delegation marched into the federal courtroom of Judge Harold R. Medina, where the Communists were being tried, but Pagie decided to skip that one. They were sure to land on page one, and they did, with Muriel Draper (wife of the singer Paul Draper and a Sanders of Haverhill, a family her father would have approved of, who had blossomed as a propagandist for the Soviet Union) sitting on a courtroom desk and showing plenty of leg, as if for a cheesecake shot.

By the summer of 1949, through repeated invitations and small favors, Pagie had won the trust of Zelma Brandt, who told her she was going to England for the summer. Pagie asked if she could borrow her apartment, where the CAW files were kept, on the pretext that hers was being remodeled. Once installed, Pagie notified Murphy, who got J. Edgar Hoover to send over two FBI men with a copier as big as a washing machine to copy the files.

The files were turned over to Murphy, to Hoover, and to Ben Mandel of HUAC, who published a report on the CAW on October 23, 1949. In addition, the CAW lost its observers' seat at the United Nations and was placed on the attorney general's list of subversive organizations. Many years later Pagie said: "That's the only thing I ever did that I was ashamed of." She genuinely liked the women she was spying on and thought of them as inoffensive.

In mid-1949 Jim Angleton was not yet head of Counterintelligence, he was chief of Foreign Intelligence Operations, with six secretaries and assistants. Feeling outflanked by Wisner and his Mighty Wurlitzer, Angleton determined to start a little foreign service of his own, and his first recruit was Pagie Morris. He was hearing about her from all sides, from Murphy, from Donovan, from Dunderdale. She seemed to be resourceful and energetic, and she had intelligence experience and an adventurous nature.

In the summer of 1949, a meeting was arranged in Washington. Pagie wore a purple skirt, a tight white linen blouse with a high neck, tucked in at the waist, and white Italian sandals. A tall, skinny young man with a handsome face—high forehead, large brown eyes, jutting jaw, somewhat like an El Greco prelate—introduced himself. He wore a double-breasted charcoal gray suit and a homburg-type hat in the Washington heat, as though trying to make himself look older (he was thirty-two).

"Would you like to work with me?" Angleton asked. "Not for the CIA. Just for me. I want you to be my eyes and ears, go on special assignments, stay clear of the embassies . . . let things come your way naturally."

"What do you want me to do?"

"Gather information."

"But I'll need some kind of reason to float about."

"There's always Jay Lovestone and the A F of L," Angleton said. As it happened Pagie had met Lovestone in Murphy's office a year before, and they were already seeing each other in New York.

In this casual manner began an association that continued for twenty-five years. Pagie was paid five hundred dollars a month plus a generous expense account. Her cover was that she worked for Lovestone's FTUC and ran the Gompers library, though she knew nothing about the labor movement, except that her father hated unions. Her code name was Martha, and her cutout was Mario Brod, an Italian-American lawyer in New York whom Angleton had met in Italy during the war and kept on his payroll. Once or twice a week she would go to Brod's office with her reports, and he would tell her what Angleton wanted done. She rarely went to Washington.

In March 1948, Murphy had introduced her to a man in his early fifties, a shade under six feet, with sandy hair, cold blue eyes, and a beakish nose. He gave off a tremendous vitality and had a sense of humor that kept her laughing every five minutes. He was like some sort of wizard who knew what was going on in every country in the world. An hour with Lovestone was like a seminar in foreign relations. She had never seen that kind of machine-gun mind.

Not only was Pagie fascinated but Jay became her nominal boss, with Angleton's blessing. Pagie never forgot their first date, before the arrangement with Angleton, in May 1948. Lovestone took her to the Automat on Fifty-seventh Street, west of Sixth Avenue, at 6:00 P.M., his dinnertime, after which he went home to his apartment at One University Place and curled up with his work. Pagie had never been to the Automat before and was enchanted by the Boston pork and beans in their earthenware crocks, the pie slices in their shining cubicles, and the glass of milk standing like a still life in its gleaming chrome frame. Lovestone talked about the Italian elections, then walked her over to Madison and put her on an uptown bus (she lived at Eighty-first and Madison). Pagie always took cabs, but she had been taught not to be rude, so she got on the bus, and at the next stop she got off and hailed a cab.

The progress of their curious romance can be charted through their letters. She wrote him often on Free Trade Union Committee letterheads that said "From the desk of Jay Lovestone." In one 1950 letter, she crossed out "desk" and wrote in "bed." In another she wrote in "pillow." On September 19, 1950, Pagie wrote: "No one is to know you are back so that we can have a peaceful week-end together. . . . Please darling. . . . As to what more one could ask for I hope you know the answer as well as I do."

From Boston she wrote: "This is just to tell you that I miss you and I love you very much. . . . A kiss and a scratch." By this time he was her d.o.m. (darling old man) and she was his l.j.c. (little jungle cat). Jay responded with what for him was unbridled passion when he wrote, "missingly and kissingly with much love," and "I shall miss no end the little delightful despot with the wonderfully devilish ways."

In both Jay and Pagie, the strategies of love and espionage coincided, based on trickery, deceit, and the need-to-know principle. Jay continued to see Esther Mendelssohn and told Pagie that he was going to visit "my sister Esther," since he did have a sister called Esther. Pagie too had a roving eye, but she compartmentalized her life so that Jay knew nothing about her affairs.

Jay was from long habit crafty and security-conscious. Stalin's enmity and the 1938 burglary of his apartment had given him the reflexes of a hunted man. He told Pagie that he always left a hanger in a certain place in his closet so he would know at once that someone had been there if it had been moved.

In 1954 the FBI began tapping Pagie's phone, according to the following memo: "Have a technical coverage of home phone telephone of subject's girl friend and associate Louise Page Morris. Installed March 31, 1954. . . . This technical coverage has resulted in the acquisition of interesting information on Lovestone's contacts with government officials." It also recorded the following conversation between Pagie's maid and one of the maid's friends: "I'm quite certain that Jay Lovestone spent the night at Mrs. Morris's apartment. She must be playing him for his money." (In fact, Jay was always broke, while Pagie had some family money.) "Lovestone is old compared to that young fellow she is seeing," the maid went on. "She is crazy about that young fellow and holds on to Lovestone for what she can get out of him." (The young fellow was the Polish sculptor Nisan Trigor, who, as described earlier, went on missions for Walter Bedell Smith.)

Keeping secrets from each other helped Pagie and Jay maintain their relationship in a state of precariousness. It could be said that they conducted their private version of the Cold War, for they quarreled constantly (verbally, never physically). One evening in her apartment Pagie, Jay, and Mario Brod were discussing the advisability of financing a French magazine called *Jeune Afrique.* Jay and Brod were for it, while Pagie was against it, claiming that the editor, Simon Malley, was a phony who pretended he had visited Red China while Pagie was sure he had not. "But he sent us postcards from Peking," Jay said. "He could have had them sent by others," Pagie said. Jay called her "an old Jesuit." "Jews and Jesuits are peas in a pod," Pagie replied. She was so mad she went into her bedroom and slammed the door. Then she thought, I'll put a good one over on them.

She went to the window and opened it wide, then hid behind the long evening dresses in her walk-in closet. A few minutes later she heard a knock on the door, and they both came in, saw the window open, and looked down at the courtyard below. "My God, she's jumped," Jay said. "We'd better go down," Brod said. Pagie put on her nightgown and went to bed. She could hear them muttering in the dark below. "Where's the body?" "I don't see anything." Ten minutes later they came upstairs and found her. "Oh, you witch," Jay said, "you've given me a heart attack." "Aries people are hard to live with," Pagie said. "It's not my fault, it's the stars."

Pagie had to have her way, in matters large and small, as the following tapped conversation with Jay shows:

> PAGIE: When are you coming to see me?
> JAY: I'm coming over.
> PAGIE: Take a cab.
> JAY: It's too expensive.
> PAGIE: I'll reimburse you when you get here.
> JAY: I don't need to take a cab.
> PAGIE: I'm feeling tired, I'm going to bed.

In any event, their affair wound down into lasting friendship and close companionship around 1960, when Pagie asked Jay: "Can't you see the difference between 'I love you' and 'I'm in love with you'?" Jay, who had never married, kept proposing, and Pagie kept refusing, and Jay would say: "I know what it is, you don't want Lovestone on your tombstone."

Pagie kept Jay off balance. He had never met a woman with such a low flashpoint, who could accelerate in ten seconds from tenderness to boiling anger. "We miss you here with all your bullying, terrorizing, and scene-making," he wrote. Pagie sent him a valentine showing a porcupine with the message "I am stuck on you," with "loads of love and kisses on your dear old Beak." When Jay asked her to darn one of his socks, she gave it back to him with the needle still in it, so that he stuck himself. "Darn your own damned socks," she said. When Jay slipped in the shower and hurt his back, she said: "What's the matter with you, can't you even take a shower without slipping, you clumsy ox?" What a hypochondriac he was, Pagie told him. If he had a scratch it was a wound, if he had a headache it was a brain tumor, if he had a sore throat it was pneumonia.

For the first time in his life since Crissie Ware, Jay experienced jealousy. He tried to monopolize Pagie and bad-mouthed her friends. One was "the fat Iraqi," another was "a germ-carrier," a third was "a taker and not a giver," a fourth was "that bubble-headed banker." "Use your head," Jay told her. "Stop being a Red Cross for so many people." Pagie's warmth, her generosity, her gift for friendship, were all irritants when not directed at him. "What bothered Jay was that he couldn't boss me," Pagie recalled.

The day came when Pagie took Jay to West Newton to meet her father, a prospect she viewed with some trepidation. Jay had devoted his life to movements; he needed something larger than himself, be it the Communist Party, the AFL, or the CIA. Her father was a self-sufficient snob who despised all causes except the abolition of the income tax. He was an exploiter of the working class in his West Virginia mines, with their company stores and company housing. He had never met anyone from the labor movement, nor did he want to, for he thought organized labor was an unspeakable evil and John L. Lewis was the villain of the century.

But Pagie and Jay took the train to West Newton, and the Jewish, proletarian, onetime Communist labor man shook hands with the Boston Brahmin. Instead of coming to blows, Pagie recalled, "they got along like a million dollars," discussing touchy issues with sweet reason. Father told Jay the company store was humanitarian. Jay said it had to do with the miners' dignity. How could he ever get out from under?

Culture shock was minimal on both sides. Father put Jay up at his Boston club, the Somerset, but that night Jay called Pagie in alarm. "There's no key in my room," he said. "There aren't any keys in men's clubs," Pagie said. "But I can't sleep if my door isn't locked," Jay said, still secretly fearing Stalin's henchmen. "Put your chair under the knob," Pagie advised.

The next morning, Father called and said, "Jay, I'm coming to pick you up and take you to the oldest church in Boston, on Brown Hill. It's so old there aren't any pews—just cubicles." In Boston, gentlemen on their way to church walked with canes, and Father told Pagie, "I'm taking him a stick." "He won't know what to do with it," Pagie said, "and he's never seen the inside of a church." Father had to teach Jay the rudiments of walking with a stick, and soon the two men could be seen heading up Massachusetts Avenue, Mr. Page leading and Jay following, trying to synchronize his gait with the stick movement, and looking rather Chaplinesque.

Pagie was living a triple life—one with Lovestone and his labor friends, one on foreign assignment for Angleton, and one with her New York high-society friends. She was a fixture in the society columns and a close friend of Polly Howe, a tall, patrician blond divorcée with a lot of money and a big apartment on Fifth Avenue. Polly's passion was the duke and duchess of Windsor, who spent several months of each year in New York. Polly gave dinners for them and loaned them her house in Locust Valley, complete with servants, while she stayed in the guest cottage.

"Put me next to Mrs. Morris," the duke would say at dinner, for Pagie had spent the war years in London while he had been exiled to Bermuda. At one dinner she told him about the buzz bomb that had landed near her office: "The queen drove down in a rickety old Ford to see where the bomb had dropped. All the people who had left work when the sirens sounded trooped around and said, 'Isn't she wonderful! What a luv!'" The duke grew misty-eyed, and Pagie saw the duchess scribble a note, fold it, and give it to the waiter to pass to the duke, who read it and absentmindedly stuffed it into his jacket pocket, but missed, so that it fell on the floor. Pagie put her purse over it and retrieved it as she got up from the table. It said: "*Smile,* you fool!"

Polly Howe invited Pagie and Jay for the weekend and they all stayed in the guest cottage, while the duke and duchess gave a dinner for forty people in Polly's house and didn't even invite her. Pagie counted the cars going up the driveway. Lovestone wrote his London informant Jack Carney: "The duke is a close friend of Pagie's. He likes to sponge on a lot of people, to use their summer homes etc. I reckon he thinks he honors them by using up their money instead of his." In one of his tapped conversations, Lovestone described the duchess as pro-Nazi and said she was very friendly with a man who was a pansy.

Most of the time, Pagie was engaged in a bewildering array of assignments for Angleton, from whom she never knew what to expect. He might say, "Would you like to go to Jordan and look around?" Or, "My people want to turn so-and-so." Or, "There's a woman in Italy giving me trouble."

Once he asked her to take a Russian freighter, which also carried passengers from Marseilles to New York, telling her only that one of the passengers would approach her and ask, "Have you been to the purser?" The crew was sullen, except for a helpful cabin boy, and when she told the purser that she wanted to tip the boy, he said, "We don't accept gratuities on Soviet ships." One moonlit night she took a walk on deck and suddenly found herself surrounded by four Russian sailors, closing in on her as she stood against the rail. Just then a passenger came up and asked, "Have you seen the purser?" He turned out to be an Israeli who gave her an envelope for Angleton. Pagie was furious that she had gone to so much trouble just to act as a courier. She wondered if Angleton had an impulse for needless complications, like a gambler who feels obliged to shuffle the deck ten times.

It all had to do with Angleton's contacts as head of the Israeli account. In this case, Reuven Shiloah, the director of Mossad, came to Washington in June 1951 to work out with Angleton an exchange of information and liaison officers. When Pagie saw Shiloah in Washington, she wore gold earrings. His hand went to her ear; he unsnapped the earring, examined it, and put it back. "What a bizarre thing to do," she told Jim. "He thought the earring was bugged," Angleton explained. Angleton would later be accused of having become an advocate for the Israelis. He was a close friend of Moshe Dayan, who directed the 1956 Sinai campaign. They shared an interest in archaeology, and when Angleton went to Israel, which he did often, Dayan took him out on digs and gave him excavated antiquities. "Jim had childlike characteristics," Pagie recalled. "He'd come back from seeing Dayan and pull an oil lamp out of his pocket and say, 'Isn't that wonderful?'" When Pagie said, "They're a dime a dozen," he looked hurt.

Lovestone did not share Angleton's fondness for the Israelis. He thought they were too friendly to the Soviet Union. The Czechs and the Yugoslavs were training Israeli pilots and supplying them with arms. Jay wrote Pagie in October 1952 that "the Israeli stinkers voted with Stalin on China" in the UN. "Don't let me see those Kosher rats again."

One day Angleton called to say he had no one in Bulgaria. He gave Morris the name of a Bulgarian refugee living in Turkey who had con-

tacts with the Bulgarian trade unions and told her to go to Istanbul and
see him. Morris checked into the Park Hotel and met with a Turkish security man, who helped her find her contact. The Bulgarian refugee set
up a meeting for Morris at the border, where a Bulgarian trade union
leader would give her a report on labor conditions.

But then Turkish security decided to take over the operation. "How
can you know what the report says if you can't read Bulgarian?" the one
she knew asked. "I'll insist on a translation," she said. "We'll give you a
driver and an interpreter," the Turk said, "and some backup in a second
car in case anything goes wrong."

It took four hours on a twisting, narrow road with a sharp drop on one
side and a cliff on the other to reach the border town of Edirne. In a
smoke-filled, dimly lit café, Morris was introduced to a strapping fellow
with a handlebar mustache who wore a sheepskin coat and a wool cap.
He was annoyed that she had brought an interpreter but even more annoyed that she was a woman. The interpreter explained: "He says it does
not do him enough honor to send a woman." Morris said, "Tell him I am
not a woman but the representative of the most important trade union in
the world."

The Bulgarian finally gave her a letter proposing an agreement between the AFL and the group he represented. But the interpreter said the
letter included passages critical of Turkey. There was a long history of
rancor between the two countries. When Morris asked the Bulgarian to
cut the anti-Turkish passages out with his penknife, he snatched the letter out of her hand and put it in his pocket. What a barbarian, Pagie
thought.

At that moment the security men in the second car burst into the café
with guns drawn and arrested the Bulgarian, who was charged with crossing the border illegally. They snapped handcuffs on him and pushed him
into the second car. But when they started back to Istanbul, a car full of
armed Bulgarians blocked their way and began firing. The order of the
cars was now reversed, so that Pagie was in the second car and less at risk,
but she put her head between her knees and her arms over her head. The
Turks, firing back, whipped around the Bulgarian car and sped down the
road toward Istanbul, with Morris's car following. She felt responsible for
the man's arrest, having botched the job by getting the Turks involved,
and flew out of Istanbul on the first plane. The papers were full of stories
about the American mystery woman mixed up in the border incident.

In 1954 Morris went on a Middle and Far Eastern swing for Angleton,
to Cairo, Karachi, Bombay, Rangoon, Bangkok, Djakarta, and Taipei. In

Egypt King Farouk had been deposed and sent into exile in 1952. A group of anti-British nationalist army officers were in power. Mohammed Naguib was the titular leader, but the real power was Gamal Abdel Nasser. The British still held the Suez Canal and were dragging their feet about turning it over to Egypt. The State Department and the U.S. embassy were seen as pro-British. The Egyptians were asking for American economic and military aid, but the United States was stalling, saying it did not want its weapons to be used against its allies. Through Morris, Lovestone and Angleton were running their own sub-rosa negotiations with the Egyptian leadership.

In Cairo, Pagie dyed her hair black and wore a long dress and a head-scarf for her appointment with President Naguib at his home (she did not want to be logged as a visitor to his office). Naguib at once confided in her: "Do you know there's a plot against me?" he asked. "I don't quite know what to do. It's the colonels." "Your police force is nil," Morris said. "They're leaning on their rifles. The colonels have the army. You have nothing. You must improve the police force." Naguib responded: "I'm doing the best I can for my people."

As a result of this talk, Angleton had advance notice that Naguib was about to be deposed. Within three months he was under house arrest and Nasser came into the open, naming himself prime minister.

Morris concluded after meeting Naguib that he was a soldier and not a politician. He knew how to give and take orders, that was about all. Nasser was much more impressive, with an analytical mind that examined every facet of the political mosaic. Not only that, he was a fine-looking devil with flashing white teeth. Morris sounded him out about using the Egyptian unions to initiate peace feelers with Israel.

"For reasons of prestige," Nasser said, "there can be no peace with Israel until we get the British out of Suez."

"But what about the trade unions?" Pagie asked. "Why don't you join the ICFTU?"

"If we ask to join," Nasser asked, "will the Histadrut try to keep us out?"

"Not if George Meany has anything to say about it," Morris replied. She assured Nasser that neither the AFL nor the CIA was pro-Zionist.

"I want to do something, but where to begin," Nasser said.

Morris suggested discreet contacts between an Egyptian trade union leader and someone from the Histadrut in New York. Nasser agreed, and the contacts took place, but events overtook them with the Suez crisis in 1956.

Nasser wanted to know why American military aid was so slow in coming. "All they have given us so far are helmets and jeeps," he said. Morris said that was outside her area of knowledge.

In Bangkok, Morris saw Bill Donovan, who had been sent to Thailand as ambassador the year before. He told her he was pessimistic about America's place in the world. "Sometimes," he said, "I long for that feeling I had as a boy that when you waved the flag your enemies shuddered." Donovan knocked Allen Dulles, whom he called "churchy" and "politically dishonest." He had ruined the CIA, Donovan said, by turning it into "a reporting agency." He also had it in for Eisenhower, who was "not a great man. How could he have won the election after his affair with Kay Summersby?" Morris interpreted his logic as follows: Donovan, who had had many affairs, was not president. Therefore, Eisenhower, who had had an affair, should not have been either.

In mid-March 1954, Morris arrived in Taipei, where Bill Etter, now with the Foreign Operations Administration, had been reporting to Lovestone that the labor situation was discouraging. All power on the fourteen-thousand-square-mile island was centered on Chiang. No political opposition was tolerated. Their old friend Liu Ching-lih, of the Free China Labor League, was the nominal head of a trade union federation, but he was completely hamstrung. Etter told Morris that Liu had just been deposed from the federation and was in hiding in the port city of Chi-lung, fearing arrest. The Taiwan unions were now under the direction of the minister of transportation. Etter would take her the next day to see Liu.

When they drove to Chi-lung, on the northern tip of Taiwan, they crossed a shantytown area where the dockworkers were housed. Pagie insisted on taking a look, and Etter walked her through dormitories in windowless wooden shacks with rotting floors, alive with bugs, with no running water, no toilets, and no beds, and a smell so foul that it made her sick. Skeletal men in rags were curled up on the floor. She made the sign of the cross, for the first time in years. Next door to these shacks was a fine stone building with large windows and a garden. She asked Etter what it was. "Oh, that's Madame Chiang's dog hospital, funded by the American missions, but there are no dogs in it—all the dogs are caught and eaten."

Then they went to see Liu, and Pagie asked: "What shall I do for you?" Liu said, "Please write the minister of transportation so that he will suffer loss of face." She wrote in front of him: "In our country, we do not have a cabinet minister as the head of our unions. We have Mr. George Meany, who at one time was a plumber. I have seen the workers' quarters in Chi-lung and I will make a detailed report to Mr. Meany." She wrote in her diary: "Chi-lung: The most horrible place I've ever seen. Formosans living like lowest animals."

On March 19 she saw Chiang Kai-shek, who looked at her through half-closed eyes, as if dozing. "My trip to Chi-lung distressed me very much," she said. "Yes," Chiang said. "We have your letter. We are now arranging for you a trip to the mountains, which you will enjoy more." Pagie realized that she had to act fast, for the trip to the mountains was a way of removing her from her inquiries. She managed the next day to see Chiang's son, Chiang Ching-kuo, minister of the interior, who was reputed to be more reform-minded than his father, obsessed with return to the mainland to the exclusion of all else. Chiang Ching-kuo, a husky, bearded fellow who saw her in a small office he kept over a movie theater, said: "I know you have seen Mr. Liu. I know about Chi-lung and the letter. What are you planning now?"

Sensing that he was not unfriendly but viewed her with mild irony, Pagie said: "There must be a change, and you have the power to do it."

"My lady, please tell me how," said Chiang Ching-kuo.

"You can make Taiwan the showcase of Asia. There must be schools, hospitals, and better conditions for the workers. I will have a Taiwanese trade union ask to see you, and when you receive its delegation you can appoint a minister of labor."

"My lady," Chiang Ching-kuo asked, "are you a Christian?"

"Yes," said Pagie.

"May I say, God bless you?"

Pagie did succeed in one small thing, the naming of a minister of labor, but she knew that the chance of reform was slim and wrote Lovestone: "The mess in Taiwan is unbelievable, and a good part of the blame rests not on the big boss but on his lady."

When Pagie got back to New York in June 1954, Jay called her "the Asian." His disposition was beyond belief, Pagie reported to Angleton, whom she and Jay had code-named Scarecrow. Even Irving Brown had called and asked "What is biting him?" "The other night at dinner," Pagie wrote Angleton, "he tore everyone to pieces and then went after me—that I was childish, emotional, idiotic, Asian—that's his new insult—Red Cross nurse and so on. Finally I got fed up and said, 'Sometimes I think that you either don't like America or our government, or that you haven't rid yourself of your Communist training. I'm sick and tired of your negative approach. Half of your attacks are founded on that big stupid nose of yours, without a shred of evidence." "Emotional Asian," however, was a step up from "don't be childish," Pagie said.

Matters improved in August when her interview with Nasser paid off.

Lovestone told her that Nasser had made a speech welcoming American military aid and asking the United States to become the arbiter in the conflict with Israel. Pagie thought the AFL should make a statement, but Lovestone said it could be handled at the convention. He said the "lousy Jews," whom he described as "a foul crowd who have done nothing but beat the war drums for the past two weeks," were sure to mess things up.

In January 1955, Lovestone signed the lease for the Gompers Library, which Angleton had approved at a rent of two hundred dollars a month, and gave Pagie some money for bookcases, which she ordered from Macy's. She also bought some furniture and moved in forty cases of books that Lovestone had taken out of storage. Lovestone had seen Earl Browder, the former head of the American Communist Party, who was about to testify before the Jenner Committee. "He has a lot of documents and material," Lovestone reported. "We may want to take some for our library. This fellow is still rudderless. He needs political psychiatric treatment, and if he gets it, in the proper way, not by McCarthy type stuff denouncing this one and that one, he could be of invaluable help."

In March 1956 the FBI was monitoring Lovestone's love life, according to this phone tap report: "Subject contacted unidentified woman in Washington. . . . This was not subject's usual associate. . . . Subject addressed woman in endearing terms and said he wanted to be in her arms." The FBI then ran a check on the woman and found that she worked for the American Institute for Free Labor Development, an AFL outfit that focused on Latin America. Jay had begun a passionate affair with the woman, whose story had touched him. She was sixteen, a girl going to a gymnasium in Berlin, when the Nazis took over in 1933. She refused to sign a paper promising not to talk to her Jewish schoolmates. But under pressure she joined the Bund Deutsche Mädchen. Shocked by the unspeakable methods of trying to instill anti-Semitism in children, she told Jay, she resigned in 1936. When the Gestapo warned her divorced mother she might be placed in a Nazi reform school, they left for Brazil, where they had friends, in December 1936.

Elfie, as she was known, spent thirteen years in Brazil, then came to the United States and got a master's degree in Russian studies at Washington University in St. Louis. She found a job with the ILGWU in St. Louis as a translator and got an introduction to Lovestone in New York. He helped her get a job with AIFLD, where she started out taking Latin American labor people on tours of the United States. The affair progressed in tandem with her job, and an April 1, 1956, FBI report observed that Jay and Elfie "expressed mutual affection."

But ending up in the middle of an FBI investigation got Elfie into serious trouble. The FBI ran a check on her and located some informants who objected to the way she had acted on a 1954 tour of Brazilians in Birmingham, Alabama. These informants, who spoke both English and Portuguese, said that she "had made disparaging remarks about the U.S. and had told trainees they were not receiving the true picture of Negroes in the South and everything was staged." The informant said that he and his wife were "incensed by the attitude she had and her comments and interpretations given to the group in the Portuguese language. . . . She seemed to be anti-American and did a lot toward ruining the purpose of the trip. When in Demopolis, Alabama, the group was shown a Negro farm typical of the area. Elfie explained in Portuguese as they moved along that the colored people were mistreated in this area and that they actually lived under poor conditions. . . . Again, at the Tuskegee Institute, one of the Brazilians asked who had financed it. The tour leader said it was financed by an endowment and private donations. Elfie, who was translating for the tour leader, said in Portuguese that those who donated money did so not because they were generous but to evade income tax." As a result of these comments, Elfie was investigated by the Civil Service Commission in May 1959; she wrote to them: "I was mindful of my instructions never to hide facts and problems of the American scene of which foreign visitors might be critical." She was cleared and kept her job.

Through the phone taps the FBI in 1956 summarized Lovestone's personal life as follows:

> Relationship A: On May 24, Lovestone and [Elfie] exchanged expressions of affection. On May 31, [she] informed Lovestone of her affection for him.
> Relationship B: On April 22, Lovestone expressed his feelings of love for Esther Mendelssohn of Montreal, Canada.
> Relationship C: On April 30, Mrs. Louise Page Morris, upon being informed that Lovestone was ill, indicated that she would send him something. Further conversation indicated an intimate personal relationship.

The FBI had all the bases covered. When Lovestone went to a hotel with a lady friend, as on August 21, 1956, the FBI was there. "Lovestone checked into the Colonade [sic] Hotel in Miami Beach with a Mrs. Lovestone [Elfie], tall, slender build, late 30s, mannish haircut, dark hair, glasses, wearing Guatemalan-type clothes."

In 1960 Elfie was sent to Brazil for the AIFLD and saw Jay only when she went back to Washington. Her letters were full of recrimination:

> You fool! If you only knew how often you have broken my heart! I am tired of your pussy-footing all around.
>
> I know you won't marry me, but you should be around when I need you and not build me up and then kick me down. You say you love me but you do everything to hurt me.
>
> In my mind you are the world's worst stinker. . . . You are never around when you are needed. . . . What exactly do you mean when you give me all that song and dance about what I mean to you?

Finally, from Rio in 1966, she wrote her last letter:

> You say don't fall for any Latinos or Yankee visitors. Jay dear, that's what I need now and badly. I am lonesome and afraid. I am some-times near the point of pushing the panic button. . . . When they called me a subversive, you were gone. When mother died, you were incommunicado. . . . OK if that's the rule of the game.

Pagie, meanwhile, was finding Jay so irascible that she was glad to get away on assignment for Scarecrow. In 1959 Angleton asked her to go to Iraq. "The British say Iraq is going Communist," he said. "I want to know what's going on." An officers' movement had toppled the monarchy in 1958, bringing into power Col. Abdul Karim al-Kassem. The king and the crown prince were put to death, as was the pro-British prime minis-ter, Nuri Said. The CIA had failed to predict the coup and knew nothing about al-Kassem. Were the Russians behind it?

"I'll need a generous expense account," Pagie said. "In the Arab world you must give presents. For the men, linen batiste handkerchiefs, monogrammed, so they can't give them to their superiors, or gold ciga-rette lighters. They all smoke. For the women, silk stockings and per-fume."

"Do you have to take presents to every one of them?" Angleton asked. "Yes," Pagie assured him, "and more besides. I should also have a bedroom and sitting-room, so I can have a man visit me without having him in my bedroom."

"Have I ever said no to you?" Angleton pleaded.

As it happened she arrived in Baghdad the night of a coup. As the customs man at the airport went through her bags, searchlight beams crisscrossed the sky and she could hear gunfire. The customs man pulled out a pair of evening slippers and held them up, saying: "There's a revolution going on, and this woman comes in with pink slippers."

On the bus going into town, the driver told her to lie down on the floor. At the Aliyah Bridge an angry mob brandishing pitchforks and shovels blocked the way, and the driver took a back road to her hotel on Rashid Street. From the balcony of her room she watched the riots. Cars were on fire in the streets, and limp bodies hung from lampposts.

She was able to get through to her close friend Hashem Jawad, the foreign minister, whom she had gotten to know when he was ambassador to the UN. He came to get her at the hotel and explained that the Ba'ath Party had staged the coup but that al-Kassem was in control. The next day things had calmed down, and Jawad showed her the spot where in 1958 Nuri Said had tried to escape by wearing women's clothes. Betrayed by his shoes, he was captured and hanged, the site becoming one of Baghdad's points of interest.

Pagie suspected that the hotel concierge, a Chaldean named Issa (Jesus), was passing her mail to Iraqi intelligence. One letter from Lovestone got through, in which he tactlessly said: "Most Iraqis are first-class swindlers who use you and abuse you and you seem to enjoy it and want more. . . . Why the hell don't these damned swine give you the mail that is yours?" In addition, he reported that Scarecrow had stopped smoking, drinking, and going to parties.

Through Jawad, Morris met the head of Iraqi intelligence, Ibrahim Shahiah, who took a liking to her. One day he called her in and told her they were reading her outgoing mail. "You are writing all the time to Jaybird," he said. "Who is that?" "Jay Lovestone, my boss," she said. "And who are the 'camel thieves' you write so often about?" he asked. "All Arabs, including Iraqis. And if there's anything else you don't understand, I'll be glad to tell you."

Baghdad was a city of suspicion and rumor, essentially tribal, with groups within groups. Alliances were temporary and expedient. The power base was the army. Under al-Kassem, Pagie learned, the Russians were pouring in agents. More than a thousand were in Iraq, some at her hotel, and the barman complained that they never tipped. The head of the air force, Awkati, was a Moscow-trained Communist. Al-Kassem bought MiG 23s from the Russians and sent his pilots to Russia for training. Morris had friends in the air force who told her that in the officers' mess they cursed al-Kassem, saying, "Spit on him, the stinking Kurd and his Armenian whore."

Morris went to Iraq again in 1963, after al-Kassem was overthrown and killed, and when she got home, Allen Dulles had been replaced as director of the CIA by John McCone, a millionaire industrialist from California. Angleton had always paid Pagie out of unvouchered funds. With forty thousand dollars a year in tax-free money, she had her own little tax shelter. McCone, a stickler for correct procedure, went over Angleton's books and said that not only must Morris be put on the regular payroll but she must pay back taxes. In one of his rare outbursts, Angleton began to shout, "Nothing doing! Nothing doing!" He finally arranged it so she got a small taxable salary and a large expense account.

Many years later, when Angleton had left the CIA and material in his files revealed the connection with Lovestone and Morris, their reports were used to discredit Angleton. These field reports lacked the starchy seriousness of embassy dispatches. They tended to be raw, irreverent, sometimes crass. But much of the information they contained was valuable intelligence not to be found in diplomatic files. In that sense they could be considered vitamin supplements to the regular intelligence diet.

15

THE LOVESTONE INTELLIGENCE SERVICE

In its November 1954 issue, the magazine *Pageant* ran an article called "Who Are the Six Top Anti-Communists?" As little known as he was, Jay Lovestone joined J. Edgar Hoover and Monsignor Fulton Sheen on the list, thanks to the endorsements of Matthew Woll and David Dubinsky. "Since 1935," Dubinsky wrote, "Lovestone has done more to damage the cause of Communism in this country and abroad than any other individual among us. . . . The Communists consider him their worst enemy. Yet Lovestone has worked without fanfare. What he has accomplished is known by comparatively few people."

In the mid-fifties, after the death of Stalin, when some foreign policy experts saw the Cold War winding down, Lovestone had not budged. It was his mission to sustain a state of red alert. Whatever the Kremlin did to lessen international tensions was in his view a tactical maneuver. He continued to believe that the aim of the Soviets was to spread their system in all parts of the world. Russia remained the model for tyrannical one-party rule and the overseer of a system of satellites. Its record on human rights was as deplorable as ever. For Lovestone, the Soviet Union was still an implacable foe bent on destroying the human spirit.

In July 1955 in Geneva came the first summit conference since Potsdam ten years before. The simple fact that a summit took place gave rise to talk of "the spirit of Geneva." To Lovestone, however, the summit did not amount to "a hill of beans." Of course, he told a friend on July 14, 1955, Molotov's recent visit to the Geneva Museum of Natural History, in whose hall of dinosaurs he said he felt "most at home," could be seen as a concession to the lessening of tensions. But in the end, Lovestone thought, Geneva was "potentially far more catastrophic than Yalta." It was a tragedy to adopt a policy based on Russia's needing reassurance from attack. The fact that "people are thrilled over it shows the neurotic condition and plight of mankind today."

It seemed to Lovestone that the Russians had seized the initiative. The West was losing the Cold War. At Geneva, he said, Khrushchev had kidded Eisenhower by telling him that Marshal Georgi Zhukov's daughter was getting married when Zhukov had no daughter. Ike gave Zhukov a wedding present for his daughter, and the Russians were laughing themselves silly at having put one over. That was the level of Ike's acumen.

After Geneva, First Secretary Khrushchev and Premier Nikolai Bulganin toured the world with their dog-and-pony act. Lovestone was aghast to hear that they were visiting Britain, where they would meet the queen and lunch with Churchill. They were bound to have exchanges with British unions. Ever since the Profintern in the twenties, the avowed aim of the Kremlin had been to control the British trade unions, and now they were being invited in, even as Ike spoke about the friendly spirit in the air. Lovestone was happy to hear from Allan Morgan, the British labor attaché in Washington, that not all had been milk and honey during Khrushchev's British trip. In Birmingham, someone in the crowd shook his fist at the Russian leader. This provoked Khrushchev into saying, "When you shake a fist at us, we will shake a fist at you. Anyone who shakes a fist at us will meet the fate of Hitler. You British once shook a fist at us in your war against our revolution. We gave you a bloody nose." The Russian-speaking Foreign Office people picked up what he said, but Khrushchev's clever translator, Troyanovsky, rendered his belligerent remarks as: "You British were once at loggerheads with us, but all that is forgotten."

Every month there seemed to come an aftershock of Geneva. In September, Konrad Adenauer went to Moscow and negotiated diplomatic relations in exchange for the release of 9,626 prisoners of war. Lovestone, outraged, wondered how many of those released were Nazi war criminals.

Lovestone fought back on all fronts. He saw the October 1955 conference of unaligned nations in the Indonesian hill town of Bandung as a disaster for the free world. The Fizzlanders laughed it off as "the Darktown Strutters' Ball," but Jay took it seriously. It was at Bandung, he felt sure, that Chou En-lai and Nehru had taken Nasser over lock, stock, and barrel.

Lovestone, who had been cultivating Nasser ever since he had come to power in 1954 with the help of the striking Egyptian unions, and who had sent Pagie Morris to Cairo to establish contact, wrote him on November 18, 1955, to express his "deep concern" over Soviet arms shipments to Egypt. "You know the dangers in even a limited partnership with Moscow," he said. "The arms unloaded from the Soviet ship *Stalingrad* will be followed by Communist 'technicians' . . . trained in organizing subversion and fomenting civil war." But it did no good, as Nasser inched toward the Soviet camp.

To balance the bad news came the Hungarian uprising in October 1956, and the formation of a government under Imre Nagy that proclaimed the end of the one-party system and the withdrawal of Hungary from the Warsaw Pact. But in November, Soviet tanks attacked Budapest, thousands were killed, and a puppet regime under János Kádár was installed. Lovestone received reports from Anna Kethly, a member of the Hungarian Parliament in the twenties, later jailed by both the Nazis and the Soviets. She was a minister of state under Nagy, sent to Vienna to drum up support for the rebellion. When the Soviets encircled Budapest on November 4, she could not get back. Kethly wrote Lovestone on November 6 that "Kadar is at present not a free agent but a prisoner of the Soviet occupation authorities. No credence should be given to his statements since they originate with the Russian rulers in Hungary."

Lovestone brought her to the United States for three weeks, thinking that this sixty-seven-year-old woman, with her white hair and lined face, the only member of the Nagy government still at large, could make an impact.

On November 10 the FBI tapped a conversation between Pagie and Jay:

> MORRIS: I just talked to Anna [Kethly]. . . . Did you know what she told [Dag] Hammarskjöld [secretary general of the UN]?
> LOVESTONE: I did not want to raise it last night even.
> MORRIS: I know the whole thing. . . . Do you remember when I said to you that it was criminal to incite a revolution and a rebellion, and not to follow it through? . . . Well, the Wisner crowd incited it. . . . And Kethly went to Hammarskjöld and she said it is all very well and good to induce people to rise, but then you have to follow it through. . . . You can't make promises using the name of the United

States government and then nothing happens. . . . And the Horthy crowd has been in it. [Miklós Horthy was the right-wing admiral who ruled Hungary from 1920 to 1944.]

LOVESTONE: Well, I'm sure they're in it, you know?

MORRIS: And the accusation of the Russians is correct. . . . That's the terrible part of it.

LOVESTONE: You can't avoid that, kid.

MORRIS: If you are going to go in with it, even with the Horthy crowd, you got to support them.

LOVESTONE: No, darling. The revolution attracts forces of all kinds.

MORRIS: It didn't attract, it was instigated by, that is the whole point. . . . It was not a spontaneous socialist revolution.

LOVESTONE: Listen, darling. There is no such thing as a spontaneous socialist revolution in the pure sense. Someone incites. Somebody does this. Somebody does that.

MORRIS: Now listen to me and stop going off into your Utopian theories. This thing was an outrage, theoretically sound, but where the mistake came in was the people who assumed the leadership of it right from the beginning of it.

LOVESTONE: Well, you can't help it. That's unfortunate. Those things happen. They went beyond their strength.

MORRIS: They not only went beyond their strength, they had no right to even go as far as they did.

LOVESTONE: When people are so desperate there is no question of right.

MORRIS: Sure there is. They were absolutely certain that American tanks were coming in. These kids are dying for nothing. They had been promised and they didn't get it. This is what she told Hammarskjöld. . . . That Radio Free Europe is the crowd that's behind it.

LOVESTONE: Well, I'm trying to get some very simple things done. I wanted her to see the president, if possible.

MORRIS: You know why she's going to be prevented from seeing the president? . . . For the simple reason that the people I spoke of have gone beyond their limits, and they don't want the president to know it. They don't want that made public. That is why she isn't going to get anywhere.

Pagie was right on target, as it turned out, for on November 14 Lovestone took Kethly to Washington and got nowhere. He told Undersecretary Robert Murphy that she should address the UN, but, "Bob hemmed and hawed, squirmed and wormed," Lovestone wrote Irving Brown. "The sum and substance was that nothing could be done." While sympathetic to the Hungarians, the United States did not wish to confront the Soviets over the uprising.

The New York Times reported on November 14 that Anna Kethly claimed the right to be seated at the UN as the legal delegate from Hungary. "Documentary proof of Miss Kethly's appointment by Mr. Nagy as head of the Hungarian delegation," said the article, "is said to be en route from Austria, where it was brought by a friendly messenger." All this was masterminded by Lovestone, who arranged for the letters to be sent and had them copied. He told his secretary, "If the planes are delayed, I'll be in trouble with the UN." Lovestone could not, however, prevent the seating of the Kádár delegation, though he succeeded in establishing a five-member UN investigating commission, which published a report in September 1957. This in turn led to a permanent watchdog committee.

Nor could he prevent the arrest of Imre Nagy, or his execution on June 16, 1958. Lovestone told Henry Cabot Lodge, the U.S. ambassador to the UN: "The least we can do is throw the rascals out of the UN. . . . Our government should at least stop sending track teams to Hungary and cut out the cultural business." Lodge replied on June 19: "I share your feelings and am taking the liberty of sending your views to Washington." Lovestone felt that his view of the Soviet Union had been vindicated. The spirit of Geneva had been washed away in the Hungarian bloodbath. Stalin's successors were just as ruthless as old Joe himself.

Lovestone wrote Irving Brown on October 10, 1957, "I wish I could get optimistic about *Sputnik* waking up Washington and putting some sense in its noodle to undertake a campaign against the paralyzing complacency from which the American people are suffering. . . . All of this can be traced back to the Geneva spirit when Eisenhower said that Khrushchev and Bulganin are just as sincere in their desire for peace as he was."

In the fifties, Lovestone's priorities shifted from Europe to the nations emerging from colonialism. To tackle this job, he developed a private intelligence service, financed by Angleton. He was at odds with the State Department, which supported America's NATO allies, Britain and France, the principal colonial powers. But he found an ally in the CIA, whose function it was to penetrate the independence movements that Lovestone backed. An effective foreign policy required a foot in each camp. To side wholeheartedly with the colonial powers would throw the emerging nations into the arms of the Soviet bloc. It was exactly this "shadow foreign policy" that Lovestone could carry out.

But just at the moment when Lovestone had finally stabilized his partnership with the Fizz Kids and had his agents in place came a threat to his survival in the labor movement from his old enemies in the CIO. George Meany and Walter Reuther, in spite of many points of disagreement, were negotiating to merge their respective federations. The overriding reason was the clout of a single federation with 15 million members.

One of the merger results that the Reuther brothers hoped to achieve was the ouster of Lovestone. The FBI reported that at an AFL Executive Board meeting on February 24, 1954, CIO officials "vigorously attacked AFL foreign policy and singled out the FTUC for liquidation, saying that once it was out of the way things would be simpler. Meany protested these remarks and ruled the CIO officials out of order and removed all references from the minutes of the meeting." A March 4 FBI report said: "Lovestone has been concerned over his future status as a result of the forthcoming merger. He has a spy in the CIO who is informing him about developments. Lovestone maintains that the Communist Party will exert every effort to penetrate the merged organization."

As merger talks went into high gear in December 1954, Lovestone wrote Irving Brown that "Victor Reuther, that terribly over-estimated and self-inflated character," was conducting a campaign of "vicious slander" against Brown, saying that he was "not a trade unionist but a government man doing government work with government money. . . . For my two cents he is a first-class phony." The upshot of it was, Lovestone said, that "Victor and his like have a notion they will demand your head and mine as a price for unity with the AFL."

In October 1955, while the staffs of the two federations were being fitted together in preparation for the December merger, the battle over Lovestone still raged. On October 14, a committee of six, including George Meany, Jim Carey, and Walter Reuther, met for three days to thrash out all outstanding questions, of which the foremost was what would happen to the international work. Who would run it? Lovestone was as unacceptable to the CIO as Victor Reuther was to the AFL. When the topic was on the table, Meany said, "I nominate Brown." The CIO men jumped out of their chairs and said nothing doing. Meany said, "I did not mean Irving Brown. I meant George Brown." The latter was a colorless timeserver who had been research director of the plumbers' union before becoming an assistant to Meany. The CIO men were so flabbergasted that Carey said, "Okay, we will buy that." Mike Ross of the CIO would be his number two. Lovestone would remain as head of the FTUC. Even though Meany had rescued him from the lynching party, Lovestone wrote Irving Brown that "the George Brown affair was a pretty shoddy piece of business."

The London-born Mike Ross was fifty-seven and in poor health. He had fought in World War I and been gassed in the trenches. His lungs were damaged, and his three-pack-a-day cigarette habit did not help. He was known for coughing spasms that went on for minutes. Although Ross was a stalwart Reuther man, Lovestone got along with him very well. The reason was that Jay knew something about Mike that other people did not: He had been a member of the Communist Party in England, an allegiance he had neglected to mention when he came to the United States in 1933 and applied for citizenship. In 1931 Ross had gone to Moscow with Jane Tabrisky, a member of his Communist cell in London, and worked for the Soviet State Publishing Office for about a year. Friends of Jay's in the Moscow British colony remembered Ross as a good-humored Marxist fatalist with no great hope for the world. Men were moved by economic forces, Ross said. If Lenin had lived, things would be the same, for Stalin was not a devil but a product of Russia's past history. Ross and Tabrisky went to expat parties and talked through the night, and ate caviar and drank vodka and sang songs until daybreak, when they went home and saw the lines forming in front of the shops for a loaf of bread.

In November, according to an FBI report, Lovestone said that Meany was bitter about the unity negotiations and fed up with Walter Reuther's demands. Lovestone said that Reuther was "a first-class double-crosser." The CIO *News,* he said, was "in many respects like the *Daily Worker.*" The author of the CIO foreign affairs line, Lovestone claimed, was the concealed Communist Paul Sifton, one of Reuther's ghostwriters on the Washington staff of the UAW.

On December 1 and 2, 1955, the CIO and the AFL held their last separate conventions in New York City. At the CIO convention they sang songs of the picket line, and the actor Melvyn Douglas spoke. There was one discordant note when Michael J. Quill of the Transport Workers' Union opposed the merger on the ground that the AFL dragged its feet on civil rights. "I spoke to the AFL rep in Miami," Quill said. "How did you manage to get in the Negro delegates?" I asked. "Oh," he said, "we have a special bus for them. We bring them over every morning, and we get them out again before sundown." "And that's the way the AFL meets. The slogan there is 'no nigger on the beach after sundown.' Are we going into that kind of union?"

Notwithstanding Quill's objections, the CIO did merge, ending twenty years of separation, and the joint inaugural convention was held on December 5 and 6 at the Seventy-first Regimental Armory, where they used a single gavel. President Eisenhower addressed the convention on a phone hookup. When George Meany spoke, he excoriated fellow travelers and third world neutralists, lumping together Nehru, Sukarno, Nkrumah of Ghana, and Tito. Victor Reuther was appalled. It was just a continuation of the Lovestone Cold War aggressiveness. Victor thought that Walter had stepped down gracefully, allowing Meany to be president of the merged federation. But to equate Nehru with Tito as a Communist stooge was too much. Meany was dismissing the one major Asian nation that had a parliamentary democracy. K. P. Tripathi, the small and swarthy head of the India Trade Union Congress (INTUC), who had come a long way to attend the merger convention, said to Victor: "You would think that Meany was a spokesman for the War Department."

In the years following the merger, Lovestone remained convinced that the Reuthers were gunning for him. In a report to Scarecrow on April 23, 1956, Pagie Morris wrote that "Jay is obsessed with destroying Reuther. He can think and talk of nothing else. Everything else is at a standstill. He is bitter because he thinks he is being taken for granted. He is gathering material for George to present at the Executive Council meeting at which George will openly attack Reuther."

At a meeting on June 11, 1957, Walter Reuther openly denounced the FTUC as a dual organization, competing with the ICFTU. Jim Carey said, "I am not going to let my ulcers get me, I'm going out for a glass of milk." In the hall he ran into Lovestone and said, "You are driving me to drink milk." "That's your mental condition that is doing that, Jim," Lovestone said. "I would give you something worse." Meany finally told Reuther: "Okay, you make a motion to discontinue the FTUC. Then I'll make a proposal to pull out of the ICFTU. I challenge you to take it to the full council meeting." Reuther backed down, but to Jay it was like the Perils of Pauline.

Jay was on edge. The day after the meeting was one of those days. Pagie burned the omelette at breakfast. The coffee boiled over and the milk was sour. He had lunch with his broker and sold a stock for a fifteen-hundred-dollar loss. Right after he sold it, it began to climb. At the office, Ellie Borochowicz nagged that he was stingy about money. That evening Pagie gave a dinner for Archbishop Makarios of Cyprus, Bahi Lagdham, the Tunisian ambassador to the UN, and George Meany. "You're not going to light all the candles, are you?" Jay asked. "Of course," Pagie said. "Makarios is Greek Orthodox. They love candles." "You'd better take up the rug, your fine Arab friend will drop his cigarette ash on it— little they care." At dinner the saturnine archbishop, bearded and cas- socked, stroked the Orthodox cross that hung from his neck with his left hand while his right hand was under the table groping Pagie's legs. When he had gone, Pagie showed Meany her leg, saying, "He pinched me black and blue." "The hell I'll back that guy," Meany said. "What a fakeroo."

At the end of 1957, Mike Ross replaced George Brown as head of the AFL-CIO Department of International Affairs. Lovestone now moved under Ross, which meant the de facto demise of the FTUC, though Jay kept his office in New York. He didn't mind that much. He did the real work, while Mike coughed out his lungs and played chess. The crucial thing was that he kept his network of agents, who now worked under the cover of being correspondents for the *Free Trade Union News,* which he continued to publish.

In the shift to anticolonialism in the fifties, Lovestone at first con- centrated on North Africa, which was under French rule. In September 1951, he invited the Tunisian nationalist leader Habib Bourguiba, and the general secretary of the Tunisian union (UGTT), Ferhat Hached, to at- tend the AFL convention in San Francisco. The French pressured the State Department not to give them visas, but Lovestone got them via Ray Murphy. At the convention they both made a solid impression, and Love- stone wrote a friend: "Bourguiba is a very able and moderate Tunisian nationalist. . . . The French were riled because he came to the U.S. . . . They were aroused to a panic when the AFL intervened to get a visa for him. When they learned he would be on Voice of America and the BBC they began a vicious campaign against him."

In April 1952, Lovestone obtained another visa for Hached, timing his visit with a vote on Tunisia in the UN Security Council. Jay intro- duced Hached to his Israeli friend Eliezer Livneh, a member of the Knes- set. They went to lunch at a Greek restaurant and discussed Israeli support of Tunisian independence. On the morning of December 6, 1952, Hached was driving to his office from his home in the Tunis suburb of Rades when a car pulled up alongside and gunmen pumped four bullets into his body, killing him. Livneh wrote Lovestone that he was shocked and that he remembered Hached as "a man of Western caliber." Meany condemned the murder, which he blamed on the French terrorist group the Red Hand, and asked for a full investigation.

At that time Pagie Morris decided to specialize in the Arab world, because, she said, "I knew I couldn't play every instrument in the band."
Lovestone told her to go to the UN and help the Tunisian observer, Bahi
Lagdham. She even found him a dentist when he broke his tooth and paid
the bill. Pagie did a little missionary work, and that October the UN put
the Tunisian question on the agenda.

In 1953, to Pagie's delighted surprise, Henry Cabot Lodge was
named U.S. ambassador to the UN, after having lost his Massachusetts
Senate seat to John F. Kennedy in the 1952 election. Pagie had known the
tall and courtly Boston aristocrat since they had played as children during the summer on the Massachusetts shore. He was the first boy she ever
kissed. Cabot and his brother John, both as blond and handsome as Saxon
princes, had taken Pagie and one of her friends to a fair near Beverly.
They rode on the roller coaster, and though Pagie was elated rather than
frightened, she flung her arms around Cabot's neck and sunk her head
into his chest. Later, when they were alone, they kissed, and she thought
he was fairly passionate for a Yankee. Now, more than thirty years later,
they met again in the aisles of the General Assembly, and the old spark
was rekindled in an affair that lasted for years. Cabot's wife, Emily, was
in Boston a great deal, and they saw each other at Pagie's new apartment
on Fifty-seventh Street or in Cabot's suite at the top of the Waldorf Tow-
ers. Cabot would call and say, "I'm up to my neck, but I'll slip away as
soon as I can."

Lodge arrived at the UN at a time when new states were aborning
like calves in a stockyard. Between 1953 and 1956 the number of UN
members increased from fifty-six to seventy-three. Lodge at first went
along with the State Department policy of backing the colonial powers.
Pagie told him the United States was losing the third world while the Soviets were making new friends. When he voted in the Security Council
with France and England, she teased him: "You've got your hand up, but
why is your head hanging?"

In a phone conversation on August 27, 1954, recorded by the FBI,
Pagie told Jay that she had raised a "holy stink" with Lodge over North
Africa. She told him that the American delegation at the UN were
"a bunch of eunuchs." Lodge said, "I'm willing to listen to what you
say, but you have to give us a formula." Pagie said she would arrange a
dinner with Jay. The FBI commented: "As you know, the AFL policy has
long supported freedom from colonialism for North Africa and other
colonial people. . . . Lodge is apparently agreeable to listening to the AFL
position."

The dinner took place on September 2, and the following day Lodge called Pagie and said of Lovestone: "I think he has one of the most brilliant minds I ever heard of. I cannot tell you, I learned so much last night. He gave me ideas, new ideas, fresh ideas. I really feel this has been a valuable experience." When Pagie passed this on to Jay, he said: "I believe him, as we are not starchy people. I learned something too—your guest is not a drunkard and does not even smoke."

Lodge began to agree that the United States was losing the third world. Finally, on June 26, 1956, he wrote Eisenhower: "We are supporting the Colonel Blimps. . . . We should go much harder on the anticolonial side." At State the European Desk hands lamented that Lodge was "going native" and "laboring under the Afro-Asian influence."

Tunisian independence finally came in March 1956, and in November, Tunisia was admitted to the UN. Lovestone, who expected gratitude from the regime he had backed, was to be cruelly disappointed. In the UN the Tunisians abstained on the admission of Red China. There was no way to control these people once they were on their own, he mused. In 1963 Bourguiba brought the Tunisian unions under state control and had the leaders arrested. The bond of friendship was broken, and Lovestone observed that "between the AFL-CIO and Bourguiba, there is a complete and irreparable breakdown."

Lovestone was also instrumental in abetting Moroccan independence, bringing the trade union leader Taieb Bouazza to the United States in December 1954 and giving him funds to launch a federation, the UMT (Union des Travailleurs Marocains). But he wrote Irving Brown on January 25, 1955, that "the role of the State Department in the North African situation is much more cowardly and shameful than appears." He wanted help from Squinty, but Dulles was weighed down by the tragic condition of his son.

Nonetheless, Morocco became independent at the same time as Tunisia, and by October 1956 the country had a trade union federation. Once again there was some slippage, when in 1957 the secretary general of the UTM, Mahjoub Ben Seddik, sent a delegation to Red China.

But the toughest colony to crack in North Africa was Algeria, which was not a protectorate like the other two but an integral part of France, with 1 million French settlers out of a population of 9 million. In 1954 a war of independence broke out that would last eight years. A National Liberation Front (FLN) was formed under the leadership of Ahmed Ben Bella and Hocine Ait Ahmed.

A delegation of Algerians with observer status arrived at the UN in

1955. Lovestone assigned Pagie to shepherd them. She felt that they were alone in the world. They had very little money and could barely speak English, so she let them use her apartment for meetings and wrote their speeches. She sat with them in the General Assembly, like a baseball coach in the dugout.

Pagie arranged a dinner with George Meany, who expected a bunch of thugs, but she told the Algerians to wear clean suits, and they showed up on their best behavior, speaking their broken English; it went like a million dollars. "They're just like us," she told Meany, "except that they don't have any tea to throw into the harbor." As a result the AFL-CIO passed a resolution supporting the FLN against the French.

The war continued with increasing ferocity, and by 1956 the French had half a million troops in Algeria. In the meantime Irving Brown was helping the Algerians start a trade union, the UGTA. This displeased the hard-line resident minister, Robert Lacoste, who declared Brown persona non grata. In the French National Assembly on May 29, Lacoste called Brown "the master corrupting force in North Africa." Meany protested to the French premier, Guy Mollet, on June 14 that he was shocked by the unfounded and inflammatory attack.

In the fall of 1956, Morocco and Tunisia offered to broker the peace process in Algeria. The five top FLN leaders, including Pagie's friend Ait Ahmed, went to Rabat in October to talk to the king, who then provided a chartered plane to fly them to Tunis for talks with Bourguiba. But when the plane flew over Algerian airspace on the way from Rabat to Tunis, the French forced a landing in Algiers, and the five leaders were captured and locked up in a Paris prison, where they remained for the next six years, until the end of the war. Lovestone wrote Ray Murphy on October 24: "The French colonialists have done it again. Their kidnaping of the Algerian democratic leaders going to a peace conference arranged by Bourguiba and the king of Morocco will do far more damage through Africa and Asia than did the murder of Hached and the deportation of the Sultan." Lovestone urged the State Department to ask the French Foreign Office for a direct explanation and asked the Civil Pilots Association to write a protest letter.

Pagie was so mad she took Ait Ahmed's wife to meet the French UN ambassador, Willie Georges-Picot, and said: "I'd like to introduce you to a woman whose husband you arrested." Georges-Picot got red in the face and said it was none of his doing.

While at the UN, Ait Ahmed had told Pagie: "We Arabs do not make friends outside our own tribe, but we consider that you are one of us." On

February 2, 1957, he wrote her from the Santé prison: "I must confess that as far as our kidnapping, we lived terrible moments indeed. . . . I had to undergo many teams of 'interrogators.' . . . I realized that colonial domination has created a special kind of human being, the French Algerian, who has nothing to envy the Nazis. . . . They are more anti-American than anti-Stalinist. . . . When I denied ever meeting Irving Brown, I was accused of being a Communist. . . . And in spite of their Beria-like methods, dear Louise, in spite of the tragedy of our country, Cabot Lodge has found words to trust the colonial system." (Lodge had made some pro-French remarks.)

But Lodge was changing as he fell under the influence of Pagie and Jay, with whom he now collaborated on a number of issues. Lovestone was working on a new Hungarian policy, which was to have the United States and the UN recognize a government in exile. But Lodge told him it could not succeed in the UN. The Latin Americans and the Spaniards were opposed to the plan because it would create a precedent whereby governments in exile could be heard. Lodge proposed an end run around the opposition by setting up a watchdog committee in the General Assembly, which could make its own rules and hear witnesses without setting a precedent. Lovestone was also lobbying Lodge on the issue of Red China's membership in the UN. Pagie told Jay that she had spent the evening with Cabot (Jay did not know they were amorously linked), who said that he would fight to keep the Nationalist Chinese in the UN. Lodge said the British were responsible for the package deal on the admission of eighteen nations, though officially it had originated with Canada. Lovestone fumed that all Asia was being given away by one mistake after another.

Focusing on Algeria, Lovestone in 1957 was looking for someone in Congress to make a pro-Algerian statement. John F. Kennedy, the young chairman of the Senate subcommittee on UN affairs, was a likely candidate, up for reelection in 1958. Lovestone asked George Meany to tell Kennedy that any pro-Algerian remarks would help him with the labor vote in Massachusetts. On July 2, 1957, Kennedy gave his pro-Algerian speech. The United States had a dismal record, he said. American helicopters had been used against the rebels. The U.S. ambassador to France, Douglas Dillon, continued to solemnly say that the United States stood behind the French. It was time for a change in policy. Lovestone thought the speech was a clarion call and told Kennedy so when he saw him in New York a few months later.

Lovestone did not know it, but in 1957, after seven years, the FBI called off its espionage investigation and stopped tapping his phone (as well as Pagie's). A February 1957 memo said: "During the more than six years the technical has been maintained on the subject's residence, it has provided no evidence of subversive or Communist activity on Lovestone's part; on the contrary, it has shown in essence that he is anti-Communist." The FBI had started out suspecting that Lovestone was spying for the Soviets. It took the bureau seven years to realize that he was spying for us. The case was closed on May 9.

In December, when Pagie and Jay saw Allen Dulles on one of his rare visits to New York, Dulles told her: "People ask me what you do in the AFL, since you have no union background. I say you're there for decorative purposes. But I will say this—nothing I ever tell you comes back to me—not like your boss"—and he pointed at Lovestone. "Oh, he's just a dunce," Pagie said. Dulles told them there was a rumor floating about that Walter Bedell Smith would replace his brother as secretary of state. Jay said that would never happen because Pagie had something on him. In addition, Lovestone said, Eisenhower did not like Smith. Ike had told him so in Paris when he was NATO commander. "I'd rather have him on my side than against me," Lovestone quoted Ike as saying. "I don't care much for him, but that's the way he is."

General de Gaulle, who had returned to power in 1958, finally ended the war in 1962 by giving Algeria its independence. In July, Ahmed Ben Bella, the leader of the FLN, became premier of a free Algeria. He quickly veered to the left, expressing his admiration for Fidel Castro, who had taken power in Cuba in 1959.

In August 1962, Pagie was in Morocco visiting Mohammed Lagzhaoui, one of the richest men in the country and a longtime anticolonialist, who had in the early days helped finance the Algerians at the UN.

"Ben Bella is very much in our debt for letting the French kidnap him," Lagzhaoui said. "It made him a hero and kept him out of harm's way."

"Why did you build up Ben Bella?" Pagie asked.

"It was our conscience, because he was our guest."

"Rubbish," Pagie said. "So were the others. Was it because the idea of a collegial leadership worried you?"

"Well of course, if you put it that way. . . . The idea isn't pleasant and would never work. In fact, Ben Bella is quite despicable, easily flattered, vain and without depth."

"So the French and the Moroccans thought they could perhaps control him?"

"Yes, at first, but then Nasser's men got hold of him, and that was that. I went to the independence celebration in Algiers, and I've never been more furious. There was no mention of Morocco, though he heaped praise on Nasser and Castro."

In October 1962, Ben Bella came to New York to speak at the UN and announced that he was going to Cuba to see Castro. Lovestone attended a dinner for the Algerian leader hosted by Adlai Stevenson, who had replaced Lodge as UN ambassador. Jay sat next to Colonel Slimane, one of the Algerian military commanders, and asked him, "Why the visit to Cuba?" Slimane said it was to show the sympathy of the Algerian masses for another new regime. He added that the United States was losing prestige in the third world by bullying a small nation like Cuba.

An angry Lovestone wrote Averell Harriman, now undersecretary of state for political affairs: "The AFL did especially fine work in the case of Algeria . . . but now the entire Ben Bella government seeks to ape Castro . . . the Kennedy White House made a rash blunder in hastening to give him lunch when right after that he goes to see Castro."

In Algeria, Ben Bella swiftly installed a one-party system and throttled the unions. Lovestone never quite grasped that postcolonial nations had their own model, which tended toward state control of the single party and single union. American-style democracy was not in the cards in countries ravaged by war, where unemployment stood at 70 percent. Once again Lovestone felt betrayed. You held their hand and paid their bills and beat the drum for them, and as soon as they got what they wanted they stabbed you in the back.

Jay felt like a jilted suitor. Of course, when the object of desire had several suitors, one was played against the other. That was the African shell game, which Nasser had mastered so well he was teaching it to the others. But being jilted didn't stop Lovestone from trying. That was his job and his reason for being. That was why he had agents all over the hemispheres. Even if he couldn't bend governments to his will and change the fate of nations, he could bring home the bacon in terms of information, which was what the CIA paid him for.

In Japan he had Richard Deverall, surely the most bizarre—some would say pathological—of his agents. The Brooklyn-born Deverall, a devout Catholic, had been fired from the UAW Education Department by Walter Reuther, who called him "a dangerous screwball." In 1943 Deverall joined the army as a private, and he was sent to Japan in December 1945 as part of the military government under Gen. Douglas MacArthur, supreme commander for the Allied powers (SCAP). By then he was a second lieutenant in the Labor Education Branch, supervising a program for Japanese workers and employers.

With his inquiring mind and boundless energy, Deverall threw himself into a study of the Japanese language and mores. He took bicycle trips up and down the big island of Honshu, mixed with the common folk, spent hours practicing the lingo, and sat on the floor with his legs crossed, eating seaweed. He wrote Lovestone, who had asked for reports on Japan: "When you hear them singing labor songs about camellia blossoms on top of the mountain, you realize that their idiom is quite a distance away from the Soup Songs we know so well." Deverall took a five-pound box of hard candy to the burned-out area of North Tokyo and passed it out to the gangs of homeless kids there.

Brimming over with gung ho spirit, Deverall in his first field trip visited newly formed unions in twenty-five of Japan's forty-six prefectures. He found that Japanese workers had no notion of what a contract with management should be. They still saw labor-employer relations as patterned on the *oyabun-kobun* (parent-child) model. The job, as Deverall saw it, was to teach the workers to be autonomous, to free themselves from paternalism and company unions.

Deverall thought he was doing an outstanding job, and he was stunned when in June 1948 the popular head of SCAP's labor division, "Big Jim" Killen, promoted another man over him. When he asked for an explanation, Killen told him: "Many people feel that you are difficult to get on with and that you have a persecution complex. Some feel you are gunning for them." Deverall argued that the man promoted over him, Sam Romer, was a left-wing socialist with no labor experience. He said he would rather resign than lose face with his Japanese contacts.

In August, Killen went home, and Deverall asked to see his replacement, Chester W. Hepler, hoping for reinstatement. Hepler said, "The antagonism toward you is so marked that your value is questionable. Many people believe you give information to G-2. Your actions constitute frank insubordination." Deverall's hopes of return were crushed, and he left for the States in October 1948. He had in fact been reporting to G-2 on those in SCAP he thought were soft on Communism. The day before his departure General MacArthur summoned Deverall to his office and, Deverall recounted, "for forty minutes thanked me for eliminating the Communist termites from the labor division."

Back in Brooklyn in 1949, Deverall was staying with his widowed mother, Josephine, and going to graduate school at Columbia when Lovestone hired him to run the AFL Far East Bureau in Tokyo. Deverall was able, willing, and unattached. As he told Jay: "Most people have babies. Me? Well, at thirty-seven I'm still single and instead I write pamphlets."

Deverall's appointment set alarm bells ringing in the CIO, which launched a campaign to undermine him. Val Burati, a CIO man who had succeeded Hepler as chief of the SCAP labor division in Tokyo, wrote Victor Reuther on June 12, 1950, that Deverall was "a particularly vicious type of religious fanatic who sees a red in every liberal. He was a G-2 stooge while here and attempted to put the Communist label on all labor division personnel with whom he did not agree."

Backing up Burati, Edgar C. McVoy of the labor division made a charge of homosexuality against Deverall in a letter to Philip B. Sullivan, labor adviser for Far Eastern affairs at the State Department, on June 17: Deverall, he said, had been assigned a Japanese assistant, Yoshitero Kawano, with whom he went on field trips. "According to Kawano, Deverall tried to seduce him on two occasions, but Kawano refused. . . . Deverall then tried to have him fired. When Kawano was asked why he didn't bring charges against Deverall, Kawano replied that means of sexual expression varied and he did not want to bring on Deverall the kind of public onus he knew would result if it became known that Deverall was a homosexual." Instead, Kawano asked for a transfer.

Lovestone went to Meany to condemn the "scurrilous attacks" on Deverall. Thanks to Jay, he weathered the storm. Lovestone warned Deverall, who was in Bombay waiting for permission to return to Japan: "You are not out of the woods by any means. There is still terrific opposition to you. Your comrades in the CIO are waging a filthy sniping campaign. The charges they level against you through whispers, gossip, innuendoes and whatnot, run from incapability to sex perversion. . . . I forced some of your critics to speak up. Dubinsky, Woll, and myself then took good care of them."

In India, Deverall made the rounds, going to see the American ambassador, Loy Henderson, a founding member of the Riga group, who launched into a vicious anti-Nehru diatribe. He said that, to court favor with the Indians, "we should all dye ourselves brown." "Henderson has a bitch of a wife," Deverall reported. "Everyone at the embassy hates her guts. . . . Part of his trouble is that he takes out his peeves on the Indians after his wife kicks him about." This kind of gossip was not always appreciated.

Irving Brown, for one, did not much like Deverall's reports, telling Lovestone that "it would be a good idea for him to stop writing such trite crap. . . . He seems to judge everything on the basis of his own personal hatred for India. . . . Unless we can build a labor movement in India, we are finished in all of Asia."

In spite of Deverall's all too obvious drawbacks, Lovestone continued to rely on him because he was ideologically dependable. In his eyes anyone under attack from the CIO must be doing something right. Sure, Deverall was given to excess and the ventilation of personal prejudice, but he also worked like a beaver and had a good analytical mind when he chose to use it.

By the time Deverall was back in Tokyo, in mid-1952, Japan was an independent nation with an American ambassador, who turned out to be Jay's old friend Robert Murphy. It now had a union movement with seven million members, the only substantial labor movement in the Far East, though it was heavily Communist, for Japan had a large Communist Party. The Japanese federation of trade unions, the Sohyo, formed in 1950, often followed the Communist line. Deverall adopted the splitting tactics of Irving Brown and backed the small pro-U.S. Zenro federation.

But Deverall was sidetracked in his union activities by a running quarrel with the American embassy. He pursued a vendetta against a Japanese employee, accusing her of being pro-Communist and leaking secret embassy material to Tokyo's left-wing press. Deverall relayed all this to Lovestone, who wrote Murphy on August 22, 1952: "You have inherited a number of functionaries on your staff who are so-called left socialists and are in effect pro-Communist." Lovestone felt that Deverall, the spokesman for nine million AFL workers, had been treated shabbily and that Murphy should clean house.

Murphy replied in early September that "if Deverall has a complaint he is to understand that I do not live in splendid isolation and he will get better results speaking directly to me. . . . At heart he may be a timid man putting on a heavy veneer of aggressiveness and cocksuredness to protect himself. . . . One of his theories is that he must dress, act, and look more or less like a Japanese workman."

Lovestone remonstrated with Deverall, writing him: "Please Dick, no blabbing or yelling from the housetops, no shrieking out loud about suspicions, no accusations to be heard around the world, no complaints that can be peddled in the market square." The customers for his reports were George Meany and Jim Angleton, who distributed the material to Allen Dulles and to various CIA stations. Deverall's ranting and raving made the valuable information in his dispatches easy to discredit.

But getting Deverall to change was as improbable as rerouting the path of a typhoon. He seemed bent on creating havoc. He kept up his attacks on the employee, writing Lovestone that "she is known all over town as *Jinmim Sensen*, the girl with the popular front, because of her big tits (big for a Japanese). She slept with half of the labor division and the other half is lining up. She slept with Japs and foreign labor personalities. She is rotten to the core." Lovestone asked: "Tell the truth, Dick, did you ever have a crush on that gal?" Deverall griped so often to Murphy about the "multi-lateral spy" that she was finally released from the embassy.

At the same time the pug-faced, husky, balding Deverall, who covered his homosexuality with macho posturing, chomping on cigars, and roaring around on his motorcycle, told Lovestone: "I have a girl here who makes my blood tingle." He also reported that he had caught dysentery and beriberi. "For God's sake," Lovestone wrote, "don't go around picking up any more bugs. The next time you'll blame the American embassy for giving you bad salad."

By 1955 the Sohyo federation was calling for Deverall's ouster, labeling him "the McCarthy of the labor world." He had made so many enemies that he could no longer function effectively. He was finally brought down in an attempt to vilify the labor attaché Allen Taylor during what became known as the Hibiya Inn incident. The Hibiya Inn was an American-owned hotel, smack in the center of Tokyo, which had opened in 1945 with a staff of forty-five Japanese employees. On January 17, 1955, the American manager, a man named Harris, told the employees that they would have to accept a 20 percent pay cut or management would fire half the help.

Deverall saw this in the context of the larger issue of two hundred thousand Japanese employed by the U.S. and UN forces in Japan. Every incident of unfair or arbitrary treatment fueled the rise in anti-Americanism. The Sohyo leadership was looking for "blind spots," that is, small, unorganized firms that could be quickly mobilized in a crisis. The Hibiya Inn provided just such a spot.

On February 5 the workers formed their own union and called a strike. On February 8 they locked Harris and his wife in the hotel. On February 9 Taylor got into the act and negotiated with the strikers for Harris's release, which he obtained. At this point, on February 10, Sohyo arrived with a corps of flag-waving agitators who rampaged through the inn to encourage the "brilliant fighting spirit" of the hotel workers. Deverall reported that he visited the inn on February 11 and "found the place cluttered with red flags and possibly one hundred posters . . . which accused Harris of being homosexual and a raper of the females in his employ and so on and so forth."

Deverall felt that Taylor, by taking sides in a labor quarrel, had given

Sohyo a perfect opening. What had been a local dispute was now an issue between the United States and the Japanese workers. "I find the situation simply incredible," he wrote. He recommended that the incident be brought to the attention of Murphy, who was now deputy undersecretary of state. The AFL should ask Murphy's successor as ambassador, John Allison, for a report on Taylor's conduct.

Had he limited himself to his recommendation, Deverall would have acted appropriately. But he invariably went too far, and this time he publicly criticized Taylor in the February 13 issue of the English-language Tokyo newspaper *Mainicho.* "It is time that these colonial types leeching a living on the Japanese realize that they must pay the going rate or pack up and go home," he wrote. As for Taylor, he had "grossly interfered in the internal affairs of the Japanese people" by offering "the disgraceful spectacle of an American labor attaché rushing into a situation to save not labor but management."

Deverall's letter led to a protest on March 14, 1955, from Murphy to Meany, saying that Deverall had presented "an inaccurate picture of the embassy's attempts solely to protect an American citizen from violence. This, of course, it was the embassy's duty to do. Because Deverall's letter publicly reflected on our official representative in a foreign country in the name of the AFL, I am sure you would want to be acquainted with the facts."

Meany hit the roof. This could not have come at a worse time, in the middle of merger talks with the CIO, which was insisting that Lovestone divest himself of his men in the field. Lovestone told Meany: "I'm aware of Dick's shortcomings. I have time and time again written him." But Deverall was recalled to Washington. Lovestone, fed up with his envoy, told him: "I cannot help you out of your present plight. I can only tell you there are moments when God really helps those who help themselves."

Lovestone had another agent in Asia, Harry Goldberg, whom he had sent to Indonesia in 1951, when President Sukarno was steering the country on a leftward, neutralist course. Goldberg, an ex-Communist and an ex-Lovestoneite, was the kid brother of Jay's old friend Ella Wolfe. With his bow ties, three-button suits, and slightly predatory smile, he looked like a salesman. His wife, Rose, held his spiel in check, and when Harry had worn out his audience, she'd call, "Time!" If that wasn't enough, she'd say, "Harry, shut up."

Goldberg was a chronic whiner and hypochondriac, who traveled with a suitcase full of pills and who never failed to tell Lovestone about his latest ailment. "We were told that Sukarno knew we were here and what we were doing," he reported soon after their arrival in Djakarta in September 1951, "and that we should watch our step." Jay had no idea what Indonesia was like, "with the eternal damp and sweat and prickly heat and dirt, and third-rate hotels and bad food and health hazards . . . and now danger."

Although laid low by severe but mysterious pains, Goldberg established cordial relations with people of influence, writing Lovestone on November 15, 1952: "Ambassadors and official agencies somehow do not make up the gap. They just do not get around enough; their function . . . and their contacts and their purely physical locomotion are just too narrow and limited."

But Goldberg soon outwore his welcome by writing Sukarno to accuse him of "outstanding lack of statesmanship" in ruling with the support of the Communist Party. "Is it a crime to be anti-Communist in Indonesia today?" he asked. The Communists had infiltrated the government, the army, and the labor unions.

All of that may have been true, but Goldberg found himself shut out. No one returned his calls. In addition, he wasn't feeling well, and wrote Ella: "My what you call it is like a pin cushion already. Stomach pains have subsided. Still have the shoulder and body pains. This fever wears off slowly."

Lovestone moved the Goldbergs to Italy, where he needed someone to monitor the situation between Giulio Pastore's CISL, which the AFL backed, and the Socialist UIL, supported by the CIO. Goldberg was the sort who after five days in a country knew it inside and out and began to pontificate. He quickly figured out the Italians, "the playing at politics, the fencing and trying to score a point at the expense of your opponent, the trying to save face as in the inability to make mistakes, the anarchic individualism, the narrow loyalty to party first and Italy second, and above all the lack of realism in facing facts."

By March 1953, Goldberg was in the hospital with blood in his urine. Then he had back pains and had to take electric heat treatments. "It's going to be pure hell if there is no relief," he wrote Jay, "so keep your fingers crossed. I can't eat, I can't sleep, but I go on."

With his penchant for going off on tangents, Goldberg embarked on a crusade to pressure American producers making movies at Cinecittà not to hire "carbuncles"—as he called Communists. The director John Huston, he reported, was sympathetic. "I put the issue sharp and uncompromisingly," he said. "No carb labor." He had also seen the people at MGM, Paramount, and United Artists. "It's a scandal that so many American dollars are being poured into the coffers of the carbs," he told Jay. He wrote King Vidor, who was directing *War and Peace,* that "whether you know it or not, your labor policy is supporting the Communist move- ment." He added a veiled threat of reprisal in the United States if Vidor did not toe the line, which did the trick.

In November 1953, Goldberg wrote Lovestone that "the gods have struck again most unkindly. A couple of weeks ago those old pains of mine came back." It was "simply indescribable," and he was confined to his bed. The pains were followed by intestinal flu, with a fever of 102.

As with Deverall in Japan, by 1955 the American embassy in Italy was down on Goldberg. The word was out that "Goldberg's a maverick. He doesn't cooperate. He's always fighting his own government." "The boys on the second floor" were concerned about his polemic with the UIL, which had won 20 percent of the vote in the Fiat elections in Turin. Henry J. Tasca, director of the U.S. Operations Mission, asked Goldberg: "Why did you have to get mixed up in an inter-union struggle?" Goldberg saw it as "the fretting of Schmoos who've been forced to face up to basic questions." He had to explain things "diplomatically but firmly," he wrote Jay in July 1955. "They take an awful amount of educating."

Goldberg was back in the hospital in 1957 with colitis and wrote Lovestone, "Here you have to get cures from cures in hospitals." He and Rose decided it was time to go home. Goldberg left Italy thinking that "these boys haven't got what it takes. When the chips are down they give up. Italy is inevitably going to the dogs. They could have stopped Mus- solini, but they didn't."

While Harry Goldberg fought the carbuncles from Djakarta to Rome, Lovestone's man in Bombay, Mohan Das, did his best to counter the strong Nehru-fostered spirit of neutralism in India. Das, who had helped organize the eighteen-thousand-strong Bombay Transport Workers' Union, kept telling Lovestone that the labor movement in India suffered from serious underdevelopment. The pattern of collusion between union leadership and management was a function not of doctrine but of poverty.

Das was not impressed by the new U.S. ambassador in 1951, Chester Bowles, "who oozed with friendliness and goodwill and an assumed pose of naiveté and charm . . . and then dilated upon the wrong notions people had in India about red China."

"Don't mention Bowles to me," Lovestone replied. "This diplomatic dimwit thinks he can win over Nehru by pandering to his glorified igno- rance, by giving away millions of American dollars, and by avoiding all criticism of Communist China and its Kremlin masters." Lovestone was disturbed by the growing strength of the Communist Party of India, which had a posh office in Delhi, new jeeps, and cells inside the Indian Army. He was shocked that the leader of the Communist faction in Parliament could get up and say that Nehru was the Mao of India without being howled down. Das explained that "for Nehru, China and Russia are progressive nations and the United States are Wall Street imperialists. But while Nehru insults the United States he is also asking for $200 million in American aid." Lovestone replied that "there should be no aid through insults."

By July 1952 the Indian leftist press was labeling Das "an American-Vatican-Axis agent." Lovestone wrote: "It is too bad that you are not being compensated for such high office." Being a "native," Das was getting peanuts compared with Deverall and Goldberg.

Das reported that the Communist Party in India now had half a million members, with the motto "once a member, always on the register, even after death." Some employers preferred to deal with the Communists because they controlled their rank and file better and came up with a decision faster—which often meant payoffs to union leaders. Lovestone thought of the Indian Communists as "meal-ticket artists looking for a few bucks and ready to serve anybody." But Das felt that Jay did not grasp the extent to which anti-Americanism fed the national ego. There were calls in Parliament to spurn U.S. aid. As long as they had employer payoffs, as long as labor leaders did not come from the working class, as long as they were members of Parliament as in England, as long as there was no checkoff system, as long as union members paid five cents a month in dues, there could be no independent unions.

Das was himself suffering from underdevelopment, as Pagie Morris saw when she came to India in 1954 and he invited her to lunch in his small flat in a shabby section of Bombay. The lunch consisted of rice and curry. Das told Pagie: "This is what the working class lives on. When we leave, my wife will burn the flowers you've bought. She will smash the compact you gave her, and the room will be washed with cow's urine. And then you ask me why we can't do more here in India." They were bound by the caste system. Pagie was considered "unclean," and nothing could be received from her. She knew all about that, being herself a Boston Brahmin. The power of tradition was crippling.

Das took Pagie to a meeting of transport workers who worked for BEST (Bombay Electrical Supply and Tramways). They were in the midst of a heated discussion concerning a place at the depot where two tracks came to an end, separated by ten trackless yards. The freight had to be carried by coolies from one track to the other. The discussion was over who should pay the coolies—the owner of track number 1, the owner of track number 2, or the union? They had a book of trade union rules, published in London in 1933, but it did not address that particular problem. In the meantime the freight was piled high in the space between the tracks. Pagie said, "Throw the book out the window and pay the coolies." Damn the British, she thought, they left nothing but chaos.

After the independence of Morocco and Tunisia in 1956, Lovestone and Brown turned their attention to black Africa, where Britain and France were also divesting themselves of their colonies, and where free unions had to be formed practically from scratch. Though Brown was in and out of Africa, the real job fell to a black woman from the ranks of the ILGWU who became Lovestone's Africa agent.

Her name was Maida Springer, and she was born in Barbados in 1909. In 1917 her family came to New York and settled in Harlem. One of her first city memories was a line in an antidraft song, "When Uncle Sam calls out your man, just say you've got those drafting blues." She soon learned that racism has its subdivisions. Caribbeans were called King George niggers or monkey-chasers. Her classmates asked, "You got a tail?" and she pulled up her dress to prove that she didn't.

Springer found work in the garment trades as a finisher and joined the ILGWU, even though many blacks thought of unions as Jim Crow organizations where they would be denied access to skilled jobs. She belonged to Sasha Zimmerman's Local 22, which by 1933 had thirty thousand members, of whom four thousand were black. Under Zimmerman's tutelage, she joined the anti-Communist wing, distrusting the Communist courting of blacks to achieve party goals. Lovestone, who had an office in the local, was her mentor. She formed an "undying respect and admiration" for Lovestone, who recognized her ability and pushed her along in the union hierarchy.

Lovestone and Zimmerman trained Springer for leadership, sending her to take courses in contract law and parliamentary procedures. She was made education director of Local 132 and then business agent for the huge Local 22, managing sixty shops, negotiating the prices for piecework, and acting as a hiring boss. Employers called, saying, "Springer, I need an operator, I need a cleaner." One man who made high-class dresses said he needed a good operator, "But, Springer, don't send me a *shvartze* [black worker]." Springer said, "I don't know whether you want an operator or a shoemaker [a garment industry term for a clumsy worker], but have it your own way." "Oh, Springer," the man said, "I didn't mean nothing. Send her." A week later she went to check up, and the boss said, "Look at this garment, golden fingers she's got."

In 1951 Springer spent a year at Oxford on an Urban League scholarship and got hooked on African nationalism. By 1956, when the young Kenyan union leader Tom Mboya came to New York, she had become a housemother to visiting Africans. She had an old house in Brooklyn, a mother who liked to cook, a beat-up Ford to drive them around in, and two manual typewriters. Mboya stayed with her, and they became as close as kin. "Tom was his own best salesman," she recalled. "He caught on like fire . . . this beautiful black young man whose mind was like a sword." She loved the way he handled himself, telling a reporter who asked him where he learned his English, "Coming over on the plane."

Springer arranged a dinner with Lovestone in a Chinese restaurant on Third Avenue. Mboya told Lovestone about the situation in Kenya—the detentions en masse, the curfew, the attempt to destroy the unions. Jay was impressed. Mboya wanted two things: a trade union center in Nairobi and scholarships for Kenyan labor leaders. He got both. George Meany pledged $35,000 for the center, and via Lovestone he obtained eighty-one scholarships.

In 1957 Lovestone sent Springer to Africa, knowing that the British saw American trade union activities there as a sinister plot to undermine their influence. For Lovestone, however, Africa was part of the overall Cold War strategy of countering the Soviets wherever they showed up, and they were starting to show up in Africa. The Soviet foreign ministry created an African Bureau in 1958 and began to send aid to the former French Guinea. Eventually, Marxist regimes would be formed in Guinea-Bissau, Angola, Mozambique, Ethiopia, and elsewhere, and the Soviets would conduct military operations through Cuban and Libyan surrogates.

But that was all to come when Springer arrived in Ghana, the former Gold Coast and the first British colony in Africa to gain its freedom. At midnight on March 6, Springer was in Accra's Parliament Square for the independence ceremony. The crowd roared when the Union Jack went down and the red, green, and gold flag of Ghana was raised. Then, borne on the shoulders of his followers, came the charismatic Kwame Nkrumah. Once jailed by the British, he wore the striped convict suit and the white skullcap with the letters PG—Prison Graduate. Under the floodlights he danced on the wooden platform, and when he spoke of freedom tears streamed down his face. Springer found herself crying like a baby.

With his charm and evident ability, Nkrumah commanded hopeful attention from the West. Another guest at the independence ceremony was Vice President Richard M. Nixon, who showed a lively interest in Africa. After a talk with Irving Brown, he told Eisenhower that African trade unions were an important group to cultivate. Nkrumah, however, soon showed a militant leftist orientation. His true feelings about the West had been formed by the "let's see you grovel, boy" episodes of his student days at the University of Pennsylvania and the London School of Economics.

From Ghana, Springer went to Nairobi, a mile-high city like Denver. She announced the $35,000 grant to Mboya's Kenya Federation of Labor, which had fifteen thousand members and nine affiliates, to build a center. This was denounced in the local press as blood money from the racketeering Teamsters union.

Lovestone wrote Brown on March 20, 1957, that the British were denouncing Springer as a radical who had come to Africa to make trouble and was being paid $75,000 by the AFL. Springer wrote Jay that "Kenya was a shaking experience. I had forgotten what it was like to be in an atmosphere of hate, to be so acutely aware of it that the small hairs on the back of my neck began to rise."

The climate of hate was no different in Kampala, Uganda, where a half-drunk settler came up to her in the hotel bar and said, "Oh yes, you're Maida Springer. You're just here doing things you could not do in your own country." Nor was it different in October in Dar es Salaam, the capital of Tanganyika, where she found a letter from the immigration officer, S. C. Sinclair, waiting for her at the hotel. The letter told her to present herself at his office each morning with her itinerary. On November 14, the *London Weekly News* ran a dispatch from Tanganyika that said: "That busy little American Negress, who has done so much, both in cash and in kind, for Kenya's Federation of Labor, Mrs. Maida Springer, is active now in Tanganyika on a new 'goodwill mission.' The government is not quite sure yet whether she intends to hand out the cash . . . on the same generous lines as she did in Kenya."

Springer was in fact handing out cash to the sisal workers on the Pongwe Estate, who were on strike for higher wages. When the police arrested five strike leaders, eight hundred unarmed workers went to Tangatown (Dar es Salaam) to protest. The police arrested forty-eight more, nineteen of whom were sentenced to three months in jail for unlawful assembly. Springer cabled Lovestone, who sent her some money for a strike fund. Springer's friend Julius Nyerere, Tanganyika's first African university graduate, asked her: "Do you not think it is sad, Maida, that countries like yours should wait until things go wrong before they act?" Sinclair began to ask, "Have you brought any money for the unions?" So she left for London at the end of November, before they could throw her out.

In London, she saw Walter Hood, head of the Colonial Department of the TUC, who had written Governor Twining of Tanganyika on November 12 to warn him about her: "I am afraid Mrs. Springer may be assuming the role of a geopolitical go-between among African nationalist leaders in East Africa and even beyond."

Hood told Springer: "The first thing you must understand is that indigenous peoples—of the West Indies, of Africa, of Malaya—are incapable of self-sacrifice like British workers." The trouble was, he said, that too many of the colonial trade union leaders became "puffed up" and meddled in politics. They exaggerated their membership and did not collect dues. He had lived in Central Africa, he said, and, "I know the African mind.

"I've got the best job in the TUC and I don't care what the pinkies say," Hood declared. The left-winger Fenner Brockway (Lovestone's old friend from the POUM days) had complained in Parliament that when Hood was in Kenya he refused to talk to some of the African unionists until they got a scrubbing brush and washed themselves. "I don't care what he says," Hood went on. "I don't go throwing my arms around these pics [pickaninnies] simply because they're black. These people whine about being chained and handcuffed. I was handcuffed when I was fourteen."

Despite these pronouncements, intended for the benefit of the American interloper, Walter Hood had done much to help Tom Mboya. It was Hood who had arranged his scholarship at Ruskin College and Hood who had flown to Nairobi to back up Mboya when the Kenya Federation of Labor was threatened with cancellation. But he didn't want the Americans barging in on his turf. The TUC position was that only the British understood the realities of East Africa.

In April 1959, Mboya made his second trip to the United States and was received as a hero of African nationalism. In Carnegie Hall on April 15, celebrating African Freedom Day, he came onstage, said one word—*Uhuru*—and asked the audience to contemplate its meaning; they all rose in complete silence as if mesmerized. *Life* magazine said, "He is not only the outstanding political personality in Kenya, but among the most important in all Africa."

Lovestone thought the hoopla was going to Mboya's head, and he wrote Brown in June: "He has a lot of native ability and intelligence. . . .

But I am afraid the boy is a bit too conceited for his own good. . . . He has yet to apologize for his shameful mistreatment in not keeping his appointment with the UN people."

In June 1960, Maida Springer returned to Nairobi for the inauguration of the first trade union building south of the Sahara. She had devised a "shilling a brick" program, which gave the Kenyan workers a stake in the building. The Federation of Labor was established as the main mass organization in Kenya. But the stress of Africa was too much for Springer, who was laid low in 1961 with bleeding ulcers and had to be given three transfusions. "It will be a long time before she is able to be in full harness," Brown wrote Lovestone. But Jay thought she had the right idea. "It's one thing when a hungry fellow is given some fish to eat," he said. "It's another thing to teach him how to be a fisherman. Maida sensed that."

Once again, however, there was no predicting the turn a country would take after Lovestone and his people had helped them win their independence. Tanganyika became independent in 1961, and Springer's devoted friend Julius Nyerere, once president, pursued a socialist course, which despite his probity was a colossal failure. Lovestone wrote Springer on November 15, 1961: "I don't want to hide my deep disappointment with Julius Nyerere . . . he is embarking on a very dangerous course, particularly if he is responsible for the Tanganyika Federation of Labor sending students to East Germany . . . this is suicidal." As Springer tried to explain it, Africans wore their ideology lightly. It was one thing one day, another thing the next. What they wanted was "balm in Gilead."

In Kenya, *Uhuru* finally came in 1963, when the long-imprisoned leader Jomo Kenyatta was inaugurated as the first president. Mboya became minister of labor in the new government, which passed restrictive labor legislation. The Kenya Federation of Labor became a government union, and Mboya urged the workers not to engage in senseless strikes.

Springer was asked to turn the Institute of Tailoring and Cutting, which she had built with ILGWU funds, over to the government. "Now they question this unassuming program because it was underwritten by a union," she wrote Lovestone. He replied that their friend, who had fought so well against foreign despotism, was now short of breath and felt that the solution was to apply the same despotic measures as their former colonial masters. It made Jay laugh when the authors of antilabor legislation told Springer she should look at the good ingredients. "Let them start their own projects," he said.

Mboya was a Luo but had spent his whole life trying to surmount tribal rivalries. He was seen as Kenyatta's successor, but Kenyatta was a Kikuyu, as were many in his entourage, whose hostility Mboya could not quell. In mid-1969 Mboya was murdered in broad daylight on a Nairobi street. His killer was a Kikuyu who had studied for a time in Bulgaria. Years later it became known that the killer's legal fees were paid by Kenyatta's attorney general, Charles Njonjo.

Springer felt as though she had lost a son. By then she had retired, with time to ponder her African experience. She had contributed to the independence of a number of African states and then watched their downward spiral—coups, dictatorship, one-party rule, economic decay, and the rise of "kleptocracies." It was a melancholy compendium.

To some Lovestone's intelligence service seemed like Lovestone's motley crew, or his dirty half dozen. Anyone who saw their raw reports, with Deverall's attacks on the American embassy, Goldberg's complaints about his health, and Das's gossip about the private lives of Indian politicians, could easily dismiss them as a farrago of hearsay and irrelevance. But to Angleton they were a useful additive to his other sources. He liked to have fodder to pass on to Allen Dulles, which Allen in turn could pass on to his brother. Evaluations of embassy personnel came in handy, as well as examples of their failings. Gossip about foreign statesmen could be used against them at the proper time.

There was also much solid reporting. Lovestone's agents went places where the embassy people did not go and had contacts that the embassy people did not have. In New York, Lovestone the puppeteer pulled the strings, guiding them and protecting their flanks, while Angleton kept the money faucet open.

Lovestone, officially an assistant to George Meany in the AFL, was allowed extraordinary leeway in his covert assignment. Angleton left him unsupervised, as the JX files piled up in his office. The results were mixed. Aside from Brown, the best agents were the two women. Maida Springer played a valuable role in helping a number of African nations on the road to independence. She could not keep them all in the Western camp, but that was beyond her scope. Pagie Morris played a similar role in North Africa and brought back hard-to-get information from Iraq and other Arab countries. Mohan Das kept sending firsthand information about India. Irving Brown was the centerpiece of the Lovestone intelligence agency, hard-driving, well-liked, and an astute analyst. Harry Goldberg had his ups and downs but did his homework and wrote many useful reports. Richard Deverall had such a twisted personality that he could not function in a purposeful way, but he sent Lovestone hundreds of overlong reports that showed a sure grasp of Japanese politics. Love-stone called them "tapeworms," and George Meany refused to read them. As Lovestone the baseball fan liked to say, "Nobody's batting a thousand. Jesus Christ himself with his twelve apostles only batted .800."

In the fifties it seemed that the Soviets made the mistakes, with the uprisings in Poland and Hungary. In the sixties America stumbled with the Bay of Pigs and the Vietnam War, and the Lovestone intelligence service wound down. Deverall left Japan in 1955, Harry Goldberg came home in 1957, and Maida Springer retired in 1963. Irving Brown was assigned as UN rep for the ICFTU in 1962. Mohan Das occasionally reported from India, while Pagie Morris continued to travel to the Arab countries for Angleton, but the great period of churning worldwide activity was over.

16

LOVESTONE'S SECOND FRONT

Lovestone's main enemy was always the Soviet Union, but there was another enemy, inside his own camp, which he fought just as tenaciously, and that was the ICFTU (International Confederation of Free Trade Unions). It will be recalled that this organization had been created in London in 1949 as an alternative to the Communist-controlled WFTU (World Federation of Trade Unions). The ICFTU was launched with 48 million members and sixty-seven affiliates from fifty-one countries, including the CIO and the British TUC, which pulled out of the WFTU. The Communists could no longer claim that they spoke for the world's workers. The ICFTU's aim was to promote respect for trade union rights in countries where those rights were trampled and give a voice and a bit of help to democratic trade union leaders.

The first president was the Belgian Paul Finet, and the first general secretary was Jacob Oldenbroek, a Dutchman who had been the head of the powerful International Transport Workers Federation. Having spent the war years in England, he was thought to be partial to the TUC. In addition, he was somewhat haughty and diffident in manner, although cherubic and weak-chinned of countenance. But he was considered a model bureaucrat, the ideal person to set up a new organization, using diagrams with rectangular boxes and arrows. Lovestone called him Mona Lisa, because he was often inscrutable.

Although the AFL was the principal backer of the ICFTU, which received its income from affiliation fees and contributions, George Meany soon saw it as a calcified and self-sustaining bureaucracy, incapable of doing any real work. Lovestone and his bunch did a better job on a shoestring, with no overhead. When the ICFTU failed to react energetically to the invasion of South Korea, Irving Brown wrote Meany on August 16, 1950: "Unless we can show more desire on the part of the ICFTU to play a role in these hot issues, the reason for the existence of the ICFTU becomes less and less."

The ICFTU held a world congress every two years, and at the first congress, in Milan in July 1951, the AFL was dealt what it considered a low blow. Finet did not want a second term as president, and Sir Vincent Tewson, the general secretary of the British TUC, was elected. The AFL saw this as a betrayal of the 1949 small-country agreement. Tewson as president, swaying the pro-TUC Oldenbroek, would bring the ICFTU under the control of the British. The CIO, breaking ranks, had treacherously supported him. Tewson's selection, Brown said, "rather helps the propaganda of our enemies," and would be a drawback "in the kind of cold war we are now engaged in with the Communists, especially in the colonial areas."

In his speech to the Milan congress, Brown referred to the Soviet-backed aggression in Korea. Lovestone, who was also in Milan, was shocked when Tewson said to Brown after he had finished: "It is too bad you mentioned Korea. We wanted to say nothing or do nothing which might hurt the armistice negotiations." Like Lovestone, Meany saw the ICFTU as appeasers and was so angry at Tewson's election that he held back the AFL payment to the ICFTU regional fund, intended to finance foreign activities. The CIO, only too pleased to upstage its rival, contributed a hundred thousand dollars.

At the March 1952 meeting of the twenty-nine-member ICFTU Executive Board, another incident occurred when a two-man delegation from Cyprus asked to be heard. Cyprus was then a British crown colony, but a movement had sprung up among Greek Cypriots asking for union with Greece, or *enosis*. The Cypriot Workers' Union, an ICFTU affiliate, was strongly pro-*enosis* and sent the delegates to Brussels to explain its position. But Tewson, on a point of order, would not allow them to speak or even enter the hall. As they cooled their heels in the anteroom, the TUC veteran Arthur Deakin said, "Let the Greeks stay the hell out of our property."

On May 11, 1952, Brown had dinner in London with Tewson, who said, "Irving, for the life of me, I don't see how and why this worsening of relations came about. What is bothering the AFL people?" "Frankly," Irving said, "the AFL feels that you are playing a narrow British game." Meany agreed, saying, "The ICFTU is run by the British."

The AFL boycotted ICFTU meetings until the Second World Congress in Stockholm in July 1953. There the AFL had its first victory, as Tewson was replaced as president by the strong-jawed Belgian Omer Becu, in whom Meany and Lovestone had high hopes. But Oldenbroek remained in the key job of general secretary.

With the merger approaching, both George Meany and Walter Reuther attended the Third World Congress of the ICFTU in Vienna in July 1955. At this congress the AFL finally prevailed on two important matters. Concerned with the Soviet peace offensive, the "spirit of Geneva," and the "new look," the AFL pushed through a resolution banning contacts between ICFTU affiliates and Soviet bloc countries. To offset the influence of Oldenbroek, the AFL called for a new position, director of organization, who would handle the bulk of the foreign work. But it took the ICFTU a year to pick a man for the job, the leader of the Canadian steelworkers, who had once wanted to be a missionary, Charles Millard. In the meantime the AFL policy of withholding payment seemed to be working, for Brown wrote Lovestone in October 1955 that "Tewson is scared stiff to do anything which does not please Meany. . . . Our position of strength in this case is to the tune of $280,000 a year."

In 1956 a new ingredient was added to the ICFTU mix, which precipitated quite a few violent reactions. Richard Deverall was stagnating in New York. Lovestone and Meany did not want to leave him unemployed, in spite of the stains on his blotter. Lovestone thought up the idea of planting him in the ICFTU secretariat as a sort of Trojan horse. When Oldenbroek came to the AFL-CIO Executive Council meeting in Bal Harbour, Florida, in December 1955, on a fence-mending foray, Meany did a little arm-twisting. Oldenbroek offered Deverall the important-sounding position of special assistant to the assistant general secretary while observing that "you have made a good many enemies in various parts of the world." Deverall arrived in Brussels on March 19, 1956, and was assigned to the dour and anticlerical German socialist Hans Gottfurcht, one of the assistant general secretaries. When Deverall asked what his duties were, Gottfurcht told him: "You were hired without my knowledge or consent and I have heard terrible stories about you, but I will reserve judgment. I have no idea what you can do. Read the files and in time you can carve out a job."

Within the ICFTU, Deverall was generally regarded as a spy planted by Lovestone. He found himself to be a chief of service with no service, no secretary, and no duties, barred from meetings and kept in Coventry. His in-basket was empty. Life at the office was a series of small humiliations. "No, Mr. Oldenbroek is too busy to see you." "I'm sorry, but you are not invited to the reception."

"I'm throttled here in Brussels eating my heart out," Deverall wrote Lovestone. He had been "iron-curtained" by slander and ostracism. He was now working on a glossary of labor terms. Be patient and keep your powder dry, Jay counseled. Don't sound persecuted. "As they say in the needle trades racket, don't eat your heart out."

Partly in retaliation and partly for something to do, Deverall reported on the office atmosphere. Most of the employees, he said, were loafers, rotten, or incompetent. Oldenbroek, who had deserted his first wife and picked up a blond in London, was a sick man, absent a lot. Fred Strauss, the director of finance, spied on his employees, listening in on their phone conversations and keeping dossiers on them. People were giving notice right and left, and the new people were useless. One of the rare times when Deverall was allowed to have a typist from the pool for half an hour, "Cominform" came out "common form." The men in the upper echelon all kept mistresses. One of Oldenbroek's assistants had sired bastards in the office, and "Oldenbroek once temporarily fired him after his legal wife came into the office with a loaded pistol intent on killing her erring husband and/or one of his other 'wives.'" When the African and Asian *stagiaires* (trainees) arrived in Brussels for their three-month program, "the young British and Belgian girls in the office are led to entertain them at night. The first *stagiaire* program produced one pregnancy and a late abortion."

Deverall's steady undermining of the ICFTU fell on receptive ears in the AFL. In June 1956 the beefy Charles Millard was named director of organization. Lovestone observed that "Mr. Millard is a fourth-rater. His own union, the steelworkers, wanted to get rid of him. He is incapable of handling the job."

In November 1956, when the Hungarian crisis broke, the ICFTU launched its International Solidarity Fund. The money poured in, but since they didn't know how to spend it, they turned a small amount over to a social relief agency in Vienna and earmarked the rest for other activities. The fact that funds were collected for a specific purpose and not disbursed for that purpose made Lovestone very unhappy, since the AFL had sent fifty thousand dollars to the Hungarian fund.

What most upset Lovestone that year, however, what made him call the December board meeting of the ICFTU "the most detestable and disgusting that I have ever heard of" was the Pissas affair. Michael Pissas was the leader of the anti-Communist union in Cyprus, the Cypriot Workers' Union. He was one of the two who had come to Brussels in 1952 and not been allowed to speak. In 1956 Cyprus was in an uproar. After the failure of a conference in London in September 1955, the EOKA guerrilla movement under George Grivas launched a campaign of terrorism—bombings, assassinations, ambushes, grenades at garden parties. In October, Field Marshal Sir John Harding arrived with twelve thousand troops, including such famous British regiments as the Gordon Highlanders, to restore order. Harding declared a state of emergency. There was a curfew, and it was unlawful to show the Greek flag.

On March 9, 1956, Archbishop Makarios was deported to the Seychelles islands, a British crown colony off the east coast of Africa. On March 10, Pissas was arrested and sent to a detention camp ten miles from the Cypriot capital of Nicosia. Under Harding's emergency law, anyone suspected of anti-British activities could be detained without a trial, and more than five hundred, including about fifty members of Pissas's union, were so detained in two camps.

Lovestone wrote Meany on March 13, 1956, that "it was crude stupidity on the part of the British colonialists to arrest and deport the leader of the Cypriot national movement [Makarios]. . . . The arrest of Pissas is very significant. . . . The British have established a totalitarian regime. [Prime Minister Anthony] Eden needs to show strength to bolster his position in the conservative party."

Pissas was detained for more than nine months on charges of fomenting strikes. He pointed out that the Communist union was better off than his own. There was collusion between the British and the Communists, who were against Makarios because he was a Greek Orthodox archbishop. The Communists, who saw the *enosis* movement as church-sponsored and denounced the Grivas operations, were left alone by the British, while Pissas's union headquarters was raided and vandalized.

Pissas appealed to the ICFTU, where the pro-British element led by Tewson backed the Colonial Office position of "freedom by degrees." Instead of protesting Pissas's detention, the ICFTU sent an emissary to Cyprus to broker an agreement. Evert Kuper had been to Cyprus before and was on good terms with the British.

Kuper arrived in October 1956 and saw Pissas, who gave him a detailed description of the ill treatment in the camp. In February 1957 two former camp guards presented a statement to the House of Commons that inmates had been beaten with rifle butts. In a press conference convened at the House of Commons by the Labour MP for Eton and Slough, Love-stone's old anticolonialist friend Fenner Brockway, the guards told their story.

After talking to Pissas, Kuper saw Sir John Harding, who said that Pissas could not be put on trial, for that would endanger the lives of wit-nesses. The EOKA had stepped up its assassinations. A U.S. vice consul had been killed by a bomb thrown into a restaurant. A British correspon-dent had been shot down in the street in broad daylight. But if Pissas signed a statement denouncing the EOKA, he would be released from the camp and deported. Harding drafted a statement, which Kuper took to Pissas in the camp, and Pissas said: "If I sign this I shall be shot dead by the resistance fighters in twenty-four hours." Then Pissas himself drafted a statement, which Kuper took back to Harding. Kuper shuttled between Pissas and Harding until proposal number 6 was found acceptable by both: Pissas would abstain from all political activity and agreed to leave Cyprus within two weeks of his release.

Pissas was released on December 22 and went to Brussels, where he blamed the ICFTU for making a deal with the British, saying: "I believe that the British government was encouraged to insist on terms for my re-lease by the attitude of Mr. Kuper." Pissas was covering his own behav-ior so as not to incur the wrath of the EOKA people, who were calling him a traitor to the cause.

But Lovestone, always looking for reasons to find the ICFTU at fault, was all too ready to believe Pissas, although he had in fact signed the agreement without any pressure from Kuper, who had acted as an honest broker. Jay wrote Irving in December: "I have been active in the labor movement since 1912 [when he was fifteen—a bit of hyperbole]. This may shock you because this was just about the time when you began to know the difference between a ball and a bat. Then you had not even heard of Babe Ruth! You certainly were not a Yankee fan! In all these years I have never seen or heard anything as shocking as the statement which was offered for Pissas to sign. That statement was worthy of Vorkuta [a Soviet gulag] and Berchtesgaden. It is strictly a Nazi-Communist type of document." The AFL seized on the Pissas pledge as another stick to beat the ICFTU with, calling it a "yellow dog" contract (by which an employee agrees not to join a union while employed).

Back in Brussels, Pissas wanted to go to the UN, which was debating the Cyprus question in February 1957, and hold a press conference. He was told that to do so would be a violation of the agreement he had signed. If he spoke out he would make it more difficult to get anyone else released from the camps. Thus, when he went to New York, the two ICFTU men at the UN, Arnold Beichman and Bill Kemsley, were told not to help him and there was no press conference. Kemsley wrote Jay Krane of the ICFTU Organization Department on April 30, 1957: "Re Pissas. You can have the guy. I wouldn't trust him across the street. . . . He denied he had spent any time in Lovestone's office. . . . To be as kind as one can, he is a conceited, immature ass."

In the meantime the British were ready to pull out of Cyprus, wanting only a couple of military bases, while the Greeks wanted *enosis* and the Turks wanted partition. In March 1959, Makarios returned to Cyprus, and in 1960 came the transfer of power from the British to the Republic of Cyprus. Pissas also returned and became an official in the Makarios government. AFL-CIO activities in Cyprus became irrelevant in the light of continued fighting between Greeks and Turks.

Irving Brown proposed in 1957 that the upcoming Fourth World Congress of the ICFTU be held for the first time outside Europe, perhaps in Tunis. The North African location would underline the confederation's presumed anticolonial sentiments. But when the ICFTU leaders met in March to discuss the congress, Tewson said Tunis was too hot in the summer. Sometimes the temperature rose to 114 degrees Fahrenheit. It would be impossible to sleep. Why not hold the congress in Brussels? Oldenbroek suggested.

Brown, however, prevailed, and the congress was set for Tunis in July. Irving felt he had the green light from Vice President Nixon, who had recommended after his African tour in March 1957 that America raise its profile on the continent. As Lovestone wrote Deverall on April 29: "When Nixon is right he is right despite his name being Nixon. . . . Be fair! Nixon did a good job in Africa and I would rather have him against colonialism than for colonialism. . . . All of us should welcome the fact that the vice president has come around to show some inkling of Africa."

The Tunis Congress of the ICFTU in July was a spectacular affair, attended by a large number of African nations, who kept their anti-Americanism in check, and covered by *Life* magazine. In one way it was a third world hoedown, a forum for the aspirations of developing countries. The anticolonialism of the new African nations collided with the views of the TUC. A. Philip Randolph of the Pullman Porters Union gave a rousing anticolonialist speech, while Sir Vincent Tewson responded with the British go-slow approach.

For Lovestone the high point had nothing to do with Africa—it was

Anna Kethly's speech on Hungary and Tewson's subsequent denunciation of it. On July 11, in the spirit of Tunis, Kethly placed the Hungarian question in a colonial context. "The Hungarian revolution," she said, "was not only an internal affair of a small nation, it was the greatest and strongest protest against dictatorship and the specific colonial exploitation of our modern times. . . . Not only in Asia and Africa do we find colonies," she said, "but we have to watch the Soviet satellite states and the small republics within the Soviet Union, Ukraine, Georgia, Armenia. These states and republics suffer under the same economic and national oppression and exploitation as the African and Asiatic people under colonial rule."

For Tewson this equation of Soviet imperialism with British colonialism passed the bounds of decency. He smelled Lovestone's hand in Kethly's speech, delivered in English, a language she barely spoke. Tewson detested Lovestone, who, as he had once put it, "was preaching Communism in reverse by the reprehensible methods and practices of his erstwhile Communist masters." Tewson believed that Lovestone had ghosted Miss Kethly's speech as an oblique way to attack him. He waited until Kethly and Lovestone had left the congress to deliver his reply:

> It occurred to me that it was rather strange that she was speaking in English. She might have been more comfortable if she had spoken in German and that had been translated. . . . There were some phrases in that speech which I seemed to have heard before. I have heard in tittle-tattle that the British TUC is the stooge of the Foreign Office and the Colonial Office. . . . I am not going to deny that because there are sufficient people who know how totally untrue it is. But there is one very strange feature, that we no longer hear of Soviet imperialism, we now talk of Soviet colonialism. . . . I do not know whether it was prompting. I make no charge. . . . But it is extremely unfortunate, probably owing to language difficulties, that Anna Kethly, in referring to certain republics under the Soviet Union, [said they were like African or Asian colonies]. I would not like a phrase like that to be used, because I think there is a profound difference between Soviet oppression and the conditions which apply in many colonial territories, and in the British territories overseas without exception.

Just as Tewson had seen Kethly's speech as a veiled attack on him, Lovestone saw Tewson's reply as "an outburst against me by crude and obvious inference," as he wrote George Meany from Rome on July 16. Lovestone was informed that "the only American who applauded Sir Vincent was Victor Reuther . . . it was hardly credible that someone from the American delegation should applaud an attack on his own delegation from this rude and stupid sir. . . . I assure you that neither I nor anyone else had the slightest thing to do with the contents or translation of her speech." If Lovestone had nothing to do with Anna Kethly's speech, then someone else did, for she was quite incapable of writing a speech in English by herself. Lovestone told Kethly that he regretted Tewson's "indecent, ungentlemanly, and unwarranted attack on you." He thought her speech had shaken up the Africans and Asians, who had no experience of Communism. They had a tendency to say, "Communism has never bothered us, but colonialism has." As for Tewson's attempt to build a theory of good and bad colonialism, it only served to reveal his prejudices.

After Tunis, Lovestone continued to attack the ICFTU for turning the Hungarian fund into a multipurpose fund. The ICFTU now had $850,000 in the Hungarian kitty, which they used to pay lawyers' fees in Africa, print newspapers in Asia, and do many other things. Not one ruble had they spent on Hungary. In the spring of 1958 events took a turn in Lovestone's favor, for another scandal broke in Brussels, calling into question once again the organization's competence. This time the scandal culminated in the arrest of Irving Brown by the Belgian police.

It had all started at the Tunis Congress, when a young Algerian named Dekkar, the head of the postal and telegraph workers' union, made an impassioned speech calling for Algerian independence. His character and dedication were impressive, and Jay Krane invited him to Brussels for a three-month training stint. In September 1957 he arrived with seven other trade union leaders from North Africa. The Algerians in the group, however, including Dekkar, were wanted by the French police and therefore traveled on Tunisian passports, using aliases. Dekkar was ostensibly a Tunisian named Charfi.

In Brussels, Charfi and the others were placed under the care of Albert Nebbot, the ICFTU director of education, who quartered them in a grubby pension behind the Gare du Nord and gave them a per diem of four dollars a day. Charfi said, "I am a trade unionist, not a little Algerian peasant boy," and the Algerians staged a sit-down strike until they were given better lodgings.

In mid-December the program was over, but Charfi's training scholarship was extended, and he stayed in Brussels into the spring of 1958. Deverall reported that he was lionized by the British clique around Krane (who was American). There were plenty of parties with "a generous flow of whiskey, and after-party sports."

On the evening of March 19, 1958, Charfi had dinner in a Chinese restaurant with Deverall and Brown. At about 9:00 P.M. they left, and Deverall walked ahead and turned the corner, stopping to admire the opera house, which was being washed. Behind him, Brown and Charfi were approached by three plainclothesmen, who arrested them. Brown was held for two hours incommunicado and then released, but Charfi was detained on the ground that he was traveling under false papers. It occurred to Brown that Charfi had been in Brussels for six months. Why arrest him now, if not to implicate Brown?

Deverall later learned that Nebbot had informed the police that Charfi was an Algerian traveling under a Tunisian passport. The crux of the case was whether the Belgians would recognize his Tunisian passport. The French police asked for his extradition. If it was granted, Deverall wrote Lovestone, Charfi was "a dead duck." Charfi was moved to a prison outside Brussels, which was not a good sign. The French police gave the Belgians proof that he was an Algerian wanted for "political activities." In May 1958, Brown went to Tunis and put pressure on Bourguiba to ask for Charfi's release through diplomatic channels. His move paid off; Charfi was released on May 30. Once again the ICFTU had shown itself to be completely muddleheaded.

In Brussels, Oldenbroek accused Deverall of sending reports to New York. "You write tons of reports," he said, "and they are full of lies." But Deverall was not deterred, reporting to Lovestone in June 1959, as the tenth anniversary of the ICFTU approached, that the organization was in bad shape, losing membership in Africa and Asia, and clearly stamped as a British colonial agent. Oldenbroek was losing his grip, Deverall said, and got drunk at a beer party. Millard had phlebitis and had collapsed in his office. Krane was hospitalized with a mysterious disease.

Krane was the one who had instigated the slander campaign against Deverall, but Dick nonetheless went to the Brugmann Hospital to see him, more out of curiosity than compassion, bringing a box of peaches. He wrote George Meany: "I was absolutely shocked to find him all alone in a small bare room with a fever of 106 degrees, emaciated (he had lost almost twenty-five pounds), with a wandering mind, and not much resistance to fight the ailment which has had him in bed for four weeks. . . . I found his situation tragic and dispatched a huge bouquet of flowers to adorn his dismal room." When Krane got out of the hospital, he was a shell of a man, barely able to sustain a conversation, and he died in 1961.

At the Tenth Anniversary Congress, at the Palais des Congrès in Brussels in December 1959, 132 affiliates from one hundred countries, representing 57 million members, sent delegates, but instead of a celebration the urgent topic was the removal of Oldenbroek. Meany made it quite clear where the AFL-CIO stood when he said, "We are not going to let the dead hand of bureaucracy, no matter where it exists, keep us from helping these people in Africa and Asia." At a closed meeting Oldenbroek proposed, as a face-saving device, that if the congress reelected him he would resign the following June. On April 20, 1960, Deverall wrote Lovestone: "Maybe we should just shoot Oldenbroek. One of my Algerian friends in Paris, Tony the killer, would do the job for a railroad ticket and 10,000 French francs [$19]." Murder did not prove necessary, however, for Oldenbroek resigned in July and was replaced as general secretary by the Belgian Omer Becu, who had briefly served as president.

The honeymoon with Becu was the shortest on record. He was immediately tagged as evasive and indecisive. He took office in August 1960, and on November 30, at a farewell dinner for Oldenbroek and Tewson, Meany rose and said that he had campaigned vigorously against Oldenbroek and that this was the biggest mistake of his life. "If I had known then what I know now, I would not have supported the removal of Oldenbroek," he said. Victor Reuther, reporting to his brother, said that "these words struck utter consternation and confusion among all members of the board." Victor could recall no meeting at which morale was so low and bitterness so widespread.

Meany continued to express dismay over the African operations of the ICFTU. At the Executive Board meeting in Brussels from March 11 to 14, 1963, he said that instead of giving money away blindly he wanted to see the documents on receipts and outlays. The spending was out of control. The ICFTU was financing almost every nation on the continent of Africa. Here was the United Labor Congress in Nigeria asking for $36,000 without explaining what it wanted the money for. The only supporting document said, "We are faced with a difficult situation." This was not union building, said Meany, it was welfare. And here was the Kenya Federation of Labor, which had been given money for a delegates' conference but did not produce any vouchers. And here were the Libyans asking for $6,000 when there was no freedom to organize in Libya, where the mails didn't even work—how had they arrived at that amount, Meany wondered, when they could not even correspond with the people there? Becu said that because of the restrictions they had to be very discreet.

Each year Meany's annoyance level rose. At a 1964 Executive Board meeting in Brussels, where French was spoken, the ICFTU budget was being reviewed. At each line item the chairman read, everyone said *d'accord* (agreed). Meany sat there listening until there was an item he objected to, and then roared, "*D'accord,* my ass." Meany felt that the whole financial operation was out of hand. They had accounts in banks drawing interest instead of tapping the surpluses for expenditures. The capital accumulated in the Solidarity Fund for Hungary stood at $2,051,688.

Meany's first public explosion came at the AFL-CIO Executive Council meeting on March 1, 1965, at Bal Harbour, Florida. He demanded a full accounting of all monies donated to the ICFTU Solidarity Fund. He insisted that all unspent monies be returned. He vowed that no further funds would be given until all unspent funds were returned and accounted for. In his press conference the next day, he said the ICFTU was "infiltrated by fairies." Becu wired Meany for an explanation of this attack on staff morals. Meany said he had been misquoted.

In July, Meany attended the Eighth World Congress of the ICFTU in Amsterdam. Becu was reelected general secretary, though he would suffer a heart attack that November and be forced to resign in 1967. But the real news was the interview that Meany gave in the July 8 issue of the Amsterdam daily *Het Parool* (*The Word*). In it he charged that $2.5 million from the ICFTU Solidarity Fund had vanished. "I have been in Brussels and looked at the books," he said, "but the money is not satisfactorily accounted for."

The next day the congress was in a turmoil. Becu said he was "flabbergasted" at accusations that reflected on the integrity of the ICFTU secretariat. Louis Major, a Belgian known to the Americans as the Congo Kid for his defense of his country's record there, said it was "irresponsible to make accusations for which there were insufficient foundations." The Dutch delegate Derk Roemers shouted, "Repeat your charges before this congress if you dare, otherwise you must take them back and apologize." This remark was greeted by loud and prolonged applause.

Meany took the floor and said: "I have spoken the truth, and I think it is wrong for the ICFTU to have placed $2.5 million in investment funds when the money was intended to be used in assisting trade unions in developing countries. When I investigated, I found that the ICFTU had placed unspent balances of the Solidarity Fund—going back as far as seven years ago—into a capital fund entitled Allocated but Unspent, and a reserve fund, from the dues of affiliates. . . . Funds should be spent or given back, and the AFL-CIO council has asked for the return of its share of the ISF reserve, the sum of $818,000, which we have received." When Meany had finished, Major said he was badly informed and so obsessed with anti-Communism that he did not know the difference between a Communist and a Socialist. Meany returned to the platform and referred to Major as "the head of the Socialist party, or whatever he is."

In fact, the financial mismanagement was worse than Meany had revealed, for the money in the reserve fund had been earmarked for pensions for the top ICFTU officials. It was hidden in bank accounts from New York to Australia, where $600,000 was invested at 6.5 percent. Meany later called it "a bit of financial chicanery" to use hidden accounts for a pension fund. As a result of this scandal, Fred Strauss, the financial manager of the ICFTU, was fired. Lovestone observed that "Strauss is no more, and justifiably so."

Lovestone was shocked when, in 1966, Herman Patteet, who had replaced Strauss as head of finance and administration, canceled the stipend of $160 a month that Anna Kethly was receiving from the Solidarity Fund. He observed that Patteet "apparently thinks it is a good idea to commemorate the tenth anniversary of the Hungarian revolt by starving the last surviving leader of that uprising." Patteet, a Flemish Belgian, was considered a playboy and a self-promoter by the Americans, but Oldenbroek liked him. Now, when Becu was resigning as general secretary and the front-runner to succeed him was the Dutchman Harm Buiter, Patteet had nominated himself by letter to various national centers.

But in 1967 Patteet self-destructed. On October 20 two policemen came into his office and arrested him on charges of forgery and embezzlement. When there was a congress, he hired ten interpreters, billed for twenty, and pocketed the difference. He ordered two hundred plane tickets for delegates from the Belgian airline Sabena but used only one hundred and fifty and got refunds on fifty. He sent postal money orders to fictitious names, which he then collected. Patteet confessed to embezzling 2.5 million Belgian francs, or about $75,000. He pleaded guilty at his trial in January 1968 and was sentenced to three years, of which he served two. Lovestone observed on February 5 that "he received a very light sentence for the simple reason that he is well connected with top politicians in Belgium. . . . This generous verdict will not have a good effect in the U.S. It only proves that a lot of other fellows pretty high up are well-connected with the crook." Overwhelmed by feelings that his life was ruined, Patteet upon his release from prison committed suicide by putting himself in front of an oncoming train.

When the AFL-CIO finally broke away from the ICFTU, in 1969, it was not because of financial irregularities but because Walter Reuther pulled his United Auto Workers out of the federation. Reuther constantly complained about the AFL-CIO foreign policy. In early 1967 he resigned from the AFL-CIO Executive Council and made veiled threats of pulling out—the UAW, with 1.3 million members, was the biggest AFL-CIO affiliate. In 1968 the UAW stopped paying per capita dues to the federation, placing the funds in an escrow account. Meany suspended the union on May 15, even though it meant a loss of $1 million a year in per capita dues. On July 1, 1968, the UAW formally pulled out and formed an alliance with the Teamsters union.

The trouble with the ICFTU came about when Buiter, the new general secretary, maneuvered to keep the UAW inside the ICFTU even though it had seceded from the AFL-CIO. According to Lovestone, Buiter was "a typical new bureaucrat with dirty ice water in his veins and began to serve as Reuther's agent." In fact, the ICFTU wanted the UAW dues. In October 1968, Buiter came to Washington and told Meany that the world congress of the ICFTU in July 1969 would admit the UAW if it came to a vote. Meany was livid that the general secretary of the ICFTU should exert pressure on a parent body and ask it to bow to the wishes of a secessionist union.

By January 1969, Brown wrote Meany that Buiter had painted himself into a corner. All he was trying to do now was save his skin, even if it meant wrecking the ICFTU. Instead of being lured into a showdown at the July congress, the AFL-CIO announced its withdrawal from the confederation on February 22, at the Executive Council meeting in Bal Harbour, Florida. After twenty years of membership, Meany said, he was "completely frustrated." This affair was "the last straw."

As Lovestone explained to Anna Kethly, "Reuther split away from the AFL-CIO. He did not take anybody with him, but he made an alliance with [Jimmy] Hoffa, who is in jail as a crook. The Reuther-Hoffa axis is now trying to split the AFL-CIO. We take the position that the ICFTU should not admit into its ranks any organization which seeks to split an affiliate of the ICFTU. . . . If the ICFTU think they can get more money by admitting Reuther, they can have Reuther and Hoffa but they can't have us."

On April 3, 1969, at a meeting of the AFL-CIO International Relations Committee, Joseph Beirne, the chairman, noted that the ICFTU was "an organization which had been set up as a movement to give assistance to workers, but had actually become a banking institution looking for countries in which funds could be invested purely for the sake of obtaining interest."

When the world congress took place in Brussels that July, John Windmuller, a Cornell professor who was an expert on the ICFTU, reported that it was a dreary and somnolent affair in the absence of the AFL-CIO. Lillie Brown, Irving's wife, who attended as an observer, said it was a sad show, completely dead, with only Victor Reuther to liven things up. He sat in the press section, looking like an overaged hippie with his white beard. Harm Buiter made every mistake in the book, taking the Africans to task for trying to achieve "their so-called unity." Less than a year later, on May 9, 1970, Walter Reuther died in a small-plane crash, at the age of sixty-three. A few years later the AFL-CIO came back into the ICFTU fold. By then everything had calmed down.

In the late 1950s cracks began to show in the Cold War armor of the AFL. The pleasant sense of certainty became harder to sustain. Events seemed to be conspiring against the cold warriors. Lovestone still pulled the strings behind the scenes, but the puppets now took on lives of their own. On a number of fronts his troops were in disarray.

Lovestone's views on the Soviet Union had of course not changed. It was a one-party system, purged on top and paralyzed at the bottom, self-sealed from the rest of the world. On May 23, 1958, Lovestone had lunch with Herzog Bar Yacov, the Israeli labor attaché, at the Salle du Bois in Washington. Bar Yacov passed on the story that before Stalin died he left two letters with Khrushchev. The first one was marked "to be opened when things are bad." The second one was marked "to be opened when things are very bad." A few years later Khrushchev opened the first letter, which read, "When things are bad blame me." Thus Khrushchev gave his 1956 speech to the Twentieth Congress listing Stalin's crimes. But as things got worse Khrushchev opened the second letter, which said, "When things are very bad, do what I did," which explained the Soviet suppression of the Hungarian uprising.

The reality was quite different, for in 1959 Khrushchev launched a peace offensive, sending his vice premier and best glad-hander, Anastas Mikoyan, to the United States for a two-week visit. Jim Carey of the CIO on January 7 hosted a lunch for Mikoyan at his electrical union headquarters on Sixteenth Street, which George Meany refused to attend. Meany clung to his Cold War stance but now began to seem a little behind the times, for the lunch went off well, with both sides giving as good as they got.

Walter Reuther told Mikoyan that the Berlin crisis was made in Moscow, that East Germany was a puppet state, and that Hungary showed what happened to satellites. Mikoyan responded with questions about Guatemala. Carey said, "We'll answer your questions about Guatemala when you have answered ours about Hungary."

"You do not even have a labor party in America," Mikoyan said.

"And you don't have a capitalist party," Carey rejoined.

Those sitting at the lunch thought they had "knocked the stuffing out of Mikoyan," but Lovestone rated it a coup for Moscow, the first time a Soviet official was able to confer with top officials in the AFL-CIO.

Lovestone was still bent on preventing Soviet incursions in all corners of the globe. He sent Pagie Morris to Iraq in February 1960, warning her: "Don't study too much Arabic. The world has had its Mohammed and one is enough." In Washington he joined George Meany to greet a Nigerian labor leader, a husky fellow with a name as big as himself, Jay said, who engaged in a lot of glib generalities. "Why don't you join the ICFTU?" Jay asked. "If we join," the Nigerian said, "we want to be able to pay our dues. This is why I want checkoff. After I get checkoff, I will join the ICFTU." Lovestone told him this was nonsense and asked: "Have you any Communists in your midst?" "There may be one or two," the Nigerian said, "but I am in control. They won't do anything as long as I am around." "I hope so," Lovestone said, but he knew it was hopeless.

Attacks in the Soviet press always gave Lovestone a lift, validating his efforts, and the March 1960 issue of *Trud,* the Soviet trade union magazine, had quite an elaborate diatribe, which said: "Lovestone loves secrecy and leads the dirty war against the USSR. . . . Lovestone never rests. From morning to night he is busy with the collection and processing of intelligence information of an anti-Communist nature." To show the extent to which he would go, *Trud* said that Lovestone had gotten wind that Iceland was preparing a consignment of filleted fish for the Soviet Union. He rushed to the State Department and painted a frightening picture: Iceland cod are heading for Murmansk! That means Russian goods will arrive at Reykjavík! There are American Air Force bases in Iceland! Lovestone urged that the United States buy up all the Icelandic fish, said *Trud.* He was portrayed as the archvillain in the worldwide struggle between the two blocs.

In May 1960, Jim Angleton, who was run-down and smoking too

much, had a TB alarm and was packed off to a sanitarium in Virginia, where Jay and Pagie went to cheer him up. A November 9 item in Angleton's FBI file reads: "You will recall that in May of this year Angleton was confined to a sanitarium because of a tubercular ailment. . . . He returned to his home on November 4, where he will continue his convalescence."

In June, New York was hot and humid, and Jay was sweltering because of power failures in his building. He wished the Kennedy-Nixon presidential campaign was over. He had never seen so many dangerous generalities floating about. If he were ever made dictator of the United States, he told Pagie, the first words he would banish from the English language would be *bold, imaginative,* and *positive.* Jay was not happy with either ticket. He couldn't see himself voting for Nixon, and he didn't want to help some of the so-called brain trust around Kennedy, who won in November by 120,000 votes out of 69 million cast.

Lovestone did not particularly like the tone of the new administration. He thought Kennedy had appointed Dean Rusk, who was not known for his boldness, because he wanted to be his own secretary of state. Adlai Stevenson had been named ambassador to the United Nations and had pressured Kennedy to appoint Chester Bowles, who to Lovestone represented all the evils of the appeasement line, as undersecretary of state. Jay did not think Kennedy had to pay that high a price, for Stevenson supporters had sat on their hands in California, which was the main reason Kennedy failed to carry Los Angeles County and lost California to Nixon.

Lovestone had a talk with Stevenson at the UN and asked him if he'd made a deal with the Soviets to strike from the agenda any discussion of the Hungarian item. Stevenson denied it, saying the entire session had been taken up by the Congo question. It was indeed a boring session, Lovestone said, with none of the usual dictators and leading noisemakers around. But he remained convinced that Stevenson was a "phony idealist who had fallen for all the Hammarskjöld rubbish."

On January 26, 1961, Lovestone testified before Pat McCarran's Senate Internal Security Subcommittee concerning the secret gathering in Moscow of eighty-one Communist parties the previous December. "This threat is very serious," he said. "The Communists have recovered much of the ground they lost in the Polish revolt and the Hungarian revolution." The Moscow summit, he said, came up with "an extremist, adventurous program for world conquest" and was a declaration of war against the United States, which was described as "an enemy of the peoples of the whole world."

Sen. Kenneth Keating of New York asked if it would not be a good idea to promote a less hostile atmosphere.

"I am all for it," Lovestone said. "But let's not lose our perspective. Welcome even the tiniest mercies, but do not forget that you are dealing with a merciless opponent."

Sen. William Dodd of Connecticut asked why the Russians had chosen this point in time to attack the United States.

"They are drunk with confidence, with conceit, with power," Lovestone answered. He also insisted that the foreign Communist parties were still under Moscow's yoke. "If Mr. Khrushchev tells the Communist Party of the United States to eat grass and say they are eating banana shortcake," he said, "they will eat grass and say they are eating banana shortcake." The American party, however, was moribund. There was hardly anyone left to eat the shortcake.

Lovestone was endeavoring to maintain the anti-Soviet line among conservative congressmen and particularly the powerful committees. To some extent he was preaching to the converted. But he also sensed that in the country at large and in the fledgling Kennedy administration, his Cold War orthodoxy was outmoded, for he told Pagie Morris that his was a voice in the wilderness. Excerpts from the hearings were televised on CBS, and Lovestone was extensively quoted, but he felt sure that it would only lead to more hostility toward him. Jim Angleton was back in harness in February, trying to fit into the New Frontier. As his wife, Cicely, put it, "Prince Hamlet is in the White House." Scarecrow gave Jay some startling news: President Kennedy was planning an invasion of Cuba. After Batista's fall in January 1959, Fidel Castro had moved quickly to turn the AFL-backed thirty-three-union federation, the CTC, into an anti-American mass movement. By 1960, to Lovestone's chagrin, the CTC was under government control and its three million members were instruments of the state. Lovestone saw Cuba as "a Russian military intelligence operation." But he did not believe a half-baked invasion was the answer. Through Mario Brod in New York, Angleton had some Mafia sources who knew Cuba, and they all told Brod that it would never work. Through George Meany, Lovestone warned the president against the operation, but in vain.

When the Bay of Pigs invasion ended in disaster in April 1961, Lovestone felt that the Kennedy administration had underestimated the total control Castro had over the Cuban people and the terrific military machine the Russians had built up. There was no reason on earth for any Cuban to stick his neck out given JFK's statement that the United States would not intervene. Thus the foredoomed cause of 11,400 amphibious infiltrators, who were, in any event, at cross-purposes and deeply penetrated, Lovestone had been told, by shady Ukrainian instructors and other iron curtain refugees.

"The time has come," Lovestone wrote a friend on May 2, a few days after Castro had declared that Cuba was a Communist state, "to consider Castro Cuba for what it really is . . . a totalitarian dictatorship and servile satellite of Moscow. . . . A military and political base directed by the Moscow-Peiping axis." The Bay of Pigs fiasco made the Kennedy administration look like bunglers in their first three months and caused Allen Dulles to be replaced as head of the CIA by the California businessman John Alex McCone.

As the sixties dawned George Meany was no longer granted the undisputed authority that had once been his. The Reuther camp was in a contentious mood, and in January 1961 a story in *The Washington Post* attributed to "Reuther's aides" described Irving Brown as "an operative of the CIA and not an independent unionist." "This slander is repeated without the slightest disclaimer," Meany wrote Reuther on January 11, "although there is no truth in it and no grounds for it in fact." Lovestone informed Meany that Victor Reuther was behind the article.

Victor Reuther was always in there twisting the knife, thought Jay. At the final meeting of the President's Committee on Government Contracts, a few days before Eisenhower was replaced by Kennedy, he'd had the gall to tell Ike that the AFL unions were racist. Meany could not attend and sent Boris Shishkin, head of the AFL-CIO Civil Rights Committee. Vice President Nixon made the presentation, but the president, who had not been briefed, interrupted to say that civil rights law ought to deal only with the right to vote. The ballot would then provide the correct solution. Nixon made a small gesture of impatience. Noticing the gesture, Ike recovered by saying he did not mean to exclude legislation covering discrimination in employment on government contracts, which was, after all, the purpose of the meeting. He went on to say that as he traveled in the South he spoke to southern employers, who assured him that though they were themselves opposed to discrimination based on race, such discrimination was widespread among unions. Was this true? he asked.

"Mr. President," Shishkin said, "the shoe is on the other foot. Labor is making tremendous progress in eradicating discrimination in employment in the South . . . but many southern employers conduct organized race-hate campaigns in their fight against unions."

Then Reuther jumped in: "Mr. President, the truth is that there is still much discrimination based on race by unions in the South. Let me point out this difference. The industrial unions have by and large succeeded in eliminating all racial discrimination. This is because those unions operate under industrywide agreements, nationwide in scope. Craft unions, on the other hand, are established locally. Many of them are small and negotiate locally and are more subject to local pressures. As a result most discriminatory practices in the South are confined to craft unions." The message was that the CIO industrial unions were rid of racism, while the AFL craft unions in the South were still primarily racist. Lovestone was disgusted. At the White House, in front of the president and vice president, the AFL was charged with racism by its supposed partner, the CIO.

Things were bad all around, Jay thought. At the UN, Khrushchev was acting like a bully, bluffing and making warlike noises. He had the Afro-Asians licking his boots and chasing after him. McCloy reported from Germany that Khrushchev had told him: "I am ready to bomb Germany to dust. I have yet to avenge 20 million Russian deaths caused by the Germans." In Paris, James Gavin was ambassador. It was part of the college boys' technique, Lovestone thought, to choose a general because de Gaulle was a general, which was general nonsense. JFK had visited Paris on his 1961 European swing, and Lovestone's information was that de Gaulle's parting words were "Et surtout, monsieur le président, n'écoutez que vous-même" (Above all, listen only to yourself).

The chairman of the British TUC, Ted Hill, joined a Defend Cuban Freedom Committee and went to Moscow in the spring of 1961 to attend the British Trade Fair. Lovestone heard that he had told some Soviet trade union people: "I am so glad you people got into outer space first rather than the Americans." At home the leaks from the White House were appalling. One insider told Lovestone that the ship of state was the only ship that leaked from the top down. So many chatterbox academics were fluttering around that everything was a talking point.

Lovestone was, however, gratified that the president, in July 1961, had sent via Lyndon Johnson a personal letter to the representative of China (Taiwan) pledging all-out opposition to the seating of the Peking regime in the UN. "Thank God Kennedy's policy is different from that of the junior Harvard boys," he observed. Lovestone remained frozen in his anti-China position at a time when many influential voices were arguing that there were two Chinas and neither one was going to go away. Diplomatic recognition was not a reward for democratic virtues. We had relations with Soviet Russia and Franco's Spain. We had negotiated with China over Korea. It was time, said these voices, to admit China.

Such reasoning infuriated Lovestone and got him into hot water in

1964, when he was accused of insulting the Israeli deputy prime minister, Abba Eban. Lovestone had never considered Israel a reliable ally in the struggle against the Communists. As far back as 1954, when he had a member of the Knesset, Eliezer Livneh, on the CIA payroll, Lovestone had written Angleton to "cut out the wailing wall builder. He is not producing a tinker's damn. . . . He has made it altogether one-way traffic in his relations. . . . You may think I am ruthless, but life is unsound otherwise." Livneh was putting out a magazine called *Beteram,* to which Lovestone had contributed fifteen thousand dollars in 1953.

On May 26, 1964, on the fifteenth anniversary of Israel's admission to the UN, Abba Eban said in a radio address that he "regretted that Communist China is not yet a member of the UN." An irate Lovestone wrote Ben-Zion Ilan, the Histadrut representative in Washington, that "apparently your Deputy Premier studied how to irritate friends and undermine friendship." Ilan forwarded the letter to Eban, who protested to Meany on June 12, asking whether "legitimate dissent should take the form of insulting remarks such as those of Jay Lovestone." Eban also wrote Lovestone: "You have no right to indulge in coarse personal discourtesy." In the labor movement, however, there was a higher tolerance for coarse language than in the State Department, and Meany ignored Eban's complaint.

The times they were a-changin', but Lovestone did not change with them, commenting when George Kennan spoke in favor of containment in early 1962 that he was "confused and conceited—a pathetic soul." On March 20, Lovestone was invited by his old friend Bob Murphy, now a director of the Corning Glass Company, to attend a Corning conference on world affairs. The panelists included President Kennedy's national security adviser, McGeorge Bundy, Julian Huxley of UNESCO, John Dos Passos, Tom Mboya, the French intellectual Raymond Aron, and the Spanish intellectual Salvador de Madariaga. Representing the Eastern Bloc was Janez Stanovnik, the director of the Yugoslav International Affairs Bureau.

At one point in the discussion, Stanovnik said that the multiparty system was a sacred cow. "Individuals should be free," he said, "but the precise framework of this freedom in each society will be decided in accordance with its own tradition." This was too much for Lovestone, who exploded: "What I can't understand," he said, "is how does it come about that in the United Nations the Yugoslavs vote with the Russians, even when the Russians spit in their faces? Very often, when the Russians spit in their faces, they think it is the morning dew." What would the Yugoslavs have done without U.S. aid, sent without any conditions?

"This is the way which will bring you the shortcut to isolation and defeat," an angry Stanovnik replied. Suddenly, thought the Corning vice president Richard H. Andrews, the Cold War, instead of being discussed "cooly and detachedly," was being fought out in the room. The tone became confrontational, and it was found preferable to move on to the population problem.

Recapitulating at his round table the next day, Dos Passos, himself an old leftie, called the Stanovnik-Lovestone exchange the high point of the conference, "a marvelous scene which gave dramatic form to what we have to face." On the one hand, the "Balkan Socialist, who had framed his side of the story so perfectly," and, on the other hand, the onetime Marxist, "using the old Marxist vituperation before the overfed dinner guests." Lovestone reported to Angleton that after dinner several guests had told him: "It is just too bad so few of us stand up to those phonies."

In the summer of 1962, Lovestone learned that when Algeria had celebrated its independence in June, the four-member American delegation had not included a trade unionist—after all that he and Pagie Morris and Irving Brown had done to bring about independence. It was an insult to labor, Lovestone told Averell Harriman, who was now undersecretary of state for political affairs, all the more shocking because one of the four delegates was Joe Kraft, Washington correspondent for *Harper's* and the author of the book *The Struggle for Algeria.* Kraft, Lovestone said, was "a Ben Bella stooge, and a deep admirer of Castro. . . . What is disgusting is that no one in Washington has the political acumen to recognize the importance of having a prominent American trade unionist in this delegation of four. . . . Not even the most emotional and diploma-ridden semiskilled intellectual or glib-eral can speak for labor." To smooth Jay's feathers Harriman sent over G. Mennen William, the undersecretary for African affairs, who explained that the omission of labor had been an oversight on his part and not a matter of policy.

Searching for opportunities where America could recapture the Cold War initiative, Lovestone learned in March 1963 that President Kennedy was planning a summer trip to Germany and would visit Berlin on June 26, the opening day of the convention of the German Building Trades Union. He drafted a memo asking George Meany to suggest to JFK that they both address the convention in Berlin's vast Congress Hall: "It would have a splendid effect on the German trade union movement. . . . It would also have an enormous and stirring effect on the workers, not only of West Berlin but also East Berlin and the entire Soviet zone of Germany. It would electrify the whole German labor movement . . . and enhance the image of the administration in Europe."

Meany mentioned his Berlin trip to JFK, who said, "I'll arrange it so that you can fly up with me." Meany said, "Fine, how about coming to the convention with me?" "I'll jump in for fifteen minutes," Kennedy replied.

On the morning of June 26, 1963, the motorcade arrived at Congress Hall at 11:15 A.M., led by Konrad Adenauer in a car with Willy Brandt, the mayor of Berlin, and JFK. Meany and Lovestone greeted them at the curb. Kennedy spoke for about ten minutes, saying: "Wherever there are men still enslaved, I am not free." East Berlin was now behind walls. The president received a standing ovation, with the thousands of workers shouting in chorus, "Kenn-ah-dee! Kenn-ah-dee!"

Then it was on to the Rathausplatz, City Hall Plaza, with U.S. flags on every lamppost, where the president told the crowd, "Today, in the world of freedom, the proudest boast is *Ich bin ein Berliner.*" Lovestone had given him the line "I too am a Berliner" (*Ich auch bin ein Berliner*), but Kennedy could not pronounce the *auch,* so he said "I am a Berliner," which Lovestone found amusing, for in the local slang a "Berliner" was a jelly donut.* In the plane from Berlin to Dublin, Kennedy told Ted Sorensen: "We'll never have another day like this, as long as we live."

Lovestone felt the same way. He had engineered the presidential visit to the convention, which showed the German workers that America was behind them. It was also a powerful signal to the Soviets. "All the efforts and work paid off," he wrote Pagie. "The president did a beautiful job. . . . Willy [Brandt] is a windbag inflated by ambition."

On his way home aboard the *Queen Mary,* Jay peeped in on the purser's cocktail party but decided that the company was beneath him—after all, he had only a few days before been in Berlin with President Kennedy and spent an hour with Chancellor Adenauer. Nor did he respond to the advertised "Dance Instructions by the Arthur Murray Family." The poor British! he thought. There was thunder and rain off the banks of Newfoundland, and pestiferous fog slowed them down to rowboat pace. He thought of putting an ad in the ship's paper: "Sun Wanted, Any Price Any Time."

Pleased to be home, he bought half a pound of roast beef for $1.45 at the Stage Delicatessen to give to Pagie's cat, Saida. He took Pagie out for a night on the town, but when he saw her off-the-shoulder dress he said:

---

*The nuance is apparent. Though with *"Ich bin ein Berliner"* Kennedy might have been saying "I am a jelly doughnut," *"Ich auch bin ein Berliner"* ("I, like you, am a Berliner") would clearly have implied "I am one of you" and not "We are all jelly doughnuts." By inserting *auch,* Lovestone was avoiding the double entendre.

"You can't go out like that—naked." "This is the first time you've noticed what I wear," she responded. It was, she reflected, a romance but a very odd one. They fought all the time but got along beautifully.

President Kennedy spoke at the AFL-CIO convention in Miami that November and quoted Abraham Lincoln: "All that serves labor serves the nation." The president was off to Dallas, and Lovestone in a brief chat asked: "Mr. President, why do you go to that unfriendly area?" "Mr. Lovestone," Kennedy replied, "I was elected by the enormous majority of 120,000 votes." When Lovestone heard the news of the fatal shooting on November 22, while en route to New York following the convention, his thoughts went back to the evening of June 25 in Berlin, when he had gone out to dinner on the Kurfürstendamm with his friends Ernest and Helen Nagy of the U.S. mission. Hawkers were selling Kennedy buttons, and sidewalk artists had chalked the president's likeness on the pavement. There was a carnival feeling he had never seen before in Berlin. In spite of what had happened now, Lovestone thought, nothing could take that memory away.

Lovestone considered that Johnson was better equipped to take over than Truman had been when he succeeded FDR or than Teddy Roosevelt had been when he took over from a nonentity like McKinley. He learned from Angleton that the KGB had rushed its files on Lee Harvey Oswald to the FBI, fearing an anti-Soviet backlash. Jim was so tense that Jay was worried, though he had probably been that way all his life. He exuded pessimism but in the most articulate way.

For Lovestone, 1963 was a year of tragedy mixed with promotion. Kennedy went to Berlin, and a few months later he was assassinated. Then in December, Mike Ross died, and Lovestone succeeded him as head of the AFL-CIO International Affairs Department. A part of Lovestone was flattered by the appointment, which was a recognition of his efforts over many years. He was now an openly prominent personage, who figured on Washington invitation lists. In April 1964, Dean Rusk invited him to a dinner for King Hussein of Jordan. "The Jordanians," Jay told Pagie, "first wanted to know whether I was a Zionist." But another part of him was dismayed, for in a sense he had lost his cover, he was now a moving but visible target.

The New York Times, in announcing the appointment on December 20, noted the importance of international affairs for the AFL-CIO, which spent about one fourth of its annual income of $10 million in the foreign field. Other newspapers made the point that picking Lovestone meant the continuation of the Meany foreign policy of uncompromising anticolonialism and virulent anti-Communism. Jay maintained his headquarters in New York, coming to Washington, where the genial and thorough Ernie Lee held the fort, two or three days a week.

While Lovestone's appointment seemed to crown a long career, it was in fact the beginning of a ten-year decline. He no longer ran a team of agents. The breadth of his activity was sharply curtailed. The sniping from the CIO would continue and intensify. Above all, his full support with Meany for the Vietnam War would contribute to his demise, dividing the labor movement as it divided the nation.

Lovestone and his people plunged into the Vietnam caldron in 1961, when Irving Brown went to Saigon and discovered a well-organized union, the CVT (Vietnamese Confederation of Workers), which claimed three hundred thousand members and was led by the energetic Tran Quoc Buu, five foot three and the father of ten. A Catholic anti-Communist from North Vietnam, Buu had organized the transport workers and longshoremen of Saigon, the workers on the big rubber plantations, and the tenant farmers in the countryside. The question was how to keep unions going in the midst of a war, with battles raging in rural areas. And what could Lovestone do to help?

Lovestone arranged for Tran Quoc Buu to come to Washington in May 1964 to brief President Johnson. Buu's message was that the way to win the support of Vietnam's fourteen million people was by meeting the needs of the peasants. He said he had one hundred trained organizers operating in five rural provinces.

In the last week of July, Brown went to Saigon and conferred with Ambassador Maxwell Taylor, another admirer of Buu. Brown decided that the AFL-CIO could put the CVT on its feet, figuring that it would cost ten thousand dollars a month at the outset. Soon the CVT had a print shop and a weekly paper, thirty motorbikes for the rubber plantations, and ten outboard motors for the fishermen's union.

But Buu drew the ire of Saigon's government of generals by calling a waterfront strike, and on September 13, 1964, he was arrested and charged with treason for interfering with the war effort. In October, Meany wrote Ambassador Taylor that the AFL-CIO was shocked by the charges. Taylor replied on October 19 that "we share your own high regard for Mr. Buu and will be of any assistance to him that we can." The charges were dropped.

In November, in another show of support, an AFL-CIO delegation consisting of George Baldanzi of the CIO United Textile Workers and Tom Altaffer, who was actually a CIA agent working under labor cover, arrived in Saigon. On December 8 Buu took them to visit a fortified agricultural center in the Mekong Delta, which was guarded by armed CVT militiamen. On the night of December 24, the Vietcong attacked the center, which was celebrating Christmas Eve. A three-hundred-man Vietcong contingent charged to the sound of bugles. When the smoke of battle lifted twenty minutes later, three militiamen and an eight-year-old boy lay dead. The school was destroyed, the administrative center was sacked and burned, and twenty-six carbines were gone.

Six CVT militiamen were taken prisoner for enrollment in Vietcong forces. The CVT camp leader, Quey, was paraded in front of the assembled villagers, who were told to criticize him. Their only reproach was that he scolded them for laziness. His captors then tied a rope around his neck and led him off. Ten other militiamen avoided capture by hiding in the river. "More than likely," Altaffer concluded in his report to Meany, "they will never again attempt such isolated living under our military protection."

Escalating in tandem with the war was the antiwar movement, which caught fire in the labor ranks. Meany and Lovestone found themselves unable to keep the rank and file in line on Vietnam. When Walter Reuther's UAW came out with an antiwar resolution, Lovestone called it "a diseased tapeworm, a rehash of newspaper clippings in spots cancerous." At the AFL-CIO convention in San Francisco in December 1965, protesters carrying antiwar banners were allowed into the galleries during a speech by Secretary of State Rusk. From the floor delegates shouted, "Throw the bums out" and "Get a haircut." Meany himself finally asked, "Will the sergeant at arms clear these kookies out of the gallery?" Lovestone and Meany continued to back the government's Vietnam policy in two 1966 resolutions of the AFL-CIO Executive Council, both of which pledged "unstinting support."

Lovestone found himself having to defend Vietnam to his European friends. In June 1966 he went to Germany to see the now-retired ninety-year-old Adenauer, observing that "his mind is sounder and clearer and his carriage stronger than five years ago. Amazing!" Adenauer proposed that the United States pull out of Vietnam, which came as a shock to Jay. He added that he had no faith in Secretary of Defense Robert Strange McNamara, "a computer-minded man of insufficient political capacity." Adenauer felt that the war was turning America's focus away from Europe. "I don't know what can be done to disabuse him of such false notions," Lovestone told a friend after his visit with der Alte. "The U.S. must be involved wherever the enemy attacks." As Jay saw it, if we lost

Southeast Asia, de Gaulle would find many takers for his argument that the United States could not be counted on to defend Europe.

In Saigon, at the fifth congress of the CVT in April 1967, Buu said that "ours is the story of a labor movement within a country which is fighting Communism." The largest unit, the Tenant Farmers' Federation, now had seventy thousand members. In the U.S. embassy officials were fond of saying that Tran Quoc Buu was the Samuel Gompers of the Vietnamese labor movement. He was also, according to Frank Snepp, the CIA man who wrote *Decent Interval,* the pride of the CIA station. Buu, said Snepp, had been turned into a "collaborator" and was used "quite profitably" as an instrument for keeping the unions loyal to President Nguyen Van Thieu. Buu was "malleable," Snepp noted, and in 1971 he was built up as a token candidate to save President Thieu from the embarrassment of running unopposed. The main purpose of the CIA in Saigon, said Snepp, was to "bribe, inveigle, and hire" enough agents to keep the Thieu regime afloat.

In 1967 Lovestone saw his carefully designed system of operations come apart. He had controlled it with a panel of secret levers that no longer seemed to work. In Germany the once-reliable DGB was attacking George Meany, who at the age of seventy-two was recovering from major surgery on a hip socket. In France, de Gaulle, "the worst prima donna in Europe," was blasting America's Vietnam policy. The attacks at home now included those of the liberal wing of the Democratic Party. In his April inaugural address as president of Americans for Democratic Action, John Kenneth Galbraith called the AFL-CIO leadership "aged and deeply somnolent."

Lovestone found himself under greater scrutiny in the press. In fact, he was much less involved in spook activities than in the fifties, when he was an anonymous toiler for the Fizz Kids. But part of the fallout from the Vietnam War was greater attention to CIA activities. Largely as the result of a war which the AFL-CIO backed to the hilt, Lovestone became the focus of attacks in the press.

On February 20, 1967, came a Drew Pearson column inspired by Victor Reuther, which said that the CIA paid out $100 million a year to the labor movement. "No CIA money for labor is spent without Lovestone's approval," Pearson wrote, "and few labor attachés are appointed to American embassies abroad without his OK."

For Meany to admit that the AFL foreign operations had been funded by the CIA for more than seventeen years would in the present climate amount to political suicide. The Reuther brothers would be all over him, and a labor movement already torn would shatter like a fragmentation grenade. So Meany in a press conference in Bal Harbour, Florida, called Pearson "a liar by choice" and said that the AFL-CIO had "absolutely not" received any funds from the CIA. The AFL-CIO, he said, had been building strong anti-Communist unions before the CIA existed. (That much was true.) Meany promised a probe, and the following exchange with reporters took place:

"Hasn't Jay Lovestone said anything today about Pearson's story?"

Meany: "I don't know. I haven't interviewed Jay. Put this in your pipe. No matter who else may be involved, anyone wants to bet—you will find out, they turn this thing upside down—that Jay Lovestone had nothing to do with the CIA and never did have. That you can bet on."

Lovestone knew he could count on George, who would never throw him to the wolves, but he dreaded the ripple effect, the reactions from abroad. The labor movement was bound to be tarnished. "We shall have brought on our heads the wrath of every fake liberal and semiskilled intellectual," he told Meany.

The topper came in May, when *The Saturday Evening Post* ran an article called "I'm Glad the CIA Is Immoral." This one did the most harm because it was impossible to refute or discredit as the work of a crypto-Communist or semiskilled intellectual. Its author was Tom Braden, who had founded the Department of International Organizations, the very CIA man who had in the early years worked directly with Lovestone and Brown. His article was presented as a defense of the CIA, but it revealed information that was particularly damaging to his onetime AFL colleagues.

Braden wrote that he still had in his possession a receipt for fifteen thousand dollars from Irving Brown, signed Norris A. Grambo, which had been used to pay off Pierre Ferri-Pisani and his enforcers, who were protecting Marshall Plan shipments in France in the early fifties. As for Lovestone, Braden said he was the conduit for "the secret subsidy of free trade unions which soon spread to Italy. . . . But though Lovestone wanted our money, he didn't want to tell us precisely how he spent it."

Once again Meany was forced into deniability mode, this time angrily. In a May 9 press conference he called Braden's article "a damn lie." "Not one penny of CIA money has ever come into the AFL or the AFL-CIO to my knowledge over the last twenty years. . . . If it had come in I would have known about it. . . . Lovestone had absolutely nothing to do with the CIA. . . . I've talked to him many times, and I can tell you he does not have anything to do with this."

In the meantime, as a form of damage control, President Johnson appointed a committee of three to review relations between the CIA and private U.S. organizations, which included labor unions. The committee recommended that "it should be the policy of the U.S. government that no federal agency shall provide any covert financial assistance or support, direct, or indirect, to any of the nation's educational or private voluntary organizations." The target date for termination of such aid was December 31, 1967.

The true purpose of the directive was not to end the arrangements but to save as many of them as possible by changing their sources of funding from covert to overt—in the case of labor, from CIA to AID. But there was one exception: Lovestone's connection with Jim Angleton and Pagie Morris continued. Now it was strictly between Jim and Jay. George Meany thought it had stopped, and Angleton's CIA bosses looked the other way.

Lovestone was seventy and getting a bit fleshier, a bit more jowly, his blondish hair turning gray and his eyebrows bushy. He maintained his single-minded focus on his work, his crusading spirit, and his enemies list. He continued to see Esther Mendelssohn in Montreal and Florida, but she was past seventy, and the once-beautiful actress had turned into a stooped and crotchety old woman. His affair with Pagie Morris had wound down, though they continued their shared domesticity in the little house they had bought together in Oak Beach, Long Island, next door to Jones Beach and across from Fire Island. There they spent many happy weekends in the pine-paneled cottage, with Pagie gardening and Jay poring over reports, often inviting the Meanys or the Dubinskys (though Pagie reprimanded Jay for his ineffectiveness around the house—he wasn't even capable of taking out the garbage).

In March 1968, Irving Brown arrived in Saigon with $35,000 for the CVT and $45,000 for the eight thousand union families who had to be relocated as a result of the January Tet Offensive. The money for Buu was to buy Japanese tractors to replace water buffalo in the rice paddies and diesel engines to replace the children who operated the big waterwheels with pedals, as if riding giant bicycles.

Lovestone saw the positive side of the Tet Offensive, telling Ellie Borochowicz that "the stepped-up guerrilla action in the cities has been a rude shock and painful awakener to some people who I thought were three-fourths dead. So far, that's the only asset in the picture." In Washington he found sharp differences in the Pentagon over estimates of Vietcong strength. He expected some fur to fly, which would lead to resignations.

Lovestone was in Paris in May 1968 for the student-worker revolts that almost toppled de Gaulle. He wrote Meany that the Force Ouvrière had tipped the scales. André Bergeron, the new head of FO, calmly went on TV before millions to state that this was an economic strike and not a bid to overthrow the regime, which reinforced Premier Georges Pompidou's efforts for a settlement. As a result, Jay said, FO membership increased by fifty thousand.

In August, Soviet troops invaded Czechoslovakia, which made Lovestone wonder what had happened to all those people who said Communism was no longer Communism. With the Democratic convention coming up, he hoped there would be enough people in the Humphrey ranks to stop catering to the McGoverns. Lovestone sat in front of his TV set in New York watching the faces of the experts—Galbraith, Senator Morse, Senator Halfbright—all on the defensive, admitting that the doves would have to eat crow. All those who said the day of détente had arrived would have to think twice.

The overriding issue, however, remained Vietnam. Much of the country was in open revolt against the war. The campuses were in an uproar, and Jay warned his grandniece, Nina Matis, an undergraduate at Smith College, that antiwar activities were "destructive nihilism." "The right to dissent is something quite different from the right to disrupt," he said. The antiwar virus had even contaminated the GOP, Lovestone reported, and New York's Republican mayor, John Lindsay, had advised the student body of Queens College on how to avoid the draft and had attended a rally at which the Vietcong flag was displayed.

At the Democratic convention, with Johnson out of the race and Hubert Humphrey beating Gene McCarthy, the antiwar legions turned the city of Chicago into an armed camp. Lovestone observed that "while not all the demonstrators were Communist, while many were hippies, nuts and whatnots, the strategy pursued by the mob was strictly Communist-inspired." His mind seemed to be trapped in a time warp. Communism continued to be the single lens through which he judged all events. But was Dr. Spock a Communist? Richard M. Nixon, having won in November 43.4 percent of the vote against 43.0 percent for Humphrey, announced a policy of "Vietnamization" and troop withdrawal.

Back in Saigon in June 1968, the AFL-CIO representative Fernand Audie presented Tran Quoc Buu with the first ten tractors. Audie wanted to display the CVT as the one nonpartisan mass organization to have held together in Vietnam. But in October 1969, Buu, on orders from the CIA, announced that he was starting his own political party. Already on the CIA payroll, Buu also sought AFL-CIO "direct cash support" from Ernie Lee, Lovestone's number-two man, to launch his party.

Seeing that Buu seemed to be juggling conflicting agendas, Audie reported that he was mercurial and overprogrammed, and that he suffered from the "last man he talked to" syndrome. Chafing under Audie's supervision, Buu charged that he was having an affair with a Vietnamese woman and speculating on the black market. Whether or not the charges were true, Audie was recalled in April 1970, his hostility to Buu having made him ineffective.

Meany, having been wooed by Nixon at lunch and on the golf course, announced in 1969 his unconditional support for the president's policy of escalation. In May, Lovestone was happy to report that labor was having nothing to do with the "senile children" of the Students for a Democratic Society. At a National Trailways bus strike in Philadelphia, "a dozen SDS longhairs tried to join the picket line with their own slogans and our fellows told them to get out."

After the invasion of Cambodia in April 1970, Lovestone still felt that Nixon's foreign policy was closer to the AFL-CIO than that of the Democratic Party. He formed a friendship with Charles W. Colson, Nixon's hatchet man and special counsel. Colson was horrified when, on May 9, 1970, following the killings at Kent State, 150,000 students descended on Washington. Colson saw a mist of tear gas form outside the White House windows. It was the start of the siege mentality.

In late May, with Lovestone's help, the AFL-CIO came through. A hundred thousand hard-hats marched through the streets of New York, shouting, "Support the troops." Two days later a hard-hat delegation was photographed with the president in the Oval Office to illustrate the alliance between organized labor and a Republican president.

Lovestone served as Colson's labor adviser. When he protested the naming of a CIO man to the Saigon embassy, Colson promised "to take very strong steps to see if this kind of thing can be avoided in the future." Thanks to Colson, Lovestone, at least on one occasion, had access to FBI documents that were sent to the White House. "Appreciate your reaction," Colson noted when he sent Jay a secret FBI report dated September 30, 1970, which had to do with Communist Party efforts to find a labor leader who would "blast" Nixon. George Morris, a columnist for the *Daily Worker,* had proposed Victor Gotbaum of the State, County, and Municipal Employees, according to the FBI.

Colson also asked Lovestone to help out with dovish AFL-CIO leaders. One such turncoat was the once-stalwart Joe Keenan, who had turned antiwar and joined the Common Cause Policy Council. In October 1971, Colson asked Jay if he could get Keenan to resign from the council. "I had thought Keenan was a strong Meany supporter and a right-thinking guy," Colson said. "I would not think the AFL-CIO would want one of their leading Executive Council members prominently involved in such irresponsible conduct."

Lovestone's greatest source of anxiety at the time was Nixon's China policy. "There are those in Europe and the U.S.," he wrote a friend, "who think it was a clever move on Nixon's part to organize his mission to Peking on the notion that it will peeve and pique Moscow and intensify dissensions between Brezhnev and Mao. This is the most rancid type of wishful thinking. The painful reality is that Mr. Nixon is prepared to work a 48-hour day to allay Moscow's suspicions and therefore makes every concession to Moscow."

In October 1971, Lovestone's worst fear, the thing that he had been fighting for more than twenty years, came to pass. Red China had enough votes to be seated at the UN. This was a lifesaver for Mao, Jay thought, breaking his isolation after the failure of the Cultural Revolution. To think that China would now have a seat on the Security Council with veto power was enough to give Jay apoplexy. Already the Mao crowd was demanding that 148 Chinese employees be added to the UN secretariat, he fumed, and Chinese would become one of the principal languages, adding hugely to the payroll.

Yet there was nothing Lovestone could do but soldier on. He operated from a sense of certainty, the centerpiece of which was that Communist regimes could not be trusted and should only be dealt with in an adversarial way. This was the lesson of his own life experience. As he often said, "I may be wrong, but I'm never in doubt." He continued to believe that criticism of American policy in Vietnam was wrong. You could not throw the baby out with the bathwater. A strong U.S. deterrent was the only way of not being conquered by Soviet imperialism. But my God, he thought, the flood of adoration for Hanoi in our newspapers and literary world!

In February 1972, as Lovestone had feared, Nixon made his historic trip to China and agreed with Mao that nations with different political systems could cooperate to their mutual benefit. In June, George McGovern won the nomination at the Democratic convention in Miami Beach, and for the first time since its founding in 1955, the AFL-CIO did not support a Democratic candidate. As Lovestone explained it, labor wanted a candidate who could beat Nixon. The New Politics wing of the party had imposed McGovern, assuming that the dumb labor people would back anybody. In November, McGovern carried only one state— Massachusetts. Lovestone noted that just 55 percent of eligible voters had gone to the polls. Millions had sat on their hands.

In the postelection period Lovestone saw Nixon moving to the left on Vietnam. After secret talks with the North Vietnamese, in January 1973 American troops began to pull out. The cost of Vietnam had become unacceptable, while the objective was now seen as marginal. The war ended the domestic consensus that had sustained Cold War policies since World War II. The labor movement itself was split in two.

Tran Quoc Buu was in trouble, accused of embezzling millions of dollars. He had apparently been collecting money from the Belgians, the French, and the Germans as well as the AFL-CIO and the CIA. Heinz Palla, who had administered German funds in Saigon for three years, said in *Der Spiegel* that Buu was receiving money from twenty-four labor organizations. He had gotten $6 million worth of German aid alone, plus half a million a year from the AFL-CIO. Dr. Palla charged that Buu had sold agricultural equipment and fertilizer on the black market. Buu's wife, he said, owned a pig farm, a feed mill, and a bottle factory.

Now that Buu was the leader of a political party, the Saigon press picked up the story, calling it Laborgate. In a press conference on May 22, 1973, Buu denied the charges and said he had not spent a single penny for himself. He wondered why Dr. Palla had cast "so mean aspirations [*sic*] on another." But whether the charges were true or not, Buu lost a good deal of his funding, as well as his stature as a political and labor leader. In any case, in the context of America's pullout, building a free Vietnamese labor federation became a lost cause for the AFL-CIO.

Well, Jay thought, if General Giap captured Washington, he would seek asylum in the Everglades, where the snakes were more honorable. In December 1972, when the Nixons scaled the Great Wall, he reflected that our business circles had always been our greatest appeasers. Thank God the AFL had avoided those pitfalls, being opposed to every form of dictatorship, be it Communist, Nazi, Fascist, Falangist, Peronist, or Big Dollar. Jay told friends he found himself doing a lot of shrugging, which he described as the vertebrate reflex indicating helplessness.

In 1973 Lovestone had a new secretary in his New York office—

Miriam Welsh, the wife of Eddy Welsh, the "bronze Apollo" who had gone with Jay to Moscow in 1929 for the face down with Stalin. "Miriam is very good," Jay wrote Ellie Borochowicz, "but . . . one of her letters mailed via the mail-room on Friday late, containing important items and checks, was lost. . . . She has also studied how to postpone carrying out instructions. . . . I will have to talk to her like a Dutch uncle."

On April 25, 1973, Lovestone conferred with Henry Kissinger at the White House, where he found the atmosphere somber, as though buried in black crepe. They were circling the wagons in the midst of the Watergate investigation, which Jay thought of as a cesspool that would spout thick, black mud. He had known Kissinger since 1960, when he was at Harvard and wrote an article for the *Free Trade Union News*. At the time Jay had sent him a fawning letter: "Your stuff tops them all. . . . Cutting was the hardest job I ever had. . . . I actually had to employ a committee to get up enough courage to reduce your paper to the allotted space."

Kissinger told Lovestone that he had hoped Meany would come too, "but I know you're the strong man." "You mean stubborn," Lovestone said. He wanted to discuss the European situation in the light of Nixon's visit to China. "The workers of Europe now say that if Brezhnev and Mao are good enough for Nixon, they are then surely good enough for us."

"We really didn't give them that much," Kissinger said, adding that Leonard Woodcock of the United Auto Workers wanted to see him urgently. Did Lovestone know why?

"You know why," Lovestone responded. "He wants you to help him bring into the United States a Soviet so-called delegation. If you yield, we will fight you to the finish."

"We'll go along with your position for a categorical no," Kissinger said.

"Irreparable damage will follow the granting of Most Favored Nation status to Russia," Lovestone said.

"I wish we could say and do what you are doing," Kissinger said. "The situation is so bad that we see only the trade unions as a stabilizing force."

Lovestone said that Chancellor Willy Brandt and his finance minister, Helmut Schmidt, were now lecturing the United States on the morality of Vietnam. "I know of no American," he said, "even of the Mansfield stripe, who would not squirm when a German official gives him moral lectures. Of course, they do not have one critical word for the Hanoi hooligans who in the Tet Offensive slaughtered not only the patients but even the German medical staff of the hospital in Hue."

Kissinger said that Brandt was "a small man trying to play a big role, and always crying." Vietnam, he added, was "a cruel mess, complicated and politically catastrophic."

When the conversation turned to Watergate, Kissinger said, "The matter is serious, but it probably grew out of somebody picking up in some file a contingency paper and then thinking it was a good idea." This explanation for the break-in was one of the few times in his career that Kissinger could have been accused of whimsy.

"The battle among the Janissaries may be costly," Lovestone said, "but if it results in the elimination of the German mafia [H. R. Haldeman and John Ehrlichman], which is not responsive to the people or the electorate, it will do the country a lot of good." When Jay saw Kissinger's reaction at the mention of "German mafia," he added, "Don't worry, Henry, you are not a part of the German mafia. You are not even an honorary Aryan."

Lovestone's thoughts on Watergate, as expressed to Irving Brown that June, were that the mess involved nothing venal but was only the typically American form of criminally insane adventurism. The foul atmosphere and political pollution would be around for some time. Every country had its own form of lunacy, Jay added. In Her Majesty's kingdom, ministerial pipelines to prostitutes had destroyed more than one cabinet member (as in the Profumo case). In France corruption was on cash terms, and selected prostitution was a way of life. In Germany the mess would come through Soviet and DDR espionage. On Germany, Lovestone was prescient, for in 1974 Willy Brandt had to step down as the result of a spy scandal involving one of his personal aides.

As it came out that Kissinger in January of 1973 had signed a secret peace agreement in Paris with the North Vietnamese, which called for a ceasefire and the withdrawal of all U.S. forces, Lovestone turned against him, calling him the False Rabbi and "the architect of disaster." "For my two cents," he said, "the False Rabbi could make a very good salesman for toothpaste."

By late 1974 even Meany's faith in the war had been shaken. In an appearance on *The Dick Cavett Show,* when Cavett asked if he had been right in backing Johnson and Nixon on the war, Meany replied in the negative. Cavett asked: "Is it hard for you to admit that?" Meany said, "If you're wrong, you're wrong, and I've lived a long time and I've made a lot of mistakes." Meany felt that neither Johnson nor Nixon had leveled with him, and he realized that as a result of his "unstinting support" in Vietnam, the AFL-CIO was more divided than ever.

Kissinger later acknowledged that the agreement with the North

Vietnamese provided for a "decent interval" between the U.S. withdrawal and the collapse of South Vietnam. In late 1974 Congress voted to reduce aid to South Vietnam by half, which hastened the end of the regime.

Among the six thousand–odd Vietnamese who were airlifted out of Saigon in those last chaotic days of April 1975 were Tran Quoc Buu and his enormous family. With the help of Lovestone and Ernie Lee, Buu was flown to Guam and then to Fort Smith, Arkansas. He decided to settle in Paris, which had a large Vietnamese community, and took out enough money to open a restaurant, L'Escale du Vietnam. As a promotional gimmick, each evening a couple among the diners was chosen and crowned "king and queen of Vietnam," amid great hilarity.

A truly extraordinary coincidence took place in 1974: Both Lovestone and Angleton were terminated by their respective employers. For twenty years they had been joined at the hip in furthering their Cold War worldview. They saw each other or talked nearly every day, synchronizing their plans and advancing their credo. The one issue they divided on was the Sino-Soviet split, which Angleton held was a deception. When their mutual friend Lily Solomon Lawrence said to Jay, "You and Jim share the same ideology," he replied: "Let me tell you something I don't share—the *meshugas* about the Chinese and the Soviets. Plus, I don't believe Harold Wilson [British prime minister from 1964 to 1970] is a Soviet agent." The labyrinthine world of counterespionage led Angleton down some paths where not even his sidekick Lovestone would follow.

Angleton served as chief of counterintelligence under six CIA directors—Allen W. Dulles, John A. McCone, William F. Raborn, Richard M. Helms, James R. Schlesinger, and William E. Colby. Given that the assignment of ferreting out enemy agents within one's own organization required and bred the reflex of distrust, the root error was maintaining the same man in the job too long. "Now," said a veteran CIA man, "we have a five-year limit on the job because it drives you buggy."

Angleton built up his own fiefdom, almost an agency within the agency, immune to the usual outside controls. Every four years the CIA inspector general carried out an inspection of the covert side, which included an audit, but Angleton managed to have certain parts of his operation—namely the Israel account and the Lovestone account—excluded from that review. The auditor would say, "Everyone gets audited, why not you?" Angleton would go to the director and say, "Turn these guys off. We don't want them looking into this Lovestone thing. It might be embarrassing." (When asked, Richard Helms denied having any influence on the boundaries of the internal audit.) The CIA was not mandated to collect domestic intelligence; by having agents inside the AFL-CIO it was breaking the law.

Actually, the heyday of the Lovestone-Angleton partnership was the Dulles years, when Lovestone had half a dozen agents in the field. In the sixties the Vietnam War cast a pall over their activities, though Lovestone remained the anti-Soviet workhorse, turning out reports and memorandums. But Cleveland Cram, a CIA station chief with a Harvard doctorate in history who was brought out of retirement to write an account of Angleton's tenure in CI, examined the JX files and saw that "as time went on it wasn't so much the reports from his operatives as it was the political gossip that he could pass on from the labor bigwigs like Meany, who played golf with Eisenhower, and who told Jay, who told Jim, who told Allen, who ate it up. More and more, Lovestone's real raison d'être was this sort of political gossip."

Both friends and foes agree that Angleton was wrecking his health with his workaholic routine, combined with smoking and drinking. He smoked five packs of Virginia Slims a day and could go through a quart of bourbon in an evening. In December 1968, according to his FBI file, Angleton was at the home of a friend when he was seized with an attack of hemorrhaging. He was rushed to the George Washington University Medical Center, where his condition was diagnosed as a bleeding ulcer.

The CIA veteran David Blee said: "I wouldn't have written an insurance policy on Jim, but then he quit drinking cold turkey and went on Anabuse. He went to the other extreme and would ask, 'Any sherry in that soup?'"

His friends noticed some slippage in his power of concentration. "He could be very convincing with his castles in the air," Sam Halpern recalled. "But everyone makes mistakes. That's why they have erasers on pencils. If I disputed what he said, he'd say, 'Sorry, Sam, you're not cleared for this, I can't talk about it.' That was his last line of defense."

Angleton's troubles began in December 1972, when James Schlesinger replaced Richard Helms as CIA director and picked William Egan Colby as deputy director for plans. Schlesinger launched a major purge of personnel, and Colby recommended those to be let go. One of the names on his list was Angleton's, who Colby felt epitomized the clandestine mystique that Schlesinger was trying to get rid of.

Colby decided to whittle Angleton down gradually. He shut down the mail-intercept program and removed Angleton as liaison with the FBI. In May 1973, however, there was a cabinet shake-up, and Schlesinger became secretary of defense. Colby, who had worked his way up in the agency since his days in the OSS, was named director.

One of Schlesinger's last demands at the CIA had been that the inspector general compile a report on "potential flap activities"—instances where the CIA was acting in violation of its charter, as in the bugging of American journalists and operations against the antiwar movement. The 693-page report became known as "the family jewels." It was not completed until after Schlesinger's departure.

Once Schlesinger was gone, Colby assigned one of his trusted officers, Horace Feldman, to look into Angleton's activities, and Feldman discovered the Lovestone connection and the JX reports, which had escaped the inspector general's review. "It was excluded for some reason," Feldman told Colby. "Excluded," Colby asked in astonishment, "how?" "It's supposed to be independent," Feldman said. "What's going on?" Colby asked. "Here we have a senior officer in the labor movement, a domestic organization outside our mandate, and he is in our pay. And he publishes a newspaper, the *Free Trade Union News*. This is a clear violation of our charter. Lovestone is collecting information on U.S. citizens."

"Jim fought, fought, fought. He had Horace in tears," Colby recalled when I interviewed him a few months before his death at the age of seventy-six in a canoeing accident, in April 1996. "But Horace doggedly investigated and gave me his report, and I said, 'This operation has outlived its usefulness and must be terminated immediately.' It looked as though the CIA was trying to influence American foreign policy via the labor movement. And another thing, how could we run a proper agency with all the contacts Jim made on his own, such as Mrs. Morris?"

But Angleton was not about to surrender his assets, and Colby was not sure of the best way to handle him. Even though he was the director, he and Angleton were equals in experience and years of service. When he called Angleton in he had to listen to his "nature of threat" lecture. Colby looked for results in the counterintelligence field and found none. It seemed to him that Angleton was sabotaging operations for no reason. "It was Jim's nature to see something behind everything," Colby recalled. "He believed all defectors were fakes. But I would rather have five fakes if I could get five good ones as well—at least test them. After all, it was our role to find out what was going on inside the Kremlin.

"Looking back on it," Colby said, "I handled Jim pretty badly. I was pushing him toward the door. I took things away from him one at a time:

the FBI account, the Israeli account, the Lovestone account. I offered him a way to retire with a larger pension if he took advantage of it right away. But he didn't take the hint, and every time I spoke to him he would argue."

On December 18, 1974, Seymour Hersh of *The New York Times* asked to see Colby, telling him he was on to a story "bigger than My Lai," which had to do with domestic spying by the CIA. Colby saw Hersh on December 20 and tried to play down the importance of the CIA activities. But with the story sure to come out, Colby saw that Angleton would become an embarrassment to the agency. So after Hersh's departure Colby called Angleton in and said: "We've talked about this for a long time, and now I have to tell you that you must leave." "And that was it," Colby recalled. "He left."

Angleton called Pagie Morris to tell her that their collaboration was over and that in his opinion Colby was a mole. "I can't understand how a Catholic who confesses to a priest can be a 'sleeper,'" Jim said. "For Jim," Pagie recalled, "anyone who undermined him had to be a Soviet agent. Even Jay, who loved him dearly, said, 'He is getting more paranoid every day.'"

Overnight Angleton's counterintelligence empire, so painstakingly constructed through twenty years, collapsed. "The business," as he called it, had been his consuming passion, and now it was taken away from him. "Jim was a defeated man," said his friend Lily Lawrence. "He felt he'd been crucified."

Those who had worked with him saw not the debacle of his last years but his overall record. "Angleton could be cantankerous and cross-grained," Bill Hood said. "He abused his body and kept eccentric hours. But he was a dominant figure in the world of counterintelligence. He established what CI should be. He had a deep understanding of tradecraft and a grasp of complex operations. He made counterintelligence a career. As Buck Clayton said about Charlie Mingus, 'He was a fascinating bunch of guys. And he could play.'"

While Angleton was fighting his rearguard action in 1974 to avoid the ax, Lovestone was also in trouble. It will be remembered that in 1973, Lovestone complained that his new secretary, Miriam Welsh, had mislaid a letter including "important items and checks." That letter, which contained a check from Angleton for Pagie Morris, had somehow ended up in the Washington office of the AFL-CIO International Department. There it was opened, and that was how George Meany found out that Lovestone was still maintaining his arrangement with Angleton, seven years after he had been told to terminate it, following the revelations of Tom Braden and others. This accident of the letter was Lovestone's demise. In addition, he was now seventy-seven, and Meany felt he had outworn his usefulness.

Early in 1974 Meany summoned Ernie Lee and told him: "You're going to be head of the International Department."

"Does Jay know?" Ernie asked. "It's a disfavor to him."

"We're going to make the change," Meany said.

As a way of dumping Lovestone, Meany made him an offer he knew Jay would refuse. On March 6 he informed Lovestone that he wanted him to close his New York office, stop publication of the *Free Trade Union News,* and transfer himself and his archives to Washington. When Lovestone argued that he could not relocate his archives and his library of six thousand books, he was dismissed.

On May 16, Rosie Ruane, who had worked in the International Department since the merger, first with Mike Ross and then with Ernie Lee, wrote Irving Brown: "I got word very privately yesterday that the deal is all set. Ernie takes over as director July 1. . . . I hope it isn't left for Jay to read about in the paper, because he still has hopes, I think."

Lee, who felt bad about taking Lovestone's place, arranged for Meany to keep him on as a consultant two days a week in Washington, on a per diem of seventy-five dollars plus expenses. Lovestone took it but resented it. "For so long," Lee recalled, "Jay was indestructible. He never stopped, and it was hard to think he ever would. But by 1974 he was gaunt and deteriorated. In the labor movement, you don't stick a shiv in somebody because they're ill and old."

On June 28, 1974, Ruane wrote Brown: "Jay left yesterday afternoon with tears flowing down his cheeks when he said goodbye to Ernie." She was off to clean out his desk.

Lee took over International Affairs at the tail end of the Vietnam War. George Meany was fully aware of the dissent in the rank and file over his support of the war. "Vietnam was like a trip to the morgue to watch an autopsy," Lee recalled. "After that, you don't go onstage and do a buck-and-wing." With Lovestone gone, so was his missionary zeal. Ernie Lee headed the department from 1974 to 1982 and kept a low profile. His way of doing things was less dramatic than Jay's, and less quarrelsome. The days when the AFL-CIO had an aggressive global foreign policy were over.

Lovestone's secret role in steering American foreign policy away from détente had begun right after the Second World War. Those were the heroic days, when the AFL worked alone and there was a genuine danger that Germany, France, and Italy would go Communist. The formation of anti-Communist unions in Europe was a program the CIA could build on. When the AFL leaders agreed to the partnership, there was a sense of urgency about the fate of Europe that seemed to justify it. But it continued long after the urgency was gone and eventually embarrassed the American labor movement, for repeated denials are acutely embarrassing.

The CIA connection and the AFL's unconditional support for the Vietnam War seemed to show that organized labor had become an arm of the government. In fact, the Lovestone-Meany policy was often at variance with the State Department. On issues such as the Soviet Union and China, it was to the right of Nixon. Yet it is proper to ask what business a labor union had mixing in foreign policy at all, except through international labor organizations. The union membership knew only in the vaguest terms how their dues were spent in the foreign field. The force of Lovestone's beliefs and personality kept this operation going far longer than it should have. Lovestone was an ideologue, and the trouble with ideologues is that they tend to discount any change that disturbs their system of beliefs. The world changed, but Lovestone remained frozen in his positions. He belittled the role of character in Soviet leadership. It was quite obvious that Khrushchev was not Stalin and that Brezhnev was not Khrushchev; that with each leader the regime had changed and that some form of accommodation had become possible. But to Lovestone, himself the victim of a purge, the Soviet Union would always act as he had seen it act under Stalin, in a brutal and treacherous manner. He had a vested interest in the Cold War—it was his livelihood and purpose—and he kept fanning its embers long after the fire had gone out.

18

THE LAST YEARS OF LOVESTONE

Lovestone turned seventy-eight in December 1975. Still physically vigorous and mentally alert (although Ernie Lee thought otherwise), he refused to think of himself as retired, replying to letters of condolence: "I am not retiring in the actual sense of the word. In reality I am switching the terrain of my activities."

The Vietnam War was over, Watergate had driven President Nixon from office, and the conservative midwesterner Gerald Rudolph Ford had succeeded him. Still consumed by his mission of foiling the Soviet Union, Lovestone railed at "the butchery of America's defense capacities and the miserable mess being created in the Middle East by the Arab Rabbi," on whom he was conferring the degrees of B.A. (bachelor of ambiguities) and D.D. (doctor of disaster). "Kissinger is the grave-digger #1 of Western freedom," he wrote a friend. "His behavior in the SALT negotiations with the Russians is disastrous. . . . He has a mortal grip on America's first unelected president."

The Russian novelist and Nobel Prize winner Alexander Solzhenitsyn had been deported from the Soviet Union the year before and was living in Switzerland. Lovestone resolved to give him his first American platform by having the AFL-CIO invite him to an important banquet in Washington. George Meany liked the idea, which seemed to Lovestone the culmination of thirty years of AFL anti-Soviet efforts. For it was in 1945 that the AFL had protested the Russian move to conscript German labor for the coal mines. Then Lovestone had raised the matter of the gulags in the UN, receiving no support from the State Department until 1950. And now, Solzhenitsyn, a victim of those very gulags, would be their guest on June 30, 1975, in the ballroom of the Washington Hilton. The AFL-CIO would take him under its wing so that he could not be attacked by the Communists as a tool of capitalism.

Born in 1918, Solzhenitsyn was in the army in 1945, when he was arrested for making disrespectful remarks about Stalin in a letter to his wife, Natasha, which was opened and read by military censors. For this peccadillo he was sentenced to eight years in Siberian labor camps, to which were later added three years in exile. In 1962, under Khrushchev, he was allowed to publish his first novel, *One Day in the Life of Ivan Denisovich.* Lovestone at the time thought it was a trick to make the regime seem more liberal. That was the only book Solzhenitsyn was able to bring out in his own country. The others, such as *Cancer Ward, The First Circle, August 1914,* and *The Gulag Archipelago,* were published abroad. In 1970 he won the Nobel Prize in literature but was not allowed to go to Stockholm to receive it.

President Ford did not respond to Lovestone's invitation to dinner. "Ford is silent, or dumb—whichever you prefer," Lovestone said. A memo to Ford from Secretary of State Kissinger and National Security Adviser Brent Scowcroft, warning him not to receive Solzhenitsyn at the White House or attend the dinner hosted by Meany, was leaked to Lovestone. "The Soviets would probably take White House participation in this affair as either a deliberate negative signal or a sign of administration weakness in the face of domestic anti-Soviet pressure," the memo said. "Solzhenitsyn is a notable writer, but his political views are an embarrassment even to his fellow dissidents. A meeting with the president would offend the Soviet Union" in the midst of delicate arms control negotiations. Lovestone ranted against Kissinger's "Metternich-style indignities." He reported to Meany that when Nixon had said of Solzhenitsyn, "he's to the right of Barry Goldwater," Kissinger had replied, "No, Mr. President, he's to the right of the tsars."

The dinner was a great success, a historic occasion. Meany and Solzhenitsyn saw eye to eye—both were against détente. Neither Ford nor Kissinger was among the twenty-five hundred guests, though two members of the cabinet did show up—Secretary of Defense James Schlesinger and Secretary of Labor John Dunlop. So did Daniel Patrick Moynihan, the U.S. ambassador to the UN, who was courting the New York Jewish vote for his forthcoming Senate bid. Lovestone reported that it was "overwhelmingly a trade union group, with some academicians as icing on the cake." He felt that Solzhenitsyn had done a terrific job, holding the audience spellbound. While Meany was applauded for hosting the dinner, Lovestone remained in the background, noticed by only a few at a table far from the dais.

Lovestone kept up his connection with Pat Moynihan. In 1976 they had lunch at the Century Club, and Jay urged the ambassador to seek the Senate nomination. "He's a good speaker with perhaps a little too much of the Irish ham in him," Jay told a friend. "By that I mean he acts and poses quite often for the sake of the fun he gets in doing so."

Lovestone continued to go to Washington two days a week on his consulting job and was busy in New York organizing his papers, which had been bought for thirty thousand dollars by the Hoover Institution at Stanford University. In May 1976 he reported that the floor of his apartment at One University Place was covered with piles of paper. "I'm delousing them," he said. He called the Hoover "my mausoleum." Grace Hawes, the archivist assigned to the Lovestone collection, found some uncashed checks, which she mailed him in the hope they were still cashable.

Hawes in the meantime drew up a list of the pseudonyms he had used over the years: Beacon, Beets, Birch, Gaynor, Judd, Langly, Lawson, Nelson, Powers, Robertson, Robin, Thornton, and Wheat. Lovestone would write occasionally to ask how she was doing with "my earthly remains." He now called himself "a Dustbinologist."

That June of 1976, Lovestone woke up one morning in his room at the Hilton Hotel on Sixteenth Street in downtown Washington feeling decidedly queasy. He called Sam Schurr, an economist who specialized in energy and natural resources and a dependable friend who was married to Lovestone's niece Beatrice, and said: "I think I'm having a heart attack. Can you come over?" Schurr arrived to find Jay in bed, dictating to a secretary but coughing and having trouble breathing. "You'd better go to the hospital," Schurr said. "I'm not going to any hospital until a doctor tells me I've had a heart attack," Lovestone retorted. "You can't always get a doctor to come here," Schurr responded.

Jay then called his friend Fritz Kraemer and said, "Fritz, I'm sorry to disturb you, but I've had a heart attack and no doctor will come to the hotel and I need an ambulance." Kraemer, who worked for the Pentagon, made a couple of calls, and fifteen minutes later an Army doctor was in the room with an electrocardiograph and an ambulance waiting downstairs. The doctor said: "Get this man to a hospital."

Schurr helped Lovestone down to the ambulance, but he refused to get in, so they drove to Sibley Hospital in Schurr's car. Schurr had his personal physician waiting; the doctor checked Lovestone in the emergency room, and said: "This man has convulsive heart disease." A nurse took his pulse and gave him a shot, but Jay seemed agitated. "You've got to relax, Mr. Lovestone," the nurse said. "How can I relax," he replied, "when the Italian elections are on Sunday?"

Lovestone's niece Bea was the daughter of his sister Sarah and Charles Gray. She had met Sam Schurr in New Brunswick in 1935, when she was a high school senior and he was a freshman at Rutgers.

When he got out of the hospital, Lovestone stayed for six weeks in Sam and Bea's house in Bethesda. His stay required considerable organizational skill, for Bea had to arrange the visits of his devoted lady friends so they did not overlap. Pagie Morris came from New York, Esther Mendelssohn from Montreal. Pagie told Jay, "You're fine, you healthy bastard." Pagie was no problem, but Bea found Esther hard to take. Now in her eighties, she was demanding and hypercritical. When Bea took her to a restaurant, she was so rude to the waiter that Bea said: "You really can't talk to people like that." Esther said: "The trouble with you is you want people to like you." Bea was glad to see her leave.

In Washington, Lovestone had a few like-minded friends, who formed a coterie of die-hard cold warriors. The main three, aside from Angleton, were Fritz Kraemer, Ed Rowny, and Henry "Scoop" Jackson. Kraemer is best-known as the "discoverer" of two secretaries of state, Henry Kissinger and Alexander Haig. He says of himself, "I am by nature a talent scout."

For twenty-seven years Kraemer had a small, obscure office, crowded with newspapers and books, in the Pentagon's Plans and Policy Division. As an adviser to the top brass and the secretary of defense, he became a sort of shadow foreign minister, the same position Lovestone held in the labor movement. For the von Stroheimish Kraemer, the Pentagon made an exception to its ban on monocles, which were seen as Teutonic.

Kraemer was born in 1908, the son of a Prussian state prosecutor. He emigrated to the United States in 1941 because of his loathing for Hitler. Drafted in 1943, he was sent to Camp Claiborne in Louisiana. It was there that he met another German immigrant, the nineteen-year-old Henry Kissinger. Kraemer informed his superiors that Kissinger was a bright young man with a sense of history and helped him get into the Counterintelligence Corps.

Kraemer was one of the few men in Washington of whom it could be truly said that he was not interested in advancement or personal gain. "I have a Prussian sense of service to the nation," he says. In Lovestone, whom he met in the fifties, he found a kindred spirit, "an autonomous personality with an instinct for politics. He reminded me of Eric Hoffer, that brilliant stevedore who once said, 'Where freedom destroys order, the yearning for order destroys freedom.' Lovestone was a man with a fiery soul but also with the discipline of the analyst. In the Pentagon there are some excellent analysts, but they are soulless, they don't get the intangibles. Take a brilliant fool like McNamara, who wanted only to bracket quantifiable factors. He ended up with an equation that had nothing to do with reality. People like McNamara are briefed by briefers, but Lovestone informed himself, he read a prodigious amount, he talked to people, he pieced together the mosaic. Lovestone was a fortress. When others wavered, one would say, 'There's always Lovestone.' "

Kissinger in his early years as Nixon's national security adviser often sought Kraemer's advice. In 1969 border clashes between Russia and China gave Nixon the chance to act on his brainchild, the opening to China. Back channels were opened, and Kissinger called Kraemer to "come over at once." When Kraemer got there Kissinger said, "Nixon wants me to go to China and work on détente. What do you think?" "I think it's a good idea to align yourself with the left-wing member of a Communist alliance," Kraemer said. "But no concessions on Taiwan."

"Later," Kraemer recalled, "I was aghast that the same man who had the vision to make the opening to China would use barracks language on the tapes. The only explanation I could find was that men like Nixon who were in the army but never went to the front used foul language to prove their manliness." Kraemer also became disillusioned with Kissinger's banal hankering after priority. How vulgar it was, he thought, to display signed photographs of the famous.

Kraemer stayed close to Lovestone, writing him when Seymour Hersh's book on Kissinger came out:

> My own view of Henry Kissinger is very harsh. But Seymour Hersh's and my criticism are solar systems apart. For me, Kissinger is an ugly tragedy. For Hersh he is an occasion for sensation and hypocritical muckraking. And Professor Stanley Hoffmann [the reviewer] is a man to whom I once talked at Harvard many decades ago but to whom today I would not even speak. These over-clever intellectuals, who are so predictable, unoriginal, so miserably bourgeois, make me ill . . . think of it . . . Kissinger, Hersh, Hoffmann, all climbers, and essentially small, all of them.

Lovestone and Kraemer formed a mutual admiration society. They agreed that they were living in an age of pygmies, of ignorant people hungry for power and unwilling to learn even the basics. "The Schwarzkopfs and the Colin Powells," Kraemer said, "they are nobodies. The quality of their minds seems to be in inverse proportion to the acclaim they receive."

Also a part of the Lovestone circle was Edward L. Rowny, the son of Polish immigrants whose grandfather had served in the tsar's army. A big, pudding-faced, affable man, Rowny graduated from Johns Hopkins in 1937 and then entered West Point. He saw combat in Italy in 1944 and 1945 as a battalion commander. After the war he was assigned to the Strategic Plans Section of the War Department and earned master's degrees at Yale in engineering and international relations.

It was as an arms negotiator for fifteen years, under five presidents, that Rowny knew Lovestone, whom he credits with helping him to understand Soviet negotiating strategies. "It was Lovestone," he recalled, "who showed me the Soviet use of intellectuals as 'useful idiots' and the deliberate corruption of language, as when they call their one-party system 'democratic.' This 'semantic infiltration' used the rhetoric of the West to lull our fears." "Don't be deceived by the Soviet fear of being invaded," Lovestone told him, "and remember that they see compliance as a matter of form." Rowny much admired Lovestone's 1971 pamphlet "Who Is the Imperialist?" (actually written by Herb Weiner). "The State Department thinking," Rowny recalled, "was that the Soviets were not expanding but merely protecting their borders, but Jay showed that they were the real imperialists; he turned the equation on its head."

Sharing the Lovestone-Kraemer-Rowny worldview was the Democratic senator from Washington, Henry "Scoop" Jackson, who was friends with all three and who articulated their Cold War ideology on the Hill. Jackson wasn't merely pushing for more planes for Boeing, he was a true believer, who had as little faith in Soviet motives as he had complete faith in Pentagon reports. Like Lovestone, he played in the uncommitted nations commodities market. Even more than Lovestone, he pushed for a military buildup and warned of "ballistic blackmail."

Lovestone worked on Jackson's foreign policy speeches, supported his presidential aspirations in 1968 and 1976, and helped him write his pamphlet on negotiating with the Russians. Jackson swallowed whole the domino theory, as did Lovestone, and saw Vietnam as an expansionist bid by Red China. Lovestone arranged for Jackson to talk to labor groups, one of which he addressed in New York as follows: "Our party has room for hawks and doves but not for mockingbirds who chirp gleefully at those who are shooting American boys."

After his June 1976 heart attack and his convalescence with Sam and Bea, Lovestone went to Stowe, Vermont, for a much-needed rest and listlessly followed the presidential campaign. Meany was backing Jimmy Carter without enthusiasm, and Jay wrote a friend on May 4 that "Carter is a total fraud. He boasts that he prays to the lord 25 times a day. I'm ready to pray 75 times a day to rid us of this peanut king. He represents 20th century Knownothingism catering to the contempt for Washington." But as the campaign wound down, Lovestone came to believe that "Carter is not stupid, i.e., he wasn't born stupid and I don't think he studied to be stupid. It just takes time to ascend from the village level to the cosmopolitan level."

In August, Lovestone started going to Washington again. Angleton invited him with Sam and Bea to eat some salmon just caught in Canada. Jay told Jim that the AFL-CIO had endorsed Carter, but "it is more formal than enthusiastic. We are saddled with Carter."

In 1977 there was "more upholstering of my system," when Lovestone had a hernia operation. In January he saw Kissinger, but as Lovestone reported to Jim Schlesinger, "the Arab Rabbi is so puffed up with himself that he cannot see beyond the outer rim of his inflated ego." As for Carter's national security adviser, the beetle-browed Zbigniew Brzezinski, Lovestone told a friend that "he is at best a profuse but not profound footnote artist. I heard him say on the air the other night that if Italian or French Communists joined the cabinet [of their respective governments], they should be judged by their behavior, which is like telling somebody, 'Take kerosene, you'll like it.' . . . This concoction of illiteracy and calculated idiocy needs no rebuttal."

Lovestone kept up with old friends like Bert Wolfe, who was now established at the Hoover Institution in the budding field of Kremlinology. Jay wrote him that sending his papers there made him feel "like an archaeologist engaged in excavating his own bones to refresh his skeleton about the years gone by."

Ah yes, mused Wolfe, the years gone by. He had broken with the Comintern because he thought the human race was too civilized for war. From 1939 to 1967 he had been a nonperson as far as the party went. Then in 1967 he was promoted to bourgeois falsifier and hireling of big business. As they heaped it on, he thought, "My cup runneth over." Now he was reading the obituaries of his contemporaries and the reviews of his books in Russian newspapers. When one was less vicious than usual, he would say, "From a pig a hair"—an old Jewish proverb expressing astonishment that from the abominated pig you could make a good hairbrush with the bristles.

It was his old friend Boris Souvarine who observed that the Communists had invented a new cause of death—suicide from disenchantment. Sergei Esenin, the greatest poet since Pushkin, took his own life in 1926. He drank, but it was Bolshevism, not vodka, that killed him, Bert believed. In 1930 the great poet of the revolution, Vladimir Mayakovsky, killed himself. Andrei Golub, less well known, left this note in 1924: "I am leaving this world and I have the pleasure of returning to you my party card." The symbolist poet Vladimir Piast hanged himself around 1930, and the great poetic innovator Marina Tsvetaeva killed herself in 1941. Also Evgenia Bosch, "heroine of the revolution in the Ukraine"; Yuri Lutovinov, member of the Central Committee; M. S. Glazman, Trotsky's secretary; and Adolph Ioffe, first Soviet ambassador to Germany and China. On May 13, 1956, Aleksandr Fadeyev, the general secretary of the Union of Soviet Writers, killed himself. For ten years he had performed abject deeds for Stalin in the world of letters, Bert reflected, receiving two Orders of Lenin. He was the one who said in Breslau in 1948 that "if hyenas could type and jackals use fountain pens, they would write like the poet T. S. Eliot and the playwright Eugene O'Neill."

In 1977 Wolfe was so thin that he took a padded chair with him to restaurants to cushion his bony frame. In his and Ella's Spanish-style house, there was a wall heater in the bathroom, and one morning while he was shaving, Bert's silk bathrobe touched the lit heater and caught fire. It was like being burned at the stake—Bert had third-degree burns all over his body. He was taken to the burn unit at Stanford Hospital but died of his injuries. "The sands of time are running out," Lovestone thought when he heard of Bert's death.

On June 30, Solzhenitsyn spoke at the Harvard commencement, and Meany was proud that it was the AFL-CIO who had launched him in America, recalling how he "provoked the knee-jerk minds of the day, immersed as they were in an unhealthy mixture of post-Vietnam guilt and fashionable anti-anti-Communism." But mixed with Meany's pride was disgust that Jimmy Carter, whom he had endorsed, now recognized Red China, that violent oppressor of human rights. This was truly the end of the Cold War and the Meany-Lovestone antidétente axis.

In March 1979, Eugenie McMahon Meany died at the age of eighty-two after a long illness. Meany joked about being bossed by his wife, but her death shattered him. Three weeks later he caught a chill at the outdoor signing of the Camp David Agreement between Israel and Egypt and was hospitalized with bronchitis. Unknown to anyone outside his family, Meany had leukemia and was on chemotherapy. Ernie Lee once took him to George Washington Hospital, where he had a blood transfusion in his fingers and then took a plane to the West Coast to give a speech. There was no stopping him.

On the patio of his house, sitting in an aluminum chair, Meany leaned back, tipped over, fell out of the chair, and hit his knee on a flagstone. On April 22, 1979, he was hospitalized with bursitis, and the doctors gave him cortisone, to which he was allergic. When Meany got home, Lee, who lived down the street, sent his kids over to teach him to play chess. But from that point on it was downhill. In May, Meany missed the AFL Executive Council meeting, for the third time in his twenty-three years as president. In September he missed the Labor Day picnic he was supposed to host. In November, at the AFL-CIO convention, he nominated Lane Kirkland, the onetime first mate, as his successor and saw him elected unanimously. Then he tapped the gavel the carpenters had given him fifteen years before and struck the mahogany block, which broke in two. It was the last labor gathering he attended, for he died on January 10, 1980, at the age of eighty-five. For two days his casket was on view in the lobby of the AFL-CIO headquarters as thousands filed by.

For Lovestone, Meany's death was the end of an era, both in trade union matters and in the political history of the country, and the memories crowded in pell-mell—the time he and Meany had paid a call on Lucius Clay in Berlin, and while they were talking the general's cat crawled up one of his arms, across his shoulders, and down the other arm without the general batting an eyelash. Or the time he and Meany were talking to Saragat in Rome and Jay said, "You can take the Italians tragically but never seriously." Saragat looked quizzical for a moment, then burst out laughing.

Under Lane Kirkland the AFL-CIO remained active in foreign affairs but in a more subdued way, and without the partnership of the CIA. Kirkland's principal foreign interest was the Solidarity movement in Poland, to which the AFL-CIO contributed ten thousand dollars in September 1980. On September 24, Lovestone reported to Kirkland that he had attended a lunch at the Council on Foreign Relations in honor of the Polish ambassador to the UN, Nagorski, "a slick, smooth operator, a well-trained seal who is a member of the Central Committee of the Polish Communist Party. This was the first time I shook hands with a Commu-

nist in over fifty years." When Lovestone gave Nagorski an invitation to
the ILGWU convention to pass on to the Polish trade unions so they
could send a fraternal delegate, his face showed "acute embarrassment."
Lovestone asked the ambassador why the Polish unions were not allowed
to exchange fraternal delegates with foreign unions. "He shrugged and
squirmed a bit and said, 'Not now.'" As Lovestone explained it, the strategy was to delay the formation of free trade unions, and "should there be
any resistance, the Polish government always has its gallant allies, represented by two crack Soviet army divisions, permanently stationed in
Poland."

After Ronald Reagan's inauguration in January 1981, Lovestone
found himself regretting the loss of Jimmy Carter, who had stood up to
the Russians in 1980 after the invasion of Afghanistan. Carter had pulled
out of the Olympics, which were nothing without the Americans, and ordered the grain embargo, which contributed to Soviet problems with
Poland. Jay was going to miss the little peanut. As for Reagan, Lovestone
was tempted to write him a letter suggesting that in the long run it would
be bad for him to be surrounded by rich men, who cared only about their
personal profits.

In June 1981, Lovestone broke one of his own long-standing rules
and allowed himself to be interviewed by Peter Worthington, a columnist
for (and later editor of) the *Toronto Sun*. Worthington, who wrote a series
of three admiring articles, came to see Jay in his cluttered office in the
ILGWU building at 1710 Broadway. On the wall behind his desk was the
map of slave labor camps that the AFL had published in the 1950s and
that Solzhenitsyn had marveled at for its accuracy.

Worthington called Lovestone "a living legend" and compared him
with George Orwell in his understanding of Communism. "His record of
anticipation in world affairs," Worthington wrote, "has been consistently
more accurate than the State Department's." One might have thought
Lovestone would have been pleased. He wasn't. He told the labor writer
Arnold Beichman that he didn't like the "glorification" in Worthington's
articles. Why, Beichman wondered, did Jay shrink from publicity? "After
all, how else can your views be disseminated?" he asked. "I could not
have gotten through any worthy project," Jay replied, "unless it came
under the name of some person holding high office in the federation. The
attainment of a worthwhile task is the highest reward. Recognition is at
best glossy advertising."

Lovestone continued to go to Washington, not only because of the
consulting fee but out of a deeper need to remain involved. On August 28,

1981, he had lunch with Alexander Haig in the secretary's office, and they lamented the state of the world together. The secretary of state had a high opinion of his commander in chief, with which Lovestone differed. "Future historians will rate Ronald Reagan as somewhat below President Millard Fillmore," he told Fritz Kraemer. Breaking the air controllers' strike, he felt, was a major blunder that would alienate labor. "The labor ranks will never use a scab plane," Jay said. "Mr. Reagan suffers from an acute and incurable god-complex."

Warren Beatty had asked Lovestone to appear as one of the "witnesses" in his movie *Reds,* in which Beatty played John Reed, but when Jay saw the film in the spring of 1982, he was glad that he had said no. "I did the right thing by not getting involved in any shape, manner, or form," he told a friend. "The few sound words uttered in the second part of the film, where Reed is portrayed as critical of Zinoviev, are in small measure due to my influence on Mr. Beatty." As for his objections to the "absurd romantic stuff," Lovestone said, "Beatty's only answer to me was that no major film can be produced in Hollywood without the bed and the couch."

In December 1982, Lovestone was contacted by "King Henry" Kissinger, who was under attack from Lyndon LaRouche and his U.S. Labor Party and wanted Jay's help in getting LaRouche off his back. LaRouche had written that the strikes in Poland were organized by Lovestone. "I wish he was right for a change," Jay said. He heard from Jim Angleton that Kissinger had also called him in an agitated state, asking him to run a background check on LaRouche, who was hounding him and having him paged on airplanes. Angleton said Kissinger had given him his numerous private phone numbers, including the one in his bathroom. Lovestone told Angleton, "You are now Kissinger's Rebbe."

And then in 1982 Lovestone's own rebbe, David Dubinsky, died at the age of ninety. That was a heavy blow. Lovestone knew that he owed his political rehabilitation and his career in the AFL to Dubinsky. In 1940, when Jay scuttled his movement, Dubinsky got him into the William Allen White Committee to Defend America, some of whose distinguished members, such as Winthrop Aldrich of the Chase Bank, wondered what an ex-Communist was doing there. Then in June 1941, Adm. William Standley, the chief of naval operations, who was about to leave for Moscow as American ambassador, addressed the committee to convey the War Department's gloomy prediction that it would take Hitler six months to knock the Soviet Union out of the war. But Lovestone argued that in six months the Russians would be sucking the Germans in and de-

stroying them. He gave his reasons so forcefully that the admiral asked
for a memo to take back to Washington. Dubinsky told Jay that his memo
was responsible for the shift in the War Department's evaluation of Russia's chances. Lovestone also remembered the trip to Berlin in 1948 with
Dubinsky and his wife, Emma, to see how the population was surviving
the blockade. As they flew over the Soviet zone, the crew gave them para-
chutes and showed them how to pull the ripcords, and Emma asked the
captain: "For Lovestone and Dubinsky, have you got a parachute that
goes up, not down? If the Communists get them, they'll be better off
dead."

In 1983 Sasha Zimmerman died, another soldier with whom Lovestone had been in the trenches, and one of the first to support the Allies,
before Jay, in 1939, when Zimmerman had campaigned for Bundles for
Britain.

These losses made Lovestone grouchy, and he complained about
everything, often with good reason. In February 1983 he was eighty-five,
and it was bitter cold, the most miserable winter in half a century, he
thought. The sidewalks were sheets of ice, and he slipped en route to the
grocery store, bruising his nose, but got home safely. His apartment was
overrun with mice and in such deplorable condition that he took his land-
lord to court. Another blow, which convinced him that Kirkland wanted
him out, was that his Washington office was turned over to the AFL-CIO
legal counsel, Larry Gold. In addition, Jay had lost his one friend in the
Reagan administration, Al Haig, who had been replaced by George
Shultz. Lovestone grudgingly admitted that "Shultz is the ablest man in
the cabinet, but he is also as agile and slippery as an eel before it is
smoked."

When he could no longer take the New York winter, Lovestone
would fly down to Palm Beach and stay with Esther Mendelssohn in her
apartment at the Ambassador, on Ocean Boulevard. Nathan had died in
1980, and Esther had let herself go. She dressed like a bag lady and was
an embarrassment to the management, accusing the help of stealing her
Canadian passport. When Esther and Jay went down Worth Avenue, with
the shuffling small-stepped walk of the elderly, holding hands, they
seemed to illustrate that all ills are gathered together in old age. At the
Petite Marmite, Jay ordered tea and made a scene when the waiter
dropped the cardboard tag attached to the tea bag into the tea.

While Lovestone was in Palm Beach in December 1983, he caught a
cold, which led to pneumonia and a high fever. He was taken to St.
Mary's Hospital, and when the doctor asked him who should be called,

he said, "Call the secretary of defense," thinking of Jim Schlesinger—but the doctor thought he was raving and brought in a psychiatrist, who pronounced him delirious.

Lovestone was not a model patient; he shouted and raged and fought with the nurses. Finally his sister Esther's children, Bob and Mildred Matis, came to get him and flew him back to New York on January 7, 1984. Lovestone was disruptive during the flight and asked to be taken to Pagie Morris's apartment at the Ritz Tower. Pagie had her hands full; Jay was unable to walk without assistance and fell down when he tried to get up. She took care of him day and night for ten days, until she collapsed. His secretary, Gloria, came over to help when she could and gave Pagie checks to pay the bills.

Finally, through Lovestone's friend Leonard Schiller, a onetime organizer for the UAW who had worked for the AFL in India and Africa, a night nurse was found. Pagie was leaving for Europe in February, and she and Schiller took Jay back to his apartment, which was in a terrible state—cockroaches everywhere, a pile of dirty laundry in the bathroom, and the living room and bedroom piled high with newspapers and junk. Most of the lamps had no bulbs, and there was no gas for the stove. It took Pagie and Gloria a week to throw out the incredible accumulation of junk. Pagie counted twenty pairs of cracked and worthless old shoes, not to mention the suitcases falling apart, still bearing the labels of defunct ocean liners.

Schiller was an old pal of Lovestone's, a big, thick-lipped, coarse-featured man of dubious reliability who had recently been working as an FBI informant. But Schiller was all Jay had, for Pagie was in Europe, the honest and dependable Sam Schurr had moved to California, and there had been a falling-out with Bob and Mildred Matis.

Before her departure, Pagie gave Schiller the name of her lawyer, Francis X. Morrissey, Jr., a member of a well-connected Boston Irish legal clan whose father had been a lawyer for the Kennedys. On March 21, 1984, Schiller took Lovestone to see Morrissey. "Jay needed a lawyer because he had no will," Morrissey recalled. "But more than that, he needed to be taken care of. He was confused and frightened."

Morrissey reluctantly gave Schiller power of attorney over Lovestone's bank account so he could pay the household bills and find a housekeeper and caregiver. Jay had a fit when Schiller withdrew fifteen thousand dollars from his account. Yet much of the time the two were like an old borscht belt vaudeville team, kidding around and one-upping each other. Jay told the cleaning woman, "Watch out for him, he's a stool pigeon," or "Don't tell him anything, he works both sides of the street." Schiller would come back with "J. Edgar Hoover thinks you're still a Commie."

The woman Schiller found to take care of Lovestone was Valerie from Belize, who was fortyish, sultry, and buxom, and invariably wore tight pants, Morrissey recalled. She flirted with Jay, and was playful when she gave him baths. When Pagie got back from Europe, she overheard Valerie trying to get Jay to buy her a house. She was definitely a bad influence, thought Pagie.

Fritz Kraemer wrote to buck Lovestone up: "You have inspired more people than you can possibly know, and you are one of the few dedicated only to a cause and not to their egotistical personal ambitions." But in 1985 there were further medical problems, and a pacemaker was inserted in Lovestone's chest. He had a form of Parkinson's that leads to rigidity, was in and out of the hospital, and finally needed a wheelchair to get around.

Frank Morrissey got wind of a scheme by which Schiller and Valerie planned to strip Lovestone's bank account. Morrissey removed Schiller's power of attorney and got rid of Valerie. He hired Malcolm Starks, a strong and genial Air Force veteran and physical therapist, and James Moore, a licensed practical nurse who had just retired after thirty-six years at Sloan-Kettering.

There were times when Lovestone hallucinated—he was on the phone to Stalin, or he was escaping from Moscow. When he got too excited, Moore was able to calm him down. Starks took him for walks and also, in his wheelchair, to Palo Alto to see Grace Hawes or to Montreal to see Esther, and kidded him about being a Casanova. Esther was in a nursing home, not in the best shape herself. She grabbed hold of Starks's necktie and would not let go. Starks reported to Frank Morrissey: "You won't believe this, she still wants to take him to bed. Their love is still strong."

In September 1986, Lovestone was discontinued as a consultant. He would be eighty-nine that December and was in no shape to go to Washington two days a week, but the disappearance of this last vestige of his professional life was nonetheless a cruel blow.

Trouble did not come as a single spy but in battalions. In September 1986, Irving Brown, who had replaced Ernie Lee as director of international affairs in 1982, suffered a stroke from which he never recovered. He had another stroke eight months later, and in 1988, when Ronald Reagan awarded him the highest civilian honor, the Presidential Medal of Freedom, he was unable to attend the ceremony. He died on February 10, 1989, in his Paris apartment on the boulevard Arago, at the age of seventy-seven. Lane Kirkland said: "We have lost a giant. No other individual did more than Irving to protect and advance workers' rights in every nation around the world."

Irving had been his field marshal, Jay recalled. His hair had never turned gray, though he had a few too many chins from eating in three-star restaurants. *Time* magazine had called him "the most dangerous man." The Budapest daily *Nepszava* called him "a trade union gangster." And when he was admonished for hiring Pierre Ferri-Pisani and his goons, he said, "They weren't thugs, but they weren't choirboys either." When Philip Habib, the State Department man from Brooklyn, was asked about Irving's CIA connections, he said, "We didn't use the sonofabitch, the sonofabitch used us." Irving had been a lion of a man, powerful, wily, relentless, with blue-collar erudition, and he picked up languages like lint.

In his last years Brown had been moving funds to the Polish strikers. By 1985 the Soviet Union was collapsing under its own weight, and Brown was a voice for a new AFL-CIO policy to explore the situation created by the advent of Mikhail Gorbachev. Lovestone was adamantly opposed to any change in policy, but Lovestone was out of the picture.

Brown saw the ground moving. *Perestroika* was the result of economic chaos and the arms race. Reagan with his military buildup was forcing the Soviets to spend too much on defense. Nixon's opening to China had given the Russians four thousand miles of troublesome borders. Russia's resources were stretched to the limit, there was dissent in its bosom, it was surrounded by hostile satellites, and the machinery was creaking to a halt. In dizzying succession came elections, the First Congress, and the formation of political parties, which meant the splintering of the once-monolithic Communist Party and the end of the dictatorship of the proletariat.

The Cold War was over, not only because of *glasnost* but because the cold warriors were becoming extinct. Cicely Angleton reported on February 20, 1986, that her husband had lung cancer and was under heavy medication. "He has no pain," she wrote Lovestone,

> but the old steroids make him hungry all the time. . . . ("If you gave me the leg of a chair, I'd put sauce on it and swallow it," says he). . . . The radiation is over, and that's a mercy. Fry your brains, that's what they do. . . . Right now he has a breathing machine which he plugs into the wall and then gurgles around and makes misty

clouds. It's called Medi-Mist. Looks like he's smoking a water-pipe or hookah, old Chinese wise man. He is so fond of you . . . and speaks of you very warmly and admiringly. . . . Shalom and love. Cicely—Jim's wife.

In early May 1987 the sixty-nine-year-old Angleton called Pagie Morris and said: "I'm on my way out." Pagie tried to remain composed, though tears streamed down her face. She said: "I can't imagine life without you."

Angleton died on May 11, and Lovestone wrote Cicely that "words fail me. I feel that I am writing not with a pen but with tears. . . . Jim was not only a man of ability, but a man of great and genuine talent."

Lovestone had pneumonia again in 1987, and Rosie Ruane wrote on June 12: "I am sorry to hear about your galloping pneumonia. I had already heard about the wheelchair . . . but that's not so bad is it?" She added that Harry Goldberg was in bad shape, going blind, and had no one to look after him. Lovestone, in his bilious mood, wrote in the margin of her letter: "Harry is a phony who can go live with his sister Ella Wolfe."

Esther Mendelssohn, sitting in her chair at the nursing home, speaking in a whisper and asking for Jay, was ninety-five when she died in 1988, leaving him the apartment in Palm Beach and some money. The apartment was sold to help pay for his upkeep.

Lovestone in 1988 had an infection of the urethra, which altered his metabolism and provoked violent fits. He slept a great deal and upon waking feverishly hallucinated. Morrissey saw the garbled flashbacks as a code that had to be deciphered. "They brought a van instead of a car, that's how I knew I was going to prison, so I slipped out the back way" referred to his 1929 escape from Moscow. Then he told Morrissey that Reagan had come to see him to discuss foreign policy. "You dreamt that, Jay," Morrissey said. "Being on your back all day affects a man," Lovestone replied.

In the March 1989 Soviet elections, Boris Yeltsin came to power. It was clear that the Soviet Union no longer posed a military threat. The Warsaw Pact was coming unraveled. The Soviets were moving their troops out of Central Europe. German reunification was approaching. On November 9, 1989, the Berlin Wall came down.

Lovestone had made a bet with his friend Ed Rowny on when the system would collapse: Lovestone believed it would happen at the turn of the century while Rowny picked the year 2006, the dawning of the Age of Aquarius. Both men agreed that the system would implode as the result of economic chaos, the old guns-or-butter argument. Until that happened the United States should do all it could to hasten the collapse.

In 1989 Lovestone was going blind; he couldn't read the papers anymore. Starks saw the life leaking out of him. When Morrissey dropped by one day in the fall of 1989, Jay said, "Watch my eyes. A man dies like a fish. His eyes die first."

When he was hospitalized in February 1990, he threw a fit, yelling, "Help, I'm being kidnapped." Lovestone, the lifelong atheist, was shouting, "Oh God, save me." In the hospital he kept repeating, "Why am I here?" Morrissey brought him home. "I promised him he would not die alone," he said. When Starks saw him he said, "He won't last the night." But he lasted until the night of March 7, when Moore put him to bed and heard him gasping for breath. He called 911, but Lovestone was dead of heart failure by the time the ambulance arrived. He had turned ninety-two in December 1989.

On April 1, Arnold Beichman wrote in the *National Review* that "Lovestone was a master strategist in the war against Communism." Ed Rowny in *The Wall Street Journal* on March 28 said that Lovestone had lived long enough to witness the collapse of the Soviet empire and the repudiation of the Leninist one-party state. There were many "summer soldiers and sunshine patriots" in the Cold War, Rowny said, but Lovestone had stood fast.

On April 11 a memorial service was held for Lovestone in the hall of the AFL-CIO Washington headquarters. Among those present was Philip M. Kaiser, Truman's assistant secretary of labor and Carter's ambassador to Hungary, who told a friend: "There were more CIA men there than labor men." Of the half dozen speakers it was Fritz Kraemer who expressed the most genuine fondness for Lovestone. The amazing thing, he said, was that Lovestone never expected credit. "He didn't need glorification," Kraemer said. "He led a simple, almost austere life, not like those who are only concerned with their miserable success."

Then Lane Kirkland said that "Jay got off the Communist boat and found a home in the labor movement. In the final months of his life he saw the workers of the world rise to their feet, and it was for him a vindication." In June 1991, Kirkland went to Moscow to see Yeltsin. "If someone had told me two years ago that I'd be going to the Kremlin to see Yeltsin, I'd have said they were crazy," he mused.

A month after Lovestone's death, Yeltsin called for the retirement of the Central Committee and the rescinding of Article Six of the Soviet Constitution, which mandated the Communist Party's leading role. The Soviet Union had in fact ceased to exist, and the Russian Republic would soon emerge. It was as if Lovestone had died once his mission was accomplished, in a world where the Soviet Union was no longer a threat.

Lovestone's low profile led the press to invest him with more influence than he had. Sanford Gottlieb of *Labor's Daily* called him in 1958 "an obsessed cloak-and-dagger man, labor's undercover agent—but one who has been setting his own policy." More accurately, Lovestone was, in David Dubinsky's words, "the unofficial Secretary of State for the labor movement." He did not act alone. His policy was also the policy of George Meany and the AFL leadership. The role of the AFL in foreign affairs, especially in the period after World War II, was a formidable asset in stopping Soviet expansion in Western Europe. Lovestone was at the heart of that effort.

The seed that Lovestone's Free Trade Union Committee planted is now acknowledged to have been one of the principal factors that gave democracy a chance for survival in Europe after the war. Stalin's plan to control the democracies of Europe through the labor unions almost worked in Germany, where our military authorities were under orders to give the Communists a free hand, and in Italy, where Mark Clark was under instructions to turn over fascist funds and party headquarters to Communist-controlled resistance groups.

Even someone like the labor attaché Morris Weisz, who was not fond of Lovestone, accepted the priorities. Weisz was with the Marshall Plan successor organizations in Paris from 1952 to 1957 and saw Irving Brown operate, flashing his wad of bills with his usual nonchalance. Today, Weisz says: "Faced by the funds available to our Communist enemies on the labor front, there was no other source but government funds to do this necessary work. I simply felt that Brown was too obvious in the way he exposed his bankroll and that in selecting his recipients he occasionally mistook greed for genuine support."

Lovestone started out trying to be a good Communist. In the party he learned to hide behind surrogates, for anything proposed by the despised Communists was doomed to failure. He found fronts, such as the farmer-labor parties and the leaders of the trade delegation to the Soviet Union, to carry out the orders of the Comintern. Formed by party factionalism, he also learned the splitting tactics that he applied unsuccessfully to the UAW in Detroit and successfully in postwar France and Italy.

Through factionalism and intrigue, Lovestone rose to the leadership of the American party, but he imprudently bucked the system and was banished by Stalin. He did not have the temperament to be a good Communist. He was not docile, he was not blind; it was not in his nature to rubber-stamp the grossly mistaken Comintern premises.

Like all true heretics, he then claimed to be the keeper of the flame and founded his own movement, which had so few followers that he knew most of them by name. In the thirties he played a rather self-serving double game, attacking the American Communist Party while trying to ingratiate himself with Stalin. The time finally came when he could no longer swallow Stalin's government by terror, and he dismantled his movement, having learned that nothing can be accomplished without the backing of a powerful organization.

Lovestone then found the backing of two such organizations—the AFL and the CIA. He recycled himself as the gray eminence, a role well-suited to his passion for behind-the-scenes plotting. He became George Meany's foreign secretary and a CIA spy. In Meany he found a boss who gave him a free hand to formulate the AFL's foreign policy, but he railed against the CIA as fervently as he had against the Comintern. His partnership with the Fizz Kids made him detest the organization, particularly when they left him in the lurch in China. Only when Lovestone teamed up with Jim Angleton did he find a mind and a sense of mission commensurate with his own.

Lovestone had a deep and vastly cross-referential understanding of the dynamics of the Soviet system. He knew that in spite of the changing faces in the cast of characters, the core would not change until the single party was done away with. But it was the very depth of his knowledge that helped to explain the rigidity of his views. He refused to acknowledge that the nature of the conflict changed after the death of Stalin. He failed to grasp that the opening to China would complicate its relations with Russia to the advantage of the West. He continued to sound the trumpet of Soviet menace when the regime was collapsing. "Lovestone's failure," as Weisz observed, "was that he became the mirror image of the knee-jerk liberal; he had knee-jerk anti-Soviet reactions instead of fostering the U.S. interest."

It should also be noted that in the period from 1945 to 1960 the Soviet threat was real and Lovestone's categorical cold warriorism served as a useful corrective to the liberal "we all want peace" refrain. It's not such a bad idea to have a Cassandra in the chorus. Lovestone and others like him were instrumental in warning that the Soviets did not play by the same rules we did. They controlled a global party that was used for subversion and destabilization. With the help of the CIA, Lovestone fought them on their own ground.

He never quite shook off the conspirator's suspiciousness instilled in him by the party. Nothing was what it seemed to be. In fact, he was often right, but that did not make his automatic mistrust an attractive trait. His devotion to his work excluded all other interests. Even Einstein fiddled. George Meany painted by numbers, and Irving Brown loved good food and wine. But Lovestone was holed up in his office behind piles of reports, working the phones, hatching his plots, spreading his tentacles, whispering his orders. He was the coach rather than the player, the master kibitzer, the prompter in the box, not the actor on the stage.

Personally, Lovestone made no effort to be liked. He seemed to judge everyone in terms of ideological reliability. His closest friends were his political allies, like Jim Angleton and Fritz Kraemer. His admirers came from the hard-line anti-Soviet camp, and over the years he made many enemies, for he was abrasive and tactless, too quick to insult and belittle those he disagreed with. Two women—Pagie Morris and Esther Mendelssohn—saw another side of him, attentive, witty, loyal (up to a point), and even passionate, occasionally. But that was a side he did his best to conceal from others. Asked today to sum Jay up, the ninety-three-year-old Pagie Morris shakes her head and says: "There never was anyone like Jay, though he had an apparatchik mentality, deceitful and omissive."

In a culture that worships fame, Lovestone's instinct was to stay in the shadows, to curse celebrity and "glorification." Through others he became a stealthy manager of the Cold War. To those who had no second acts, to those whom fame consumed, to those who self-destructed or who fell by the wayside, he could at least say: "I lasted."

ACKNOWLEDGMENTS

Special thanks to Louise Page Morris for her recollections, papers, and letters; to Sam H. Schurr, for sharing his vast knowledge of the Lovestone files; to Ella Wolfe, for sharing her recollections; to Mildred Lazarus and Robert Matis, for family photographs; to Burton Hersh, for making available his files; to Morris Weisz, for his oral histories and for arranging a number of introductions; to Herbert Weiner for his Lovestone material; to John E. Haynes and Herbert Romerstein for their helpful advice on negotiating the Comintern files; to Paul R. Porter, Daniel L. Horowitz, Cicely Angleton, Andrew J. Kauffman, and Dr. John Windmuller for their comments on chapters; to Ben Rathbun for his material on Irving Brown; and to my researchers Sally Nishiyama, Amber Morgan, Gabriel Morgan, and Datia Lotareva in Moscow.

Special thanks also to the following libraries and archives: Anne Van Camp, archivist, Elena Danielson, and the fine staff at the Hoover Institution on War, Revolution, and Peace; M. Lee Sayrs, archivist at the George Meany Memorial Archives; William LeFevre, archivist at the Archives of Labor and Urban Affairs, Wayne State University; Richard Strassberg at the Martin P. Catherwood Library, Cornell University; the Department of Archives and Manuscripts, Catholic University; the AFL papers, State Historical Society of Wisconsin; Peter Filano, archivist, the Tamiment Collection, New York University; the National Archives (OSS files); and

Kiril Mikhailovich Anderson, director of the Russian Center for the Preservation and Study of Documents of Recent History (RTsKhIDNI), Moscow.

Thanks and gratitude to the following for interviews and/or correspondence: Cicely Angleton, Arnold Beichman, Anita Billick, Alfred Bingham, David Blee, Tom Braden, David Brombart, David Burgess, William Colby, Cleveland C. Cram, Dale Good, Gloria Greenfield, Sam Halpern, Hannah Haskell, Richard Helms, William Hood, Daniel L. Horowitz, Philip M. Kaiser, Andrew J. Kauffman, Don J. Kienzle, Mildred King, Lane Kirkland, Fritz Kraemer, Lucille Lawley, Lily Solomon Lawrence, Mildred Lazarus, Ernest S. Lee, James McCarger, Robert Matis, Cord Meyer, Bruce Millen, James Moore, Louise Page Morris, Francis X. Morrissey, Walter Pforzheimer, Paul R. Porter, Ben Rathbun, Herman Rebhan, Victor Reuther, Edward L. Rowny, Rosie Ruane, Sam Schurr, Bert Seidman, Ali Shakrani, Albert Shanker, Helen Solanum, Maida Springer, Malcolm Starks, Patricia Stryker, Virginia Tehas, Gus Tyler, Michael Warner, Herbert Weiner, Morris Weisz, Miriam Welsh, Louis A. Wiesner, John Windmuller, Ella Wolfe, and Peter Worthington.

Finally, particular gratitude to Peter Osnos, my first editor, who signed up the book. To Robert D. Loomis, my second editor, who turned a Zeppelin into a P-40. To Ian Jackman, my third and final editor, whose careful reading and sympathetic support greatly improved the book; and to my agent, Lynn Nesbit, who believed in this project and navigated it through the shoals.

SOURCES

ABBREVIATED TITLES OF SOURCES FREQUENTLY CITED

AFL: State Historical Society of Wisconsin papers
CIO: Archives of Labor and Urban Affairs, Wayne State University
CP: Comintern and U.S. Communist Party papers, Russian Center for Recent History, Moscow
FBI: Jay Lovestone's FBI file, consisting of 5,700 pages
GM: George Meany Memorial Archives
ILG: ILGWU papers, Cornell University
JL: Lovestone papers, Hoover Institution
OSS: OSS labor section files, National Archives

PREFACE

p. ix   Cuneo on Lovestone: JL, Cuneo file.
p. x   Worthington on Lovestone: Worthington to author.

CHAPTER 1: THE BLOND BEAST

p. 3   Jewish immigration: Irving Howe, *World of Our Fathers,* New York, 1967; Rose Cohen, *Out of the Shadows,* Ithaca, N.Y., 1995; Mark Zborowski, *Life Is with People,* New York, 1952; Abraham Cahan, *The Education of Abraham Cahan,* New York, 1969.
p. 5   Jacob Liebstein's arrival in New York: FBI.
p. 5   Jacob's youth: Grace Hawes interviews with Lovestone, JL; Robert Matis and Mildred Lazarus to author.
p. 6   Morris Liebstein: JL, Morris Liebstein file.
p. 7   Charles Gray: JL, Gray file.
p. 8   "I pray for the tsar": Sam Schurr to author.
p. 10   City College: JL, City College file; Max Horn, *The Inter Collegiate Socialist Society,* Boulder, Colo., 1979; Harry Rogoff, *An East Side Epic: The Life and Work of Meyer*

London, New York, 1930; James Traub, *City on a Hill,* New York, 1994; Sherry Gorelick, *City College and the Jewish Poor,* New Brunswick, N.J., 1981; Will Rudy, *The College of the City of New York,* New York, 1949; Morris Raphael Cohen, *A Dreamer's Journey,* Boston, 1949.

p. 12   Bert and Ella Wolfe: Ella Wolfe to author; Bertram Wolfe papers, Hoover Institution.

p. 13   Liebstein becomes Lovestone: JL, Biographical file.

CHAPTER 2: PRESENT AT THE CREATION

p. 16   Lovestone meets Dubinsky: ILG, Dubinsky oral history.

p. 16   Gitlow and Lovestone: Benjamin Gitlow, *I Confess,* New York, 1946.

p. 16   Formation of Communist Party: Theodore Draper, *The Roots of American Communism,* New York, 1957.

p. 16   Formation of the Comintern: CP; C.L.R. James, *The World Revolution,* Westport, Conn., 1973; Duncan Hallas, *The Comintern,* London, 1985.

p. 17   Ruthenberg: Oakley C. Johnson, *The Day Is Coming,* New York, 1957.

p. 19   Palmer raids: Edwin P. Hoyt, *The Palmer Raids,* New York, 1969; Paul Avich, *An Oral History of Anarchism,* Princeton, 1995.

p. 21   Winitsky trial: JL, trial transcript, Winitsky file.

p. 23   Control Commission decision: CP.

p. 24   Second Comintern Congress: CP.

p. 24   Death of John Reed: CP; Angelica Balabanoff, "John Reed's Last Days," *Modern Monthly,* Jan. 1937.

p. 25   "apathy, disgust": JL, Communist Party files.

p. 25   William Z. Foster: CP; Edward P. Johanningsmeier, *Forging American Communism,* Princeton, 1994.

p. 26   Profintern congress: CP.

p. 27   Formation of Workers' Party: CP; Draper, *Roots of American Communism.*

p. 27   "for the first time": JL, Communist Party files.

p. 28   Bridgman raid: JL, Communist Party files; Bert Wolfe papers, Hoover Institution.

p. 29   Fourth Comintern Congress: CP.

CHAPTER 3: LOVESTONE IN LOVE

p. 30   Lovestone in Berlin: JL, Communist Party files.

p. 33   "I have the social blues": Bert Wolfe papers, Hoover Institution.

p. 33   Mother Bloor: Ella Reeve Bloor, *We Are Many,* New York, 1940.

p. 33   Harold Ware: JL, Ware file; Lem Harris, *My Tale of Two Worlds,* New York, 1986; Lowell K. Dyson, *Red Harvest,* Lincoln, Nebr., 1982; Lem Harris, *Harold Ware,* New York, 1978; Herbert Romerstein, *The KGB Against the Main Enemy,* New York, 1989.

p. 34   Clarissa Ware: JL, Ware files; Benjamin Gitlow, *The Whole of Their Lives,* New York, 1948.

p. 36   "All this about Cris": JL, Ware file.

p. 38   John Pepper: CP; JL, Communist Party files; Theodore Draper, *The Roots of American Communism,* New York, 1957.

p. 39   Farmer-Labor coalition: JL, Communist Party files; Draper, *Roots of American Communism;* Edward P. Johanningsmeier, *Forging American Communism,* Princeton, 1994.

p. 40   Lenin's death: CP.
p. 41   "Things are wretched": Wolfe papers.
p. 43   Nathan Mendelssohn: JL, Mendelssohn file.
p. 44   Esther Mendelssohn: JL, Mendelssohn file.
p. 45   "Sex is terrible": Anita Billick to author.

CHAPTER 4: THE CHICAGO YEARS

p. 48   Succession battle: CP.
p. 49   Lovestone in Russia: JL, Communist Party files.
p. 49   Hotel Lux: Arkadi Vaksberg, *Hotel Lux,* Paris, 1993.
p. 50   Louise Geisler: JL, Geisler file; Bert Wolfe papers, Hoover Institution.
p. 53   Gusev in Mexico: Ella Wolfe to author.
p. 53   Faction fight at the convention: CP; JL, Communist Party files.
p. 55   Passaic strike: JL, Communist Party files.
p. 58   Delegation to Russia: JL, Communist Party files; JL, Lauck file; Walsh papers, Berg
          Collection, New York Public Library; Rexford G. Tugwell, *To the Lesser Heights of
          Morningside,* Philadelphia, 1982.
p. 61   Lovestone and Nellie: JL, Nellie file.
p. 62   "Since when": CP.
p. 65   Death of Ruthenberg: CP; JL, Communist Party files.

CHAPTER 5: LOVESTONE SUPREME

p. 68   Lovestone in Moscow: JL, Communist Party files.
p. 68   Arthur Ewert: David P. Hornstein, *Arthur Ewert,* Lanham, Md., 1993.
p. 69   Faction fight: CP; JL, Communist Party files.
p. 70   Stalin-Bukharin fight: Stephen F. Cohen, *Bukharin and the Bolshevik Revolution,*
          New York, 1974. Edvard Radzinsky, *Stalin,* New York, 1996.
p. 70   Comintern plenum: CP.
p. 71   Lovestone 1928 campaign: CP; JL, Communist Party files.
p. 72   Sixth Comintern Congress: CP; JL, Communist Party files; Theodore Draper, *The
          Roots of American Communism,* New York, 1957.
p. 73   Lovestone to Bukharin: CP.
p. 76   Cannon conversion: James P. Cannon, *The First Ten Years of American Communism,*
          New York, 1962.
p. 78   Bert Wolfe to Moscow: JL, Communist Party files.
p. 78   Bert and Ella in Moscow: Ella Wolfe to author.
p. 79   Open Letter: CP.
p. 80   Dengel and Pollitt in New York: CP.
p. 82   Lovestone delegation: CP; JL, Communist Party files.

CHAPTER 6: IN THE JAWS OF THE BEAR

p. 85   Lovestone and Ewert: David P. Hornstein, *Arthur Ewert,* Lanham, Md., 1993.
p. 85   "Never will I be found": Benjamin Gitlow, *I Confess,* New York, 1946.
p. 85   Ewert in Brazil: Hornstein, *Arthur Ewert.*
p. 86   American Commission sessions: CP.

p. 102   Lovestone in Berlin: JL, Communist Party files.
p. 103   Kate Gitlow: Ella Wolfe to author.
p. 103   Communist Party in 1929: Harvey Klehr and John Earl Haynes, *The American Communist Movement,* New York, 1992.

CHAPTER 7: STARTING FROM SCRATCH

p. 105   Formation of Lovestone movement: JL, Communist Party (Opposition) file.
p. 106   Lovestone and Stalinism: Robert J. Alexander, *The Right Opposition,* Westport, Conn., 1981.
p. 107   Lovestone and European groups: Alexander, *Right Opposition.*
p. 108   Lovestone and Russell: JL, Communist Party (Opposition) file.
p. 108   Lovestone in Berlin: JL, Communist Party (Opposition) file.
p. 109   Esther Mendelssohn and Lovestone: JL, Mendelssohn file.
p. 110   Lovestone and Zimmerman: ILG, Zimmerman oral history.
p. 111   David Dubinsky: ILG, Dubinsky oral history; JL, Dubinsky file; Max Danish, *The World of David Dubinsky,* New York, 1957; Abe Raskin, *A Life with Labor,* New York, 1977.
p. 112   Soviet policy: CP.
p. 112   Communist Party in America: Harvey Klehr and John Earl Haynes, *The American Communist Movement,* New York, 1992.
p. 112   Soviet fronts: Benjamin Gitlow, *I Confess,* New York, 1946.
p. 113   Lovestone and the Socialists: JL, Communist Party (Opposition) file.
p. 113   Irving Brown: Ben Rathbun, *The Point Man,* London, 1995.
p. 115   Homer Martin: CIO, Homer Martin file.
p. 116   "you seem to have resigned": Bert Wolfe papers, Hoover Institution.
p. 116   Show trials: Edvard Radzinsky, *Stalin,* New York, 1996; Leonard Shapiro, *The Communist Party of the Soviet Union,* New York, 1959.
p. 116   Lovestone and Spain: JL, Communist Party (Opposition) file; Alexander, *Right Opposition.*
p. 117   Communist Party in the thirties: Klehr and Haynes, *American Communist Movement.*

CHAPTER 8: LOVESTONE BREAKS WITH COMMUNISM

p. 119   "Yonder see": JL, biographical file.
p. 120   Bukharin and the show trials: CP; Stephen F. Cohen, *Bukharin and the Bolshevik Revolution,* New York, 1974; George Katkov, *The Trial of Bukharin,* New York, 1969.
p. 120   Lovestone and Edna Mann: JL, Mann file.
p. 121   Lovestone and the POUM: JL, POUM file.
p. 122   Wolfe in Spain: Ella Wolfe to author.
p. 124   Lovestone and the UAW: CIO, Victor Reuther files; JL, UAW file; Henry Kraus, *Heroes of Unwritten Story,* Urbana, Ill., 1993.
p. 125   Lovestone to Lauck: JL, Jett Lauck file.
p. 126   Milwaukee convention: CIO, UAW file; Kraus, *Heroes.*
p. 127   Lovestone and Anschluss: JL, Austria file.
p. 129   Toohey report: CP.
p. 130   Martin demise: CIO, Homer Martin oral history, Victor Reuther file.
p. 131   Brown to Lovestone: JL, UAW file.

p. 132 Lovestone to Wolfe: Bert Wolfe papers, Hoover Institution.

p. 133 Zimmerman on Lovestone: ILG, Zimmerman oral history.

p. 134 Wolfe defects: JL, Wolfe file.

p. 135 Brockway and Carney correspondence: JL, Brockway and Carney files.

p. 137 Lovestone applies to the OSS: OSS files, Lovestone application, National Archives.

p. 138 "It is positively shocking": FBI.

p. 138 Arrest of Nathan Mendelssohn: JL, Mendelssohn file; FBI.

CHAPTER 9: LOVESTONE JOINS THE AFL

p. 141 "The son of a bitch": ILG, Dubinsky oral history.

p. 141 George Meany: Virginia Tehas to author; Ernest S. Lee to author; J. C. Goulden, *Meany,* New York, 1972; Archie Robinson, *George Meany and His Times,* New York, 1981.

p. 144 Formation of FTUC: AFL, FTUC files.

p. 144 Labor attaché program: Dan Horowitz to author.

p. 144 Sam Berger: Graenum Berger, *A Not So Silent Envoy,* New York, 1992.

p. 145 Ben Mandel: JL, Mandel file.

p. 146 Ray Murphy: Andrew J. Kauffman to author; Louise Page Morris to author; Lucille Lawley to author; JL, Murphy file.

p. 146 "Anyone can commit": JL, Murphy file.

p. 146 Margaret Buber Neumann: Kauffman to author.

p. 148 Murphy and Hiss: JL, Murphy file.

p. 150 Chipman to Lovestone: JL, Murphy file.

p. 150 Smith to Durbrow: JL, Murphy file.

p. 151 Woll to Truman: JL, Woll file.

p. 151 Lovestone and Acheson: JL, Acheson file.

p. 151 Fry to Dubinsky: AFL.

p. 152 WFTU: CIA report, June 14, 1948, "The Significance of the World Federation of Trade Unions in the Present Power Conflict," Truman Library, Independence, Mo.; Anthony Carew, "The Schism Within the World Federation of Trade Unions" (lecture; Tamiment Collection, New York University); CIO, WFTU file; JL, WFTU file.

p. 152 Meany at Blackpool: GM.

p. 153 Carey: Herb Weiner to author.

p. 153 Lovestone and FTUC: JL, FTUC file.

p. 154 "Irving was the consummate": Dan Horowitz to author.

p. 154 Lovestone and Spain: JL, Spain file.

p. 155 *The Nation* dinner: JL, Shaplen file.

CHAPTER 10: THE GERMAN COCKPIT

p. 156 Lovestone and Murphy: JL, Murphy file.

p. 156 Lovestone and front groups: JL, front groups file.

p. 157 Truman to R. J. Thomas: CIO, Thomas papers.

p. 158 Clay and McSherry: Porter to author; ILG, Dubinsky oral history.

p. 158 Wolf: Paul R. Porter to author.

p. 158 Wheeler: Morris Weisz to author; George Shaw Wheeler, *Who Split Germany?* East Berlin, 1962.

p. 159   Wiesner: Wiesner oral history by Don R. Kienzle; Louis A. Wiesner, "Organized Labor in Post-War Germany," CIA report, 1950.

p. 159   June meeting: Porter to author; Wiesner oral history.

p. 159   Rutz to Lovestone: GM, Rutz papers.

p. 160   Germany, Soviet zone: Wiesner report; Henry Kirsch, *German Politics Under Soviet Occupation,* New York, 1974.

p. 160   Lovestone to Keenan: JL, Germany file.

p. 160   Bingham and Jeffrey: Bingham to author; JL, Germany file.

p. 160   Brown to Lovestone: JL, Brown file.

p. 161   Jeffrey to Lovestone: JL, Woll file.

p. 161   Wheeler activities: GM, Rutz papers; ILG, Dubinsky papers; civil service hearing.

p. 161   Bingham to Lovestone: JL, Germany file.

p. 161   Lucius Clay: Jean Edward Smith, *Lucius D. Clay,* New York, 1990.

p. 162   Steinhardt to Clay: Smith, *Lucius D. Clay.*

p. 162   Lovestone to Woll: JL, Woll file.

p. 162   Wheeler in Bratislava: JL, Wheeler file.

p. 162   Wheeler's travels: Morris Weisz to author.

p. 163   Bingham break-in: Alfred Bingham to author.

p. 163   Rutz to Lovestone: GM, Rutz papers.

p. 164   Brown report: GM, Brown papers.

p. 164   Bingham to Lovestone: JL, Germany file.

p. 165   Clay antilabor: GM, Rutz papers; JL, Germany file.

p. 165   "the Russians are moving": JL, Brown file.

p. 166   Rutz in Stuttgart: GM, Rutz papers.

p. 166   Schumacher: JL, Schumacher file; GM, Rutz papers; Lewis J. Edinger, *Kurt Schumacher,* Stanford, 1965.

p. 169   Lovestone to Forrestal: JL, Office files.

p. 169   Lovestone report: JL, FTUC file.

p. 169   Paper shortage: GM, Rutz papers.

p. 169   Lovestone and Dubinsky to Berlin: JL, Germany file; ILG, Dubinsky oral history.

p. 170   Lovestone to Draper: JL, Germany file.

p. 170   Rutz on Clay: GM, Rutz papers.

p. 170   Lovestone on election: JL, Wallace file.

p. 171   Clay exploded: GM, Rutz papers.

p. 171   Meskimen to Lovestone: JL, Germany file.

p. 171   Woll to Clay: JL, Woll file.

p. 171   McCloy: Kai Bird, *The Chairman,* New York, 1992; JL, Rutz papers.

p. 173   CIO and WFTU: CIO, WFTU file.

p. 173   "Carey joined hands": JL, Brown file.

p. 173   Lovestone in London: Herbert Weiner to author.

p. 174   Berger on Lovestone: Graenum Berger, *A Not So Silent Envoy,* New York, 1992.

p. 174   Break with WFTU: JL, WFTU file; CIO, WFTU file; Weiner to author.

p. 175   Formation of ICFTU: JL, ICFTU file; GM, ICFTU file.

Chapter 11: Irving in Orbit

p. 177   Brown and Lovestone: JL, Brown file.

p. 178   Dimitrov to Stalin: Edvard Radzinsky, *Stalin,* New York, 1996.

p. 178   Situation in France: Herbert Luethy, *France Against Herself,* New York, 1955; Sanche de Gramont, *The French,* New York, 1969; Artemis Cooper and Anthony Beevor, *Paris After the Liberation,* New York, 1994.

p. 178   Brown to Lovestone: JL, France file, FTUC file.

p. 179   Brown to Woll: JL, Brown file.

p. 180   Lovestone, Brown, and Caffery: JL, France file.

p. 180   Brown and Jouhaux: JL, Brown file.

p. 181   Marshall Plan: Cooper and Beevor, *Paris After the Liberation.*

p. 182   Formation of Force Ouvrière: JL, Force Ouvrière file.

p. 182   Caffery cable: Irwin M. Wall, *The United States and the Making of Post-War France,* New York, 1991.

p. 183   Jay and Esther: JL, Mendelssohn file.

p. 183   Jay and Natalie Davies: JL, Davies file.

p. 184   Lovestone and Hoffman: JL, Marshall Plan file.

p. 184   Lovestone and Czechoslovakia: JL, Ray Murphy file.

p. 185   Brown and Ferri-Pisani: JL, Ferri-Pisani file.

p. 186   Lapeyrade to Lovestone: JL, Force Ouvrière file.

p. 186   Lovestone to Ferri-Pisani: JL, Ferri-Pisani file.

p. 186   Lovestone in Paris: JL, France file.

p. 187   "with one nostril closed": JL, Brown file.

p. 187   Bruce to Hoffman: JL, France file.

p. 187   "the Communist Party machinery": JL, France file.

p. 187   Donovan to Forrestal: JL, Donovan file.

p. 188   Lovestone on Acheson: JL, Acheson file.

p. 188   Brown on Cachin: JL, Brown file.

p. 188   Jouhaux and the Third Force: JL, Force Ouvrière file.

p. 188   Lovestone to Lafond: JL, Force Ouvrière file.

p. 189   Lovestone to Meany: JL, Force Ouvrière file.

p. 189   Postwar Italy: Daniel L. Horowitz, *The Italian Labor Movement,* Cambridge, Mass., 1963; Ronald L. Filipelli, *American Labor and Postwar Italy,* Stanford, 1989; Federico Romero, *The United States and the European Trade Union Movement,* New York, 1991.

p. 190   "trade union opposition": JL, Italy file.

p. 191   1948 Italian election: James E. Miller, "Taking Off the Gloves," *Diplomatic History* 7 1948; Robert T. Holt and W. van de Velde, *Psychological Operations,* Chicago, 1960.

p. 191   "They will have to repeat": JL, Italy file.

p. 191   Lovestone in Rome: JL, Italy file.

p. 191   Lovestone and Saragat: JL, Italy file.

p. 193   Formation of CISL: JL, Brown file.

p. 194   End of Marshall Plan: Charles L. Mee, Jr., *The Marshall Plan,* New York, 1984.

Chapter 12: Lovestone Joins the CIA

p. 195   "I want someone": Michael Warner, ed., *The CIA Under Harry Truman,* Washington, D.C., 1994.

p. 196   "The new CIA": H. Bradford Westerfield, *Inside the CIA's Private World,* New Haven, 1995.

p. 196   Wisner: Burton Hersh, *The Old Boys,* New York, 1992; W. M. Leary, *Perilous Missions,* University, Ala., 1984.

p. 197   Woll to Wisner: JL, Woll file.

p. 198   FTUC books: JL, FTUC file.

p. 198   Lovestone to Wisner: JL, Wisner file.

p. 199   Slave labor: JL, Slave Labor file.

p. 199   Wisner and Israel: JL, Wisner file.

p. 200   Finland: JL, Finland file.

p. 202   China and Etter: JL, Free China Labor League file.

p. 208   "This information": JL, Woll file.

p. 208   Borochowicz and Korea: Borochowicz papers, Tamiment Collection, New York University.

p. 209   "the stunning blow": JL, Korea file.

p. 209   "the White House has asked": JL, Korea file.

p. 209   Offie: JL, Offie or "Monk" file; Offie, FBI file; Orville H. Bullitt, ed., *Correspondence Between Franklin D. Roosevelt and William C. Bullitt,* Boston, 1972.

p. 211   Hull and Dunn letter: JL, "Monk" file.

p. 211   Cochran report: Offie, FBI file.

p. 212   Report of Offie's advances: Department of the Army, Offie file.

p. 212   McCarthy and Offie: Thomas C. Reeves, *The Life and Times of Joe McCarthy,* New York, 1982.

p. 213   Offie's enemies in OPC: James McCarger to author.

p. 214   W. B. Smith: L. L. Montague, *Walter Bedell Smith,* University Park, Pa., 1992.

p. 214   AFL-CIA summit: JL, "Monk" file.

p. 217   "we got together": JL, Brown file.

p. 218   Lovestone and Dulles: JL, Dulles file.

p. 218   Pinky Thompson: McCarger to author.

p. 219   Offie to Lovestone: JL, "Monk" file.

p. 220   Braden: Braden to author; JL, Committee for a United Europe file.

p. 221   Lovestone sees Smith: JL, "Monk" file.

p. 221   "Memorandums of Understanding": JL, Dulles file.

p. 222   "Allen would ask me": Thomas Braden to author.

p. 222   Victor Reuther to Europe: Victor Reuther to author.

p. 223   Braden to Detroit: Braden to author.

p. 223   Lovestone to Europe: JL, Meany file.

p. 223   Blowup with Thompson: JL, "Monk" file.

p. 223   Dulles and Malaxa: JL, "Monk" file.

p. 224   Malaxa: Seymour M. Hersh, *The Dark Side of Camelot,* New York, 1997.

p. 224   World Series: JL, Brown file.

p. 225   Dulles and family: Peter Grose, *Gentleman Spy,* Boston, 1994.

p. 225   "I was collecting intelligence": Sam Halpern to author.

p. 225   "She asked me": JL, "Monk" file.

p. 226   FBI surveillance of Offie and Lovestone: Offie, FBI file.

p. 232   "Carmel looked like a monkey": Louise Page Morris to author.

p. 232   phone taps: Lovestone FBI file.

p. 234   Lovestone to Cuneo: FBI file.

p. 234   Spencer Miller flap: FBI file.

p. 237   Hoover to Adams: FBI file.
p. 238   Lovestone to Woll: FBI file.
p. 238   Lovestone to Stark: FBI file.
p. 239   Dulles and Angleton: FBI file.
p. 241   Clardy and Miller: FBI file.
p. 241   Lovestone and Riesel: FBI file.
p. 242   Van Nassan: FBI file.

Chapter 13: Jay and Jim

p. 245   Braden and Dulles: Thomas Braden to author.
p. 245   Angleton and Lovestone account: Confidential source.
p. 247   Angleton and Lovestone friendship: Cicely Angleton and Louise Page Morris to author.
p. 248   Angleton and *Furioso:* e. e. cummings papers, Houghton Library, Harvard University.
p. 249   Pound to Angleton: cummings papers.
p. 249   Angleton interviewed by FBI: FBI file, James J. Angleton.
p. 249   Angleton and X-2: William Hood to author.
p. 251   Angleton and senators: Church Committee hearings.
p. 254   Lovestone and Angleton correspondence: JL, Angleton file.

Chapter 14: The American Mata Hari

p. 259   Louise Page Morris: Interviews and papers.
p. 263   Donovan and daughter-in-law: Louise Page Morris to author.
p. 264   Congress of American Women: Morris and Andrew Kauffman to author.
p. 265   Angleton and Morris: Morris to author, corroborated by CIA sources.
p. 267   Pagie and Jay correspondence: Louise Page Morris papers, Hoover Institution.
p. 272   Morris in Egypt and Far East: Morris papers.
p. 275   Morris to Angleton: Morris papers.
p. 276   Elfie: JL, "Elfie" file; FBI.
p. 278   Morris in Iraq: Louise Page Morris reports.

Chapter 15: The Lovestone Intelligence Service

p. 281   Geneva summit: JL, 1955 file.
p. 286   AFL-CIO merger: Victor Reuther to author; FBI.
p. 286   Meany proposes George Brown: JL, merger file; Rosie Ruane to author; Ernest Lee to author.
p. 287   Mike Ross: JL, Michael Ross file.
p. 288   Lovestone and Carey: JL, Carey file.
p. 288   Lovestone on edge: Louise Page Morris private papers.
p. 289   Morris and Makarios: JL, Cyprus file.
p. 289   Lovestone and Tunisia: JL, Tunisia file.
p. 290   Morris and Lodge: Morris to author; Henry Cabot Lodge, *Memoirs,* New York, 1976.
p. 291   Lovestone and Morocco: JL, Morocco file.

p. 291   Lovestone and Algeria: JL, Algeria file; Morris and Algerians, Morris private papers.
p. 291   Algerian delegation in New York: JL, Algeria file.
p. 292   Irving Brown in Algeria: GM, Brown papers.
p. 295   Deverall: Deverall papers, Catholic University.
p. 296   Deverall resignation from SCAP: Deverall papers.
p. 297   CIO fights Deverall appointment: CIO, Victor Reuther papers.
p. 297   Charge of Deverall's homosexuality: CIO, Val Burati papers.
p. 298   Deverall in Tokyo: Deverall papers.
p. 298   Lovestone to Deverall: JL, Deverall file.
p. 300   Deverall ouster from Japan: Deverall papers.
p. 300   Goldberg in Indonesia: JL, Indonesia file.
p. 301   Goldberg in Italy: JL, Italy file.
p. 302   Das: JL, India file.
p. 304   Springer: Maida Springer to author; JL, Africa file; Yevette Richards, "My Passionate Feeling About Africa: Maida Springer-Kemp and the American Labor Movement," Ph.D. diss., Yale University, 1994.
p. 305   Mboya: JL, Mboya file; Springer to author; Anthony Clayton and Donald C. Savage, *Government and Labor in Kenya,* London, 1974; Sanford J. Ungar, *Africa,* New York, 1978.

CHAPTER 16: LOVESTONE'S SECOND FRONT

p. 311   Beginnings of ICFTU: JL, ICFTU file.
p. 312   Cyprus delegation: JL, Cyprus file.
p. 312   Brown dinner with Tewson: JL, Brown file.
p. 313   Deverall in Brussels: Deverall papers, Catholic University.
p. 315   Pissas affair: JL, Cyprus file.
p. 317   Kemsley to Krane: GM, ICFTU file.
p. 317   Tunis Congress: JL, ICFTU file.
p. 319   Charfi affair: JL, ICFTU file; GM, ICFTU file.
p. 321   Meany's distress: GM, ICFTU file.
p. 323   Patteet scandal: David Brombart to author.
p. 323   AFL breaks with ICFTU: JL, ICFTU file.

CHAPTER 17: DECLINE AND FALL

p. 326   Lovestone and Bar Yacov: JL, Israel file.
p. 326   Mikoyan lunch: JL, Mikoyan file.
p. 327   Lovestone and Nigeria: JL, Nigeria file.
p. 327   Lovestone and *Trud:* JL, Soviet Union file.
p. 328   Lovestone and 1960 campaign: JL, Brown file.
p. 328   Lovestone on new administration: JL, Dohrn file.
p. 328   Lovestone and Stevenson: JL, UN file.
p. 328   Lovestone testifies: JL, Anti-Communism file.
p. 329   Lovestone and Cuba: JL, Cuba file.
p. 330   Meany to Reuther: GM, Meany file.
p. 330   Reuther at White House: GM, Shishkin report.

p. 331   Khrushchev to McCloy: JL, McCloy file.

p. 331   Ted Hill: JL, TUC file.

p. 331   Leaks in White House: JL, Kennedy file.

p. 331   Lovestone on China: JL, China file.

p. 331   Lovestone and Eban: JL, Eban file.

p. 332   Lovestone at Corning conference: JL, Robert Murphy file.

p. 333   Lovestone and Kraft: JL, Algeria file.

p. 333   Lovestone and Berlin trip: JL, Berlin file.

p. 335   Kennedy at AFL-CIO convention: JL, Kennedy file.

p. 335   Lovestone promoted: JL, International Affairs file.

p. 336   Lovestone and Vietnam: JL, Vietnam file.

p. 336   Buu in Washington: JL, Buu file.

p. 336   Brown to Vietnam: JL, Brown file.

p. 336   Baldanzi and Altaffer in Saigon: JL, Vietnam file.

p. 337   San Francisco convention: JL, Conventions file.

p. 337   AFL-CIO Executive Council: CIO, Walter Reuther papers.

p. 337   Lovestone sees Adenauer: JL, Germany file.

p. 339   Meany press conference: GM, Meany papers.

p. 340   Brown in Saigon: JL, Buu file.

p. 340   Lovestone to Borochowicz: Borochowicz papers, Tamiment Collection, New York University.

p. 341   Lovestone to Paris: JL, Force Ouvrière file.

p. 342   Audie and Buu: JL, Buu file.

p. 342   Colson to Lovestone: JL, Colson file.

p. 343   Red China enters UN: JL, UN file.

p. 344   Buu in trouble: JL, Buu file.

p. 345   "Miriam is very good": Borochowicz papers.

p. 345   Lovestone and Kissinger: JL, Kissinger file.

p. 347   Buu leaves Vietnam: Ernest Lee to author.

p. 347   "You and Jim": Lily Lawrence to author.

p. 347   Inspector general audits: Confidential source.

p. 348   Colby fires Angleton: Colby to author; William Colby, *Honorable Men,* New York, 1978.

p. 350   Angleton calls Morris: Louise Page Morris to author.

p. 351   "You're going to be": Lee to author.

p. 351   Lovestone departure: Rosie Ruane to author.

CHAPTER 18: THE LAST YEARS OF LOVESTONE

p. 353   "Kissinger is the grave-digger": JL, Kissinger file.

p. 353   Lovestone and Solzhenitsyn: JL, Solzhenitsyn file.

p. 355   Lovestone and Moynihan: JL, Moynihan file.

p. 355   Lovestone and Hawes: Grace Hawes to author.

p. 355   Lovestone heart attack: Sam Schurr to author.

p. 356   Lovestone and Kraemer: Fritz Kraemer to author.

p. 358   Lovestone and Rowny: Edward Rowny to author; Edward L. Rowny, *It Takes One to Tango,* McLean, Va., 1992.

p. 358   Lovestone and Jackson: JL, Jackson file.

p. 359   Bert Wolfe: Bert Wolfe papers, Hoover Institution.

p. 360   Wolfe's death: Ella Wolfe to author.

p. 360   Death of Meany: Ernest Lee to author.

p. 361   Lovestone to Kirkland: JL, Kirkland file.

p. 362   Worthington articles: Peter Worthington to author.

p. 363   Death of Dubinsky: JL, Dubinsky file.

p. 364   Lovestone in Palm Beach: Gloria Greenfield and Mildred King to author.

p. 365   Lovestone back to New York: Robert Matis and Mildred Lazarus to author.

p. 365   Pagie takes care of Jay: Louise Page Morris to author.

p. 365   Lovestone and Schiller: Sam Schurr and Morris to author.

p. 365   Lovestone and Morrissey: Francis Morrissey to author.

p. 366   Lovestone and Valerie: Morrissey to author.

p. 366   Lovestone's last days: Malcolm Starks and James Moore to author.

p. 367   Death of Brown: JL, Brown file.

p. 368   Death of Angleton: JL, Angleton file.

p. 369   Death of Lovestone: Morrissey to author.

p. 369   Memorial service: Schurr to author.

p. 370   Lovestone and Weisz: Morris Weisz to author.

INDEX

ABOUT THE AUTHOR

TED MORGAN is the author of biographies of Franklin Roosevelt, Winston Churchill, Somerset Maugham, and William S. Burroughs, and of the histories *A Shovel of Stars* and *Wilderness at Dawn*. He lives in New York City.

ABOUT THE TYPE

This book was set in Times Roman, designed by Stanley Morrison specifically for *The Times* of London. The typeface was introduced in the newspaper in 1932. Times Roman has had its greatest success in the United States as a book and commercial typeface, rather than one used in newspapers.